# OXFORD MODERN LANGUAGES AND LITERATURE MONOGRAPHS

*Editorial Committee*

C. DUTTLINGER   S. GILSON   G. HAZBUN

A. KAHN   I. MACLACHLAN

C. SETH   W. WILLIAMS

# Complicity in Fin-de-siècle Literature

HELEN CRASKE

# OXFORD
UNIVERSITY PRESS

Great Clarendon Street, Oxford, OX2 6DP,
United Kingdom

Oxford University Press is a department of the University of Oxford.
It furthers the University's objective of excellence in research, scholarship,
and education by publishing worldwide. Oxford is a registered trade mark of
Oxford University Press in the UK and in certain other countries

© Helen Craske 2024

The moral rights of the author have been asserted

All rights reserved. No part of this publication may be reproduced, stored in
a retrieval system, or transmitted, in any form or by any means, without the
prior permission in writing of Oxford University Press, or as expressly permitted
by law, by licence or under terms agreed with the appropriate reprographics
rights organization. Enquiries concerning reproduction outside the scope of the
above should be sent to the Rights Department, Oxford University Press, at the
address above

You must not circulate this work in any other form
and you must impose this same condition on any acquirer

Published in the United States of America by Oxford University Press
198 Madison Avenue, New York, NY 10016, United States of America

British Library Cataloguing in Publication Data
Data available

Library of Congress Control Number: 2023949806

ISBN 9780198910190

DOI: 10.1093/9780198910220.001.0001

Printed and bound by
CPI Group (UK) Ltd, Croydon, CR0 4YY

Links to third party websites are provided by Oxford in good faith and
for information only. Oxford disclaims any responsibility for the materials
contained in any third party website referenced in this work.

*For my parents.*

# Acknowledgements

*Complicity in Fin-de-siècle Literature* emerges from a doctoral thesis funded by the Arts and Humanities Research Council and All Souls College, Oxford. A Junior Research Fellowship at Merton College, Oxford, provided the time, funds, and intellectual atmosphere required to revise and publish it in book form. It has been a privilege to benefit from such generous institutional support and to learn from my distinguished colleagues.

As a writer and scholar, I am indebted to the mentors who have guided my academic development: Sue Badger, Natalie Crawford, Allyson Emby, Ian Maclachlan, and Nick White. Special thanks go to my former doctoral supervisor, Andrew Counter, for the time, guidance, and inspiration he has given me. A range of readers generously offered advice about the book's content and translations: Eva Besson, Ben Craske, Fra' John Eidinow, Julien Schuh, and Rebecca Sugden. Jen Altehenger, Stephen Rainbird, Audrey Southgate, Anna Tankel, and Amanda Thomas have been stalwart friends throughout the book's fruition. For his companionship during the highs and lows, I cherish Eamonn O'Keeffe.

Above all, I would like to thank my parents, Nigel Craske and Josephine Craske, for their love and support. This book is dedicated to them.

# Contents

List of Figures ix
Note on Sources x

Introduction: Complicity as a Literary Concept 1
Complicity: A Fin-de-siècle Phenomenon? 3
Literature's Accomplices: Readers, Authors, and Critics 6
Chapter Outlines 14
Complicity: A Lens for Crossing Cultural Brows 17

1. Legal Complicity: Fin-de-siècle History and Case Studies 19
   Outraging Public Decency 23
   Underwriting Obscenity: *Prête-noms* at *Le Fin de Siècle* 26
   Political Sedition 31
   Illicit Associations: The Trial of the Thirty 34
   Literary Implications 38

2. Framing Literature: Guilt and the Fin-de-siècle Novel 39
   Illness and Cure: Literary Influence in Bourget's *Essais* 40
   The Psychological Novel: Conscience or *Complaisance*? 52
   Implication and Exculpation: *Le Disciple* (1889) 66

3. Writing Murder: Fictional Accomplices, Complicit Fictions 79
   Complicit Narratives: *Nono*, *La Bête humaine*, and *Complices* 83
   Locating Guilt: Crime Scenes 85
   Sharing and Displacing Guilt: Confession Scenes 95
   Complicit with Injustice: Trial Scenes 100
   'Murderer Literature' 106
   Murder: A Writer's Profession 115

4. Scandal and Collusion in Avant-Garde Media 122
   Partners in Crime: Rachilde and Jean Lorrain 125
   Collusive Genres: *Romans à clef* and Little Magazines 127
   Avant-Garde Polemic in *Le Zig-Zag* (1885) 130
   *Réclame* and *réclamation* 137
   *Déshabillage*, or Public Striptease 147
   Compromising Revelations in *Romans à Clef* 150
   Collaborative Exposure: Vulnerability and Risk 158

5. Saucy Magazines: An Erotic Network 168
   The 'revue légère' *Don Juan* (1895–1900) 168
   Seduction, Solicitation, and Collaboration 172

Titillation, Polemics, and Obscenity 181
Selling Sex: Periodicals as *Proxénètes* 195

Epilogue 209

*Bibliography* 212
*Index* 222

# List of Figures

Figure 3.1. 'Brevet d'assassin', *Journal des assassins*, 1 June 1884 (BnF) — 118
Figure 5.1. E. Cros, 'Petit lever', *Don Juan*, 18 November 1896 (BnF) — 185
Figure 5.2. Maison Claverie advert in *Don Juan*, 18 November 1896 (BnF) — 197
Figure 5.3. Advertising Page, *Don Juan*, 18 November 1896 (BnF) — 201

# Note on Sources

Some material from Chapter 4 previously appeared as 'Partners in Crime? Scandalous Complicity Between Rachilde and Jean Lorrain', in *Nineteenth-Century French Studies* 48, nos. 3–4 (2020): pp. 326–43, doi:10.1353/ncf.2020.0002, published by the University of Nebraska Press. A section from Chapter 5 previously appeared as 'Periodicals as *proxénètes*: Erotic Complicity in *Don Juan* (1895–1900)', in *French Studies* 76, no. 3 (2022): pp. 366–84, doi:10.1093/fs/knac099, published by Oxford University Press. I am grateful to both journals for granting permission for this material to reappear in book form.

Unless otherwise stated, all translations are my own.

# Introduction
## Complicity as a Literary Concept

Il nous semblait, hélas! qu'à nous la raconter, Michel avait rendu son action plus légitime. De ne savoir où la désapprouver, dans la lente explication qu'il en donna, nous en faisait presque complices. Nous y étions comme engagés.[1]

[We felt that, by telling us this story, Michel had somehow justified the way he had behaved. By not condemning his actions at any point during his long explanation, we were as good as being accomplices. We were in some way implicated.][2]

In André Gide's *L'Immoraliste* (1902), the protagonist recounts his life story to a group of friends, highlighting his recent divergence from established moral norms. The novel concludes with Michel's audience reflecting on the narrative they have just heard. By listening to Michel's confession in its entirety, the friends mirror, via *mise en abyme*, the reader approaching the end of *L'Immoraliste*. Both experiences, the text implies, involve a moral uneasiness that shows literature's capacity to implicate readers in transgressive content. The friends' inability to pinpoint precisely what moral position they ought to take, and their unwillingness to admit the full extent of their collusion with Michel's 'immoral' ideas and behaviour, speaks to the uncertainty of textual impact and reader response in turn-of-the-century France. If readers can become indirect participants in a shared illicit action, as Gide's novel suggests, what would it mean, for our understanding of literary culture, to consider reading not only as a seductive or transgressive activity, but also—and above all—as a fundamentally *complicit* one?

Responding to this question, *Complicity in Fin-de-siècle Literature* examines how literary works forge relationships of implication and collusion between writers, readers, and critics. It does so by analysing how notions of shared responsibility and guilt structured the production and perception of literature in fin-de-siècle France. This was an era when writers, publishers, and editors, could—and did—face trial alongside one another as accomplices in literary crimes such as obscenity, libel, and political sedition. French authors of the period regularly countered

---

[1] André Gide, *L'Immoraliste. Roman* (Paris: Mercure de France, 1902), p. 178.
[2] André Gide, *The Immoralist*, trans. Alan Sheridan (London: Penguin, 2000), p. 123.

accusations of seducing and corrupting their readers, in textual responses ranging from the vehement defences penned by mainstream authors, to the tongue-in-cheek polemic typical of the avant-garde.[3] Working with a range of genres and styles, fin-de-siècle writers employed specific techniques to encourage readers' identification with transgressive ideas and actions. By doing so, they constructed alternative forms of solidarity, especially in literary cultures situated outside the acceptable mainstream. It is above all the tendency for complicity to leap from within to beyond the written page that this book seeks to comprehend.

In both English and French, the word 'complicity' refers to an individual's implication or involvement in an illicit action committed by another person.[4] While denoting shared criminal responsibility and guilt, 'complicity' can also evoke forms of cooperation, solidarity, and amicability that do not necessarily retain an illicit undercurrent. This is particularly the case in French, where the figurative definition of 'complicité' includes: 'Connivence, coopération, action commune' ['Connivance, cooperation, common action'], and the extended definition of 'complice' ['accomplice'] reads: 'Individu qui participe à toute action menée avec un certain secret' ['Individual who participates in any action undertaken with a degree of secrecy'].[5] These wider definitions, which render complicity closely synonymous with collusion and connivance, have paved the way for the habitual modern French usage, which mitigates the word's legal connotations and highlights instead its relational or convivial aspect. A similar slippage occurs in the English locution 'partners in crime': although it can be used to evoke actual criminal accomplices, it more frequently describes—in a playful, humorous way—a particular kind of amical relationship. Because of its conceptual fluidity, ranging from shared legal responsibility to collusive friendship, 'complicity' conveys the ambivalent ways in which transgressive material can be employed and received in a range of literary forms.

When applied conceptually to literature, complicity works on both the thematic and the self-reflexive (or 'meta-literary') levels, which facilitate two interconnected lines of enquiry. The first involves analysing the representation of shared crime or guilt by writers and critics, in order to appreciate the close imbrication of legal, moral, and aesthetic discourses. As an approach, the thematic understanding of complicity relies on a contextualised, literary-historical awareness of critical

---

[3] I use the term 'avant-garde' to denote individuals who oppose or reject mainstream channels for recognition and success, using marginal media to secure their reputation and gain alternative forms of cultural capital. Typically associated with autotelic (as opposed to bourgeois or social) approaches to art, 'avant-garde' literature constantly changes in response to earlier models, including those within the avant-garde itself. For further discussion of the term, see Pierre Bourdieu, *Les Règles de l'art: genèse et structure du champ littéraire* (Paris: Seuil, 1998), pp. 175–7 and 352–6.
[4] See *A New English Dictionary on Historical Principles: founded mainly on the materials collected by the Philological Society*, edited by James Murray, 11 vols (Oxford: Clarendon Press, 1888–1933), II (1893), p. 728, and Larousse, Pierre, *Grand dictionnaire universel du XIXe siècle*, 17 vols (Paris: Administration du Grand Dictionnaire universel, 1866–77), IV (1869), pp. 784–5.
[5] Larousse, *Grand dictionnaire universel*, IV (1869), pp. 784–5.

reception and debates about the 'immoral' or transgressive potential of literature. It contributes to a longstanding critical tradition that examines the relationship between literature, morality, and the law. This tradition considers how societies define literary responsibility, crime, and guilt at given moments in history by analysing legal codes, trial documents, and judicial debate alongside incriminated literary texts.[6] Drawing on law and literature studies, my book examines relevant legal contexts in order to establish a historically grounded analysis of transgression and collusion. At the same time, it extends beyond legal history by viewing reading as a relationship and literature as a cultural network. It is here that the meta-literary side of complicity comes into play. Through it, the book's second line of enquiry considers how the presentation of illicit themes *within* literature intersects with, or enables, illicit solidarity created *through* literature. By employing this second approach, I combine close reading with a *poetics* of complicity to assess how specific literary techniques, texts, or genres create collaborative and collusive relationships between readers, writers, and critics. This type of analysis poses questions about content, form, and reception: to what extent are readers implicated in what they read? How are they encouraged to share responsibility for ideas and works considered immoral, if not outright illicit? Is this process associated with particular literary techniques or genres? If so, why might this be the case, and how effective are they?

## Complicity: A Fin-de-siècle Phenomenon?

Writers in late nineteenth-century France penned a broad range of morally compromising works, which encouraged collusive bonds between writers, critics, and readers. This process relied on a vision of the reader as an active, collaborative figure, presumed or constructed to be complicit with the perceived transgression of literary works. While closely bound up in fin-de-siècle concerns about literary bad influence and authorial responsibility, 'complicity' provides a vision of reader-text relations that nonetheless diverges from the viewpoints of moralising critics and self-justifying authors of the period, who depicted readers as victims to be pitied or exhorted to defend themselves against literature's pernicious effects.[7] Moralising visions of literary influence contributed to longstanding debates about the value of artistic and cultural production, which have evolved from discussions of mimesis in ancient philosophy to more recent concerns about video games

---

[6] Notable examples of this approach include: Yvan Leclerc, *Crimes écrits: la littérature en procès au XIXe siècle* (Paris: Plon, 1991), Elisabeth Ladenson, *Dirt for Art's Sake: Books on Trial from* Madame Bovary *to* Lolita (Ithaca: Cornell University Press, 2007), and Gisèle Sapiro, *La Responsabilité de l'écrivain* (Paris: Éditions du Seuil, 2011).

[7] On representations of the fin-de-siècle reader, see François Proulx, *Victims of the Book: Reading and Masculinity in Fin-de-Siècle France* (Toronto: University of Toronto Press, 2019), pp. 56–85.

and social media. Such debates play a familiar part in critical narratives analysing nineteenth-century France, which witnessed a persistent conflict between 'l'art social' ['social art'], with a morally improving purpose, and the autotelic *l'art pour l'art* ['art for art's sake'].[8] During the early nineteenth century, writers such as Germaine de Staël (1766–1817) and Victor Cousin (1792–1876) theorised a vision of art that sought to unite aesthetic and moral concerns.[9] In the Avant-Propos to *La Comédie humaine*, Honoré de Balzac (1799–1850) asserted literature's necessary contribution to improving society.[10] However, other writers rejected this attempted union between moral purpose and artistic beauty. Théophile Gautier (1811–72) famously claimed: 'Il n'y a de vraiment beau que ce qui ne peut servir à rien [...]. L'endroit le plus utile d'une maison, ce sont les latrines' ['Nothing is truly beautiful unless it serves no purpose [...]. The most useful place in a house is the lavatory'].[11] Reflecting the century's shift away from a patronage model of artistic creation to the industrialised mass production model facilitated by evolving print media technologies, these debates fed attendant concerns about 'industrial' literature, literary 'prostitution', and bad influence.[12]

Despite benefiting from a policy shift towards greater press freedom that culminated in the 1881 *Loi sur la liberté de la presse*, writers in the Third Republic continued to face criticism and litigation for their alleged immoral influence over readers.[13] This can partly be explained by a conservative moral backlash provoked by the socio-political upheaval of the Franco-Prussian War and the Paris Commune (1870–1). Another contributing factor was the popularity of new intellectual trends, such as philosophical pessimism and scientific positivism, which heightened concerns about the loss of traditional values in the face of analytical methods considered atheistic and immoral. Furthermore, an increasing number and broader range of readers exacerbated the perceived negative influence of such trends. At the fin de siècle, French literacy rates increased in the wake of educational reforms, and new mass media outlets targeted different classes of reader. These changes dovetailed with concerning developments in academic and literary circles. For example, the burgeoning disciplines of psychology, sociology, and criminology inspired the evolution of literary genres—including

---

[8] Gisèle Sapiro offers an encompassing overview of these debates in *La Responsabilité de l'écrivain: littérature, droit et morale en France (XIXe–XXIe siècle)* (Paris: Éditions du Seuil, 2011).

[9] Sapiro, *La Responsabilité*, pp. 168–9.

[10] Honoré de Balzac, *Œuvres complètes*, 24 vols (Paris: Michel Lévy Frères, 1869–76), I (1869), p. 10.

[11] Théophile Gautier, *Mademoiselle de Maupin, double amour*, 2 vols (Paris: Eugène Renduel, 1836), I, p. 47.

[12] On Charles Augustin Sainte-Beuve's use of the term 'littérature industrielle' ['industrial literature'], and the incorporation of literature into journalism as a way of seducing readers, see Éléonore Reverzy, *Portrait de l'artiste en fille de joie: la littérature publique* (Paris: CNRS Éditions, 2016), pp. 25–7.

[13] On the gradual easing of press restrictions from the 1860s and 1870s, see Raisa Rexer, *The Fallen Veil: A Literary and Cultural History of the Photographic Nude in Nineteenth-Century France* (Philadelphia: Philadelphia University Press, 2021), pp. 124–5.

the Naturalist novel, crime fiction, and the *roman psychologique* ['psychological novel']—in which the depiction of taboo topics, such as murder and adultery, became the norm. These genres were immensely popular and became the predominant novelistic modes in the period. Their practitioners regularly responded to accusations of moral complicity both thematically within their works and rhetorically in the prefaces and articles surrounding them. At the same time, writers at the margins of 'acceptable' literary production played up to the moral panic expressed in mainstream criticism by writing about illicit themes in a subversive and often tongue-in-cheek manner. They published works through smaller, avant-garde publishing houses and subversive literary reviews, which provided alternative means of achieving recognition and attaining cultural capital. Functioning as a backdrop, censor, and stimulus to artistic production of the period, a series of laws defined and regulated literature's capacity for committing, aiding, or abetting crime. Analysed in more detail in Chapter 1, these laws confirmed the widespread fear of moral contagion (or 'bad influence') in the period, the complexities involved in attributing literary responsibility, and the active legal awareness of writers and editors attempting to find loopholes in the system. Changing regulations for press-related crimes relied on specific, technical understandings of complicity that had a tangible impact on how literary works were written, produced, and received in the period.

While emphasising the specificities of the fin-de-siècle French context, this book proposes a methodology that transcends its own linguistic, geographical, and temporal parameters. As a concept and tool for literary study, 'complicity' can be used to analyse the predominance of illicit themes, the processes involved in critical reception, the formation of socio-literary networks, and the relationship between literature and media culture. Each of these elements can be considered in isolation, but they are most effectively understood through their interaction with one another. To examine these interactions, I draw on methods associated with close reading, literary history, sociology of literature, and cultural studies. The first employs close textual and intertextual analysis to examine how fin-de-siècle fiction depicted criminal acts and collusive characters, and what this suggests about contemporaneous visions of shared guilt. The second asks questions about reception, considering how critics framed literature as an implicating medium through which writers became morally complicit with the illicit ideas and behaviour they depicted (and supposedly encouraged in the malleable reader). Inspired by Bourdieu's sociology, the third analyses literary relationships and networks, exploring how literature functioned as a medium to create bonds between writers, readers, and critics via shared references, in-jokes, and forms of address. The fourth focuses on the intersection of different cultural forms and on literature as a marketable product sold to both elite and popular consumers. Each chapter combines the four approaches, but with a different level of emphasis, in response to the content, genre, and style of the material it analyses. This four-pronged approach offers a new terminology and conceptual framework through which to analyse literary influence and reception, applicable to different historical periods and national settings.

## Literature's Accomplices: Readers, Authors, and Critics

To draw out the broader applicability of complicity, I combine the term's general and legal definitions with theoretical discussions about the relationship between readers, authors, and critics. A key hypothesis guiding this book is that literary complicity requires the recognition of illicit textual content by readers, a presumption of malicious or corrupting intent on the part of authors, and the reader's capacity to translate their understanding of textual content into illicit action. In this process, the reader can be understood as a function played in the act of interpretation (the 'implied' reader). They also have the required knowledge and shared cultural references to understand the text in an 'acceptable' way, whether this notion relies on the concept of authorial intention or institutionally agreed upon processes of interpretation (the 'competent' reader). Finally, the reader is also a figure discussed by critics, often as a source of socio-political anxiety associated with the 'bad influence' model of literature. This figure combines the historically situated 'actual' reader, capable of translating their textual understanding into real-life action, and the projection of a generally *in*competent reader, who is insufficiently trained to interpret literature in an intellectually distant (and ideologically 'safer') way.

The functional vision of 'implied reader' was most famously promulgated by the German reception theorists Hans Robert Jauss (1921–97) and Wolfgang Iser (1926–2007).[14] Both thinkers proposed models for understanding reading as a communicative act between message (text) and receiver (reader): a dualistic relationship producing a form of 'directed perception', which influences individual acts of interpretation and wider trends of literary history.[15] For Jauss, the reading process involved an encounter between a reader's 'horizon of expectations'— the historically situated understanding of genre, form, and themes brought to a text—and the 'textual strategies' of any given work. Sufficient distance between the two could lead to a 'horizon change', whereby audience reactions evolve and appropriate—or reject—different aesthetic forms. By analysing this process, Jauss re-assessed the status of canonical works, emphasised how the critic's historical situatedness could influence aesthetic judgement, and asserted the 'socially

---

[14] Key precursors to German reception theory included: Russian formalism, Prague Structuralism, phenomenology, hermeneutics, and the sociology of literature. See Robert C. Holub, *Reception Theory: A Critical Introduction*, new edition (London: Routledge, 2003), pp. 13–52.

[15] Hans Robert Jauss, 'Literary History as a Challenge to Literary Theory', trans. Elizabeth Benzinger, *New Literary History* 2, no. 1 (1970): pp. 7–37 (p. 12), https://www.jstor.org/stable/468585.

formative function' of literature.[16] Whereas Jauss pursued a broad social vision of literary reception, Iser analysed response at a closer, textual level.[17] Borrowing concepts from John Langshaw Austin's speech act theory, Iser argued for a pragmatic approach to literature, assessing the conditions for successful communication between text and (implied) reader. In this relationship, the implied reader's role is to 'reduce the indeterminacies' of the text—to fill in the textual 'gaps'—and contribute to producing its meaning, guided by the text's 'strategies' and appeal to conventions. When discussing literary evolution, Iser valorised 'novel' literature that challenges or negates previous conventions, thereby encouraging readers to re-assess the social world rather than to accept or reproduce it.[18] Unlike Jauss, therefore, he left little room for appreciating the text-reader relationship constructed via so-called 'trivial' literature, which reaffirms previous conventions and the status quo.[19]

Although Jauss and Iser's postulations about the implied reader are broadly useful to discussions about complicity as a form of literary response, they are limited by their very abstraction. At what point, we might ask, does their vision of response truly differ from more general understandings of interpretation?[20] If complicity is understood as a synonym for textual reception, does this not risk falling into a generalisation, whereby all literary texts—regardless of content, genre, or style—can be said to rely on readers' complicity? To address such concerns and achieve a workable methodology, I combine several interpretations of reader response in this book. There are specific elements of Jauss's and Iser's approaches that resonate with my discussion of complicity and are worth highlighting. For example, Jauss's reassessment of the literary canon, combined with his emphasis on the critic's historically situated position, parallels this book's inclusion of cultural production beyond the canon and its attempts at critical self-awareness. Iser's attention to specific textual strategies and literary conventions anticipates how subsequent chapters employ close reading and genre-based analysis to discuss the ways in which texts create complicity through specific themes and techniques. In this way, the concept of 'implied reader' is most directly relevant to the current study through the manner in which it was wielded by its early proponents, within their broader analytical paradigms.

Located somewhere in-between the abstract 'implied' reader and the real-life 'actual' reader, the 'informed' or 'competent' reader is a construct used by theorists such as Stanley Fish and Jonathan Culler to evoke individuals—both real

[16] Jauss, 'Literary History', pp. 9, 14–5, 20, and 37.
[17] On Jauss's 'macrocosm of reception' and Iser's 'microcosm of response', see Holub, *Reception Theory*, pp. 82–3.
[18] Wolfgang Iser, 'The Reality of Fiction: A Functionalist Approach to Literature', *New Literary History* 7, no. 1 (1975): pp. 7–38 (pp. 22–9), https://www.jstor.org/stable/468276.
[19] Holub, *Reception Theory*, pp. 94–7.
[20] On this question, see also Holub, *Reception Theory*, p. 100.

and imagined/projected—who have the linguistic and cultural knowledge to interpret literary texts in ways that are acceptable to other readers within the same 'interpretative communities'.[21] Both critics stress the interpersonal, institutionalised, and historically contingent nature of literary interpretation, especially in academic circles (to which, as literature professors, they inevitably belong). My own vision of literary complicity amalgamates elements of the 'implied', 'actual', and 'competent' readers. By doing so, I draw on the notion of a 'targeted' reader ('lecteur visé'), proposed more recently by Ariane Bayle, Mathilde Bombart, and Isabelle Garnier, in their study of 'connivence' ['connivance'] in early modern French literature.[22] The volume's contributors adopt a historically situated approach to reader-writer and reader-text relations, which moves beyond postulating an 'implied' reader to acknowledging the existence of 'actual' readers and their authorial counterparts. This reduces the danger of making the reader synonymous with pre-existing notions of textual appeal.[23] While recognising the reader's role in filling a text's 'blanks', the contributors' historicist approach emphasises authorial intention as a guarantee for a text's hidden meanings. By doing so, they maintain a level of interest in authorship that is almost entirely absent from the work of Culler and Fish. Importantly, Bayle et al. focus primarily on how texts function upon their original publication, 'sans exclure pour autant d'éventuels réemplois ou relectures dans d'autres contextes où se cristalliseraient d'autres connivences, pas forcément prévues par l'auteur' ['without necessarily excluding potential re-uses or re-readings in other contexts, where other forms of connivance, perhaps unforeseen by the author, might crystallise'].[24] In this way, *L'Âge de la connivence* shares my emphasis on historically situated readings of transgressive texts, while hinting at the ways in which complicity or 'connivance' might be built into the structure of works and thus function every time the work is read, even by entirely *un*targeted readers.

The term 'targeted' reader acknowledges the multi-faceted nature of textual reception, which involves various interconnecting bonds and not just the

---

[21] On acceptability, Culler writes that '[the] question is not what actual readers happen to do but what an ideal reader must know implicitly in order to read and interpret works in ways which we consider acceptable, in accordance with the institution of literature'. Jonathan Culler, *Structuralist Poetics: Structuralism, Linguistics and the Study of Literature* (London: Routledge & Kegan Paul, 1975), p. 124. On interpretative communities, see Stanley Fish, 'Interpreting the *Variorum*', *Critical Inquiry* 2, no. 3 (1976): pp. 465–85 (pp. 483–4), doi:10.1086/447852.

[22] Bayle et al. define 'connivence' as a secretive form of mutual understanding that is actively constructed to bond authors to their public, or to one another. This process relies on the real or posited existence of an excluded third party ('tiers exclu'), in relation to which the conniving relationship plays out. The 'tiers exclu' could be a naïve reader incapable of perceiving the hidden, transgressive meanings of a text, or the potential censor whose accusatory gaze must be tricked or avoided. See Ariane Bayle, Mathilde Bombart, and Isabelle Garnier, 'La connivence, une notion opératoire pour l'analyse littéraire', in *L'Âge de la connivence: lire entre les mots à l'époque moderne*, edited by Ariane Bayle and others (Geneva: Droz, 2015), pp. 5–36 (pp. 7–9, 15, and 28).

[23] On the similarity between the implied reader and structures of literary appeal, see Holub, *Reception Theory*, p. 85.

[24] Bayle et al., 'La connivence', pp. 23–5.

reader-text relationship proposed by Jauss and Iser. In particular, it considers the role played by authors—and to a lesser extent, editors and publishers—in the construction of literary complicity. Like readers, authors represent a 'function' or role required in the production of textual meaning. They are also real-life individuals, who are liable for the content they publish, and who can be taken to court for press-related crimes.[25] As an 'actual' individual, the author is a participant in literary culture, by associating with particular social *milieux*, responding to pre-existing traditions, and enacting intertextual exchanges. As players in the literary game, 'actual' writers also take on imaginary or projected roles, typically in the form of media personae, which are forged by textual, often collaborative, means. Finally, like the reader, the author is a figure discussed by critics and a source of socio-political anxiety, due to their perceived capacity for illicit or immoral influence over real-life (if partly phantasmatic) readers.

By viewing authors as potential accomplices within a broader vision of literary networks, *Complicity in Fin-de-siècle Literature* draws heavily on the work of Pierre Bourdieu (1930–2002). It does so by framing complicity as a socio-cultural phenomenon, which feeds into and shapes the bonds created between writers and their audiences, including other authors: the teammates, rivals, and arbiters of taste playing for, and judging success in, the literary 'game'.[26] When analysing literary culture through a sociological lens, Bourdieu suggests that writers' choices and strategies result from the back-and-forth relationship between their individual dispositions ('habitus'), their position in the field (which is determined by the accumulation of 'capital', whether economic, social, cultural, or symbolic), and the state of play in that social arena (or 'field').[27] He speaks of writers' strategic 'position-takings' within this social arena, founded on an intuitive 'feel for the game'—something which is strengthened when the field in question matches an individual's pre-existing habitus.[28] The key message in Bourdieu's work is that critics and theorists should think *relationally* when analysing socio-cultural phenomena. This approach is well suited to my primary theme, since the notion of 'complicity' expresses how individuals can be united by a specific relational bond—in this instance, a bond based on implication and collusion. For Bourdieu,

---

[25] On the 'author function' and the importance of legal liability, see Michel Foucault, 'Qu'est-ce qu'un auteur?', in *Dits et écrits*, edited by Daniel Defert and others, 4 vols (Paris: Gallimard, 1994), I, pp. 789–821.

[26] See Bourdieu, *Les Règles de l'art*.

[27] Karl Maton and Patricia Thomson define 'habitus' and 'field' in *Pierre Bourdieu: Key Concepts*, edited by Michael Grenfell (London: Routledge, 2014, 2nd ed.), pp. 48–64 and pp. 65–80, respectively. 'Habitus' refers to individuals' ways of acting, feeling, thinking, and being (p. 51). 'Field' refers to the social space upon which the competitive game of capital accumulation takes place, each with its own logic or 'doxa', and which exerts influence on the individuals who play within it (pp. 67–9). The term 'doxa', examined by Cécile Deer in the same volume (pp. 114–25), evokes the 'pre-reflexive, shared but unquestioned opinions and perceptions conveyed within and by relatively autonomous social entities—fields' (p. 115).

[28] See John R. W. Speller, *Bourdieu and Literature* (Cambridge: Open Book Publishers, 2011), pp. 61–2, and Karl Maton in Grenfell, ed., *Pierre Bourdieu*, p. 57.

as John Speller has noted, the literary analyst's task is 'to explain why particular authors have adopted particular strategies'.[29] The following pages respond to this undertaking by asking: why did fin-de-siècle authors, from across the literary field, consistently return to notions of immoral influence and illicit solidarity? Which socio-historical factors facilitated their engagement with these questions? And what impact did complicity-related textual strategies have on writers' careers, relationships, and reception?

There is clearly a productive intersection between Bourdieusian sociology and the forms of 'complicity' studied in this book. However, Bourdieu used the term in a different way, which reflected his wider philosophy regarding analytical criticism. Throughout *Les Règles de l'art*, the terms 'complicité', 'collusion', and 'connivence' evoke an unquestioning allegiance with a field's prevailing doxa, on the part of writers, readers, and critics. Citing the examples of bourgeois theatre and journalism, Bourdieu demonstrates how shared presuppositions create collusion between authors and their readers or audience.[30] The 'interested participation' of the individuals involved requires ideological complicity with preexisting values, and this 'fait que le jeu vaut la peine d'être joué, [et] est au principe du fonctionnement du jeu' ['make[s] the game worth the trouble of playing it' and is 'the basis of the functioning of the game'].[31] Importantly, Bourdieu applies this logic to modern critics as well as to those from the past, asserting the need for self-reflexivity in order to understand how scholars are bound up in what they analyse. He takes issue with critics who fail to historicise the processes involved in literary production and its reception, arguing that the most 'objective' form of analysis involves accounting for the preconceptions, interests, and impulses of the knowing subject ('sujet connaissant').[32] This requires critics to suspend 'la relation de complicité et de connivence qui lie tout homme cultivé au jeu culturel pour constituer ce jeu en objet' ['the relationship of complicity and connivance which ties every cultivated person to the cultural game, in order to constitute the game as object'].[33] While scholars may take issue with the idea that being taken in by the doxa of literary works is a completely negative phenomenon, since it contributes to the pleasure of reading and interpretation, many would agree that self-awareness and critical reflexivity are important skills to hone. Maintaining this dualism, I suggest that by analysing the processes by which literary complicity is created—for

---

[29] Speller, *Bourdieu and Literature*, p. 67.
[30] Bourdieu evokes the 'complicité éthique et politique' ['ethical and political complicity'] between author and audience in bourgeois theatre (*Règles*, p. 108), and the 'affinité élective' ['elective affinity'] between journalist, newspaper, and readership in nineteenth-century journalism (*Règles*, p. 235). For English translations, see Pierre Bourdieu, *The Rules of Art: Genesis and Structure of the Literary Field*, trans. Susan Emanuel (Stanford: Stanford University Press, 1996), pp. 71 and 165, respectively.
[31] Bourdieu, *Règles*, pp. 316–17 (*Rules*, pp. 227–8).
[32] See Bourdieu, *Règles*, pp. 274 and 291 (*Rules*, pp. 194 and 207).
[33] Bourdieu, *Règles*, p. 320 (*Rules*, p. 230).

both contemporaneous and modern readers, critics included—scholars can better understand its impact and appeal.

When analysing the construction of complicit bonds, it might be tempting to view readers, authors, and critics as neutral figures, with whom all individuals can identify and relate. But as Bourdieu's analysis of social distinction and cultural capital suggests, this is rarely the case in the literary field.[34] It is therefore important to consider which personal, social, and cultural factors may affect and limit a 'complicit' response to literary works. As a primary form of distinction between individuals, gender identity impacts most—if not all—of these factors, and it was particularly ubiquitous in fin-de-siècle French literary culture.[35] Hierarchised gender distinctions can emerge through textual and extratextual means, including the depiction of relationships between characters, the predominance of certain themes, forms of appeal or address, and critical framing. In literary analysis, it is therefore useful to ask: are the main characters chiefly men or women? What is the power dynamic between them? Which relationships are prioritised in the narrative, and which are minimised or occluded? Are there intertextual references to other literary, historical, or cultural writings, and what kind of reader would appreciate these references? Is there an authorial preface, or an embedded narrator-narratee structure, that addresses a particular type of reader? The answers to these questions are frequently bound up in genre-based traditions and can be affected by an author's sense of belonging to, or desire to dissociate from, a specific literary 'school'. For example, nineteenth-century French adultery novels typically focused on relationships between men and women, and depicted the myriad ways in which female sexual desire could be restricted or released, celebrated or condemned. In a similar but reversed dynamic, the novel of formation usually centred on the education and career of male characters, whose trajectories depended on the creation of bonds with other men, as well as the manipulation (and eventual renunciation or denial) of more ambiguous feminine influences.[36] If not directly mirroring reality, these genres indirectly reflected the period's sociopolitical anxieties, and contemporaneous responses to them demonstrated how gender distinctions shaped fin-de-siècle debates about appropriate and inappropriate reading. Such debates, analysed at greater length in Chapter 2, focused on the social, political, and moral dangers of women reading 'immoral' texts, but

---

[34] Bourdieu analyses how different classes respond to the same cultural artefacts in *La Distinction: critique sociale du jugement* (Paris: Éditions de Minuit, 1979). See chapter five, 'Le sens de la distinction', pp. 293–364.

[35] Other forms of identity difference, such as class, age, and ethnicity, affect the types of complicity formulated in any given literary text. However, gender identity is the clearest distinction made in the works under study. Other defining characteristics, less frequently thematised, remain beyond the scope of this book.

[36] For a critical re-assessment of this male-centred tradition, see Juliette Rogers, *Career Stories: Belle Époque Novels of Professional Development* (Pennsylvania: Penn State University Press, 2007).

they also sought to bolster socially acceptable forms of masculinity against the perceived onslaught of 'degeneration' post-1870.[37]

On both the thematic and meta-literary levels, fin-de-siècle complicity was a gendered phenomenon. In works of the period, thematic transgression went hand in hand with questions of gender identity, notably through the depiction of adultery, murder, 'perversion', and eroticism. Gender also played an important role in the construction of meta-literary complicity between writers and readers, the latter of whom were implicitly or explicitly posited as men. This process relies on mediated forms of male bonding that Eve Kosofsky-Sedgwick has referred to as 'homosociality'. Drawing on René Girard's vision of triangulated desire, Sedgwick states that homosociality between men requires the presence of a woman, who, as an object of desire and source of rivalry, facilitates the indirect bond between two competing men. The homosocial model binds desire, identification, and emulation in a complex correlation, while denying women power in their silent, mediating position.[38] Sedgwick notes that 'in any male-dominated society, there is a special relationship between male homosocial (*including* homosexual) desire and the structures for maintaining and transmitting patriarchal power.'[39] Describing a form of complicity in its own right, Sedgwick's analysis hints at how fin-de-siècle writers relied on male homosocial bonding, constructed through a shared desire for, and denigration of, occluded female figures. *Between Men* underscores the importance of considering whether specific works were targeted chiefly at men, and relied on extratextual homosociality between (male) reader and (male) author, or whether women were also targeted as potential and actual readers.

It is not a coincidence that this book analyses material that frequently depicts men bonding with other men over women who are demeaned or destroyed. In adultery narratives, women are seduced and abandoned. In crime fiction, they are raped and murdered. In newspapers, women writers are mocked and reviled. In erotic ephemera, actresses and courtesans are the source of gossip and the butt of smutty jokes. As Alistaire Tallent notes, recounting stories about sexually available women can create an 'intimate imaginary connection' between men, particularly when the stories appear within male-to-male discursive textual frames.[40] Citing more extreme cases, such as fictional depictions of rape and femicide, Andrew Counter argues that the threat of sexual violence can function as a homosocial

---

[37] For further discussion of these questions, see Martyn Lyons, *Readers and Society in Nineteenth-Century France: Workers, Women, Peasants* (Basingstoke: Palgrave, 2001), and Proulx, *Victims of the Book*.

[38] Eve Kosofsky Sedgwick, *Between Men: English Literature and Male Homosocial Desire* (New York: Columbia University Press, 1992), pp. 1–27.

[39] Sedgwick, *Between Men*, p. 25.

[40] Alistaire Tallent, 'Intimate Exchanges: The Courtesan Narrative and Male Homosocial Desire in "La Dame aux camélias"', *French Forum* 39, no. 1 (Winter 2014): pp. 19–31 (p. 28), doi:10.1353/frf.2014.0001.

'signifying structure' that 'reinscribes the female body as a sign which allows a certain communication for and between men'.[41] Even the seemingly innocuous literary technique of irony can imply homosocial and misogynistic complicity with ideologies of gender difference.[42] Probing this question further, Amy Staples has considered the impact of modern critics' gender when analysing misogynistic texts from earlier periods, citing Wayne Booth's response to Rabelais's smutty jokes as an exemplary warning about the ongoing influence of homosociality in academic scholarship.[43] Put succinctly, there are subtle as well as obvious forms of misogyny in many literary traditions, and women readers—including modern feminist critics—can find themselves uncomfortably placed in relation to male authors' misogyny and the 'boys' club' mentality pressurising them to become ideologically complicit with it.

That said, the concept of 'homosociality' is not limited to describing relationships between men, and women readers are not necessarily doomed to become complicit with male homosocial misogyny. The forms of identification, desire, and emulation between men analysed by Sedgwick exist in comparable—if not identical—ways between women. In her influential work on the topic, Sharon Marcus studies female homosociality in Victorian England, focusing on the depiction of female friendships, desirable femininity, and marriage plots. She claims that 'we need to abandon the persistent assumption that erotic interest in femininity can only be masculine', noting how, for example, fashion plates in women's magazines 'solicited a female gaze for images that put women, their bodies, and the objects that adorned them on display'.[44] By consuming these texts, women readers could experience 'enhanced subjectivity' and 'mastery' in response to objectified female figures, in a similar way to their male counterparts.[45] To support this reading, Marcus theorises the erotic as 'a set of dynamics rather than as a function of fixed gender relations or literal sex acts', and assumes that 'women can and do feel the same forms of desire as men'.[46] Although some may disagree with Marcus's claim that '[e]rotic fantasies have no fixed relationship to gender roles, to sex acts, or to social power dynamics', it is clear that her reading of Victorian culture facilitates a more nuanced understanding of women's responses to an array of textual

---

[41] Andrew Counter, 'Tough Love, Hard Bargains: Rape and Coercion in Balzac', *Nineteenth-Century French Studies* 36, nos. 1–2 (Fall–Winter 2007-8): pp. 61–71 (p. 68), https://www.jstor.org/stable/23538479.
[42] Ross Chambers, 'Irony and Misogyny: Authority and the Homosocial in Baudelaire and Flaubert', *Australian Journal of French Studies* 26, no. 3 (1989), pp. 272–88.
[43] Amy Staples, 'Primal Scenes / Primal Screens: The Homosocial Economy of Dirty Jokes', in *High Anxiety: Masculinity in Crisis in Early Modern France*, edited by Kathleen Perry Long (Penn State University Press, 2002), pp. 37–54.
[44] Sharon Marcus, *Between Women: Friendship, Desire, and Marriage in Victorian England* (Princeton: Princeton University Press, 2009), pp. 12 and 119.
[45] Marcus, *Between Women*, p. 120.
[46] Marcus, *Between Women*, p. 115.

and visual material.[47] Due to its conceptual breadth, Marcus's approach can be applied to other periods and geographical contexts, although her examples solicit comparisons with countries sharing close cultural ties to Britain.[48] In fact, the latter decades of the Victorian era constituted a privileged moment for elaborating on how gender intersected with literary complicity.

Throughout this book, theoretical notions such as homosociality, the literary field, and targeted readers help to establish a wide-ranging critical understanding of complicity as a literary phenomenon. Rather than providing central and immutable tenets, however, they feature as conceptual motifs that draw out the broader implications of particular case studies. Woven into the book's four-pronged methodology—combining close reading, literary history, sociology of literature, and cultural studies—these ideas nuance its analysis and indicate areas of crossover and comparison between different cultural forms. By using a selection of theoretical concepts in dialogue with general definitions and historically specific legal terminology, *Complicity in Fin-de-siècle Literature* provides a roadmap for employing complicity as a critical lens, while demonstrating the method's value by carefully applying it to a specific range of texts.

## Chapter Outlines

Legal definitions of shared crime and guilt are central to understanding complicity as a phenomenon in fin-de-siècle literature. To explain why this is the case, the first chapter considers how the legal framing of literature's social and moral value intersected with subversive writing and interpretative practices in the period. It highlights two key elements of legal complicity relevant to literary production: incitement and collaboration. By analysing the evolution of these notions in two contentious press crimes—outraging public decency and political sedition—the chapter teases out some of the strategies and techniques by which fin-de-siècle writers, both individually and collectively, responded to politicians' and jurists' vision of literature as a source of illicit influence and subversive solidarity. Examining a combination of legal statute, judicial procedure, and press depictions of criminal trials, the chapter discusses the processes involved in attributing—and avoiding—criminal responsibility in fin-de-siècle literary culture. Closely studying legal definitions of complicity, and how they were interpreted in particular case studies, helps not only to situate fin-de-siècle literary production against its legal backdrop, but also to formulate conceptual analogies that feed into the textual analysis of subsequent chapters.

---

[47] Marcus, *Between Women*, p. 115.
[48] As confirmation of the close ties between Britain and France in the period, most of the images Marcus cites are French. See Marcus, *Between Men*, pp. 122–6, 128–30, 133–4, 136–7, and 154.

When fin-de-siècle writers treated shared responsibility and guilt as a theme, they often did so in response to the 'bad influence' model of reception. Premised on readers' mimetic responses to literature, the model served to accuse writers of complicity with the 'immoral' or illicit behaviour they depicted. To examine the importance of such accusations in the formulation of literary complicity, Chapter 2 analyses the works and reception of Paul Bourget (1852–1935)—an exemplary figure whose contribution to debates about the formative and potentially corrupting influence of literary production shifted throughout his career. First, it considers how Bourget reframed the 'bad influence' model in the *Essais de psychologie contemporaine* (1883) by depicting literary influence as a set of symptoms indicative of social and moral illnesses, but also as their potential cure. Second, it examines the ambivalence of his position in the mid-1880s, when he wrote a series of psychological novels centred on adultery, such as *Un crime d'amour* (1886). Analysing this novel alongside Bourget's critical reception in the period suggests that the author's increasing notoriety depended on his reputation hovering ambiguously between acceptability and immorality. Finally, the chapter turns to Bourget's most famous novel, *Le Disciple* (1889): a *roman à these* ['thesis novel'] through which the author responded to his implication in a highly mediatised murder trial. Studying the novel's presentation of seduction and corruption, its confessional structure, and its reception, facilitates a re-evaluation of readers' capacity to respond to—and reject—the novel's 'thesis'. The chapter concludes that literary guilt at the fin de siècle was less a discernible, pre-existing category than a product of extra-literary and meta-literary interactions, with authors, readers, and critics frequently attributing and avoiding blame through the framing mechanism of prefaces and journal articles.

The intense media debate about literary influence and writers' responsibility that greeted the publication of *Le Disciple* channelled fears about the widespread fin-de-siècle interest in stories about violent crime. With the birth of criminology and increasingly sensational media reporting on infamous murderers (such as Joseph Vacher and Jack the Ripper), the rise of crime fiction in the late nineteenth century heightened political and judicial concerns about literature's capacity to encourage readers to commit copycat crimes. Yet the sensational appeal of violent crime, associated with denigrated 'popular' genres such melodrama and the *roman-feuillleton* ['serialised novel'], was irrepressible, and lead one fin-de-siècle critic to hail the emergence of a 'littérature des assasssins' ['murderer literature']. Charting the imbrication between popular, scientific, and literary representations of crime, Chapter 3 considers how writers of the period appropriated the theme of criminal complicity, whether this be to critique the judicial status quo or to valorise an alternative literary aesthetic. The first and larger part of the chapter compares three novels—Rachilde's *Nono* (1885), Émile Zola's *La Bête humaine* (1890), and Hector Malot's *Complices* (1893)—whose plotlines, character development, and primary themes centred on criminal complicity in the act of murder.

It examines how the novels' murder scenes create a haunting sense of guilt, which recurs via structural parallels charting the plot's descending spiral of crime. Then it considers how confession creates bonds of complicity between characters and encourages further crimes, in a way that reflects fin-de-siècle debates about the influence of crime fiction on readers' behaviour. Finally, it analyses the displacement of blame onto scapegoat characters who happen to fit—or deliberately play up to—popular and pseudo-scientific received ideas about criminality. Using the term 'murderer literature' as a springboard, the chapter's second part explores the ways in which writer-journalists such as Rachilde (1860–1953), Octave Mirbeau (1848–1917), Maurice Beaubourg (1859–1943), and Romain Coolus (1868–1952) transformed the question of murder and criminal complicity into a source of literary solidarity. Analysing a combination of journal articles and longer fictional works—including Beaubourg's *Contes pour les assassins* (1890), Rachilde's *La Sanglante Ironie* (1891), and Mirbeau's *Le Jardin des supplices* (1899)—this section examines the self-referential approach typical of avant-garde writers, drawing out the meta-literary implications of a recurrent analogy between criminal association and literary endeavour.

By depicting adultery and murder, fin-de-siècle writers fed off the popularity of illicit topics while also responding to, critiquing, and in some cases subverting the 'bad influence' model of literary reception. This is particularly the case for avant-garde writers, who occupied, or were seen to occupy, a subversive and 'criminal' space in the literary field. Set apart from mainstream literature, whose values and moral guidelines they rejected, such writers attracted criticism and litigation for their depiction of illicit themes, notably sexuality. The book's latter two chapters suggest that this marginal, criminalised status provided a specific sense of communal identification or illicit solidarity between writers associated with the avant-garde. Chapter 4 analyses a group of writers—at their centre: Rachilde, Jean Lorrain (1855–1906), and Oscar Méténier (1859–1913)—whose media exchanges created a sense of collusion by inviting readers 'in the know' to unravel half-veiled secrets. It explores the group's relationships through a polemical media exchange in a little magazine called *Le Zig-Zag* and two *romans à clef* by Méténier: 'L'Aventure de Marius Dauriat' (1885) and 'Décadence' (1886). By analysing these works in conjunction with selected correspondence, the chapter shows how biographically revealing texts created complicity not only between the writer and the reader, but also between the writers themselves, as they mutually constructed media personae based on the titillating appeal of taboos surrounding gender and sexuality. Highlighting the close imbrication between self-promotion and self-defence in these exchanges, Chapter 4 concludes that the strategy of biographical unveiling was a productive but problematic source for avant-garde solidarity, since there were both benefits and risks involved in publicly revealing 'compromising' material.

As the media exchanges between Rachilde, Lorrain, and Méténier suggest, the boundary between the acceptable and the illicit is notably ambiguous when sex is involved. Following this logic, Chapter 5 demonstrates that the production of erotic material established networks of complicity between fin-de-siècle writers, reviews, and businesses. To do so, it analyses *Don Juan* (1895–1900): a saucy magazine that published a range of literary and artistic works, from the popular to the avant-garde. This exemplary but previously unstudied review offers a window onto the networks of illicit erotic businesses vilified by jurists from 1882 onwards. The chapter's analysis shows that *Don Juan* created forms of erotic complicity between text, contributor, and reader by wielding sex appeal, shared humour, and textual structures appealing for response and involvement. First, it explores how the review framed the reading experience as a form of erotic exchange between reciprocally desiring partners, in a reformulation of earlier traditions of gallantry and *libertinage*. Second, it considers how the review's textual and visual content hovered between socially acceptable frothy eroticism and illicit obscenity, notably crossing this boundary in 1896, when the review's director Alfred Hippolyte Bonnet faced trial for 'outrages aux bonnes mœurs' ['outraging public decency']. Finally, it suggests that the review enacted a form of 'pimp journalism' by encouraging and enabling readers to engage in both imagined and actual erotic relations. Through its manipulation of different advertising formats—such as personal ads, book catalogues, and veiled advertising or 'réclame'—*Don Juan* provided space for erotic exchange, both real and imagined. By doing so, it blurred the generic and structural boundaries between advertising and main copy, pecuniary interest and artistic expression.

## Complicity: A Lens for Crossing Cultural Brows

Discussing a range of revealing case studies, the book's chapters cover well-known literary schools and genres—such as Naturalism, Decadence, and the psychological novel—as well as more obscure literary forms, including biographically revealing novels, little magazines, and saucy magazines. Within this corpus, critically recognised writers—including Émile Zola (1840–1902), Rachilde, Jean Lorrain, Paul Bourget, and Octave Mirbeau—appear alongside lesser-known literary figures, such as Oscar Méténier, Maurice Beaubourg, and René Emery. My analysis therefore spans across the literary and social spectrum, from the avant-garde highbrow to the popular low brow and passing through the bourgeois middle. On delineating one 'brow' from another, Diana Holmes notes: '[no] text is essentially and forever middlebrow [...]: novels may and do shift from one "brow" to another at different periods and under different regimes of publishing and readership'. Nevertheless, Holmes delineates a 'middlebrow poetics', based on mimesis and immersivity.[49] Historically denigrated by a critical canon that valorises the 'difficulty' of French modernism, 'middlebrow' works typically appeal to a non-specialist readership. Rather than viewing such readers as deluded victims of immersive and vicarious pleasure, Holmes suggests (alongside Jean-Marie Schaeffer) that they can choose to participate in 'a voluntarily shared, playful act of make-believe, a contract between author and reader rather than an imposture'.[50] This vision of a playful and voluntary contract resonates with elements of literary complicity, although the latter evokes a type of immersivity that encourages readers to identify with illicit or immoral content, in a way that does not necessarily help to 'make provisional sense' of characters' or readers' lives.[51]

By analysing a corpus that combines cultural 'brows', my book adds aesthetic transgression—the act of crossing boundaries of 'taste' and 'value'—to its thematic and meta-literary counterparts. These elements frequently intertwined, and writers' adoption of them could shift over time. For example, Paul Bourget moved from promoting an avant-garde appreciation of literature in his early criticism to publishing middlebrow (if slightly risqué) adultery novels, before finally adopting a conservative moralising stance in a series of *romans à thèse* (Chapter 2). Following a different route, some writers of the period—from the mainstream (Zola) to the avant-garde (Rachilde, Mirbeau, Beaubourg)—appropriated popular crime narrative while satirising 'scientific' criminology (Chapter 3). Others employed scandal and titillation to construct controversial media personalities, combining an avant-garde interest in illicit topics with publicity strategies associated with denigrated forms of popular entertainment (Chapter 4). Meanwhile, inexpensive illustrated magazines such as *Don Juan* published contributions from avant-garde authors and popular writers of titillating fiction, which appeared alongside gossip, satire, and erotica (Chapter 5). Such examples demonstrate how mainstream and avant-garde writers appropriated themes and techniques associated with both popular and middlebrow literature, thereby revising the typically oppositional vision of these phenomena.[52] By bringing together material from different levels of cultural production, and from a range of less studied primary and archival sources, *Complicity in Fin-de-siècle Literature* widens our knowledge of late nineteenth-century French literature and the literary field more generally. Each of its chapters, read individually or combined, seeks to situate canonical literature in relation to its non-canonical counterparts, by revealing the widespread appeal of illicit topics and subversive solidarities across the literary spectrum.

---

[49] Diana Holmes, *Middlebrow Matters: Women's Reading and the Literary Canon in France Since the Belle Époque* (Liverpool: Liverpool University Press, 2018), pp. 2–3. In this study, Holmes focuses on novels, leaving the relation between 'brow' and periodical culture largely untreated.
[50] Jean-Marie Schaeffer, *Pourquoi la fiction?* (Paris: Éditions du Seuil, 1999), p. 148, cited in Holmes, *Middlebrow Matters*, p. 18.
[51] Holmes, *Middlebrow Matters*, p. 13.
[52] See Holmes, *Middlebrow Matters*, p. 35.

# 1
# Legal Complicity
## Fin-de-siècle History and Case Studies

The symbolic power of complicity in fin-de-siècle France was bound up in the term's legal definition and its impact on literary production. Two key factors structured this relationship: first, the association of complicity with incitement, and second, the framing of press crimes as collaborative action. According to Article 60 of the 1810 Penal Code:

> Seront punis comme complices d'une action qualifiée crime ou délit, ceux qui, par dons, promesses, menaces, abus d'autorité ou de pouvoir, machinations ou artifices coupables, auront provoqué à cette action, ou donné des instructions pour la commettre.[1]
>
> [Those who incite or give instruction to commit an action defined as a crime or misdemeanour—whether through gifts, promises, threats, abuses of authority or control, plotting, or trickery—will be punished as accomplices in this action.]

Subsequent laws cited this definition, which applied to all criminal accomplices. It notably featured in the ground-breaking *Loi sur la liberté de la presse* (29 July 1881), which defended the principle of press freedom and significantly reduced the number of punishable press crimes.[2] According to its stipulations, those involved in publishing textual or visual material could be legally inculpated primarily by their complicity with other crimes, through the act of incitement:

> Seront punis comme complices d'une action qualifiée crime ou délit ceux qui par des discours, cris ou menaces proférés dans des lieux ou réunions publiques soit par des écrits, des imprimés vendus ou distribués, mis en vente ou exposés dans des lieux ou réunions publiques, soit par des placards ou affiches déposés aux regards du public, auront *directement* provoqué l'auteur ou les auteurs à commettre la dite action *si la provocation a été suivie d'effet.*[3]

---

[1] *Code pénal de l'empire français. Edition conforme à celle de l'imprimerie impériale* (Paris: Prieur, Belin fils, Merlin, and Rondonneau, 1810), p. 8.

[2] The 1881 law abolished crimes of opinion (*délits d'opinion*) such as outraging religious morals, attacking the Constitution, and inciting hatred or disdain for the government. However, it retained other crimes, such as outraging public decency and defamation.

[3] Article 23, *Loi sur la liberté de la presse du 29 juillet 1881* (Paris: Dubuisson, 1881). My emphasis.

[Those who *directly* incite an author (or authors) of an action defined as a crime or misdemeanour—whether through speech, shouting, or threats uttered in public spaces or gatherings, whether through written works or printed material that is sold, distributed, put up for sale or exhibited in public spaces or gatherings, whether through signs or posters placed in public view—will be punished as accomplices in this action, *if the incitement was acted upon*.]

By stating that the accused must have *directly* incited a committed crime ('provocation [...] suivie d'effet'), the 1881 law removed a level of ambiguity that had been present in previous legal statutes.[4] In particular, this limited the capacity to charge someone for exerting a broader, less specific influence over a crime's author—a form of indirect responsibility that Sapiro refers to as 'complicité morale' ['moral complicity'].[5] However, there were certain crimes for which incitement alone could be punished, without requiring the incited crime to be 'suivie d'effet' ['acted upon']. These included murder, pillage, arson, military misdemeanour, and crimes against state security.[6] In these cases, outlined in article 24 of the 1881 law, incitement becomes a separate crime, which does not require the 'suivie d'effet' proof outlined in the preceding article on complicity.

The legal distinctions regarding levels and types of criminal encouragement reflected the widely held view that literature could have a direct and indirect influence over people's actions, potentially to the detriment of social and moral order. This idea structured fin-de-siècle debates about literary 'bad influence', where morality critics depicted writers as exerting a corrupting force over their readers. As Gisèle Sapiro has noted, the debate about literature's capacity to encourage moral decline has a long history, with a key source—at least in Western tradition—being Aristotle and Plato's discussions of mimesis. Understood as both representation and imitation, mimesis relies on the identification of the reader or audience with the aesthetic object. Whereas Aristotle emphasised the role of catharsis in enabling readers to distance themselves from the impact of mimetic identification, Plato insisted upon its capacity to encourage subversive and immoral tendencies. The latter's view became increasingly medicalised during the eighteenth and nineteenth centuries, when scientists and doctors examined the immoral influence of literary production, typically employing metaphors relating to poison, infection, and contagion.[7] In such a vision of literary relations, the

---

[4] See articles 1 and 8 of the 17 May 1819 law, cited in Yvan Leclerc, *Crimes écrits: la littérature en procès au XIXe siècle* (Paris: Plon, 1991), pp. 19–20.

[5] Gisèle Sapiro, *La Responsabilité de l'écrivain: littérature, droit et morale en France (XIXe–XXIe siècle)* (Paris: Éditions du Seuil, 2011), pp. 50–2.

[6] On the question of 'provocation non suivie d'effets' ['incitement without effect'] in the judicial debates preceding the 1881 law, see Sapiro, *La Responsabilité*, pp. 330–3.

[7] Sapiro, *La Responsabilité*, pp. 127–30.

reader played a passive and victimised role.[8] This was particularly the case for readers defined by reigning ideologies as naturally inclined to corruption, such as women, children, and the working classes.[9] Jurists and politicians cited these individuals less for their real-life existence than for their capacity to symbolise the passive, impressionable reader in general. Yet their vision of the reader was ambiguous, hovering somewhere between a potential criminal and a victim of illicit influence. This blurred the link between cause and effect when attributing responsibility: were writers fundamentally corrupting or were readers fundamentally corruptible? In the latter case, vehement responses to 'immoral' literature at the fin de siècle betrayed an underlying fear that the reading population was inherently criminally inclined, requiring only a small amount of encouragement to transgress social, moral, and legal norms.

As well as evoking writers' capacity to incite others to commit illegal actions, complicity also refers to the collaborative structure of press crimes, which implicated various people involved in the publication of illicit material. On this question, the 1881 law outlined the individuals who were jointly responsible for press-specific crimes such as obscenity, libel, and political sedition. Importantly, the law stated that press managers and publishers were considered the primary culprits and authors their accomplices. This distinction existed because the law punished the act of publishing, rather than writing, illicit material. Article 42 describes the hierarchy of individuals considered liable for press crimes, in the following order: '1° les gérants ou éditeurs, quelles que soient leurs professions ou leurs dénominations; 2° à leur défaut, les auteurs; 3° à défaut des auteurs, les imprimeurs; 4° à défaut des imprimeurs, les vendeurs, distributeurs ou afficheurs' ['(1) the managers or publishers, regardless of their profession or description; (2) in the absence of managers or publishers, the authors; (3) in the absence of authors, the printers; (4) in the absence of printers, the sellers, distributors, or billposters'].[10] Gisèle Sapiro has argued that the legal status of writers as accomplices, rather than the primary 'authors', of literary crimes contradicted what many considered the obvious moral responsibility an author had for the content and potential impact of their works.[11] An annotated version of the law acknowledged this conflict: 'La responsabilité morale retombe tout entier sur l'écrivain, tout le monde le sent. [...] Mais, au point de vue des principes de la législation, les choses changent d'aspect' ['Everyone feels instinctively that moral responsibility falls entirely on the writer. [...] But things look different from the

---

[8] For an extensive account of the reader as victim, see François Proulx, *Victims of the Book: Reading and Masculinity in Fin-de-Siècle France* (Toronto: University of Toronto Press, 2019).

[9] Martyn Lyons examines a similar list of unruly readers that fuelled Third Republic anxieties about indiscriminate and subversive reading practices in *Readers and Society in Nineteenth-Century France: Workers, Women, Peasants* (Basingstoke: Palgrave, 2001).

[10] *Loi sur la liberté de la presse*, p. 20.

[11] Sapiro, *La Responsabilité*, p. 24.

viewpoint of legislative principle'].[12] That said, legal theory and judicial practice notably diverged in the case of novelists tried for obscenity, who would often receive harsher sentences than their publishers. Such sentences confirmed the 'common-sense' view that associated literary authorship with criminal authorship, based on a more individualistic vision of responsibility. When it came to periodical publications, however, judgements tended to follow the statutory hierarchy of responsibility. Press directors frequently received tougher penalties than book publishers and the writers or artists who penned the offending material.[13]

This distinction made sense because the publication of newspapers, reviews, and magazines involved more collaborative processes than book production. Furthermore, the increased accessibility and lower cost of periodical formats heightened fears of bad influence over morally corruptible readers. Legal statute in the period effectively ratified broader suspicions concerning mass media's appeal to, and influence over, vulnerable readers across socio-political divides. At the same time, the imbrication of moral, socio-political, and legal concerns about the dangers of reading had a significant impact on literary production, due to the strategies and techniques via which fin-de-siècle writers, both individually and collectively, responded to this negative perception. For example, some writers chose to avoid certain themes, genres, or publication formats—such as melodrama, adultery fiction, or the *roman-feuilleton* ['serialised novel']—as a result of their wariness about being associated with a morally or aesthetically 'tainted' medium. Conversely, other writers deliberately published works of this kind, in order to reach a wider audience, to revitalise earlier models, or to transgress socio-political and aesthetic norms. Such strategies are clearly at play in Bourget's tacit permissiveness with erotic themes in Chapter 2, the denigration of murder fiction's association with *romans-feuilletons* and melodrama in Chapter 3, the critique of biographical unveiling as striptease in Chapter 4, and the saucy magazine's blend of gossip, smut, and radical politics in Chapter 5. Although few of these examples attracted prosecution, their creation and reception were moulded by the legal frameworks that delineated acceptable from unacceptable publications and punished individuals responsible for the latter.

Despite benefiting from unprecedented levels of freedom granted by the 1881 press law, fin-de-siècle writers and publishers could therefore still, according to that law's stipulations, face trial alongside one another for crossing certain moral, social, and political boundaries. In particular, two forms of boundary-crossing provoked debate about the nature and levels of shared criminal responsibility in the literary domain: outraging public decency and political sedition. Both crimes became the focal point for later legal amendments that restricted press freedom

---

[12] *Lois annotées ou Lois, décrets, ordonnances, avis du Conseil d'Etat, etc., avec notes historiques, de concordance et de jurisprudence*, IX (Paris: Recueil Sirey, 1881–5), p. 221.
[13] See Leclerc, *Crimes écrits*, pp. 78–80 and Sapiro, *La Responsabilité*, pp. 457–9.

as part of a reactionary response to perceived breakdowns in socio-political order. These amendments affirmed the transgressive potential of literature while highlighting and modifying its complicit status.

## Outraging Public Decency

The crime of outraging public decency has historically provided a keystone to the moral regulation of print media. Referring to a range of subversive positions on society, it links most clearly to the related notion of 'obscenity'.[14] Although never systematically defined in legal statute, 'obscenity' usually evokes the depiction or discussion of sexual behaviour considered contrary to a set of moral codes inherited by tradition and ratified by public opinion. The era's most famous literary trials centred around the question of obscenity, thereby demonstrating the close association between sexual morality and socio-political order in nineteenth-century France. The mid-century trials against Charles Baudelaire (1821–67) and Gustave Flaubert (1821–80) reflected an accepted perception that 'obscene' works encouraged immorality by representing illicit behaviour without overtly condemning it. This view remains in circulation today, through discussions about pornography, violent video games, and the regulation of social media content. It was notably present in the 1881 *Loi sur la liberté de la presse*, which, despite abolishing related crimes such as outraging public and religious morality, retained 'outrage aux bonnes mœurs' ['affront to public decency'] and gave harsher penalties for it than an earlier legal precedent set in 1819.[15]

These penalties were soon deemed insufficient to deter writers and publishers from producing and selling 'immoral' works. On 8 August 1882, only a year after declaring press freedom, France passed a new law to clamp down on obscenity. The reactionary measure reflected a surge of moral panic in the minds of jurists and politicians, who viewed the new freedoms as having opened the floodgates to a wave of immoral publications. As Raisa Rexer has noted, journalists in the mainstream press propagated this apocalyptic vision from 1880 onwards, in the process of attacking titillating popular literature for political and economic reasons.[16] After the chamber of deputies debated and modified the government's initial proposal,

---

[14] On the link between obscenity and press freedom, see Nicholas Harrison, *Circles of Censorship: Censorship and its Metaphors in French History, Literature, and Theory* (Oxford: Clarendon Press, 1995), and Elisabeth Ladenson, *Dirt for Art's Sake: Books on Trial from* Madame Bovary *to* Lolita (Ithaca: Cornell University Press, 2007).

[15] The 1881 law raised maximum prison sentence from one to two years, and the maximum fine from 500 to 2,000 francs. See Sapiro, *La Responsabilité*, p. 334. To translate the term 'outrages aux bonnes mœurs', I use the terms 'affront to public decency' or 'outraging public decency'. This crime differed from 'outrage à la pudeur', which is akin to 'gross indecency', 'indecent exposure', and 'indecent assault'.

[16] Raisa Rexer, '*L'Année pornographique*: The French Press and the Invention of Pornography', *Romanic Review* 111, no. 2 (2020): pp. 260–87, doi:10.1215/00358118-8,503,476.

the leftist Republican senator Louis Devaux (1819–84) presented a report to the senate declaring the urgency of passing a new law:

> Les publications obscènes se sont multipliées, dans ces derniers temps, avec une telle fréquence et sous tant de formes, que le Gouvernement, en proposant aux Chambres un complément nécessaire de la législation existante, n'a fait que répondre à l'opinion publique révoltée d'une situation intolérable. Il n'est plus possible, en effet, aujourd'hui, de faire un pas sur la voie publique sans la trouver encombrée de crieurs, de colporteurs de ces productions scandaleuses que l'on étale effrontément sous les yeux des femmes, des jeunes filles, des enfants; qu'on leur distribue même gratuitement quelquefois, dans l'espérance que cette détestable semaille, prodiguée sans pudeur, fournira plus tard une honteuse mais lucrative moisson.[17]

> [In recent times, obscene publications have multiplied with such frequency and variety that the Government's proposal to the Chambers, suggesting a much-needed complement to existing legislation, simply responds to public outcry against an intolerable situation. Indeed, it is no longer possible, nowadays, to go out in public spaces without finding them crowded with hawkers and pedlars of these scandalous publications, which are brazenly displayed in front of women, young girls, and children, and sometimes even offered to them free of charge, in the hope that these foul seeds, lavishly and immodestly sown, will later reap a shameful but fruitful harvest.]

The force of Devaux's assertions relies on his use of hyperbole and a stream of adjectives conveying reactionary moral judgement, such as 'intolerable', 'scandalous', and 'shameful'. He refers to women and children as the primary victims of cynical manipulators seeking financial gain from the encouragement of immoral instincts, thereby demonstrating both the legislators' paternalistic approach and the tangible—if condemnable—public interest in 'indecent' works, which bolstered lucrative sales.

To counter this trend, the August 1882 law created a special status for 'outrages aux bonnes moeurs', which increased the crime's penalties and made it easier to prosecute. Maximum fines increased from 2,000 to 3,000 francs, in a clear attempt to punish perpetrators in the same way they might benefit from the crime—that is, financially.[18] In line with the penal code's stipulations, accomplices could face identical sentences as the primary offenders. Most importantly, trials would henceforth take place in the correctional courts rather than in the assizes: that is, behind closed doors (*à huis clos*) and without a jury.[19] This change

---

[17] *Lois annotées*, IX, p. 376.
[18] *Lois annotées*, IX, p. 376.
[19] *Lois annotées*, IX, p. 377.

addressed two major concerns: first, that the lengthy processes required by the assizes prevented justice being applied swiftly enough to be effective, and second, that juries were too lenient. The law also granted the correctional courts the power to seize incriminated texts and arrest the accused and their accomplices as a precautionary measure. This stipulation had already been the case for obscene images, but the 1882 law extended it to cover nearly all forms of written production, with one key exception: books remained under the 1881 law's jurisdiction, so their authors and publishers appeared before the assizes courts.

The 1882 law represented a key moment in the history of press censorship in France, demonstrating how concerns over literature's immoral influence eclipsed the desire for broader press freedom.[20] It also raised debates about the rise of mass media formats and how to define literary value in its wake. The book's exemption from the 1882 law's jurisdiction suggested that the format was more closely associated with aesthetic and moral value than periodicals. On this question, senator Devaux expressed the widespread association between press ephemera and pornography:

Le danger pour les penseurs et les écrivains n'existe pas, car ils n'auront jamais à comparaître comme tels devant la juridiction correctionnelle, et si le zèle d'un magistrat du parquet les confondait par accident avec les folliculaires flétris aujourd'hui du nom de pornographes, la magistrature elle-même les relèverait d'une aussi lamentable méprise.[21]

[There is no danger for writers and thinkers, since they will never face the criminal courts in this capacity. If a particularly zealous prosecutor accidentally mistook a writer or thinker for one of these hacks denounced nowadays as 'pornographers', the judicial authorities would release them from such a terrible misunderstanding.]

The derogatory term 'folliculaires' ['hacks'] here evokes a particular *type* of journalism, which suggests that publication format alone was not sufficient to define obscenity. The difficulties of associating publication format with literary, social, and moral value led to a discussion in the chamber of deputies regarding the status of respected and conservative reviews such as *La Nouvelle Revue* and *La Revue des Deux Mondes*. Were these titles to be treated as the equivalent of books or aligned with pornographic ephemera? Politicians left this question unanswered during the debates, presuming that it would be resolved by later jurisprudence.[22] By

---

[20] On the conflict between the Third Republic's democratic ideals and its restriction of press freedom—ostensibly to protect 'acceptable' sexual morality—see Hannah Frydman, 'Freedom's Sex Problem: Classified Advertising, Law, and the Politics of Reading in Third Republic France', *French Historical Studies* 44, no. 4 (2021): pp. 675–709, doi:10.1215/00161071-9,248,720.

[21] *Lois annotées*, IX, p. 377.

[22] *Lois annotées*, IX, p. 376.

distinguishing between different types and levels of published material, the 1882 law encourages a broad understanding of cultural production and its relationship with legal and moral discourses. This vision, adopted in the following pages, recognises the importance of considering a range of incriminated material—and not just a limited selection of assizes trials—when analysing the impact of format, genre, and content in debates about literature's transgressive and implicating potential.

Devaux's attack against the journalists and peddlers selling salacious literature to an avid public implies the existence of a thriving network of businesses seeking to profit from the appeal of illicit erotic material. Despite the hyperbolic bent of his discourse, Devaux's vision of illicit erotic networks was not entirely fabricated. Reviews such as *Le Courrier français* (1884–1914), *Le Fin de Siècle* (1891–1909), and *Don Juan* (1895–1900) published titillating literature, drawings, and advertisements for semi-clandestine businesses including sex shops, medical quacks, and abortionists. In the period, these reviews continued to thrive regardless of the restrictions brought in by the 1882 law. How did they manage it? One answer is that those involved in the 'obscenity industry' ('industrie de l'obscénité') employed canny methods of avoiding litigation or mitigating its impact.[23] For example, there is evidence to suggest that the editorial team of *Le Fin de Siècle*—a saucy magazine that regularly faced trial for obscenity throughout the 1890s—paid people to sign off as the review's manager (*gérant*) and therefore take primary responsibility for any risqué content. This tactic demonstrates an implicit understanding, and attempted manipulation, of the hierarchy of responsibility described in the 1881 press law. As previously mentioned, article 42 attributed criminal responsibility first to the manager or publisher of an inculpated publication, and only afterwards to its writer(s), printers, and sellers. Writers were usually charged as accomplices and not as the main perpetrator. This structure left a degree of ambiguity regarding the role of the editor-in-chief (*rédacteur en chef*), who might not have been considered a review's manager or publisher but who would make key decisions regarding its content. In the early 1890s, the editor-in-chief of *Le Fin de Siècle* exploited this ambiguity to displace responsibility and avoid litigation—an approach that, no matter how canny, was not always successful.

## Underwriting Obscenity: *Prête-noms* at *Le Fin de Siècle*

On 15 July 1891, the writer-journalist Louis Octave Besse (1870–1911) faced trial for outraging public decency in an article he contributed to the 17 June 1891 issue of *Le Fin de Siècle*, entitled 'Crime'. The courts charged him as the accomplice

---

[23] See Maxence Rodemacq, 'L'Industrie de l'obscénité: commerce pornographique et culture de masse à Paris (1855–1930)' (Master's dissertation, Sorbonne University, 2010), and 'L'Industrie de l'obscénité à Paris', *Romantisme* 167, no. 1 (2015): pp. 13–20, doi:10.3917/rom.167.0013.

of Urbain Hippolyte Heurtier, an impoverished sixty-one-year-old who signed as the journal's *gérant*. When interrogated by the police, Heurtier explained that, after working for a railway company for many years, he had spent the previous six or seven years of his life unemployed. Further intelligence revealed that Heurtier's son paid his father's rent (30 francs per month). When asked to explain his involvement in the review, Heurtier responded as follows:

> Je suis gérant du journal *Fin de Siècle* depuis 3 mois. Je n'ai aucun traité avec la direction, mais en exécution de conventions verbales, je reçois 10 francs par numéro que je signe comme gérant.
>
> J'avais remarqué, dans la nouvelle intitulée: 'Crime', le passage que vise plus particulièrement la poursuite. Les expressions: *'Les cuisses s'ouvrent à sa virilité'* et: *'la fusion des ventres'* m'avaient paru quelque peu osées. J'en avais fait l'observation au rédacteur en chef, M. Emery qui m'avait répondu: 'Qu'à la rigueur on pourrait supprimer ces passages', ils ont été maintenus, ce que plus tard M. Emery a attribué à un oubli.
>
> En général la direction ne me soumet, préalablement, ni les manuscrits des 'nouvelles', ni les originaux des dessins.[24]

> [I have been the manager of the newspaper *Le Fin de Siècle* for three months. I have no contract with the editors, but on the basis of a verbal understanding, I receive ten francs for each issue I sign as manager.
>
> I had noticed the passage targeted by the prosecution, in the story entitled 'Crime'. The phrases *'thighs opening to his virility'* and *'the fusion of bellies'* seemed to me somewhat risqué. I made this observation to the editor-in-chief, Mr Emery, who responded that 'if necessary, the passages could be suppressed'. But they were not, and this is something that Mr Emery later attributed to a moment of forgetfulness.
>
> Generally speaking, the editors do not send me any manuscripts of the 'stories' or original drawings in advance of their publication.]

Although it was common practice at the time for newspaper managers and editors to avoid the appearance of guilt by claiming not to have seen the article or drawing in question, Heurtier here openly acknowledges having read the incriminated article.[25] However, in this instance, Heurtier's admission serves to highlight the fact that he had little or no influence over the review's content. Instead, he cites the editor-in-chief René Emery as the primary decision-maker. By claiming to have remarked upon the potential immorality of the inculpated article to Emery—a comment that the latter either forgot or deliberately ignored—Heurtier shifts the

---

[24] 'Interrogatoire sur mandat de comparution', Archives de Paris (AP), D2U6 93, 15/07/1891—HEURTIER, Urbain; BESSE, Louis Octave.

[25] Leclerc, *Crimes écrits*, p. 79.

blame away from himself. It is difficult to know the precise level of involvement Heurtier had in the review, since he could simply have been using his testimony to avoid culpability. Having said that, he had very few connections with journalism and no prior convictions, but instead had several years of financial hardship under his belt. These factors suggest that he was unlikely to be the mastermind of operations at *Le Fin de Siècle* and that he was paid to sign as the manager to displace blame from those more practically involved in the day-to-day running of the review.

A few months after the court's judgement against Besse and Heurtier, between December 1891 and January 1892, Paris's correctional courts implicated René Emery in a series of trials against *Le Fin de Siècle*. As a recidivist, Emery faced increasingly harsh sentences, which over the course of three trials reached an accumulated total of five months in prison and 7,000 francs to pay in fines.[26] He therefore stood to gain from any subsequent attempt to mitigate his responsibility—a fact confirmed by the procedural documents from another trial that took place on 25 May 1892.[27] On this occasion, Emery faced prosecution for being an accomplice in the crime of outraging public decency, after having penned an article for *Le Fin de Siècle*, suggestively entitled 'Gorges à l'air' ['Bare Breasts']. He appeared alongside Henry Julien, who had signed as the manager. When interrogated about his involvement in the review, Julien stated:

> Je n'ai jamais lu, pas même jusqu'à ce jour, l'article dont il s'agit; d'ailleurs M. Emery ne me soumet jamais la copie des articles qu'il insère dans son journal. Je ne suis gérant que pour la forme car je suis employé au journal 'Le Soleil'.
>
> Je touche 50 fr. par mois, uniquement pour signer 'Fin de Siècle' comme gérant.[28]
>
> [I have never read the article in question, even to this very day. Besides, Mr Emery never sends me a copy of the articles he includes in his newspaper. I am 'manager' for form's sake only, being employed at another newspaper, 'Le Soleil'.
>
> I am paid 50 francs a month, simply for signing as the manager of 'Le Fin de Siècle'.]

A court report on Julien's background affirmed his impoverished status: 'Il est marié, et a quatre enfants: il paraît être dans la misère' ['He is married, has four

---

[26] On the 1885 and 1891 laws on recidivism, see Jean-Lucien Sanchez, 'Les Lois Bérenger (lois du 14 août 1885 et du 26 mars 1891)', *Criminocorpus*, Histoire de la criminologie: Autour des *Archives d'anthropologie criminelle 1886–1914* (2005), doi:10.4000/criminocorpus.132.

[27] The Archives de Paris retains only a limited selection of the correctional court's 'documents de procédure' ['procedural documents']. Further details regarding the earlier trials against *Le Fin de Siècle*, other than those found in the official judgement, are therefore not available because the relevant files have been destroyed.

[28] Henry Julien's 'Interrogatoire sur mandat de comparution', AP, D2U6 95, 25/05/1892—JULIEN, Henry, Alexandre; EMERY, René, Marie.

children, and seems to be destitute'].²⁹ This evidence supports Julien's claims to be a pretend figurehead with a purely financial incentive to sign as manager. It seems that Julien was desperate enough to risk taking responsibility for the review's content in any potential litigation, or that he was simply unaware of the structure of responsibility in legal statute.

By signing as manager, Julien acted as a shield for the person truly responsible: René Emery. In the interrogation cited above, Julien attributes the review's ownership and management to Emery by evoking 'the articles he [Emery] includes in *his* newspaper' (my emphasis). This attribution of responsibility aligns with the latter's implication in the earlier trials against Le Fin de Siècle, as well as by his relatively high earnings. On 27 April 1892, the police seized copies of the indicted issue at the review's offices on rue de Provence and interrogated the editor-in-chief. When questioned about his financial revenue ('moyens d'existence'), Emery responded: 'Je n'en ai pas d'autre que la direction du journal "Fin de Siècle" et j'estime mon gain à 10 000 francs par an' ['I have no other means than those earned from being editor of "Le Fin de Siècle", and I would estimate my income to be 10,000 francs per year'].³⁰ Emery's annual wage was therefore significantly higher than the pro rata annual sum of 600 francs that Julien received. This disparity suggests that Emery had a more central position at the review and that he was one of the primary recipients of any profits it made. In administering justice against Julien and Emery, the correctional court recognised the latter's greater share of responsibility and his status as an unrepentant recidivist by sentencing him to thirteen months in prison and a 3,000-franc fine. As a first-time offender benefiting from attenuating circumstances, Julien avoided prison, but he still received an equally heavy fine.³¹ Emery's prison sentence was the fourth pronounced against him in five months, and to avoid serving them he subsequently fled to Belgium.³²

If Julien's involvement in the review was indeed a mitigation strategy—which the evidence above implies—it was clearly unsuccessful, and its failure necessitated a more drastic course of action. The magistrates involved in the May 1892 trial clearly saw through the diversion tactics, recognised Emery's involvement in a series of earlier crimes, and punished him more harshly than the supposed primary culprit Julien. I suggest that this reversal of the statutory hierarchy was less a question of punishing Emery's authorship of an illicit text than an acknowledgement of Emery's more influential role as editor-in-chief of a paper that repeatedly transgressed the boundaries of acceptable morality. In this way, the collaborative nature of press publication was central to courts' decisions on the appropriate sanctions for publishing illicit material, and to the attempts to displace legal

---

[29] 'Rapport', AP, D2U6 95.
[30] 'Procès verbal', AP, D2U6 95.
[31] AP, D1U6 428, 25.05.1892—JULIEN (Henry, Alexandre) and EMERY (René, Marie).
[32] See Rodolphe Bringer, *Trente ans d'humour* (Paris: France-Édition, 1924), p. 33, and *Lettre de René Emery à Rachilde* (Paris: Bibliothèque Littéraire Jacques Doucet, LT Ms 10207, [ND]), [NP].

responsibility—sometimes successful, sometimes unsuccessful—made by those profiting from such material.

Strategies employed by the editorial team at *Le Fin de Siècle* to avoid litigation highlight the importance of authorial naming not only in the attribution of liability for press crimes, but also in the attribution of responsibility and blame more broadly understood.[33] Not all risqué or subversive textual content would fall under legal statute, but the boundaries between legal/illegal, acceptable/unacceptable were porous enough to associate a broad range of works with the threat of press litigation and the indictment of public opinion. For example, some writers acknowledged, offset, or satirised the negative impact of prosecution and critique by publishing their works anonymously, or under pseudonyms, in a clear parallel to Emery's 'prête-nom' ['front-man'] strategy. Strategies of naming, misnaming, or *not* naming also structured authors' publication of (auto)biographical material, in which the revelation of certain kinds of information may compromise themselves or others in the public domain. Compromising revelations could damage a writer's reputation and, in extreme cases, could attract libel suits. Although the dangers of signing compromising material were less serious than in previous centuries, writers in fin-de-siècle France still navigated the risks of taking legal, moral, and aesthetic responsibility for what they published.[34] As Chapter 4 demonstrates, some writers played up to these risks, re-appropriating the appeal of transgression for self-promotional ends. In some ways, this strategy diluted the association with real-life legal retribution, since its consequences were sufficiently anodyne for writers to adopt them in a playful, insouciant manner. Nonetheless, it reinforced the link between literary crime and titillation, by reminding readers of the blurred distinction between them.

The blurred boundary between different forms and levels of transgression—whether moral, political, or legal—is implicit in the *Fin de siècle* 'prête-nom' case study. Despite indirectly acknowledging his legal responsibility through strategies of displacement, René Emery outwardly denied the charge of 'outrage aux bonnes mœurs' when questioned in the lead-up to the May 1892 trial. Instead, he claimed that jurists had targeted *Le Fin de Siècle* for political reasons, as part of a wider clamp-down against anarchist propaganda:

> Je suis persuadé que Monsieur le Juge d'Instruction s'est trompé. Il n'y a dans le numéro aucune ligne qui puisse être incriminée. Les dessins n'ont absolument

---

[33] For further discussion of authorial naming, see Michel Foucault, 'Qu'est-ce qu'un auteur?', in *Dits et écrits*, edited by Daniel Defert and others, 4 vols (Paris: Gallimard, 1994), I, pp. 789–821.

[34] In the seventeenth century, libertine writers were imprisoned or burnt at the stake, both actually (Claude le Petit) and in effigy (Théphile de Viau). For an historical analysis of libertinism, press censorship, and trials against subversive authors during this period, see Adam Horsley, *Libertines and the Law: Subversive Authors and Criminal Justice in Early Seventeenth-Century France* (Oxford: Oxford University Press, 2021).

pas d'inconvenant. On a cru sans doute que le journal était un organe anarchiste. Je déclare formellement qu'il n'en est pas.[35]

[I am convinced that the examining magistrate has made a mistake. There is not a single line in the issue worthy of incrimination. The drawings are above reproach. Perhaps people believed that the paper was a mouthpiece for anarchism. I can state categorically that it is not.]

Emery's reference to anarchism may seem at first glance incongruous with the charges laid before him. The article in question contains predominantly erotic content, juxtaposing the feasting and orgies of a Flemish *kermesse* with the banality of policed Parisian fairs. The closest it gets to political commentary is by denigrating the police's role as moral enforcer.[36] That said, the tradition of *libertinage* had long established a close association between sexual transgression and subversive politics, and *Le Fin de Siècle* clearly inherited and reformulated this tradition.[37] Furthermore, 'Gorges à l'air' was published at a moment in France's history when political tensions were rocketing, and when any publication promoting transgressive ideas might be tarred with the same brush as more extreme political opinions. René Emery's comment therefore hints at the second key area of contention in fin-de-siècle definitions of press freedom and complicity: literature's capacity to incite violence and social unrest.

## Political Sedition

The relationship between literary production and political sedition was a controversial question in the 1890s: a period when France experienced significant socio-political upheaval through a series of scandals (including the Panama Canal scandal and the Dreyfus affair) that incited media storms, divisive debate, and violent protest.[38] Members of the government, the army, and the financial sector implicated themselves in underhand dealings and attempted cover-ups, which shook public confidence in the authority they represented. Combined with widespread socio-economic inequalities, these scandals provided fertile ground for the dissemination of anti-establishment thought, notably anarchism: a political philosophy which valorised the individual over the collective and called for the abolition of the state. Because of the emphasis it placed on individuality,

---

[35] 'Procès verbal', AP, D2U6 95.
[36] René Emery, 'Gorges à l'air', *Le Fin de Siècle*, 23 April 1892.
[37] For further analysis about how the titillating erotic content in such reviews often blended with or disguised more transgressive political commentary, see Chapter 5.
[38] On the antisemitic demonstrations and attacks committed during the Dreyfus Affair, see Pierre Birnbaum, *The Antisemitic Moment*, trans. Jane Marie Todd (Chicago: University of Chicago Press, 2003).

anarchist thought was popular among avant-garde writers and artists.[39] Notable anarchist sympathisers included the Impressionist and Neo-Impressionist painter Camille Pissarro (1830–1903), the writer-journalist Octave Mirbeau, and the art critic Félix Fénéon (1861–1944).[40] At the same time, anarchism gained support from a network of working-class militants and became a hot topic discussed across socio-political divides.

During this period, France witnessed a wave of anarchist violence, referred to as 'propaganda by the deed', which included a series of bombings, committed from 1892 to 1894, and the assassination of President Sadi Carnot in 1894. François Claudius Koenigstein, alias Ravachol, committed the first major attacks in response to police violence and judicial severity in the Clichy affair.[41] With the help of some accomplices, Ravachol ignited two bombs on 11 and 27 March 1892, targeting two magistrates involved in the affair: Edmond Benoît and Léon-Jules Bulot, respectively. After raising the suspicions of a waiter at a restaurant on the Boulevard de Magenta, Ravachol was arrested on 30 March and faced trial on 27 April.[42] The day before the trial proceedings, anarchists retaliated by bombing the restaurant where Ravachol had been denounced. Condemned to a life sentence of hard labour, Ravachol faced a second trial for murders predating the bombing, for which he was found guilty and executed (on 11 July 1892). Ravachol's execution initiated a vicious cycle of escalating violence, in which acts of anarchist vengeance provoked judicial repression. On 9 December 1893, Auguste Vaillant set off a bomb in the National Assembly, injuring several but killing none—an act for which he was nonetheless sentenced to death. The unusual severity of this sentence increased public sympathy for Vaillant and incited further reprisals. A week after Vaillant's execution, on 12 February 1894, the young anarchist Émile Henry detonated a bomb at the Café Terminus at the Gare Saint-Lazare. Tried and found guilty on 27 April, Henry was guillotined on 21 May 1894. To avenge both Vaillant and Henry, the Italian anarchist Sante Casario stabbed President Sadi Carnot to death at a public ceremony in Lyon on 24 June 1894—a crime for which Casario was executed on 16 August the same year.

---

[39] See Juan Ungersma Halperin, *Félix Fénéon. Aesthete & Anarchist in Fin-de-Siècle Paris* (New Haven: Yale University Press, 1988), p. 263 and Alexander Varias, *Paris and the Anarchists: Aesthetes and Subversives During the Fin de Siècle* (Basingstoke: Macmillan, 1997), p. 135. See also Patrick McGuinness, *Poetry and Radical Politics in Fin-de-Siècle France: From Anarchism to Action Française* (Oxford: Oxford University Press, 2015).

[40] Félix Fénéon was arrested on suspicion of anarchist activity during a period of state orchestrated repression in the mid-1890s.

[41] On 1 May 1891, the same day as a violent repression of a workers' protest in Fourmies, three anarchists were arrested at a protest march to Clichy, outside Paris. They were beaten in police custody and subsequently faced trial for their involvement in the protest. Two received harsh prison sentences and one was acquitted.

[42] Note that 27 April 1892 was the same day that copies of *Le Fin de Siècle* including 'Gorges à l'air' were seized by the police.

Although all of these attacks provoked debate and controversy, it was Vaillant and Casario's crimes that, by directly targeting political authority, provided the pretext for a state-sponsored clamp-down on anarchist activity and propaganda. Between 1893 and 1894, France passed a series of anti-anarchist laws, known as the *lois scélérates* ['villainous laws'], that restricted press freedom even further than the 1882 obscenity law.[43] The government passed the first 'loi scélérate' on 12 December 1893, only three days after Vaillant's bombing at the National Assembly. This law increased sentences for those found guilty of inciting murder, pillage, arson, military misdemeanour, and crimes against state security. It also criminalised the justification (or 'apologie') of such crimes, thereby targeting anarchist propaganda while implicating writers and journalists who publicly expressed anarchist inclinations. Furthermore, it allowed preventative arrest of the accused in cases of both incitement and 'apologie'.[44] The second, which was submitted the same day as the first but passed a few days later (on 18 December 1893), rewrote articles of the penal code to condemn anyone directly or indirectly involved in groups formed 'dans le but de préparer ou de commettre des crimes contre des personnes ou les propriétés' ['with the aim of preparing or committing crimes against individuals or property']. People accused of this crime could be charged regardless of the association's duration. The new codification also encouraged members of criminal groups to become informants in exchange for exemption from punishment, which in this case was long-term hard labour.[45] The third and final law came into effect on 28 July 1894, a month after President Sadi Carnot's assassination. It moved trials for incitement or apology of crime from the assizes to the correctional courts when the crimes in question were committed as an act of anarchist propaganda. These juryless courts had the power to suppress, either partially or completely, the publication of anarchist-related trial proceedings in the name of preserving public order.[46] Clearly, the published written word was a key target of the *lois scélérates*, due to its perceived ability to encourage, justify, and publicise acts of political revolt. The laws implied that, by employing these tactics, anarchist leaders and sympathisers might attract wider support from a belligerent press and an increasingly disillusioned public: an outcome the French government clearly wanted to avoid.

---

[43] The pejorative nickname 'lois scélérates' was popularised by Francis de Pressensé and Émile Pouget in their pamphlet *Les Lois scélérates de 1893-4* (Paris: Éditions de la Revue blanche, 1899), made up of articles published in the avant-garde little magazine *La Revue blanche* (15 Jan. 1898, 1 July 1898, and 15 July 1898).
[44] 'Loi portant modification des articles 24, paragraphe Ier, 23 et 49 de la loi du 29 juillet 1881 sur la presse', *Journal officiel de la République française*, 13 Dec. 1893.
[45] 'Loi sur les associations de malfaiteurs', *Journal officiel de la République française*, 19 Dec. 1893.
[46] 'Loi ayant pour objet de réprimer les menées anarchistes', *Journal officiel de la République française*, 29 July 1894.

In many ways, the *lois scélérates* were successful in enabling an anti-anarchist clamp-down. Within three months of the first two laws passing, anarchist journals such as *La Révolte* and *Le Père Peinard* had disappeared, and propaganda in favour of anarchism virtually ceased. Militants were either rounded up and arrested or fled France.[47] Nevertheless, the concept of criminal association between theorists, writers, and criminals remained a hotly contested issue. To what extent could a writer who has expressed anarchist sympathies be implicated in anarchist-related crimes committed by another person? How direct or indirect was their involvement? And should they be punished alongside the main perpetrators? As previously mentioned, the first *loi scélérate* confirmed writers' complicity with anarchist violence by aligning 'apologie' with 'provocation'. Consequently, anarchist theorists and pro-anarchist authors could be considered complicit in crimes committed by anyone espousing anarchist views. The open-ended nature of 'indirect' involvement described in the second law further enabled the courts to bring together sympathisers and militants, especially when they moved in the same social circles. This newly instated capacity to punish theorists and sympathisers alongside militants and criminals was tested—and contested—during an infamous trial-cum-media-event known as the 'Procès des trente' ['Trial of the Thirty'].

## Illicit Associations: The Trial of the Thirty

During the government clamp-down in early 1894, the police arrested hundreds of individuals for their involvement in anarchist activity. Out of these, thirty appeared together at a trial, charged primarily with the crime of 'association de malfaiteurs' ['criminal association/conspiracy']. The group included anarchist theorists (Jean Grave, Sébastien Faure, and Paul Reclus), writers and journal editors involved in anarchist activity (Félix Fénéon, Émile Poujet, and Louis Matha), and pro-anarchist thieves such as Philippe Ortiz and Paul Chericotti. Throughout the trial, the theorists refuted the idea that they were involved in an 'association', as they claimed the notion was fundamentally anti-anarchist. However, the prosecution emphasised the links that existed between members of the group, notably by exploring a network of anarchist periodicals. For example, Julien Ledot and Charles Chatel were accused of having contributed to anarchist propaganda through their involvement in *La Révolte*, *La Revue libertaire* (formally *La Revue anarchiste*), and *Le Père Peinard*. When questioned regarding his alleged authorship of a column in *La Révolte* entitled 'Mouvement social', Ledot answered as follows:

---

[47] Jean Maitron, *Le Mouvement anarchiste en France. 1. Des origines à 1914* (Paris: Maspero, 1975), pp. 251–2.

L'ACCUSÉ.— Qui vous dit que ces articles sont de moi. Ils ne sont pas signés.
M. LE PRÉSIDENT.— Mais on ne signe pas dans votre journal.
L'ACCUSÉ.— Alors poursuivez le gérant.
M. LE PRÉSIDENT.— Mais vous étiez le directeur.
L'ACCUSÉ— C'est possible; mais légalement vous n'avez pas le droit de me poursuivre.
M. LE PRÉSIDENT.— Vous avez dans un article inséré le 13 janvier 1894, fait un appel non dissimulé à l'emploi des explosifs; en outre vous avez servi de point d'union entre plusieurs anarchistes.
L'ACCUSÉ.— Quel est le journal qui n'est pas un point d'union entre ses lecteurs?[48]

[DEFENDANT: How can you tell that I wrote those articles? They are not signed.
PRESIDING JUDGE: But no-one signs articles in your paper.
DEFENDANT: So prosecute the manager.
PRESIDING JUDGE: But you were the director.
DEFENDANT: Perhaps, but legally you have no right to prosecute me.
PRESIDING JUDGE: In an article published on 13 January 1894, you gave open support for the use of explosives. In addition, you served as a point of connection between several anarchists.
DEFENDANT: What paper does not serve as a point of connection between its readers?]

In his replies, Ledot refuted the prosecuting lawyer's vision of anarchist journals having a specific tendency to bring people together in an illicit association by highlighting the fundamentally collaborative nature of journalism, regardless of political affiliation. By doing so, he ridiculed the prosecution's attempt to use involvement in journalism as proof of criminal complicity. Furthermore, he demonstrated a clear awareness of the legally instituted hierarchy of responsibility described in the 1881 press law, by insisting that the prosecution should direct their questions to the manager rather than to him.

A few days later, Charles Chatel redeployed this argument when he interrupted the *réquisitoire* ['final indictment'] of prosecuting lawyer Léon-Jules Bulot (one of the intended victims of Ravachol's 1892 bombings). Chatel claimed that he did not write the articles attributed to him and that his role as 'secrétaire de rédaction' ['sub-editor'] at the *Revue libertaire* meant that he was not legally responsible for its content. Bulot's response to Chatel's interruption was noticeably more confrontational than it had been during Ledot's interrogation:

Ah! Vous n'êtes point le gérant, et, en conséquence, vous n'êtes pas responsable? Vous oubliez que le gérant n'est qu'un simple garçon de bureau, la plupart du

---

[48] 'Le Procès des 30 Anarchistes', *Le Petit parisien*, 7 Aug. 1894.

temps, ignorant, et vous, vous étiez le secrétaire de la rédaction! Eh bien, dans votre situation, vous lisiez les articles, vous en connaissiez, mieux qu'un gérant, la portée; vous les avez approuvés, vous les avez laissé passer, j'ai le droit de vous en demander compte comme à l'auteur de l'article!⁴⁹

[Ah! You are not the manager, so therefore you are not responsible? You forget that the manager, most of the time, is no more than an ignorant office worker, whereas you, you were the sub-editor! Well, in your role, you used to read the articles, and you knew their content much better than a manager did. You approved them, you let them appear in print, and I have the right to ask you to account for them, as I would the article's author!]

Bulot's response highlights the stakes involved in legally distinguishing the hierarchy of shared responsibility, which did not necessarily match up with actual decision-making roles. By noting that 'the manager is often no more than an ignorant office worker, most of the time', Bulot indirectly confirms my interpretation of the paid signatories at *Le Fin de Siècle*. Furthermore, by insisting that, regardless of the hierarchy established by law, he had the right to consider Chatel responsible for the *Revue libertaire*'s content, Bulot valorises 'common-sense' views of press responsibility and suggests that jurisprudence may need to supplement the unresolved ambiguities created by legal statute. Bulot may also have been referring to the 1881 law's attribution of responsibility to managers and publishers, 'regardless of their profession or description', which suggests room for interpretative manoeuvre in the legal delineation of press roles.

Despite his best efforts, Bulot was unable to convince the jury to convict anyone other than three of the most notorious thieves. The jury's verdict reflected the views expressed by fin-de-siècle commentators, who questioned a nonspecific form of complicity that could render strangers responsible for one another's crimes. In an article written for *Le Figaro*, Albert Bataille remarked that there was insufficient material evidence to consider the group to be enacting a wider anarchist plot:

Que tous ces hommes aient formé une association, ourdi un complot, le ministère public ne pourrait essayer de le soutenir en s'en tenant aux faits matériels.

Pour conspirer ensemble, la première condition est de se connaître.

Suffit-il d'avoir obéi à une idée commune, d'avoir isolément prêché, écrit ou volé, pour réaliser ce que Caserio appelait l'idéal anarchiste?

C'est cette théorie qu'il soutiendra sans doute, car, autrement, la prévention ne tiendrait pas debout.⁵⁰

---

⁴⁹ 'Le Procès des 30 Anarchistes', *Le Petit parisien*, 10 Aug. 1894.
⁵⁰ Albert Bataille, 'Gazette des Tribunaux', *Le Figaro*, 7 Aug. 1894.

[Keeping to the material facts alone, the public prosecutions office would not be able to prove that these men had formed an association and hatched a plot.

The first condition to conspiring together is knowing one another.

Is it sufficient to have followed a common idea, to have preached, written, or stolen in isolation, to bring about what Caserio would call the anarchist ideal?

This is the theory that they will doubtless put forward, because, otherwise, preventative custody would not stand up to scrutiny.]

A few days later, another article appeared in *Le Figaro*, stating that the prosecution's approach demonstrated 'une rare maladresse' ['uncommon clumsiness'], and framing the trial as a misjudged use of repressive force.[51] Henri Bauer expressed a similar opinion when he discussed the ongoing 'vaudeville judiciaire' ['judicial vaudeville'] in *L'Écho de Paris*:

Ce procès aura démontré en quel désarroi s'agitent les pasteurs de ce siècle finissant. Incapables de réformes et d'améliorations matérielles, ils ne savent même pas défendre le vieux monde contre ses terribles assaillants. Ils brandissent malencontreusement les nouvelles armes qu'ils ont en mains et les émoussent sur les cailloux.[52]

[This trial will have shown how the moral shepherds of this closing century are flailing about in a state of disarray. Incapable of reform and material improvements, they do not even know how to defend the old world against its mighty foes. Ill-advisedly, they brandish the new weapons they have in hand, blunting them against pebbles.]

Bauer's conclusion juxtaposes impotent defenders of the status quo with its powerful assailants, ridiculing the trial as a wasted, poorly timed effort. But did the Trial of the Thirty completely miss its target? Some journalists suggested that regardless of the result, it functioned as a warning to pro-anarchist writers.[53] Others reminded readers that such embarrassing results would not be repeated because the third *loi scélérate* moved future trials from the assizes to the correctional courts (much like trials for 'outrages aux bonnes mœurs' post-1882).[54] Furthermore, although the prosecution may have failed in defending a broader definition of complicity, anarchist propaganda was significantly restricted by the *lois scélérates* and political tensions receded—however briefly—in the trial's aftermath.[55]

[51] F. M., 'Echos. La Politique', *Le Figaro*, 13 Aug. 1894.
[52] Henri Bauer, 'Le Procès des trente', *L'Écho de Paris*, 14 Aug. 1894.
[53] Anon., 'A Travers la Politique', *Le Fin de Siècle*, 19 Aug. 1894.
[54] F. M., 'Echos—La Politique', *Le Figaro*, 14 Aug. 1894.
[55] These tensions would be swiftly re-awoken during the Dreyfus affair.

## Literary Implications

As a highly debated media event, the Trial of the Thirty emphasises the influential, if polemical, notion that press publications served as a medium for illicit influence and association. Demonstrating both complicity as incitement and complicity as collaboration, the trial contributed to fin-de-siècle discussions regarding literary 'bad influence', based on readers' mimetic identification with and enactment of transgressive ideas and behaviour. It raised questions about the transmissibility of socially disruptive ideas and their translation into extreme political actions. In addition, the trial highlighted concerns about the criminal potential of collaborative press practices and the difficulty of attributing responsibility to those involved in the publication of illicit material. As both the Trial of the Thirty and the trials against *Le Fin de Siècle* demonstrate, writers and journalists attempted to avoid litigation by citing the technical distinctions made in legal statute regarding levels of press responsibility. These divisions were particularly loaded in cases against periodical culture, which French courts targeted more frequently than book culture due to its association with questionable morals and reduced aesthetic value. Undoubtedly, the Trial of the Thirty was a failed attempt at political suppression, but even in its failure it reflected a broadly accepted vision of certain literary groups as dangerous to the moral and political status quo. It did so by depicting such groups as a hotbed for radical and subversive ideas, which could easily lead to violent, illegal action. Avant-garde writers in turn re-appropriated reactionary discourses by playing up to literature's criminalised image, whether that be through public support for radical politics, the aesthetic valorisation of criminal acts, or the assertion of non-normative identities. The authors who adopted these stances may not have been as destructive as the anarchists exploding bombs in Parisian streets, but the forms of illicit solidarity they created were comparable to, and interrelated with, their more radical counterparts. Moreover, the legal regulation of literary publication intersected with social, political, and moral concerns to such an extent that its impact can be found across literature of the period, and not just at its avant-garde margins. As a result of this broad cultural intersection, the incitement and collaboration models provide valuable analogies for collusive tendencies in fin-de-siècle literary culture, as well as a guiding structure with which to analyse them.

# 2
# Framing Literature
## Guilt and the Fin-de-siècle Novel

Fin-de-siècle discussions about literature's role in society persistently examined the extent to which writers could influence, and be held responsible for, the thoughts or actions of their readers. These discussions frequently played out as a conflict between writers and their critics—notably politicians, magistrates, and journalists—who feared the negative impact of 'mauvaises lectures' ['bad reading'] on individual and public life.[1] Although similar debates had waged for centuries, the fin de siècle witnessed their increasing predominance in the wake of post-1870 socio-political upheaval and in conversation with emerging intellectual trends, such as psychology and criminology. As Robert Nye has demonstrated, a 'medical model of cultural crisis' predominated in fin-de-siècle France, when 'deviance' was perceived as having biological origins, and medicine increasingly addressed social pathologies such as crime, prostitution, alcoholism, and suicide.[2] The medicalised concept of 'degeneration'—famously propounded by Max Nordau in a sustained attack against literary bad influence, *Entartung* (1892–3)—fed into this network of interdependent socio-political anxieties.[3] In the literary sphere, discourses of social pathology, degenerate art, and 'bad influence' shaped creative works and critical responses that raised questions about moral complicity.

The title of this chapter, 'Framing Literature', provides a way of conceptualising how fin-de-siècle writers posed such questions. First, the word 'framing' expresses the idea that literature 'frames' (in the sense of 'shapes' or 'inclines') readers to think and act in certain ways, which may be perceived as negative or illicit. Central to legal definitions of complicity as incitement, this type of framing is synonymous with the concept of literary 'bad influence'. Second, the word evokes how bad influence is itself 'framed'—that is, conceived of and depicted—by authors and critics of the period. The second type of framing relies on specific literary forms and techniques, including: prefaces, polemical articles, and textual layering. Third, the word 'framing' can be used to ask whether, in the context of fin-de-siècle debates

---

[1] Gisèle Sapiro, *La Responsabilité de l'écrivain: littérature, droit et morale en France (XIXe–XXIe siècle)* (Paris: Éditions du Seuil, 2011), pp. 168–9.

[2] Robert Nye, *Crime, Madness and Politics in Modern France: The Medical Concept of National Decline* (Princeton: Princeton University Press, 2014), pp. xi–xiii.

[3] Daniel Pick notes that '[n]ational defeat, degeneration, and social pathology appeared to be caught up in an endless reciprocal exchange', in *Faces of Degeneration: A European Disorder, c. 1848–c.1918* (Cambridge: Cambridge University Press, 1989), p. 98.

about responsibility and bad influence, literature was 'framed' (i.e. falsely accused of, or made to look responsible) for 'crimes' it did not actually commit. Finding a definitive response to this question is less important than recognising that, by asking it, modern readers can appreciate how judicial, political, and moral discourses shaped literature in the period. Viewing literature through different forms of framing sheds light on how complicity was a structuring principle of the fin-de-siècle literary field, which compelled writers and critics to adopt strategies for defining and justifying their position towards it.

The content, reception, and evolution of Paul Bourget's early career provides a striking example of how writers adapted their position on literary complicity over time. Although he is less widely read nowadays, Bourget achieved mainstream success during his lifetime. As a writer and critic, he became a key figure in fin-de-siècle debates about the formative and potentially corrupting impact of literary production. Like many of his contemporaries, Bourget's early writing appropriated emerging philosophical and scientific trends, notably experimental psychology. Recurring themes throughout his works included the social implications of literary influence, the balance between scientific neutrality and moral responsibility, and the dangers of over-analysis. After publishing several poetry collections, Bourget achieved recognition with a volume of literary criticism, *Essais de psychologie contemporaine* (1883), and wider popularity with his psychological novels, including *Un crime d'amour* (1886). In the former, Bourget insisted on the centrality of literature to understanding a society's intellectual and moral atmosphere. In the latter, he charted the psychological complexities of characters engaging in illicit sexual behaviour, notably adultery. Somewhat unsurprisingly, therefore, Bourget became a target for criticism in debates about literary immorality. Responding to the hostility that punctuated the early stages of his career, Bourget eventually adopted a more conservative position, closer to Catholic moral dogma, which he developed through a series of thesis novels from *Le Disciple* (1889) onwards. In my analysis of Bourget's texts and their reception, I show how fin-de-siècle notions of literary responsibility and guilt were a product of combative—yet ultimately collaborative—extra-literary interactions: authors, readers, and critics attributing and avoiding blame via the framing mechanism of liminary material and criticism. These interactions demonstrate the role played by networks of reception in redefining shared literary and moral values, while emphasising the magnetic pull of illicit topics for writers across the literary spectrum.

## Illness and Cure: Literary Influence in Bourget's *Essais*

In the early 1880s, Bourget's writing expressed ideas associated with positivist scientific trends in sociology and psychology, notably those channelled into the study of literature by the famous historian and critic Hippolyte Taine (1828–93).

Bourget's *Essais de psychologie contemporaine* (1883) exemplify Taine's influence, through a series of essays that had originally appeared in Juliette Adam's periodical *La Nouvelle Revue*. Each essay studies, in a quasi-scientific manner, how a particular writer had shaped collective psychological tendencies in fin-de-siècle France. By adopting this approach, Bourget clearly drew on Taine's analytical framework of *race*, *milieu*, and *moment*, which charted the influence of contextual factors on a writer's literary method. However, the *Essais* extended Taine's vision while reversing its emphasis. Rather than viewing literature purely as a *product* of determining contextual factors on an individual, Bourget posited literature as a causal factor affecting wider social and psychological trends.[4] He analysed five authors who influenced the fin-de-siècle moral and intellectual atmosphere, defined by a proclivity towards pessimism, disillusion, and decadence: Charles Baudelaire, Ernest Renan, Gustave Flaubert, Stendhal, and Hippolyte Taine himself. In a second volume, entitled *Nouveaux essais de psychologie contemporaine* (1885), Bourget analysed five more writers: Alexandre Dumas fils, Charles-Marie Leconte de Lisle, the Goncourt brothers, Ivan Tourguéniev, and Henri-Frédéric Amiel. In 1899, the two collections were republished together, alongside several appendices, as a volume in Bourget's complete works.[5] Each of these texts contained liminary material that addressed the question of literary influence and (re)framed Bourget's approach towards it.[6]

Bourget's vision of the links between social and cultural phenomena attributed to authors an influential role over society's wider functioning, as well as its potential *dys*function. He explored this role via educational and pathological analogies in the *Essais*' liminary material. For example, in the first Avant-Propos, Bourget depicted literature as a primary educator of young French people: 'le *Livre* devient le grand initiateur' ['the book is becoming the great initiator'].[7] By doing so, he repeated the widely held view—propounded across the medical, judicial, and legal realms—that reading was an influential form of education.[8] When

---

[4] See also André Guyaux's 'Préface', in Paul Bourget, *Essais de psychologie contemporaine. Études littéraires*, ed. André Guyaux (Paris: Gallimard, 1993), pp. VII–XXIII (p. XIV).

[5] The appendices included the speech Bourget made upon his election to the *Académie française*, which is framed in an introductory note as the 'conclusion' to the *Essais*. Proulx describes this text as 'Bourget's long-awaited description of a cure to his era's literary maladies'. François Proulx, *Victims of the Book: Reading and Masculinity in Fin-de-Siècle France* (Toronto: University of Toronto Press, 2019), p. 49.

[6] There are differences between early editions of Bourget's *Essais* and those reprinted in Guyaux's edited volume, which reproduces the 'definitive' revised text of 1899. To cite later prefatory material (1885 and 1899), this chapter uses Guyaux's edition—henceforth: *Études littéraires*—but when referring to the 1883 *Essais* and its preface, it cites Paul Bourget, *Essais de psychologie contemporaine: Baudelaire, M. Renan, Flaubert, M. Taine, Stendhal*, 3rd ed. (Paris: A. Lemerre, 1885)—henceforth: *Essais*.

[7] Bourget, *Essais*, p. vi.

[8] Works penned by nineteenth-century French writers were viewed as an influential form of education, which offered 'discours tutélaires' ['guiding discourses']. See Denis Pernot, *Le Roman de socialisation, 1889–1914* (Paris: Presses Universitaires de France, 1998), pp. 17, 26, and 120. François Proulx has also recently emphasised the importance of the educational model of literary

describing his approach to analysing such phenomena, Bourget distanced himself from more traditional author-centred criticism: 'Je n'ai voulu ni discuter des talents, ni peindre des caractères. Mon ambition a été de rédiger quelques notes capables de servir à l'historien de la Vie Morale pendant la seconde moitié du XIXe siècle français' ['I wanted neither to discuss their talents or depict their characters. My ambition has been to compile some notes which could be of use to the historian of French moral life during the second half of the nineteenth century'].[9] By framing his criticism as a moral history, Bourget emphasised his links with Taine, who was known for his positivist and historicist approach. Having said that, Bourget's quasi-scientific neutrality sits uneasily alongside a lengthy evocative anecdote, which describes reading as an intimate bond between an author and his (adolescent) reader:

> [Le lecteur] passe tout entier dans les phrases de son auteur préféré. Il converse avec lui de cœur à cœur, d'homme à homme. Il l'écoute prononcer sur la manière de goûter l'amour et de pratiquer la débauche, de chercher le bonheur et de supporter le malheur, d'envisager la mort et l'au-delà ténébreux du tombeau, des paroles qui sont des révélations. [...] De cette première révélation à imiter ces sentiments, la distance est faible et l'adolescent ne tarde guère à la franchir.[10]

> [[The reader] is completely absorbed by the sentences penned by his favourite author. He speaks with him heart to heart, man to man. He listens to the author's pronouncements about how to relish love and practise debauchery, how to seek happiness and manage suffering, how to think about death and the mysteries beyond the grave. These words are revelations to him. [...] The gap between revealing and imitating these feelings is small, and the adolescent does not take long to cross it.]

In this section, Bourget evokes a relationship based on fraternity and mentorship, where the process of initiation or education leads to imitation. The author takes on the role of a spiritual guide, as seen in the words 'prononcer' and 'révélations'. There is an intense, almost disquieting association between the spiritual authority adopted by the author, and the centrality of eroticism to the reader's education. As François Proulx has shown, the phrase 'd'homme à homme' ['man to man'] is revealing in its depiction of reading and writing as 'a male-to-male network of apprenticeship and initiation from which women, although they may be a favoured topic of discussion, are nevertheless excluded as participants'.[11] Women's

---

influence, as well as its pathologised counterpart. See 'Contagions and Cures' in *Victims of the Book*, pp. 25–55.
[9] Bourget, *Essais*, pp. v–vi.
[10] Bourget, *Essais*, pp. vii–viii.
[11] Proulx, *Victims of the Book*, p. 72.

exclusion is a prerequisite of homosocial bonding, but also betrays fin-de-siècle anxieties about same-sex activity, particularly amongst adolescents who have not yet reached sexual 'maturity'.[12] Alongside its implicit eroticism, the episode moves away from a scientific framework to a vocabulary of intimacy and emotion typical of religious writing of the period.[13] In Bourget's reformulation of the religious model of intimacy, writers take on a guiding role that supplements more traditional forms of paternal and spiritual authority, and their influence is channelled through a close, personal, and implicitly eroticised reading encounter.

If writers adopt a position of influence traditionally associated with institutionalised moral authority, such as the Church, to what extent can they be held responsible for their readers' actions? Are readers free to reject, or re-appropriate selectively, the material they read? While Bourget avoided answering the first question directly in the 1883 and 1885 prefaces, he returned to the second question in the latter. His response offers a conflicting vision of authorial influence and readers' interpretative faculties. For example, he suggests that literature functions as 'une irrésistible, une constante propagande d'idées et de sentiments' ['a constant, irresistible form of psychological and emotional propaganda'].[14] This vision of literary propaganda seems to leave little room for interpretative independence. Yet Bourget also claims that readers have sufficient freedom to respond to their literary lessons in a way that transcends direct imitation:

> Les jeunes gens héritent de leurs aînés une façon de goûter la vie qu'ils transmettent eux-mêmes, modifiée par leur expérience propre, à ceux qui viennent ensuite. Les œuvres de littérature et d'art sont le plus puissant moyen de transmission de cet héritage psychologique.[15]

> [Young people inherit from their forebears a way of experiencing life, which, modified by their own experience, they pass on to those who follow after them. Works of literature and art are the most powerful means of transmitting this psychological inheritance.]

Bourget's vision of literary transmission is therefore not a complete imposition. Rather, it transforms upon reception by the reader, who adapts their predecessors' approach with their own experience. This process involves a level of reciprocity

---

[12] Proulx expands on the analogy between reading and homosexuality by analysing depictions of same-sex liaisons in boarding schools and adolescent masturbation (*Victims of the Book*, pp. 72–8).

[13] In a monograph analysing models of personal relationships between readers and writers, Philippa Lewis highlights how the vocabulary of intimacy, love, and friendship was regularly used by theologians and religious writers of the period as 'a model for an individual's affective relationship with the divine'. She cites Hubert Lebon's Catholic handbook, *Coeur à Coeur avec Jésus* (1857) and Ernest Renan's *Vie de Jésus* (1863) as key examples. See Philippa Lewis, *Intimacy and Distance: Conflicting Cultures in Nineteenth-Century France* (Cambridge: Legenda, 2017), p. 28.

[14] Bourget, *Études littéraires*, p. 437.

[15] Bourget, *Études littéraires*, p. 437.

that, according to Philippa Lewis, was essential to the creation of literary intimacy in the period. She notes how a friendship model defined readers' relationship to both protagonists and writers, as well as how the reading experience relied on a strong identification between readers and writers.[16] Questions of literary transmission also reflected fin-de-siècle criminological discussions about free will, in which the atavistic Italian approach, exemplified by Cesare Lombroso's 'born criminal', juxtaposed the French emphasis on environmental influence and voluntarism.[17] This is relevant because the *Essais*' description of reciprocity reduces the extent to which authors are considered solely responsible for the impact of their works, and implicitly shifts part of the blame onto readers themselves. Bourget returns to this idea in the 1899 preface, by depicting the author as a paternal figure who has limited control over his child's actions:

> Il y a donc dans l'œuvre littéraire, si son auteur lui a vraiment insufflé ce mystérieux pouvoir de la vie, une force d'action indépendante de cet auteur lui-même, et qu'il n'a pas pu mesurer plus qu'un père ne mesure à l'avance les énergies du fils émané de lui.[18]

> [If an author has succeeded in breathing the mysterious spark of life into a literary work, it contains the power to act independently from the author himself, in ways which the author could not have fully determined, much like a father cannot know in advance the strengths of a son born to him.]

This description mitigates the author's responsibility by emphasising the reader's inclinations and choices. Through the fluctuation of moral responsibility between writers and readers in the process of literary education, Bourget offers an increasingly ambiguous vision of the balance between direct influence and indirect re-appropriation. Above all, he highlights the importance of these questions to his position in the literary field by repeatedly reframing his response to them.

Alongside the educational metaphor, Bourget employed pathological analogies to discuss literature's capacity for moral 'contagion'. In the essay on Baudelaire, Bourget employed an extended analogy of society as an organism to explore the reciprocal relationship between literary and social phenomena. For example, Bourget stated that 'decadence', when considered as a social phenomenon, happens when individuals become independent of the whole and threaten society's ability to function as a coherent system. As a literary phenomenon, decadence represents a *stylistic* breakdown, where individual words and phrases take precedence over the unity of a given work.[19] In these definitions, Bourget hints at

---

[16] Lewis, *Intimacy and Distance*, p. 37.
[17] On the born criminal debate, see Nye, *Crime, Madness and Politics*, pp. 97–131.
[18] Bourget, *Études littéraires*, p. 442.
[19] Bourget, *Essais*, p. 25.

the 'bad influence' model, since he suggests that literary breakdown can lead to social breakdown, and vice versa. Rather than drawing a moralising conclusion about both forms of 'decadence', Bourget relativises the moral standard by which such conclusions are made. He does so by re-assessing the adjective 'unhealthy' ('malsain'), which was often applied to Baudelaire's poetry:

> Il n'y a pas à proprement parler de maladies du corps, disent les médecins; il n'y a que des états physiologiques, funestes ou bienfaisants [...]. Pareillement, il n'y a ni maladie ni santé de l'âme, il n'y a que des états psychologiques, au point de vue de l'observateur sans métaphysique [...]. Un préjugé seul, où réapparaissent la doctrine antique des causes finales et la croyance à un but défini de l'univers, peut nous faire considérer comme naturels et sains les amours de Daphnis et de Chloë dans le vallon, comme artificiels et malsains les amours d'un Baudelaire dans le boudoir qu'il décrit.[20]

> [According to doctors, bodily illnesses do not exist, in the true sense of the word. There are simply physiological states, either fatal or beneficial. [...] Similarly, from the point of view of a neutral observer, there is no such thing as a healthy or unhealthy soul, but simply psychological states. [...] It is prejudice alone, associated with the ancient doctrine of final causes and the belief in a clear end-point for the universe, that can make us view the rustic love between Daphnis and Chloe as natural and healthy, but the secluded love in Baudelaire's fictional boudoir as artificial and unhealthy.]

In this section, Bourget puts forward a mechanistic scientific approach that views the body and mind as a system that experiences different states as neutrally equal until valorised or demonised by external agents. He takes issue with critical language that relies on polarised notions of nature/artifice and health/illness, due to their socially constructed nature. By referring to religious faith as a mere prejudice, he also rejects the Christian framework that would condemn writers like Baudelaire. Bourget's position in the first edition of the *Essais* therefore takes a materialist and atheist bent, focusing on neutral analysis rather than moral condemnation. This stance is comparable to that taken by Émile Zola in *Le Roman expérimental* (1880), which offered a materialist and determinist vision of human psychology, attacked religious idealism, and asserted the superiority of neutral scientific reasoning. As Marie-Ange Voisin-Fougère has noted, there are resemblances between Zola and Bourget's position in the late 1870s and early 1880s: both defended realism, took an interest in the theme of heredity, admired Hippolyte Taine, and

---

[20] Bourget, *Essais*, pp. 12–13. This section of the Baudelaire essay changes significantly in the 1899 revised version, with the extended medical analogy disappearing entirely. See Bourget, *Études littéraires*, p. 8.

applied the concept of experimental science to literature. However, from as early as 1883, their positions diverged, as Bourget's writing became increasingly spiritual and idealist in nature.[21]

Bourget's changing position responded to criticism he had previously faced for highlighting intellectual, moral, and psychological tendencies—pessimism, disillusion, and decadence—that were widely perceived as having a negative influence on society's moral health. The *Essais*' apparent glorification of these tendencies (which Bourget was initially unwilling to condemn as immoral) attracted criticism from journalists and commentators across the political spectrum. For example, the academic and poet Emmanuel des Essarts (1839–1909) expressed concerns about Bourget's pessimism leading to '[le] grossier fatalisme du bétail imitateur' ['the coarse fatalism of herd mentality'].[22] While acknowledging that pessimism was part of Bourget's originality, he valorised a more optimistic outlook, asserting that '[les] plus bienfaisants penseurs sont encore ceux qui ont donné à l'humanité confiance en elle-même' ['the most benevolent thinkers are still those who have given humanity confidence in itself'].[23] For an anonymous commentator in the *Revue chrétienne*, Christian faith was the only positive alternative to demoralising intellectual trends: 'Au pessimisme de la génération contemporaine il n'y a rien à opposer, si ce n'est l'amour chrétien: l'amour qui se donne, qui croit et qui espère' ['Nothing can prevail against the pessimism of the current generation, other than Christian love: a selfless, faithful, and hopeful love'].[24] While attacking philosophical pessimism, considered the central cause of society's moral decline, critics targeted Bourget's vision of scientific determinism, his presentation of decadence in the essay on Baudelaire, and his appraisal of intellectual dilettantism in the essay on Renan. The moderate Republican politician, journalist, and future President of the Republic Paul Deschanel (1855–1922) highlighted these factors when assessing Bourget's criticism:

> Ainsi le dilettantisme des idées, en détruisant tout principe de certitude, affaiblit la volonté et la puissance d'agir [...]. L'âme se déconcerte sous l'effort du doute; la foi patriotique et l'amour disparaissent avec la loi morale. En goûtant la décadence, on y travaille, et l'on hâte (inconsciemment) la décomposition de son pays; on ne se contente pas d'assister, en spectateur impassible, à l'affaiblissement de sa race; la curiosité y trouve plaisir, s'enivre des senteurs de la corruption et y contribue.[25]

---

[21] Marie-Ange Voisin-Fougère, 'Émile Zola et Paul Bourget: Une amitié littéraire', in *Champ littéraire autour de Zola*, edited by Béatrice Laville (Pessac: Presses Universitaires de Bordeaux, 2004), pp. 177–91 (pp. 183–5).
[22] Emmanuel des Essarts, 'Variétés: Études littéraires', *Le Soir*, 15 Nov. 1883.
[23] Des Essarts, 'Variétés'.
[24] E. M., 'Un critique psychologue: M. Paul Bourget', *Revue chrétienne*, May 1884, 279–96 (p. 296).
[25] Paul Deschanel, 'Critique contemporaine: Paul Bourget', *La Revue politique et littéraire*, 23 Feb. 1884, p. 232.

[Thus dilettantism, in the realm of ideas, weakens people's willpower and ability to act, by destroying all notion of certainty. [...] The soul is unsettled beneath the weight of doubt; as moral laws disappear, so do patriotism and love. Having tasted decadence, people work towards it, and (unconsciously) hasten their country's decomposition. They are not satisfied with being indifferent bystanders witnessing the decline of their race; finding pleasure at the sight of it, and intoxicated by the scent of corruption, their curiosity contributes further to its spread.]

Deschanel here adopts the bad influence model by refuting Bourget's claim to impartial observation, based on the opportunity for experiencing corrupt pleasure from the analytical act. Furthermore, he shares his contemporaries' concerns about the harmful effects of doubt on individuals and society as a whole, by highlighting how it undermines willpower, patriotic feeling, and shared moral values.

In response to these criticisms, Bourget moved away from determinism and materialism, and approached the literary 'contagion' model from a different angle. He increasingly adopted the language of morality critics and shifted the analyst's role from neutral analysis of social ills to offering a potential cure. As early as 27 December 1883, in an article appearing in Le Parlement suggestively entitled 'Vers l'Idéal' ['Towards the Ideal'], Bourget started to distance himself from the scientific trends evoked in the 1883 Essais.[26] Two years later, Bourget reframed his earlier work in the Avant-Propos to the 1885 Nouveaux essais de psychologie contemporaine. In an ideological volte face, Bourget described a morally contaminated youth in judgemental, negative terms: '[la] jeunesse contemporaine [...] offre les symptômes, visibles pour tous ceux qui veulent regarder sans parti pris, d'une maladie de la vie morale arrivée à sa période la plus aiguë' ['the contemporary youth [...] show symptoms, visible to all those who wish to take an unbiased viewpoint, of an illness in their moral lives that has reached its most serious stage'].[27] He claimed that the 1870 Franco-Prussian War and the 1871 Paris Commune played a central role in encouraging widespread moral decline, described as a form of intellectual 'poisoning': '[Q]uelque chose nous en est demeuré, à tous, comme un premier empoisonnement qui nous a laissés plus dépourvus, plus incapables de résister à la maladie intellectuelle où il nous a fallu grandir' ['something remained inside all of us, like an initial poison that left us more depleted and less capable of resisting the intellectual illness of our growing years'].[28] While adopting the language of more conservative moral commentators, these additions responded directly to the criticisms of Paul Deschanel, who condemned not only Bourget's moral complicity with social decay, but also the absence of references, in the 1883

---

[26] Cited by Voisin-Fougère in 'Émile Zola et Paul Bourget', p. 185.
[27] Bourget, Études littéraire, p. 438.
[28] Bourget, Études littéraires, p. 440.

edition of the *Essais*, to the events of 1870–1 as an influential factor affecting the younger generation.[29] But although Bourget clearly reframed his position to fit better with contemporaneous views of literature's immoral influence, he did not—at least at this stage—distance himself from the affected group he analysed. Rather, he aligned himself with a generation of young readers and hinted at his inevitable involvement in that group's decline.[30] By using the third person plural and emphasising the universal impact of a generation's socio-political inheritance ('all of us'), Bourget occupied a dual position of critic-analyst and patient-sufferer, implicating himself in potentially contagious phenomena.

As well as changing his approach to materialism and adopting a more negative vision of literary influence, Bourget laid the groundwork for developing a religious and moralising lens more agreeable to conservative reviewers. Notably, in the 1885 Avant-Propos, he responded to his critics' questions regarding the necessity of faith to society's ideal functioning:

> Quand le premier volume de ces Essais fut publié, les critiques me dirent: apportez-vous un remède au mal que vous décrivez si complaisamment? Nous voyons votre analyse, nous ne voyons pas votre conclusion. Et j'avoue humblement que, de conclusion positive, je n'en saurais donner aucune à ces études. Balzac, qui s'appelait volontiers un docteur ès sciences sociales, cite quelque part ce mot d'un philosophe chrétien: «Les hommes n'ont pas besoin de maîtres pour douter.» Cette superbe phrase serait la condamnation de ce livre, qui est un livre de recherche anxieuse, s'il n'y avait pas, dans le doute sincère, un principe de foi, comme il y a un principe de vérité dans toute erreur ingénue. Prendre au sérieux, presque au tragique, le drame qui se joue dans les intelligences et dans les cœurs de sa génération, n'est-ce pas affirmer que l'on croit à l'importance infinie des problèmes de la vie morale? N'est-ce pas faire un acte de foi dans cette réalité obscure et douloureuse, adorable et inexplicable, qui est l'âme humaine?[31]

> [When the first volume of these Essays was published, critics said to me: do you provide a cure for the illness you describe with such indulgence? We can see your analysis, but we cannot see your conclusion. And I humbly admit that, when it comes to reaching a positive conclusion, I could not fathom how to do so with these studies. Balzac, who would gladly call himself an expert in social science, somewhere cites a phrase from a Christian philosopher: 'Men need no masters to teach them to doubt'. This superb phrase would amount to a condemnation of my book, which is a work of anxious research, were there not an element of

---

[29] Deschanel wrote that 'le livre aurait pu être écrit en 1869' ['the book could have been written in 1869'], 'Critique contemporaine', p. 232.
[30] Pernot discusses the creation of 'fraternité de génération' ['generational fraternity'] in prefaces of socialisation novels. See *Le Roman de socialisation*, p. 66.
[31] Bourget, *Études littéraires*, p. 440.

faith to be found in sincere doubt, as there is an element of truth in all naïve mistakes. Taking seriously, almost tragically, the drama that plays out in the minds and hearts of one's generation, is that not a way of confirming one's belief in the infinite importance of moral questions? Does it not amount to a leap of faith in the reality, both obscure and painful, adorable and inexplicable, of the human soul?]

Bourget here summarises his critics' argument that analytical writers may indirectly promote the social ills they describe if they do not condemn them overtly. By failing to offer a 'positive conclusion', such analyses enact a form of immoral indulgence towards social and moral ills. In this passage, Bourget evokes Balzac's use of a phrase attributed to the counter-revolutionary philosopher Louis de Bonald (1754–1840), which reads: '[un] écrivain doit avoir en morale et en politique des opinions arrêtées, il doit se regarder comme un instituteur des hommes; car les hommes n'ont pas besoin de maîtres pour douter' ['a writer ought to have settled opinions on morals and politics; he should regard himself as a tutor of men; for men need no masters to teach them to doubt'].[32] Bonald suggests that showing problems in God's design without offering solutions is irresponsible and immoral, since men are naturally inclined to incredulity. By citing Bonald, Balzac therefore endorses the view that writers must actively encourage moral behaviour and religious sentiment in their works in order to counteract this inclination. Considering Balzac's position—itself part of a defensive response to criticisms of his works' immoral influence—Bourget effectively concedes that his essays are worthy of condemnation. Nevertheless, the rhetorical questions mitigate this condemnation on the basis that his doubt was an innocent error that he could rectify and transform, with the benefit of hindsight, into an indirect act of faith.

The *Nouveaux essais*'s preface was a turning point or stepping stone, via which Bourget was able to reframe his earlier work and take up a different position in the literary field. Due to the change in perspective required for this evolution, it is not surprising that such a turning point was fraught with uncertainty and ambiguity. Several fin-de-siècle critics recognised Bourget's conflicted position in the mid-1880s, highlighting the nostalgia for religious certainty hiding deep within Bourget's earlier pessimism. They suggested that pessimism's unspoken despair at a lost ideal implied an unconscious desire for a return to the Catholic faith and the reassurance it provides.[33] The same reasoning also applies to the

---

[32] Honoré de Balzac, *Œuvres complètes*, 24 vols (Paris: Michel Lévy Frères, 1869–76), I (1869), p. 6. English translation from the 'Author's Introduction' in Honoré de Balzac, *The Complete Works of Honoré de Balzac*, 36 vols, I: *The Magic Skin*, ed. George Saintsbury (Boston: Colonial Press Company, 1901), pp. liii–lxix (p. lix).

[33] See Sutter Laumann, 'Revue littéraire', *La Justice*, 2 Mar. 1886, Paul Lallemand, 'Variété: La jeunesse contemporaine d'après les livres récents', *Le Français*, 23 Aug. 1887, and Ernest Tissot, 'Les Évolutions de la critique contemporaine: M. Paul Bourget, étude analytique', *La Revue Générale*, 15 Aug. 1888, pp. 361–72.

1885 Avant-Propos, which attempts to recuperate a positive conclusion from an otherwise negative position. Yet, as François Proulx has noted, there is a 'certain unresolved uneasiness' in the *Nouveaux essais*'s frame text.[34] This is apparent in the awkwardness of Bourget's supposedly 'humble' concession to his critics, as well as in the revealing phrase 'recherche anxieuse' ['anxious research']. Furthermore, the rhetorical questions cited above appear less like a stylistic flourish used to underscore a convincing argument than a post hoc (and somewhat begrudging) attempt to reinterpret earlier work through a moralising lens. In this way, the transitional moment in Bourget's career reveals a hesitancy and difficulty inherent to the process of ideological and aesthetic evolution. Or, to use a botanical analogy: the decaying wood of earlier positions exists alongside, and intertwined with, the bourgeoning shoots of newer, more delicate, growth.

Rather than pruning off the older growth, Bourget's literary development involved a form of intellectual grafting that demonstrates his unwillingness to leave behind fully the scientific model in favour of its religious counterpart. To this end, later prefatory material suggested that scientific approaches may support religious teaching, rather than undermining it. For example, in the preface to the 1899 *Œuvres complètes* version of the *Essais*, Bourget writes:

> La psychologie est à l'éthique ce que l'anatomie est à la thérapeutique. Elle la précède et s'en distingue par ce caractère de [...] diagnostic sans prescription. Mais cette attitude d'observateur qui ne conclut pas n'est jamais que momentanée. C'est un procédé analogue au doute méthodique de Descartes et qui finit par se résoudre en une affirmation.[35]

> [Psychology is to ethics what anatomy is to medical treatment. The former precedes the latter and is distinguished from it by a proclivity for [...] diagnosis without prescription. But the position of observer who does not conclude is only ever adopted temporarily. It is a process analogous to Descartes's methodological doubt, which ends up resolving itself in an affirmation.]

In this passage, Bourget returns to the vision of experimental literature formulated by Émile Zola in *Le Roman expérimental* (1880). As previously noted, Zola's vision of human psychology in this work was fundamentally materialist and determinist. He claimed that '[un] même déterminisme doit régir la pierre des chemins et le cerveau de l'homme' ['A like determinism will govern the stones of the roadway and the brain of main'].[36] According to Zola, proponents of experimental

---

[34] Proulx, *Victims of the Book*, p. 49.
[35] Bourget, *Études littéraires*, p. 442.
[36] Émile Zola, *Le Roman expérimental*, 5th ed. (Paris: Charpentier, 1881), p. 16. For the English translation, see Émile Zola, *The Experimental Novel, and other essays*, trans. Belle M. Sherman (New York: The Cassell Publishing Co., 1894), p. 17.

literature could contribute actively to scientific progress through observation and experimentation. They were 'moralistes expérimentateurs' ['experimental moralists'], who, like omnipotent doctors, could cure the social and moral maladies they analyse ('se rendre maître de la vie pour la diriger').[37] In the 1899 preface, Bourget expresses ideas that recur in Zola's essay, including the alignment of psychology with anatomy, and an insistence on scientific neutrality ('diagnostic sans prescription', 'observateur qui ne conclut pas'). However, by claiming that scientific neutrality is a transitional step between doubt and faith, Bourget clearly differentiated himself from his contemporary's atheistic positivism and his insistence that the true experimental scientist (and writer) does not conclude.[38]

The fact that Bourget returned to the question of experimental literature in 1899 demonstrates its importance as a springboard for his renewed moral and literary perspective. In this later preface, Bourget turned scientific neutrality and doubt into a means of attaining truth and moral 'affirmation'. He did so by tapping into the discourse of scientific discovery while also harkening back to an earlier Christian model: Cartesian doubt. Already implicit in the 'sincere doubt' of the 1885 Avant-Propos, Descartes's 'methodological doubt', mentioned in the 1899 preface, acts a bridge between Bourget's vision of religion as a mere prejudice in 1883 and as a positive source of moral 'affirmation' in 1899. Bourget strengthens the Christian credentials of his works by claiming that they contribute to an 'apologétique expérimentale' ['experimental apologetics'].[39] The word 'experimental' clearly invokes Zola's earlier essay, uniting seemingly contradictory scientific and religious vocabularies. Significantly, Bourget returns to this paradoxical notion in the preface to the Œuvres complètes edition of his early novels: 'Cette apolégétique [sic] consiste à établir [...] qu'étant donnée une série d'observations sur la vie humaine, tout dans ces observations s'est passé *comme si* le Christianisme était la vérité' ['This apologetics consists of establishing [...] that, given a series of observations on human life, everything in these observations has taken place *as if* Christianity were true'].[40] By reframing his earlier psychological approach as a stepping stone towards Christianity, Bourget adopted an idealist position and moral standpoint increasingly in line with Catholic dogma. In many ways, Bourget could therefore not have been more different from the anticlerical Zola. Yet despite being frequently posited as opposites by both their peers and modern

---

[37] Zola, Le Roman expérimental, pp. 23–4.
[38] 'Un expérimentateur n'a pas à conclure, parce que, justement, l'expérience conclut pour lui.' Zola, Le Roman expérimental, pp. 28–9. ['An experimentalist has no need to conclude, because, in truth, experiment concludes for him.'] Zola, The Experimental Novel, p. 30.
[39] Bourget, Études littéraires, p. 443. The OED defines 'apologetics' as 'The defensive method of argument; often spec. The argumentative defence of Christianity', in 'apologetic, adj. and n.' OED Online, Oxford University Press, Dec. 2022, www.oed.com/view/Entry/9321, accessed 12 Jan. 2023.
[40] Paul Bourget, Œuvres complètes. Romans I. Cruelle énigme, Un crime d'amour, André Cornélis (Paris: Plon, 1900), p. x. References to novels in this edition hereafter appear parenthetically in the text, preceded by the abbreviation OC.

scholars, Bourget and Zola employed a similar language and logic to support their supposedly antithetical viewpoints. It is also well known that, like Bourget, Zola eventually moved away from his earlier anti-idealist stance and wrote a series of utopian thesis novels.[41] Regardless of their ideological differences, then, these similarities reveal the shared structures of knowledge and interpretation that undergirded fin-de-siècle discussions about literary influence and responsibility, which served to justify a morally improving literature as much as it condemned immoral contagion.

Throughout the 1880s and 1890s, Bourget honed his vision of literary influence. From a quasi-scientific analysis of literature's impact on wider social and moral trends, he moved towards a more prescriptive position, which reinserted the traditional authorities that his earlier vision seemed to undermine. Depicting the reading relationship as both an intimate process of mentorship and an ambiguous conduit for moral contagion, Bourget returned incessantly to the question of authorial responsibility and moral complicity. The dominance of this theme was due, at least in part, to Bourget's desire to respond to others' critique of his early works, and, eventually, to reframe them according to a more traditional moral outlook. Before analysing the novel that marks this transition—*Le Disciple* (1889)—it is worth considering why Bourget faced so much criticism in the first place. To do so, the following section analyses his contributions to another literary genre: the *roman psychologique*. For although the *Essais* were key to launching Bourget's career, he became equally (if not more) well known for publishing psychological novels centred on adultery, such as *Cruelle énigme* (1885), *Un crime d'amour* (1886), and *André Cornélis* (1887). As one of the genre's leading exponents, Bourget frequently faced accusations that he was morally complicit with, or compromised by, the forms of human psychology and behaviour he depicted. This critique, which eventually encouraged Bourget to move towards writing moralising thesis novels, demonstrated remarkable staying power throughout his later career.

## The Psychological Novel: Conscience or *Complaisance*?

Emphasising interior characterisation and motivation, psychological novels examine the reasons for fictional characters' behaviour and how the intricacies of their mental lives influence external events and drive forward the story's plotline.[42] Evolving from the earlier genre of 'analytical' novel ('roman d'analyse'),

---

[41] For a recent study of Zola's later thesis novels, considered in relation to those penned by Paul Bourget and Maurice Barrès, see Béatrice Laville, *Une poétique des fictions autoritaires. Les voies de Zola, Barrès, Bourget* (Pessac: Presses Universitaires de Bordeaux, 2020).

[42] Christopher McNab, 'Psychological Novel and Roman d'analyse', in *Encyclopedia of the Novel*, edited by Paul Schellinger and others, 2 vols (London: Fitzroy Dearborn, 1998), II, pp. 1057–9.

spearheaded by Madame de La Fayette's *La Princesse de Clèves* (1678), the psychological novel flourished in France during the late nineteenth century. Its popularity increased through the influence of writers such as Stendhal and Dostoevsky, whose works appeared in French translation from 1884 onwards. It gained further impetus from scientific developments, notably the positivist and experimental psychology pioneered by Hippolyte Taine and Théodule Ribot (1839–1916).[43] Cited as Naturalism's opposite, while rivalling it as one of the most influential and successful novelistic genres at the turn of the century, the psychological novel combined mainstream appeal with the added cultural cachet of new intellectual trends. Its proponents appropriated Taine differently to their Naturalist peers, by '[spiritualisant] la psychologie en la purgeant du déterminisme qui la constitue comme science' ['spiritualising psychology by purging it of the determinism that made it scientific'].[44] Indeed, most of the leading psychological fiction writers—Anatole France (1844–1924), Paul Bourget, Édouard Rod (1857–1910), Jules Lemaitre (1854–1914), and Maurice Barrès (1862–1923)—were united in opposing Emile Zola's literary school.[45] Their works typically focused on questions of psychology, morality, and the complexities of human behaviour, through characters who typically belonged to their own social milieu.[46] By remaining within the bounds of 'acceptable' subject matter, these writers accumulated greater cultural capital and participated in more traditional literary networks than their Naturalist competitors. They benefited from the patronage of high society salons and the mainstream press, and gained official recognition in the form of elections to the *Académie française*. Yet the psychological novel also offers an intriguing example of how even the most socially legitimate literature could be accused of complicity with immorality. Bourget's early novels testify to this phenomenon by hovering on the line of acceptability, between conscience and *complaisance* ['laxity' or 'indulgence']. Their depiction of destructive psychological tendencies and illicit behaviour through a morally ambivalent lens frequently attracted criticism, thereby contributing to the dubious reputation of both the genre and its main proponent.

Published a few months after the *Nouveaux essais de psychologie contemporaine*, Bourget's *Un crime d'amour* (1886) recounts the story of an adulterous affair between Hélène Chazel and her husband's best friend, Armand de Querne. Armand, a cynical philanderer, seduces Hélène under the false impression that she has already had an affair. In fact, Hélène is deeply in love with Armand, who seems

---

[43] Alexander McCabe, 'Dostoevsky's French reception: from Vogüé, Gide, Shestov and Berdyaev to Marcel, Camus and Sartre (1880–1959)' (PhD dissertation, University of Glasgow, 2013) p. 26.

[44] Sapiro, *La Responsabilité*, p. 358.

[45] See Rémy Ponton, 'Naissance du roman psychologique: capital culturel, capital social et stratégie littéraire à la fin du 19e siècle', *Actes de la recherche en sciences sociales* 1, no. 4 (1975): pp. 66–81 (p. 67), doi:10.3406/arss.1975.3421.

[46] Ponton, 'Naissance du roman psychologique', p. 74. See also Sapiro, *La Responsabilité*, p. 358.

more in tune with her sensibilities than her husband, Alfred, an awkward but devoted mathematician. Initially blind to Armand's heartless indifference, Hélène is convinced her feelings are reciprocated. Their affair lasts a few months before Armand starts to reveal his cynical nature. When Alfred raises his suspicions regarding the affair, de Querne decides to end his relationship with Hélène in the name of male solidarity and honour. During the break-up scene, Armand reveals his true nature to Hélène, who then takes vengeance by having sex with the man he thought to be his predecessor. When Hélène confesses this 'crime d'amour' ['love crime'], Armand recognises his responsibility and feels guilt for her moral decline. To alleviate his suffering, de Querne flees to England. After returning to Paris, he meets with his former lover, who has since decided to act nobly by returning to her role as a committed wife and mother. Awed by Hélène's generosity, Armand is converted to living a moral existence.

Throughout *Un crime d'amour*, Bourget uses pathologising language to depict Armand as both a victim and perpetrator of intellectual and moral disease. By doing so, he reinscribed, in novel form, the shift towards a more negative formulation of social pathology discourses, seen in the 1885 *Nouveaux essais*' preface. Excerpts from Armand's diary provide a pathological case study, as a '[une] sinistre monographie d'une maladie secrète de l'âme' ['a sinister monograph about a soul's secret disease'] (*OC*, 163). The language of poison and contagion returns when de Querne faces his actions' negative consequences. The narrator describes de Querne confronted with '[un] être auquel il aurait de ses mains versé du poison' ['someone poisoned by his own hand'] (*OC*, 276), and states that '[son] âme n'était pas seulement morte, elle avait répandu autour d'elle la contagion de sa mort intime' ['his soul was not only dead, but contagious, spreading its inner death to those surrounding it'] (*OC*, 280). The literary implications of this depiction come to the fore via instances of *mise en abyme*, where characters' literary tastes reflect and contribute to their moral 'decline' in the novel. For example, Bourget highlights Armand's preference for '[des] romans de desséchante analyse' ['novels that contain withering analysis'] (*OC*, 164). On the surface, Bourget appears to align himself here with a conservative viewpoint of literary influence by demonising his cynical protagonist. But there is a note of self-aware irony here, since Bourget's own novels could be considered to contain 'withering analysis'. Such irony re-emerges when Hélène decides to buy risqué novels in the build-up to her moral 'suicide': '[elle] fit venir, pour les avoir sur sa table, les ouvrages dont elle avait entendu parler ces dernières années comme étant les plus audacieux' ['she sent for works that, in recent years, she had heard were the most audacious, so that she could have them on her table'] (*OC*, 247). Bourget's novel implies that Hélène does not necessarily read the books she buys. Rather, she puts them on display as an outward marker of immoral inclinations that she does not fully personify. Through these details, readers are reassured of Hélène's underlying virtue, in such a way as to enable the novel's 'moral' ending. Nevertheless, by aligning literary taste with false appearances, Bourget also suggests that at least some of the moral panic around literature, and the 'bad influence' argument that supports it, is superficial hype constructed through external framing rather than a true reflection of a work's inherent qualities.

Compared to Bourget's other psychological novels, such as *Cruelle énigme* and *André Cornélis*, *Un crime d'amour* has a morally uplifting ending that hints towards a tacit acceptance of Christian morality as an alternative to pessimism.[47] However, until Armand's final volte face, the trajectory of *Un crime d'amour* is predominantly pessimistic, offering a fatalistic view of human experience and morality. Just before the denouement, Armand's musings offer a cynical vision of human injustice and sin: 'le péché de chacun, s'il y a péché, porte son fruit empoisonné dans l'âme d'un autre, et la même solidarité gouverne tous les rapports des hommes entre eux. Les fils expient pour les pères, les justes pour les méchants, les innocents pour les coupables' ['each person's sin, if they have any sins, bears its poisoned fruit in another person's soul, and the same solidarity governs all relations between men. Sons atone for their fathers, good people for evildoers, the innocent for the guilty'] (*OC*, 281). This passage reformulates a section from *La Philosophie de la liberté* (1848), by the Swiss philosopher Charles Secrétan (1815–95).[48] The word 'solidarity' evokes a broad network of shared crime and guilt, which spans illogically—because indiscriminately—across the generations. Unable to convince himself of God's existence or of the validity of Christian morality through reason alone, Armand is finally won over by the example of Hélène's compassion and self-sacrificial repentance. Bourget here shows that the logic of influence works both ways. Through the vicissitudes of de Querne's fate, readers witness the possibility of a 'good influence' model of literature, which offers an idealistic and implicitly religious twist to an otherwise largely pessimistic tale.[49] In the novel's final lines, Armand's realisation amounts to a conversion:

---

[47] *Cruelle énigme* (1885) tells the story of a young, respectable man, Hubert Laurian, who falls in love with a married woman, Thérèse de Sauve. The story charts the progress and gradual debasement of their affair. After Thérèse is unfaithful for no apparent reason, Hubert resumes their relationship, thereby sacrificing his moral fortitude to her sensual appeal. *André Cornélis* (1887) is a Hamlet-inspired story that ends with the protagonist's despair that, having finally murdered his stepfather (who, many years earlier, had orchestrated his father's death), his revenge remains incomplete, because he was unable to destroy his mother's love for the deceased.

[48] The original passage includes the following lines: 'Qu'ont fait les enfants pour souffrir des fautes de leurs pères? Quel est le sens moral de cette solidarité qui enchaîne les hommes aux hommes, les peuples aux peuples, les générations aux générations?' ['What have children done to suffer for their fathers' misdeeds? What moral sense is there in this solidarity that binds men, peoples, and generations together?'] Cited by E. M., 'Un critique psychologue', p. 294.

[49] Belief in the potential for literature to enact positive influence, either by vaunting the merits of 'moral' characters or depicting the downfall of their immoral counterparts, was central to the thesis novel genre that Bourget adopted later in his career. It was also propounded by Catholic contemporaries who encouraged 'good' reading practices, notably through the means of Church-organised lending libraries. On the history and practices of the 'Work of Good Books' Archconfraternity, initially founded in Bordeaux in 1859, see Loïc Artiaga, *Des torrents de papier. Catholicisme et lectures populaires au XIXe siècle* (Limoges: PULIM, 2007).

> Ainsi le principe de salut qu'il n'avait pu obtenir de l'impuissante raison et que les dogmes de la foi ne lui avaient pas donné, puisqu'il n'y croyait pas, il le rencontrait dans cette vertu de la charité qui se passe de toutes les démonstrations et de toutes les révélations,—mais ce précepte de charité ne fut-il pas la révélation suprême? [...] Et Armand éprouva qu'une chose venait de naître en lui, avec laquelle il pourrait toujours trouver une raison de vivre et d'agir: le respect, la piété, la religion de la souffrance humaine. (*OC*, 290-1)

> [Thus, he found the principle of salvation—which he had been unable to attain through impotent reason and which religious teachings had failed to provide, since he did not believe in them—in this charitable virtue requiring no proof or revelation ... But was this principle of charity not itself the ultimate revelation? [...] And Armand felt something spring up within him, which he could always rely on to find reasons for living and motivation to act: respect, piety, and faith in human suffering.]

The religious lexis ('salvation', 'revelation', and 'piety') moves the novel distinctly away from psychology to morality, and from cynical doubt to restored faith. This mirrors Bourget's changing position towards literary morality and responsibility in the *Essais*, and foreshadows a similar 'conversion' that takes place in his later novel, *Le Disciple* (1889).

Rather than appeasing his contemporaries, *Un crime d'amour*'s ending attracted criticism for its lack of verisimilitude. When reviewing Bourget's novel, Édouard Rod wrote: 'que le remords puisse être fécond dans une âme dévastée par l'*incroyance*,—qui le croira?' ['who would believe that remorse could grow from a soul devasted by a lack of faith?']⁵⁰ Rod's criticism targets the volte face experienced by a character whose cynicism appears boundless for most of the novel. The Protestant theologian and critic Edmond Schérer (1815–89) also expressed his incredulity regarding Armand's conversion: 'je n'attends, pour ma part, aucun redressement de cet homme; il ne sera qu'un blasé' ['for my part, I expect no recovery for this man; he will only ever be blasé'].⁵¹ If readers doubt Armand's sudden ethical conversion, *Un crime d'amour* remains predominantly a pessimistic adultery novel, with an ambiguous moral status. The ending's lack of verisimilitude undermines any moral value the novel might otherwise have, because it seems too contrived to be believable ('who would believe [...]?'). By breaking the believability required for the realist reading pact, the sudden shift in *Un crime d'amour* provoked more doubt than certainty regarding the novel's moral status.⁵²

---

⁵⁰ Rod, 'Variétés. Un crime d'amour', *La République française*, 18 Feb. 1886.
⁵¹ Edmond Schérer, 'Variétés. Un crime d'amour', *Le Temps*, 4 Mar. 1886.
⁵² On the realist reading pact, see Susan Rubin Suleiman, *Authoritarian Fictions: The Ideological Novel as a Literary Genre*. 2nd ed. (Princeton: Princeton University Press, 1993), pp. 72–3.

While criticising *Un crime d'amour*'s denouement, Bourget's peers also questioned the moral value of his psychological novels, due to the primary position given to adulterous passion in their plotlines. For example, Edmond Schérer justified his disbelief at Armand's conversion by highlighting and condemning the work's illicit sensuality: 'Il y a là, dans les cent premières pages, [...] [des] descriptions licencieuses et qui sont là pour leur compte, d'images de sensualité que le sujet n'exigeait point et dans lesquelles il faut bien conclure que se complaît l'esprit de l'écrivain' ['In the first hundred pages, there are licentious descriptions that exist for their own account, sensual images that the subject did not require, and in which, we must conclude, the writer's mind takes pleasure'].[53] According to Schérer, a writer may evoke erotic themes to advance the plot or character development, but anything beyond this amounts to moral complacency ('se complaire'). This sensuality attracted the attention of avant-garde writers, Octave Mirbeau and Maurice Barrès, who—unlike their more conservative peers—celebrated the ambiguity of Bourget's moral position. In *Le Gaulois*, Mirbeau described the novel as a 'livre hardi' ['daring book'] containing 'certaines brutalités d'analyse' ['a certain analytical brutality'], while admitting its limited suitability for impressionable readers:

> Je n'en recommande point cependant la lecture aux jeunes filles. Je me permets seulement de la conseiller aux femmes; car, si cette œuvre entre violemment dans des questions scabreuses et délicates à traiter, elle éloigne de la dépravation, et reste toujours 'de bonne compagnie', comme on dit.[54]

> [I do not, however, recommend it as reading material for young ladies. I take the sole liberty of recommending it to grown women, for although this work enters violently into tricky questions that require delicate treatment, it staves off depravity, and always retains the tone of 'good society', as they say.]

By proscribing the act of reading for women at different life stages, Mirbeau redeploys an argument typical of moral literary criticism, while highlighting literature's dual potential for both corruption and edification. He further implies that Bourget sugar-coats erotic material so that it can pass the standards of social acceptability required by his upper-class readership ('good society'). In a similar gesture, Maurice Barrès—a fellow proponent of the psychological novel—humorously celebrated Bourget's ability to make audacious material palatable to high society: 'le piquant, c'est que Bourget se fait lire de la meilleure société. [...] [P]eut-être ce qui vaut à Bourget qu'on lui passe ses sincérités, c'est qu'il fait ses personnages toujours délicats ou de manières raffinées' ['the best part of it is that Bourget is read

---

[53] Schérer, 'Variétés'.
[54] Octave Mirbeau, 'Un crime d'amour', *Le Gaulois*, 11 Feb. 1886, p. 1.

in the highest society. [...] Perhaps the reason why people let Bourget's honesty slide is because the characters he creates are perennially delicate or have refined manners'].[55] Both Mirbeau and Barrès lace their tongue-in-cheek appraisal with a side-note of mockery, since Bourget's skill at sugar-coating risqué material implicitly denotes his status as a panderer, subservient to an edulcorated and hypocritical literary taste.

With his unusual proclivity for both quasi-scientific psychological analysis and sentimental—if not melodramatic—plotlines, Bourget seemed too risqué for traditionalist critics, and not risqué enough for the avant-garde. Barrès captures this ambivalence when he describes Bourget's writing as hovering between science and sentimentalism: 'De la tendresse vague de son cœur, il fait cet idéalisme précis, ce mystisme [sic] que nous avons exposé; de l'appétit des sens, il prend des notes' ['From the vague tenderness of his heart, he creates a particular sort of idealism, this mysticism we have uncovered. From the sensual appetite, he takes notes'].[56] Barrès suggests that, by blending scientific accuracy with idealism and mysticism, Bourget takes on the position of a religious moral guide: 'd'élégiaque devenu mystique, d'*inquiet* devenu presque directeur de conscience, [...] il tient un rang fort particulier parmi nos écrivains' ['from elegiac lamenter to mystic, from anxious analyst to would-be spiritual director, [...] he holds a very peculiar position amongst our contemporary writers'].[57] The comparison seemed so apt to Bourget's contemporaries that it recurred in critical appraisals of his work. For example, when reviewing *Cruelle énigme* (1885), Raoul Frary (1842–92) noted that '[l'auteur] apporte dans cette étude la pénétration attentive et attendrie d'un confesseur de femmes, d'un confesseur laïque bien entendu' ['the author brings to this study the penetrating and tender attentiveness of a woman's confessor (but a secular confessor, of course)'].[58] The same year, Félicien Champsaur (1858–1934) compared Bourget's writing style to 'le geste onctueux d'un petit prélat' ['the obsequious gesture of a low-level bishop'], which revealed the author's desire to become a brainwasher or 'manieur de cerveaux' ['mind-manipulator'].[59] Ten years later, upon Bourget's election to the *Académie française*, the journalist Gibrac wrote that 'il y a de l'abbé, du confesseur, même du jésuite, dans M. Paul Bourget' ['Mr Bourget has something of the abbot, of the confessor, and even of the Jesuit about him'].[60]

By comparing Bourget to a spiritual director ('directeur de conscience'), Bourget's critics tapped into a wealth of social and literary stereotypes about the ambiguity of priests' moral influence. Charged with guiding the everyday behaviour of

---

[55] Maurice Barrès, 'Notes sur M. Paul Bourget', *Les Lettres et les arts*, 1 Feb. 1886, pp. 256–63 (p. 260).
[56] Barrès, 'Notes', p. 260.
[57] Barrès, 'Notes', pp. 260–1.
[58] Roman Frary, 'Un roman d'analyse', *La France*, 2 Mar. 1885.
[59] Félicien Champsaur, 'La Vie littéraire et artistique: Brelan de critiques', *Le Figaro, supplément littéraire*, 5 Oct. 1885, p. 195.
[60] Gibrac, 'Actualité: Sous la coupole', *Le Signal*, 15 June 1895.

aristocratic and upper-bourgeois women, *directeurs de conscience* held an influential position within privileged social circles. Their critics accused them of holding a dangerous sway over women through the practice of confessional. Literary depictions of the figure abounded in works by writers such as Balzac and Zola—with a degree of sympathy in the former, and varying levels of anticlericalism in the latter.[61] In particular, anticlerical writers drew inspiration from Jules Michelet's *Du prêtre, de la femme, de la famille* (1845), which depicts priests as unwelcome intruders in the family setting, whose influence over women's personal lives distances them from their husbands. In this work, Michelet employs a lexis associated with adultery to highlight the dangers of women's shared loyalties:

Le maître de la pensée est celui à qui la personne appartient. Le prêtre tient l'âme, dès qu'il a le gage dangereux des premiers secrets [...]. Voilà un partage tout fait entre les époux, car maintenant il y en aura deux, l'âme à l'un, à l'autre le corps.[62]

[A person belongs to those who control their thoughts. As soon as the priest receives the dangerous collateral of someone's deepest secrets, he takes hold of their soul. [...] Henceforth there will be two husbands in the marriage, each taking their share: one will have the soul, and the other, the body].

According to Michelet, the Catholic practice of confessional encourages an unhealthy bond between confessor and confessant. He claims that priests experience sensual pleasure through their influence over faithful penitents: 'Il y a pour celui à qui toute jouissance naturelle est interdite [...] une sensualité maladive à exercer cette puissance, [...] à désoler pour consoler, blesser, guérir et blesser encore' ['For someone to whom every natural pleasure is forbidden [...] there is an unhealthy sensuality in holding this power, [...] in distressing someone to console them; in wounding, curing, and wounding again'].[63] However, the relationship is not purely predatory, but reciprocal and complicit: 'Ils se sont troublés ensemble, c'est une complicité... Tous deux savent (sans le savoir bien, d'instinct confus, de passion) qu'ils ont prise l'un sur l'autre, elle par le désir, et lui par la peur' ['Together, they are troubled and aroused, through a bond of complicity... Without full awareness, they both know, by some vague instinct or passion, that each of them has a hold on the other, her through desire and him through fear'].[64] In this way, a religious figure charged with guiding others' moral conscience has the power—and the inclination—to corrupt this conscience through moral *complaisance*.

---

[61] On the figure of the *directeur de conscience* in Balzac, see Jean Malavié, 'Présence du directeur de conscience dans les couples de *La Comédie humaine*', *Les Lettres Romanes* 56, nos. 3-4 (2002): pp. 223-33, doi:10.1484/J.LLR.3.53.
[62] Jules Michelet, *Du prêtre, de la femme, de la famille*, 2nd ed. (Paris: Hachette, 1845) p. 221.
[63] Michelet, *Du prêtre*, p. 267.
[64] Michelet, *Du prêtre*, p. 270.

Michelet's account is emblematic of a broad cultural attitude towards confession that supplies a metaphor that Bourget's critics wielded when attacking his perceived moral complacency. For example, Raoul Frary warned against the dangers of Bourget's position, remarking that 'M. Paul Bourget est un maître à qui nous ne souhaitons pas beaucoup de disciples' ['Mr Paul Bourget is a mentor to whom we wish very few disciples'].[65] Gibrac expressed similar concerns by directly accusing Bourget of casuistry: 'M. Paul Bourget est un casuiste; il se plaît aux problèmes les plus délicats, les plus difficiles de la morale; et c'est rarement aux bénéfice [sic] de celle-ci qu'il les résout' ['Mr Paul Bourget is a casuist: he finds pleasure in the most delicate and difficult problems in moral ethics, and it is rarely to the latter's benefit that he resolves them'].[66] Of all Bourget's critics, it was the avant-garde writer Jean Lorrain who took the comparison to its extremes in a series of lampooning articles which were republished in a collected volume entitled *Dans l'oratoire* (1888).[67] The text mounts a scathing attack against popular writers who traded on tacit permissiveness in erotic themes, which apparently appealed to and influenced their (predominantly female) readership. Lorrain aligned such writers with the perverted priests evoked by Michelet decades earlier. In the preface, Lorrain draws out the similarities between Catholic confessional and the literary production of his peers, considered a form of 'oratory' literature.[68] By using the term 'oratoire', Lorrain creates an analogy between a personal and contemplative religious space and the intimacy created through the act of reading. This space, like the literary relationship it represents, blends sensuality with mysticism:

> L'Oratoire, ce boudoir psychique, où la femme catholique est en coquetterie réglée avec Dieu: l'Oratoire, où le prêtre a régné près de sept siècles sur les sens et l'imagination de la femme: l'Oratoire, où le Christ prend de languides attitudes d'Adonis Syrien, et la dévote, des prosternements aspirants de prêtresse: l'Oratoire, lieu de mystère et de clair-obscur, [...] mi-partie sanctuaire, mi-partie gynécée, inquiétant et troublant comme un amour de moine.[69]

---

[65] Frary, 'Un roman d'analyse'.

[66] Gibrac, 'Actualité'.

[67] Jean Lorrain, *Dans l'oratoire* (Paris: C. Dalou, 1888). First appearing in *L'Événement* and *Le Courrier français* between March and July 1887, Lorrain's articles are gossip-laden critiques of partially veiled targets. The portrait of Bourget ('Mademoiselle Baudelaire!', pp. 11–21) appears alongside a series of satirical articles on other popular writers: Octave Feuillet (1821–90) in 'L'Aumonier du château' (pp. 22–31), Ernest Renan (1823–92) in 'L'Abbé de Joie' (pp. 32–41), Elme-Marie Caro (1826–87) in 'Monseigneur Psycho' (pp. 42–6), Catulle Mendès (1841–1909) and René Maizeroy (1856–1918) in 'Les Pères saphistes' (pp. 47–55), and a celebrity priest, Jacques Monsabré (1827–1907) in 'Frère Hépicus' (pp. 56–67).

[68] An oratory is a '[pièce] qui, dans une maison, est destinée aux exercices de dévotion' ['room, in a house, used for devotional practices']. Pierre Larousse, *Grand dictionnaire universel du XIXe siècle*, 17 vols (Paris: Administration du Grand Dictionnaire universel, 1866–77), XI (1874), p. 1411.

[69] Lorrain, *Dans l'oratoire*, p. 1.

[The Oratory, this psychological boudoir where Catholic women enter into a flirtatious courtship with God. The Oratory, where priests have reigned over women's imagination and senses for almost seven hundred years. The Oratory, where Christ adopts the languid posture of an Adonis and devout women kneel down before him like aspiring priestesses. The Oratory: a place of mystery, somewhere between light and darkness, [...] part-sanctuary, part-gynaecium, it is both worrying and disturbing, like a monk in love.]

Lorrain's article here frames women's relationship to oratory literature as a love affair, where writer-priests take on an ambiguously eroticised position. This vision borders on sacrilege, with Christ becoming the sexualised object of a pagan cult. The text's eroticism has uncanny similarities to Bourget's depiction of the reading relationship in the 1883 *Essais* preface. The key difference is a gendered one: Lorrain's prose evokes a female reader's attachment to a highly sensual (if sexually ambiguous) Christ-Adonis figure, whereas Bourget's preface depicts reading as homosocial (if implicitly homoerotic) bonding between men.

Lorrain's depiction of feminine devotion targets proponents of oratory literature for reducing religious sentiment to sensual titillation, and for tapping into the fantasies of (supposedly) frivolous women to further their careers. This canny manipulation of sensual mysticism contributes to the wider comparison between writers and *directeurs de conscience* in *Dans l'oratoire*. After describing the erotic appeal of the oratory mode, Lorrain cites a list of writers—'MM. Octave Fleuret, Paulin, Bourget, Caro et Jules Lemaitre'—who take on the role of Michelet's priests.[70] Such authors become *directeurs de conscience* for upper-class women and their novels become a secular replacement for the oratory space. The aim of these writers, referred to as '[R]évérends pères titillants, directeurs laïques de mondaines consciences' ['Reverend Fathers of titillation, secular directors of the high society conscience'],[71] is to arouse quasi-illicit desires in their female readership, while turning a blind eye to moral responsibility:

Ces Messieurs doivent tout éveiller d'un doigt discret et savamment mené dans leur moral organisme de femme, mais ils ne doivent qu'éveiller; [...] ils ne prêchent pas, ils chuchottent [sic]; ils ne confessent pas, ils frôlent.
*Frôleurs et Frôlées!*
Un titre pour un roman de M. Catulle Mendès... et pourquoi pas?
Le frôlement est exquis, parfois.
C'est une complicité toute de demi-teintes, de demi-gestes et de demi-sourires et, entre ouailles et prédicants, un délicieux échange de tacts et de contacts... effleurants.[72]

[70] Lorrain, *Dans l'oratoire*, p. 3.
[71] Lorrain, *Dans l'oratoire*, p. 5.
[72] Lorrain, *Dans l'oratoire*, p. 5.

[These gentlemen must stimulate everything with a discreet finger, cleverly probing into the moral body of women, but they must go no further than stimulation; [...] instead of preaching, they whisper softly; instead of receiving confession, they offer caresses.
*Strokers and Strokees!*
A title for a novel by Mr Catulle Mendès... and why not?
Sometimes, the light touch is exquisite.
It is a form of complicity made from half-tints, half-gestures, and half-smiles. Between flock and preacher, it is a delightful exchange of tactful delicacy and delicate touching...]

The extended references to physical touch—such as 'discreet finger', 'light touch' ('frôlement'), and 'delicate touching' ('contacts... effleurants')—hint at clitoral and vaginal stimulation, thereby confirming the woman-centred sensuality of oratory literature. The extract combines physical sensuality with psychological and moral ambiguity, as seen in the 'complicité toute de demi-teintes' and the 'délicieux échange de tacts et de contacts... effleurants'. The prefix 'demi' obscures the relationship between flock and preacher, where the flock represents readers and preachers represent writers. Furthermore, the French pun 'tacts et contacts' (rendered with the words 'tactful' and 'touching'), extends Lorrain's implicit accusation against writers who adopt the role of moral guide in order to corrupt their readers, while avoiding moral censure by corrupting them *tactfully*.

As the leading figure associated with tacit permissiveness in erotic themes, or 'la casuistique des sensualités' ['sensual casuistry'], Paul Bourget faced criticism above all for his feminised writing style and readership. In the portrait of Bourget, 'Mademoiselle Baudelaire!', which opens the first sub-section of *Dans l'oratoire* ('Leurs confesseurs'), Lorrain responds to an article by Catulle Mendès, who apparently used the eponymous appellation to refer to Bourget.[73] By feminising Bourget's identity and aligning it with a poet infamous for his portrayal of morbid erotic themes, Lorrain criticised the titillating appeal of Bourget's writing style and its complicity with less artistically valued forms of moral transgression:

Mlle Baudelaire! Singulier nom pour un abbé! Ah! c'est que celui-là est si peu abbé et si profondément mademoiselle, si féminin, si souple, si câlin d'allures et, dans tous ses sermons, d'une subtilité si féminine et qui plaît tant aux femmes! Ce n'est pas un confesseur, mais un confident et plutôt une confidente, que Mlle Baudelaire.[74]

---

[73] I have been unable to find the article to which Lorrain refers.
[74] Lorrain, *Dans l'oratoire*, p. 13. On Bourget's latent homosexuality, see François Proulx, *Victims of the Book*, pp. 144–8.

[Miss Baudelaire! What a strange name for an abbot! Ah, but he is so little like an abbot and so profoundly like a 'miss': so feminine, so pliable, so tender in his looks, and demonstrating, in all his sermons, so feminine a subtlety that women like so very much! This Miss Baudelaire is less a confessor than a confidant, or rather: a confidante.]

Through religious vocabulary ('abbot', 'sermons', and 'confessor'), Lorrain extends the ongoing analogy that aligns writers of the *roman psychologique* with the moral indulgence of religious confessors. Through an analogy with Michelet's maligned priest figure, Lorrain accuses Bourget of pandering to women's desire to be excused of their misdemeanours, and of doing so for personal gain. What is more, the questionable taste of Bourget's readership lowers the value of his works in Lorrain's eyes: '[C]'est à la femme, [...] à son besoin d'être plainte, attendrie sur elle-même, un peu méprisée, mais toujours excusée, cajolée, caressée, traitée en petite fille, en malade, toujours à la lectrice et jamais au lecteur, que s'adresse le jeune et très pratique futur académicien' ['It is to women, [...] to their need to be pitied and to pity themselves, to be slightly disdained, but always excused, cajoled, and caressed; to be treated like a little girl or a suffering invalid—that is, always to the female reader and never to the male reader—that the young (and very practical) future member of the *Académie française* addresses himself'].[75] In a clearly misogynistic gesture, Lorrain implies that male readers are more discerning of literary quality than their female counterparts. By framing Bourget's writing as flirtatious and frivolous—qualities often associated with women—Lorrain feminises his target while aligning him with a denigrated readership. In this way, Lorrain posits his own readership to be predominantly masculine, and willing to enter into the homosocial complicity of rejecting authors perceived as overly feminine. Even if some of his readers were women, Lorrain's critique encourages them to align themselves with the dominant homosocial model and valorise masculinity at the expense of femininity. That said, there is a degree of hyperbole and irony in Lorrain's gendered attack, due to his reputation as an effete writer of Decadent poetry and gossipy journalism.[76] Alongside irony, there is an edge of bitterness and even jealousy to Lorrain's mocking critique of Bourget's popularity with upper-class women (the 'bonne compagnie' mentioned in Mirbeau's review of *Un crime d'amour*), whose influence over literary *salons* could vastly improve a writer's career prospects.

Similar criticisms of Bourget appeared in a series of articles penned by Octave Mirbeau, whose sarcastic vitriol rivalled Lorrain's antagonism with its visceral force. In 1886, after ten years of amicable rapport, Mirbeau started to mock Bourget before making their 'rupture' public in 1889.[77] Within months of having

---
[75] Lorrain, *Dans l'oratoire*, p. 14.
[76] Chapter 4 discusses at greater length Lorrain's ambivalent approach to gender and sexual identity.
[77] See Octave Mirbeau, *Combats littéraires*, ed. Pierre Michel and Jean-François Nivet (Lausanne: Éditions L'Âge d'Homme, 2006), p. 591, footnote 14.

praised *Un crime d'amour* in *Le Gaulois* (11 February 1886), Mirbeau published a disguised portrait of Bourget in the 27 July 1886 issue of *Gil Blas*. The article depicts 'Loys Jambois': an effete artist whose declarations about the poetic value of umbrellas reveal tendencies that recur in Bourget's works, including Anglophilia, melancholy, and pessimism.[78] At this stage, the identity of his target was veiled, but Mirbeau's attacks became increasingly explicit as the pair's friendship collapsed. The official break-off happened in early March 1889, when Mirbeau spotted elements of his work-in-progress, *Sébastien Roch*, appearing in the third instalment of Bourget's *Le Disciple*.[79] In response to Bourget's apparent indiscretion, Mirbeau penned a lampooning article, 'Le Manuel du savoir écrire', which took his former friend to task for focusing on self-promotion and for achieving popularity by adopting a literary style appealing primarily to women.[80] The similarities between Mirbeau and Lorrain's critiques are unmistakable: both attacked Bourget for appealing to a female readership presumed to lack artistic judgement. This presumption confirms the fact that, at the fin de siècle, references to women readers were often ideologically loaded, with gender acting as an automatic disqualifying factor. Many writers viewed women's involvement in, and appreciation of, artistic and intellectual pursuits as libidinally interested, due to the underlying patriarchal tendency to align women with the body.[81]

Misogynistic prejudices recurred in Mirbeau's ongoing criticism of Bourget, which spanned across the century's closing decades. In the autumn of 1897, Mirbeau published a series of caricatural articles in *Le Journal*, entitled 'Chez l'illustre écrivain', which offered an extended satire of Bourget's implicitly feminised tendencies—notably his frivolity, obsession with outward appearances, and tendency to court media attention.[82] In one episode, the 'illustrious' writer converses with his valet as he awaits a mysterious rendezvous. While discussing the writer's upcoming seduction quest, the valet reassuringly exclaims: 'Monsieur sait si bien parler aux femmes timides et troubles!... On dit, partout, de Monsieur qu'il est un confesseur d'âmes!... Avec la voix et la séduction de Monsieur, rien n'est embarrassant!... Ah! Monsieur est un grand franchisseur d'obstacles' ['My lord knows very well how to speak to timid and troubled women!... People everywhere say that my lord is a confessor of souls!... With my lord's voice and his seductive

---

[78] Octave Mirbeau, 'Portrait', *Gil Blas*, 27 July 1886. This article was republished, with some modifications, as 'L'Unique—Scène de la vie décadente', *L'Écho de Paris*, 22 Mar. 1889, and 'Portrait', *Le Journal*, 24 Nov. 1895.

[79] In a letter to Paul Hervieu, Mirbeau claimed that he had discussed his upcoming work *Sébastien Roch* with Bourget, only for the latter to steal two key details about his eponymous character's First Communion. These details appeared in *Le Disciple* before the publication of Mirbeau's novel, thereby forcing the latter to edit his work to prevent accusations of plagiarism. See Proulx, *Victims of the Book*, p. 136.

[80] Octave Mirbeau, 'Le Manuel du savoir-écrire', *Le Figaro*, 11 May 1889.

[81] See Rachel Mesch, *The Hysteric's Revenge: French Women Writers at the Fin de Siècle* (Nashville: Vanderbilt University Press, 2006).

[82] Octave Mirbeau, 'Chez l'illustre écrivain', *Le Journal*, from 17 Oct. to 28 Nov. 1897.

appeal, nothing is too tricky!... Ah! my lord is a great overcomer of obstacles'].[83] In this humorous exchange, Mirbeau weaponises the priest/confessor analogy to accuse Bourget of deliberately seducing women through his literary production, and doing from a position of moral hypocrisy and complacency. He does so by structurally aligning the roles of confessor ('confessor of souls') and adulterer ('overcomer of obstacles') in the valet's exclamation, in a gesture clearly reminiscent of Michelet's *Du prêtre, de la femme, de la famille*.

Much like Lorrain, Mirbeau would later return to this analogy with reference to the 'oratoire', in an article appearing in 'Têtes de Turcs': a collection of polemical portraits published by the satirical journal *L'Assiette au beurre*. His portrait of Paul Bourget reads as follows:

Anglomane subtil et psychologue respectueux. [...] A inventé l'adultère chrétien, le canapé chrétien, le bidet chrétien, la garçonnière chrétienne, le chapelet obscène et le scapulaire transparent. [...] A transformé les cabinets de toilette de ses héroïnes en oratoire, et, dans ses bidets changés en bénitiers, on voit flotter des fragments d'hostie, au lieu de mousse de savon.[84]

[Discerning Anglomaniac and respectful psychologist. [...] Invented Christian adultery, the Christian sofa, the Christian bidet, the Christian bachelor pad, the rosary of obscenity and the see-through scapular. [...] Transformed his heroines' dressing rooms into oratories, and in his fonts—formerly bidets—you can see fragments of holy wafer floating about, instead of soap suds.]

In this eye-watering attack, Mirbeau aligns religion with obscenity and scatology through the list of Bourget's literary 'inventions'. Through a form of synecdoche, Mirbeau blends feminine intimacy and eroticism, associated with the *cabinet de toilette* as a scene of (un)dressing and seduction, with religious devotion, associated with the oratory as an intimate, devotional space. By doing so, Mirbeau mirrors Lorrain's sacrilegious depiction of the Christ-Adonis figure in *Dans l'oratoire*. The fact that, many years after the latter's publication, Mirbeau adopted Lorrain's oratory metaphor demonstrates the clear resonance it had with the widespread accusation of complicity levelled at writers who appropriated the morally ambiguous role of confessor. Yet their critiques targeted as much the upper-class literary circles to which Bourget belonged as Bourget himself: an outwardly conservative but covertly sordid literary environment in which mainstream writers could achieve fame and success through their hypocritical complicity with, and pandering to, debased or corrupting tendencies.

---

[83] Mirbeau, 'Chez l'illustre écrivain', *Le Journal*, 21 Nov. 1897.
[84] Octave Mirbeau, 'Paul Bourget', *L'Assiette au beurre*, 31 May 1902, p. 1019.

Bourget's mainstream success in the 1880s and 1890s prompted hostile responses from across literary divides, which targeted the perceived erotic source of his morally ambiguous appeal. Indeed, even after his election to the *Académie française*, Bourget could not shake his earlier reputation as a casuist panderer. When reporting on Bourget's 1895 admission ceremony for *Le Signal*, a daily newspaper run by the Protestant Eugène Réveillaud (1851–1935), one critic remarked that 'quoi qu'il fasse et quoiqu'on dise, M. Paul Bourget restera le petit maître de la littérature contemporaine' ['whatever he may do and whatever people may say, Mr Paul Bourget will remain the preening popinjay of contemporary literature'].[85] By calling Bourget a 'petit maître', the journalist signing 'Gibrac' drew from an earlier tradition of dandified male characters, typically found in eighteenth-century gallant and libertine fiction.[86] The comparison is implicitly derogatory, for it suggests foppish narcissism and, in this context, unoriginality. The staying power of Bourget's negative reputation can be seen by the fact that both Zola and André Gide (1869–1951) would go on to produce fictional characters based on Bourget, portraying him as a hypocritical Catholic seducer of women (Santerre in *Fécondité*, 1899) and a possibly homosexual corrupter of young men (Passavant in *Les Faux-Monnayeurs*, 1925). For many writers and critics of the period, then, Bourget was a divisive figure, perceived to be morally compromised by his association with psychology as a deterministic, materialist science, but also by the tacit erotic permissiveness of its novelistic counterpart. The widespread perception of Bourget's complicity with immoral ideas and denigrated readerships helps to explain the purgative attempts he later made to adopt an increasingly moralising approach to literary responsibility.

## Implication and Exculpation: *Le Disciple* (1889)

In November 1888, French newspapers obsessively reported on the sensational murder trial of Henri Chambige in Constantine, Algeria. On 25 January that year, Chambige had used a gun to kill a wife and mother of two, Magdeleine Grille, before shooting himself in the mouth. He survived his wounds and stated that he had committed the crime to uphold his side of a suicide pact with Magdeleine, of whom he claimed to be the lover.[87] Media attention intensified when newspapers revealed that Chambige had ties with the Parisian literary scene—including with Paul Bourget, whom he had met on several occasions during his time spent

---

[85] Gibrac, 'Actualité'.
[86] For a discussion of the 'petit maître' figure, see Albane Forestier, 'La figure du petit-maître est-elle subversive?', *Apparence(s)* 12 (2022), doi:10.4000/apparences.4225.
[87] On the difficulty of discerning the truth of Chambige's assertions, see Jacqueline Carroy and Marc Renneville, *Mourir d'amour. Autopsie d'un imaginaire criminel* (Paris: Éditions La Découverte, 2022), pp. 277–82.

studying in Paris (1886–7).[88] Because of Chambige's literary aspirations and connections, the affair led commentators to debate the role played by fin-de-siècle intellectual trends in encouraging individuals to commit violent crimes. Proulx notes that Bourget was 'implicated from all sides', as the primary model of literary bad influence over the accused. He explores the myriad literary references used throughout the trial, which placed moral responsibility on Bourget's shoulders.[89] Most notably, the poet, playwright, and critic Émile Bergerat (1845–1923) accused psychological writers of glorifying a perverted vision of love, which could be used to justify or encourage real-life murder. He targeted the genre's chief practitioner by mentioning Bourget's name twice in the article.[90] Around the same time, Chambige published an autobiographical account of his early obsession with pessimistic and deterministic philosophy, which gave further fodder to morality critics and ultimately prompted Bourget's novelistic response.[91]

Initially serialised in the *Nouvelle Revue*, from February to May 1889, *Le Disciple* charts the relationship between Adrien Sixte and his 'disciple' Robert Greslou. Sixte is a psychologist and philosopher whose works amalgamate ideas by influential real-life intellectuals, including Hippolyte Taine, Ernest Renan (1823–92), and Théodule Ribot. Greslou is a gifted student charged with murdering a young aristocrat, Charlotte de Jussat. The novel recounts Greslou's story through a series of narrative layers: a central nested narrative is enclosed by a frame text, which is introduced by an authorial preface. The central narrative contains Greslou's self-analytical confession, describing how he intentionally seduced Charlotte as part of a psychological experiment inspired by Sixte's theories. The 'experiment' culminates in Robert and Charlotte consummating their affair after agreeing to a suicide pact—a promise Robert fails to uphold in the moment of post-coital satisfaction. This pact provides the novel's clearest link with the Chambige affair, although Bourget changes one key element: Charlotte, unlike Magdeleine, dies by her own hand rather than by her lover's. Devastated by Greslou's cowardice, Charlotte reads his case study notebook, which reveals the former's heartless cynicism. She then commits suicide, after sending a letter to her older brother André that recounts the events leading to her death. Greslou's confession appears as a letter to Sixte, within the frame text narrating Sixte's involvement in the trial and its conclusion. This narrative appears after an overtly moralising preface, 'À un jeune homme', which Bourget added to the novel when it was published in book form.[92] The preface emphasises the importance of writers' responsibility and offers the story

---

[88] Albert Feuillerat, *Paul Bourget: histoire d'un esprit sous la troisième république* (Paris: Plon, 1937), pp. 139–41.
[89] Proulx, *Victims of the Book*, pp. 122–8.
[90] Émile Bergerat, 'La Rime en "bige"', *Le Figaro*, 8 Nov. 1888, p. 1.
[91] See Albert Bataille, *Causes criminelles et mondaines de 1888* (Paris: E. Dentu, 1889), pp. 1–28, which republishes his 'Gazette des Tribunaux' column articles from *Le Figaro* on 2, 3, and 4 Nov. 1888.
[92] The preface also appeared in *Le Figaro* upon the novel's publication: 'Le Disciple. À un jeune homme', *Le Figaro*, 17 June 1889.

as a warning to Bourget's young readership about the dangers of pessimism and determinism—the very intellectual trends he had championed a few years earlier.

Le Disciple's frame text fictionalises the process by which Bourget was compelled to respond to the Chambige affair, while its central narrative combines elements of confessional novels and novels of formation. When taken together, these textual layers offer an exemplary warning about the immoral influence and implicating power of literature, through two intertwined stories of seduction and corruption. The first recounts Greslou's seduction at the hands of Sixte's scientific works. Bourget depicts Adrien Sixte as Greslou's mentor both in the introductory preface, which asserts the formative role of writers and encourages readers to act differently to Greslou. The frame text reaffirms this vision, by depicting a magistrate who discusses the hazy distinction between legal and moral responsibility for crime, and attributes the latter to Sixte, as Greslou's 'directeur intellectuel' ['intellectual guide'].[93] However, as contemporaneous critics were swift to point out, the novel also mitigated Sixte's responsibility by depicting the multiple factors influencing Greslou's moral and psychological formation.[94] In the novel, several forms of initiation contribute to Greslou's corruption. The first form is literary, when Greslou finds a passion for reading 'clandestine volumes' of modern poetry sourced through his friend Émile, after his mother locks away his father's collection (*LD*, 108–9). The second form of initiation is sexual, when Greslou loses his virginity to a working-class woman, Marianne, in a sequence presented as the logical continuation of his earlier reading practices (*LD*, 133). The final initiation is intellectual: Greslou finds his vocation through the revelatory medium of Adrien Sixte's writings: 'Le voile tomba. Les ténèbres du monde extérieur et intérieur s'éclairèrent. J'avais trouvé ma voie. J'étais votre élève' ['The veil fell away. Light chased away the shadows of the outer and inner worlds. I had found my path. I was your student'] (*LD*, 135). The narrative attributes to Sixte the roles of intellectual mentor and spiritual guide, in a clear blending of scientific and religious vocabularies. Much like the reader-author relationship depicted in the *Essais*, Greslou's relationship with Sixte is framed with erotic imagery: his mind is 'penetrated' by Sixte's reasoning (*LD*, 135) and he is 'seduced' by Sixte's method (*LD*, 137). Furthermore,

---

[93] Paul Bourget, *Le Disciple* (Paris: Alphonse Lemerre, 1889), pp. 38–9. Hereafter references to *Le Disciple* appear parenthetically in the text as *LD*.

[94] Augustin Filon suggested that *Le Disciple*'s tragic love affair could be recounted without any reference to Sixte's determinist philosophy, in 'Courrier littéraire', *La Revue politique et littéraire*, 20 July 1889, pp. 89–92 (p. 90). Similarly, Paul Janet suggested that Greslou's character had sufficiently negative traits to produce 'un être malfaisant' ['an evil being'] without requiring any further assistance from theoretical doctrines, in 'De la responsabilité philosophique, à propos du "Disciple" de M. Paul Bourget', in *Principes de métaphysique et de psychologie: leçons professées à la Faculté des lettres de Paris, 1888–1894*, 2 vols (Paris: Librairie Ch. Delagrave, 1897), I, pp. 305–27 (pp. 312–13). Finally, an anonymous reviewer at the *Revue scientifique* rephrased Louis de Bonald when assessing Greslou's actions: '[ce] déséquilibré [...] n'a pas eu besoin d'un maître pour être un malfaiteur' ['this deranged man [...] did not need a teacher to be a criminal']. Anon., 'Causerie bibliographique', *Revue scientifique*, 17 Aug. 1889, pp. 213–15 (p. 214).

the student's philosophical awakening mirrors its sexual counterpart: 'Ah! comment vous raconter ces fièvres d'une initiation qui fut pareille à un premier amour par les félicités de l'enthousiasme et ses ferveurs? J'avais comme une joie physique à renverser, vos livres à la main, tout l'édifice des croyances où j'avais grandi' ['Oh! How can I describe that feverish initiation, which resembled first love in its enthusiastic bliss and fervour? I felt an almost physical joy, with your books in my hands, in toppling the entire belief system I had grown up with'] (*LD*, 137). The power of Greslou's 'initiation', both intellectual and erotic, is here unambiguously tied to a destructive anti-social urge, premised on the elimination of earlier beliefs associated with religious dogma.

The novel's second corruption narrative unfurls as a consequence of the first, through Greslou's seduction experiment on Charlotte de Jussat and her resulting suicide. In a relationship of influence and imitation, Greslou's intellectual seduction by Sixte's work mirrors Charlotte's romantic and erotic seduction by Greslou's *interpretation* of that work. Literature has an important role to play in this process, due to its status as a medium that facilitates illicit action. For example, storytelling features predominantly in Charlotte's seduction, where Greslou first attempts to ensnare his victim by recounting a 'fable tentatrice' '[tempting fable'] that romanticises his role as a dejected lover (*LD*, 193–4). Unsuccessful at this first attempt, Greslou turns to others' published writings in order to advance his experiment. Taking inspiration from Sixte's discussion of the process by which people unconsciously mirror literary depictions of emotion, Greslou influences Charlotte by reading Balzac's *Eugénie Grandet* aloud to the Jussat family over several evening gatherings. When Charlotte subsequently asks him for reading suggestions, Greslou reflects on the power of 'l'intoxication littéraire' ['literary intoxication'] (*LD*, 213): a popular metaphor for literary influence that hints forward to Charlotte's physical poisoning later in the story. The transition from group reading to solitary reading reflects fin-de-siècle concerns about the perceived safety of the former and perceived danger of the latter. At the same time, it blurs the boundaries between the two, by sowing seeds for the corruption of solitary reading in the pleasure Charlotte finds from its public, collective counterpart.

Although Greslou's literary seduction eventually bears fruit, the binarism between seducer and seduced is not clear cut throughout the narrative. Rather, the relationship between Greslou and Charlotte is complex and reciprocal: 'Je m'étais préparé à la séduire, et c'était moi qui me sentais séduit' ['I had prepared myself to seduce her, and it was I who felt myself being seduced'] (LD, 204). This role reversal recurs as their relationship strengthens, culminating in the sex scene that marks the success and failure of Greslou's seduction experiment. When Charlotte confesses her feelings for Greslou in this moment, she is no longer a victimised reader, but an active storyteller: 'c'est avec une voix de fantôme, une voix d'au-delà de la vie qu'elle me parlait, me racontant la longue histoire de ses sentiments pour moi' ['it was with a ghost-like voice, a voice from beyond the grave, that she spoke to me, recounting at length the story of her feelings for me'] (*LD*, 286). The otherworldly status of Charlotte's story places it beyond her seducer's power, since it is rendered sublime as the 'extase du martyre' ['rapture of martyrdom'] (*LD*, 287)—a phrase that clearly juxtaposes Greslou's subsequent cowardice.

The role reversal that occurs between Charlotte and Greslou mirrors the connection between Greslou and Sixte, further highlighting the reciprocity of the seducer-seduced relationship. In the frame narrative, Bourget deploys imagery relating to corrupted innocence to describe Sixte's reaction to Greslou's confession. In the process of reading, Sixte perceives himself to be sullied by his contact with Greslou's actions:

> A mesure que Sixte avançait dans le manuscrit, il lui semblait qu'un peu de sa personne intime se souillait, se corrompait, se gangrenait, tant il retrouvait de lui-même dans ce jeune homme, mais un 'lui-même' cousu, par quel mystère? aux sentiments qu'il détestait le plus au monde. (*LD*, 316)

> [As Sixte progressed further in the manuscript, his inner nature felt increasingly sullied, corrupted, and gangrenous, every time he recognised himself in this young man, but a version of himself somehow attached—by what kind of magic?—to the feelings he hated most in this world.]

Bourget reinforces the parallel between Sixte and Charlotte by using the words 'sullied', 'corrupted', and 'gangrenous'. The rhetorical question, presented via free indirect style, encourages the reader to empathise with the philosopher's revulsion. Sixte feels tainted because he is faced with the vision of his writings becoming 'les complices d'un hideux orgueil et d'une abjecte sensualité' ['the accomplices of hideous pride and abject sensuality'] (*LD*, 317). The adjectives 'hideous' and 'abject' offer an unambiguous condemnation of Greslou's actions, while enacting a form of self-flagellation by implicating Sixte with a denigrated criminal. Sixte's supposed 'corruption' of Greslou through deterministic psychology is clearly intertwined with the corrupting influence of Greslou's *interpretation* of this psychology. The corrupter (Sixte) is therefore capable of being corrupted, much like the seducer (Greslou) is capable of being seduced, by their respective 'victims'. By setting up these parallel structures within the novel, Bourget shows the relationship of influence and imitation between mentor and disciple, seducer and seduced, to be reciprocal and mutually implicating.

As the primary addressee of Greslou's manuscript, Sixte plays the morally ambivalent roles of mentor, doctor, judge, and confessor. These roles parallel the text's multivalent status, indicated by its various titles. Appearing on the manuscript's first page, the initial title, 'Psychologie moderne' ['Modern Psychology'], places the text within scientific and philosophical discourse, while disguising its true content from uninitiated readers. On the manuscript's second page, there is an alternative title, 'Mémoire sur moi-même' ['Report / Memoir on Myself'], which combines the language of scientific analysis (*un* mémoire: a thesis, report, or paper) with that of memory and autobiography (*une* mémoire: a memoir). Finally, the narrator re-names the manuscript 'Confession d'un jeune homme d'aujourd'hui' ['Confession of a young man today'] (*LD*, 80), thereby placing it within the genre of confessional narrative and related religious practices. Indirectly citing Alfred de Musset's *La Confession d'un enfant du siècle* (1836), the final title also hints at the close association between science and religion throughout the novel. For example, when recounting his childhood in 'Mon milieu d'idées', Greslou emphasises his 'goût précoce de la dissection intime' ['precocious taste for close self-analysis'] and his fortnightly visits to confessional (*LD*, 115). The ritualistic verbal formulae used in the confessional appeal to Greslou because of their captivating 'poésie de mystère' ['poetry of mystery'] (*LD*, 116). Yet Greslou's obsessive desire to confess borders on the pathological. During his self-analysis, 'il entra vite plus de plaisir que de repentir' ['pleasure soon prevailed over repentance'], and 'les fuyantes complications du péché' ['the elusive complexity of sin'] won out over the 'simplicités de la vertu' ['simplicity of virtue'] (*LD*, 118). Bourget here shows how Catholic devotion can enable unhealthy mental habits, which subsequently undermine religious sentiment and lead to the very sins they aim to discourage. Subsequently, once Greslou loses his religious faith, scientific and philosophical methods offer an alternative means of obsessive self-analysis. During his employment by the Jussat family, Greslou refers to his psychological self-analysis as a daily 'examen de conscience' ['soul-searching'], written in a padlocked diary. He describes this process as a form of prayer ('oraison'), 'liturgie du Moi' ['liturgy of the Self'], and the scientific equivalent of a general confession (*LD*, 170).[95] Although Greslou destroys the diary after Charlotte's death, his epistolary confession to Sixte replaces and supplements its absence in the novel.

By addressing his confession to Sixte and blending scientific and religious vocabularies, Greslou places his mentor in the role of doctor and confessor, giving him the attendant responsibility of an authority figure whose judgement is sought at times of physiological, psychological, and moral dilemma.[96] Both the doctor and the confessor are professionally bound to a code of confidentiality. This code emerges when Sixte decides to read Greslou's manuscript, which implies the acceptance of a tacit pact between reader and author. On the second page of the manuscript, Greslou insists that by reading what follows, Sixte must make an

---

[95] In Catholic practice, the 'confession générale' differs from ordinary confession. It takes place leading up to and during important moments in the Catholic calendar. Usually, it covers the whole period of an individual's life, across several sessions, and could also be undertaken in writing. See Alain Corbin, *L'Harmonie des plaisirs: les manières de jouir du siècle des Lumières à l'avènement de la sexologie* (Paris: Perrin, 2008), pp. 327–30.

[96] Michel Foucault highlights the centrality of confession to religious and scientific practices in his discussion of the 'scientia sexualis' in *Histoire de la sexualité I: la volonté de savoir* (Paris: Gallimard, 1976) pp. 78–94.

unspoken promise never to disclose its contents (*LD*, 77–8). Although initially accepting this pact, Sixte changes his mind upon reading it, since he fears becoming complicit with an injustice by remaining silent. His willingness to hand over the manuscript if Charlotte's brother does not give evidence in court therefore constitutes a betrayal of trust. A similar dilemma faces André de Jussat, who receives Charlotte's pre-suicide confession containing proof of Greslou's legal (if not moral) innocence.[97] The final chapter of *Le Disciple* describes André's unease during Greslou's trial, when he is torn between two conflicting moral imperatives: saving an innocent life or upholding the letter's injunction to protect his family's reputation. Initially seeking to save his sister's honour by concealing—and then destroying—the compromising letter, André is haunted by the voice of his conscience, 'qui nous défend de nous faire les complices d'une iniquité' ['which prevents us from becoming complicit with an injustice'] (*LD*, 338). Upon receiving an anonymous letter from Sixte questioning his silence, André decides to reveal the truth in court, before killing Greslou as an act of aristocratic vengeance. In this way, both Sixte and André break—or threaten to break—the bonds of secrecy imposed by the reading pacts set forward by confessional texts. They do so in the name of moral codes that function beyond the institutional legal context.

The reading pacts in *Le Disciple* highlight the contagious nature of guilt and the burden of knowledge for those occupying the role of confessor or judge, including the implied and actual reader. This burden is especially heavy for Sixte, who is placed almost forcibly in this position by Greslou's letter. At the start of his confession, Greslou insists on the bond ('lien') that unites him with his chosen mentor: 'Il existe de vous, le maître illustre, à moi votre élève, accusé du crime le plus infâme, un lien [...] aussi étroit qu'imbrisable' ['There exists between you, the illustrious teacher, and me, your student, who is accused of the most heinous crime, a bond [...] which is as tight as it is unbreakable'] (*LD*, 81–2). This bond is reiterated by appeals to Sixte's judgement as Greslou's intellectual and moral guide. Indeed, Sixte's authority throughout the novel resembles that held by a confessor or *directeur de conscience*: a highly ambivalent figure associated with questionable moral influence and tacit erotic permissiveness. The analogy is telling and highlights the moral ambiguity of Sixte's position. It first appears when the magistrate interrogates Sixte and refers to him as Greslou's 'directeur intellectuel' ['intellectual guide'] (*LD*, 38–9). The comparison returns when Greslou's mother acts as a go-between by delivering her son's manuscript to Sixte. Employing the logic of exemplarity and influence, she accuses Sixte of corrupting her child while at the same time insisting that he use this influence for positive ends. She compares Sixte to a Catholic *directeur de conscience* by asking him to intervene on Greslou's behalf: 'ce que j'aurais demandé au prêtre, je viens vous le demander' ['I have come to ask

---

[97] On the similarities between the two intradiegetic reading pacts, see Proulx, *Victims of the Book*, p. 143.

of you that which I would have asked of the priest'] (*LD*, 75–6). According to this logic, Sixte is best placed to save Greslou precisely *because* he corrupted him.

Established in *Le Disciple*'s frame text, the analogy between Sixte and the *directeur de conscience* strengthens in the confessional narrative, where Greslou addresses Sixte as an authoritative mentor. Much like the penitent looks to the priest for religious guidance, Greslou appeals to Sixte's scientific 'faith' to allay the doubts plaguing him in light of his feelings for Charlotte: 'Ah! mon cher maître, j'ai besoin que vous me croyiez dans ce que je vais vous dire [...]. J'ai tant besoin de ne pas en douter, moi non plus; besoin de me répéter que je n'ai pas menti alors. Croyez-moi' ['Oh, my dear mentor, I need you to believe in what I am going to tell you [...]. I badly need not to have my own doubts about it, and to tell myself again and again that I did not lie at the time. Have faith in me'] (*LD*, 276–7). Greslou's repeated appeal to Sixte's faith in, and good opinion of, his actions belies the truth value of his assertions. The imperative 'Croyez-moi' ['Have faith in me'] reads like a self-delusional bid for Sixte's post hoc forgiveness, rather than a true act of contrition. Indeed, throughout the novel, Sixte is repeatedly called upon to judge Greslou's actions in a way that presumes he will understand, justify, and pardon them. In this way, Greslou's appeals read as a plea for Sixte to turn a blind eye and enact a form of moral *complaisance*. This becomes clear when Greslou recounts his change of heart regarding the suicide pact: 'Vous qui avez décrit en des pages si fortes la vapeur d'illusion soulevée en nous par le désir physique, [...] vous ne me jugerez pas monstrueux d'avoir senti cette vapeur se dissiper avec le désir, cette ivresse s'en aller avec la possession' ['You who have described in such powerful words the haze of illusion aroused in us by physical desire, [...] you will not consider me monstrous for feeling this haze dissipate along with desire, this ecstasy leaving me at the moment of possession'] (*LD*, 288). By reminding Sixte of the principles propounded in his works, Greslou's confession forecloses the very judgement it claims to encourage.

Much like the female penitents in Michelet's *Du prêtre*, or the female readers mocked by Lorrain in *Dans l'oratoire*, Greslou seems to seek casuistry and moral laxity rather than true judgement and penance. The manuscript's closing lines confirm this by depicting Greslou's emotional urgency when he appeals to a belief system that he simultaneously disavows and manipulates:

J'ai besoin d'être compris, consolé, aimé [...]. Je m'étais flatté que j'arriverais à vous raconter mon histoire comme vous exposez vos problèmes de psychologie dans vos livres que j'ai tant lus, et puis je ne trouve rien à vous dire que le mot du désespoir: 'De profundis!' Ecrivez-moi, mon cher maître, dirigez-moi. Renforcez-moi dans la doctrine qui fut, qui est encore la mienne [...]. Dites-moi que je ne suis pas un monstre, qu'il n'y a pas de monstre, que vous serez encore là, si je sors de cette crise suprême, à me vouloir comme disciple, comme ami. (*LD*, 307–8)

[I need to be understood, comforted, and loved [...]. I had flattered myself that I would manage to recount my story to you in the same way that you set out the psychological questions in your books, which I have read so diligently, and now I can find nothing else to say to you other than the sorrowful appeal: '*De profundis!*' Write to me, my dear teacher, give me direction. Strengthen my belief in the doctrine that was, that still is, my own [...]. Tell me that I am not a monster, that there is no such thing as monsters, and that, if I emerge from this final crisis, you will be there, wanting me to be your disciple and your friend.]

Greslou's exclamation of '*De profundis!*' attributes to Sixte the power to channel divine mercy by interceding on his behalf. However, the slip from past to present tense in the phrase 'la doctrine qui fut, qui est encore la mienne' ['the doctrine that was, that still is, my own'] reveals underlying doubt regarding the validity of Sixte's scientific approach. Greslou's self-acknowledged failure to adopt Sixte's method and expositional style in his confession hints not only at a personal shortcoming, but also at the limitations of Sixte's theoretical framework when applied to real life. At the end of the confession, readers are therefore left wondering whether Sixte's intercession could ever restore Greslou's faith in a determinist and positivist outlook.

Greslou's final plea for reassurance and absolution in the central narrative paves the way for a moralising shift in the penultimate frame narrative. This culminates in Sixte adopting a praying posture in the novel's closing lines, which hint towards his future conversion. In the chapter entitled 'Tourments d'idées', Bourget describes Sixte's moral repugnance after having read Greslou's confession: 'il [Sixte] avait tressailli [...] à chaque citation d'un de ses ouvrages qui lui prouvait le droit de cet abominable séducteur à se dire son élève' ['he had shuddered [...] at every quotation from one of his works that proved to him that this vile seducer had the right to call himself his student'] (*LD*, 316). Sixte here indirectly affirms his moral complicity by recognising his influence over Greslou and feeling guilty as a consequence. For a character who, earlier in the narrative, had no qualms in suggesting that it would be scientifically valid to encourage children to practise 'vices' in order to understand human psychology better (*LD*, 50), the sudden presence of explicit moral condemnation ('abominable séducteur' ['vile seducer']) seems ironic and jarring. The text itself acknowledges this paradox: Sixte's anguished guilt is described as being 'en contradiction avec toutes ses doctrines' ['in contradiction with all of his doctrines'] (*LD*, 321). Nonetheless, at the novel's close, Sixte is clearly humbled by the tragic events he has witnessed: 'cet analyste presque inhumain à force de logique s'humiliait, s'inclinait, s'abîmait devant le mystère impénétrable de la destinée' ['this analyst, whose adherence to logic made him almost inhuman, humbled himself, bowed down, and foundered before the impenetrable mystery of destiny'] (*LD*, 359). The term 'impenetrable mystery' has religious resonances, as does the physical gesture of prayer evoked by the verb 'to bow down' ('s'incliner'). The final image of Sixte crying—after mentally reciting the Lord's Prayer and quoting from Pascal's *Mystère de Jésus*: 'Tu ne me chercherais pas si tu ne m'avais pas trouvé' ['You would not seek me if you had not found me'] (*LD*, 359)—suggests that he will eventually convert to Catholicism.[98] By hinting at religious conversion in this way, *Le Disciple*'s ending clearly resembles that of *Un crime d'amour*. Both Sixte and de Querne grapple with forces beyond their comprehension and accept the possibility of an alternative vision of human behaviour: a vision that fits neatly into traditional religious frameworks.

Although highly suggestive, *Le Disciple*'s denouement does not clearly confirm whether Sixte ultimately accepts a Christian outlook: he may cry over his disciple's corpse, but he makes no overt renunciation of his earlier philosophical position. Furthermore, Sixte's concluding prayer and Greslou's '*De profundis!*' ring somewhat hollow when analysed in the context of the entire narrative arc. Bourget's readers have often noted that the preface's moralising vision applies problematically to the text it frames, and that the novel's conclusion remains morally inconclusive. For example, Augustin Filon referred to the novel's preface as 'trop belle, peut-être, et trop éloquente!' ['too lovely, perhaps, and too eloquent!'] and stated that he was not convinced by Sixte's character.[99] He questioned the philosopher's conversion and the work's overall 'message':

> Ce 'jeune homme' auquel l'auteur adressait dès le début une si ardente et si mystérieuse supplication [...] Consentira-t-il à s'agenouiller? [...] L'auteur lui-même est-il converti? Ce livre semble un adieu à la psychologie, et parce qu'on peut la pousser plus loin, et parce qu'elle est en quelque sorte réfutée par l'absurdité de ses excès. Pourtant je ne réponds de rien.[100]

> [This 'young man' to whom the writer addresses, at the novel's opening, such an ardent and mysterious plea [...] Will he consent to kneel? [...] Is the author himself converted? This book seems to be a farewell to psychology, both because it can be taken further, and because it is, as it were, contradicted by the absurdity of its extremes. Even so, I cannot vouch for anything.]

Filon's lexis of doubt, here seen in the unanswered rhetorical questions and the verb 'to seem' ('sembler'), emphasises the difficulty of opting for a clear-cut interpretation of Bourget's novel. Édouard Rod took a similar position by noting the

---

[98] As Antoine Compagnon has noted, the latter reference is significant because, as a scientist, Pascal was aware of the limitations of science and believed in the necessity of maintaining religious faith. See 'Introduction' in Paul Bourget, *Le Disciple*, ed. Antoine Compagnon (Paris: Éditions de Poche, 2010), pp. 10–36 (p. 31).
[99] Filon, 'Courrier littéraire', pp. 90–1.
[100] Filon, 'Courrier littéraire', p. 92.

contrast between the moralising preface and the centrality of Greslou's 'malsaines analyses' ['unhealthy analyses'] to the primary narrative.[101] He also refused to make a clear pronouncement on the moral value of Bourget's works, insisting that the reader should be left free to decide between the two interpretations.[102] In this way, Rod highlighted how an extradiegetic reading pact between author and reader reflected but also surpassed the intradiegetic pact between Sixte and Greslou.[103]

By emphasising the moral ambiguity of reading pacts, both within and beyond the textual frame, *Le Disciple* became a springboard for broader debates about the 'bad influence' model and its implications for literary production. It infamously provoked a literary quarrel between respected critics Anatole France and Ferdinand Brunetière (1849–1906), and reignited the media storm associated with the Chambige affair.[104] In an article published in *Le Temps* on 23 June 1889, Anatole France argued that philosophical doctrine had little direct influence over human behaviour, stating that '[ce] n'est pas le déterminisme, c'est l'orgueil qui a perdu Robert Greslou' ['[it] is not determinism, but pride, which caused Robert Greslou's downfall'].[105] He opposed the 'bad influence' model implicit in Bourget's novel, and vociferously supported freedom of speech, asserting that 'tout système philosophique peut être légitimement exposé' ['any philosophical system can legitimately be put forward'].[106] A week later, in the *Revue des Deux Mondes*, Ferdinand Brunetière offered an opposing viewpoint. He criticised writers for failing to accept responsibility for the impact their works had on readers (whether intentional or not), and defended limitations to freedom of speech in the name of social order: 'Toutes les fois qu'une doctrine aboutira par voie de conséquence logique à mettre en question les principes sur lesquels la société repose, elle sera fausse' ['Whenever a doctrine, by consequence of its own logic, ends up questioning the principles upon which society is built, it is a false doctrine'].[107] Although initially claiming that writers should not sacrifice art for the sake of morality— '[on] n'exige pas d'eux qu'ils exercent leur art comme un sacerdoce' ['they are not

---

[101] Édouard Rod, *Les Idées morales du temps présent* (Paris: Perrin, 1891), pp. 105–6.

[102] Rod, *Les Idées morales*, p. 121.

[103] This structure of *mise en abyme* was typical of socialisation novels of the period. See Pernot, *Le Roman de socialisation*, p. 68.

[104] Leon Sachs, 'Literature of Ideas and Paul Bourget's Republican Pedagogy', *French Forum* 33, nos. 1–2 (Winter-Spring 2008): pp. 53–72 (p. 61), https://www.jstor.org/stable/40552494. See also Pascale Seys, 'Maître ou complice? La philosophie de Taine dans *Le Disciple* de Paul Bourget', in *Le Chant de Minerve: Les écrivains et leurs lectures philosophiques*, edited by Bruno Curatolo (Paris: Éditions l'Harmattan, 1996), pp. 35–47 (p. 35).

[105] Anatole France, 'La Vie littéraire. M. Paul Bourget: "Le Disciple"', *Le Temps*, 23 June 1889.

[106] France, 'La Vie littéraire'.

[107] Ferdinand Brunetière, 'Revue littéraire. A propos du *Disciple*', *La Revue des deux mondes*, 1 July 1889, pp. 214–26 (p. 220).

expected to practise their art like a religious vocation']—Brunetière revealed his conservative position by insisting that authors should condemn behaviour considered unacceptable or illicit: 'tout ce qu'ils [les auteurs] expliquent, ils l'excusent, dès qu'en le représentant ils ne le condamnent point' ['everything that they [authors] analyse, they excuse, whenever they represent something without condemning it'].[108] Liberal critics interpreted this position as a reactionary attack on intellectual freedom. On 7 July 1889, Anatole France responded to Brunetière by aligning him with the status quo: '[Brunetière] livre la pensée à la merci de la morale pratique, autrement dit l'usage des peuples, aux préjugés, aux habitudes' ['Brunetière hands over thought to the mercy of practical morality, that is: common practice, prejudice, and habit'].[109] An anonymous author in the *Revue scientifique* also opposed Brunetière's subordination of science to a 'doctrine officielle' ['official doctrine'], and encouraged writers to search for truth regardless of moral considerations regarding their work's consequences.[110] As Jacqueline Carroy and Marc Renneville have noted, this debate is striking for the way in which critics discussed Bourget's characters as if they were real people who could express thoughts and commit actions in the real world.[111] The elision of fact and fiction reflected the novel's relationship to a real-life trial, and yet it effectively re-enacted the kind of 'bad reading' attributed to Chambige. In an oddly cyclical logic, the critical framework that used *Le Disciple* to assess the moral responsibility of authors over their impressionable readers was caught up in its own impressionability.

Through his longstanding contributions to questions of literary complicity, Bourget demonstrated the power wielded by critics who framed literature as the source of social ills, while revealing their implication in the tendencies they mocked and reviled. Although he faced no legal ramifications for his implication in Henri Chambige's crime, Bourget was put on trial by his peers in the echo chamber of newspaper columns: a process to which he further contributed by publishing a thinly veiled novelistic self-defence. The 'trial' was in one sense purely rhetorical, yet it tangibly affected Bourget's career trajectory. It also reveals broader patterns in the fin-de-siècle literary field. By framing and reframing literature in response to the Chambige affair, Bourget and his peers effectively asked: what connection might there be, or should there be, between a writer and a murderer? How is one complicit with the other? Such questions haunted authors

---

[108] Brunetière, 'Revue littéraire', p. 226
[109] Anatole France, 'La Vie littéraire. La métaphysique devant la morale', *Le Temps*, 7 July 1889.
[110] Anon., 'Causerie bibliographique', p. 215.
[111] See Carroy and Renneville, *Mourir d'amour*, p. 212.

in an era that witnessed the rise of criminology, crime fiction, and mass media reports on infamous criminals. Indeed, the intense media debate about literary influence and writerly responsibility that greeted *Le Disciple* can be better understood when it is considered as part of the fin-de-siècle obsession with stories about violent crime. Examining the wider cross-fertilisation between criminological discourses and literary production in the era, the following chapter analyses works that fed off political and judicial concerns regarding literature's capacity to encourage readers to commit copycat crimes. As a popular literary subgenre, murder fiction facilitated a more playful collusive aesthetic adopted by avant-garde writers and journalists, who—unlike their more mainstream counterpart Paul Bourget—actively fostered a reputation for criminal complicity.

# 3
# Writing Murder
## Fictional Accomplices, Complicit Fictions

Crime narratives were incredibly popular throughout the nineteenth century. They featured in various mass media formats, from the centuries-old tradition of *canards* to later developments such as melodrama, Gothic fiction, and the serialised novel.[1] Broadly classified as 'popular literature', these genres depicted social, moral, or criminal transgression in a plotline that—through a series of complications and resolutions—pushed towards a return to order at the denouement.[2] By doing so, they paved the way for modern crime fiction, in which a detective deciphers clues to unravel a criminal mystery and bring justice to its victims.[3] The evolution, dissemination, and popularity of crime-centred fictions were closely intertwined with the changing press landscape throughout the century. Increased literacy rates, technological advances, and political censorship encouraged the rise of cheaper, more heterogeneous daily papers, which focused less on informing and guiding opinion than on capturing readers' attention (and customer loyalty) through a stream of sensational news items, gossip, and serialised fiction.[4] In this context, crime stories took a central role in appealing to a burgeoning readership. Reports on real-life crimes in sensational news items (*faits divers*) could make a newspaper's fortune by expanding its circulation.[5] Crime also featured heavily in popular serialised fiction, such as Eugène Sue's *Les Mystères de Paris* (1842–3)

---

[1] For a brief history of popular fiction, see Marc Angenot, 'La Littérature populaire française au dix-neuvième siècle', *Canadian Review of Comparative Literature/Revue Canadienne de Littérature Comparée* 9, no. 3 (Sep. 1982): pp. 307–33. On the *canard*, see Thomas Cragin, *Murder in Parisian Streets: Manufacturing Crime and Justice in the Popular Press, 1830–1900* (Lewisburg: Bucknell University Press, 2006).

[2] See Daniel Couégnas, *Introduction à la paralittérature* (Paris: Seuil, 1993), Diana Holmes and David Loosely, eds., *Imagining the Popular in Contemporary French Culture* (Manchester: Manchester University Press, 2013), and Bettina Lerner, *Inventing the Popular: Printing, Politics, and Poetics* (London: Routledge, 2018).

[3] Detective fiction has attracted significant attention in Francophone and Anglophone criticism. Notable examples include: David Platten, *The Pleasures of Crime: Reading Modern French Crime Fiction* (Amsterdam: Rodopi, 2011), Luc Boltanski, *Énigmes et complots: une enquête à propos d'enquêtes* (Paris: Gallimard, 2012), and Andrea Goulet, *Legacies of the Rue Morgue: Science, Space, and Crime Fiction in France* (Philadelphia: University of Pennsylvania Press, 2015).

[4] See Maria Adamowicz-Hariasz, 'From Opinion to Information: The *Roman-Feuilleton* and the Transformation of the Nineteenth-Century French Press', in *Making the News: Modernity and the Mass Press in Nineteenth-Century France*, edited by Jean de la Motte and Jeannene M. Przyblyski (Amherst: University of Massachusetts Press, 1999), pp. 160–84 (pp. 161–3 and 177).

[5] On the *fait divers*'s appeal, see Adamowicz-Hariasz, 'From Opinion to Information', p. 179 and Angenot, 'La Littérature populaire', pp. 305 and 328. *Le Petit Journal*'s circulation increased by 200,000

and Émile Gaboriau's *L'Affaire Lerouge* (1865). These genres contributed to the increasing sensationalism of press reporting, which rendered everyday existence spectacular and provided readers with a sense of participation in a wider collective through their familiarity with shared cultural allusions.[6] Criminal references spanned across popular media forms, through intertextual exchange: serialised novels were frequently adapted for the stage, and popular dramas were re-written for serialisation in newspapers.[7] Furthermore, popular genres employed similar stylistic techniques, including an emphatic use of repetition, cliché, hyperbole, and dialogue, in plotlines dominated by fast-paced, constantly moving action.[8] Writers employing such techniques appealed primarily to the reader-audience's emotive responses—via mimetic identification, suspense, and pathos—rather than encouraging intellectual distance or critique.[9] The affective impact of immersive literature was often viewed as 'a dangerous kind of openness', facilitating readers' 'seduction' via literary bad influence.[10]

The prevalence of this model explains the vehemence with which popular literary forms, and in particular crime narratives, were demonised by critics, scholars, and jurists throughout the nineteenth century, reaching fever pitch at the fin de siècle. For crime was not only a literary motif, but also a contested object of scientific study, judicial scrutiny, and socio-moral authority during the Third Republic. In a period marked by the dual rise of criminology and crime fiction, a recurrent debate was the question of criminal responsibility, as well as the role (and potential limitations) of the justice system in defining, regulating, and punishing it. Prominent contributors to such discussions included specialists in the emerging disciplines of medical pathology and criminal anthropology, as well as jurists debating penal reform during the latter half of the nineteenth century.[11] At the same time, medicine had an increasingly important role to play in the criminal justice system. It gained an unprecedented level of social and cultural

---

copies within a few weeks of reporting on the Troppmann case (see Cragin, *Murder in Parisian Streets*, p. 37).

[6] Vanessa Schwartz, *Spectacular Realities: Early Mass Culture in* Fin-de-Siècle *Paris* (Berkeley: University of California Press, 1998), pp. 32–43.

[7] Angenot, 'La Littérature populaire' p. 323, Couégnas, *Introduction*, p. 138, and René Polette, 'Mélodrame et roman-feuilleton sous le second Empire', *Europe: revue littéraire mensuelle* 703–4 (Nov.–Dec. 1987): pp. 82–9.

[8] Adamowicz-Hariasz, 'From Opinion to Information', p. 165 and Couégnas, *Introduction*. Lise Queffélec-Dumasy groups these elements of popular narrative into three dominant traits: 'redundancy, readability, and dramatisation' ('[la] redondance, la lisibilité et la théâtralisation'). Lise Queffélec-Dumasy, 'De quelques problèmes méthodologiques concernant l'étude du roman populaire', in *Problèmes de l'écriture populaire au XIXe siècle*, edited by Roger Bellet and Philippe Régnier (Limoges: Presses universitaires de Limoges, 1997), pp. 229–66 (pp. 242–4).

[9] Couégnas, *Introduction*, p. 78 and pp. 123–4, and Diana Holmes, 'The mimetic prejudice: the popular novel in France', in *Imagining the Popular*, edited by Holmes and Loosely, pp. 85–152 (91–3).

[10] Maria Scott, *Empathy and the Strangeness of Fiction: Readings in French Realism* (Edinburgh: Edinburgh University Press, 2020), pp. 25–8.

[11] Robert Nye, *Crime, Madness and Politics in Modern France: The Medical Concept of National Decline* (Princeton: Princeton University Press, 2014) pp. 97–131.

authority from increased professionalisation and vested political interests. In an era marked by civil unrest, from the spectre of the Commune to workers' strikes and anarchist bombings, there was growing support for theories that would justify a social defence approach to judicial procedure.[12] Debates raged about extenuating circumstances, notably the insanity defence, and the role of the jury in the attribution of criminal responsibility and in the severity of punishments. Reacting to jurors' perceived laxity, the government passed repressive laws such as the *Loi de rélégation* (27 May 1885), to provide harsher sentences for re-offenders. Similarly, the *Lois scélérates* (1893–4) aimed to assuage alarmist viewpoints expressed in the press about anarchism and social disorder.[13]

France's repressive approach to crime extended to its cultural representations. Scientific and judicial inquiry was not limited to real-life criminals—it also scrutinised the depiction of crime in literary production and mass media formats. Frequent targets included newspaper reports of criminal trials, popular crime narrative in serialised novels, and melodrama.[14] Critics attributed to each of these genres the capacity to influence readers to the point of encouraging them, through the aesthetic representation of transgressive actions and the heroisation of criminal characters, to reject normative morality and commit real-life crimes. Such fears escalated when the readers in question were considered inherently corruptible, and when their corruption posed a threat to the status quo—that is, when these readers were women or members of the working class.[15] To suppress the perceived danger of moral 'contagion', the French government made repeated attempts throughout the century to control the media forms attributed with its propagation. For example, in 1835, theatre censorship returned after a brief period of press freedom, notably targeting portrayals of glorified criminal characters, such as the bandit-cum-dandy figure Robert Macaire.[16] Then, as part of the 1850 censorship laws, the Riancey amendment temporarily suppressed the rise of serial fiction by adding an extra one-centime stamp on each issue of any newspaper that published a serial novel.[17] Later in the century, and despite greater press freedom post-1881, crime-centred narratives and dramas could still be targeted for outraging public decency, especially when they allied violence with sexual transgression.[18] The ongoing threat of censorship throughout the nineteenth century highlights the

---

[12] Nye, *Crime, Madness and Politics*, pp. 22–48. See also Dominique Kalifa, *L'Encre et le sang. Récits de crimes et société à la Belle Époque* (Paris: Fayard, 1995) pp. 234–70.
[13] Kalifa, *L'Encre et le sang*, p. 235.
[14] Kalifa, *L'Encre et le sang*, pp. 203–8 and 216–23.
[15] On the gender- and class-based prejudices informing discourses on criminality, see Ann-Louise Shapiro, *Breaking the Codes: Female Criminality in Fin-de-Siècle Paris* (Stanford: Stanford University Press, 1996), pp. 26–32.
[16] Odile Krakovitch, 'Robert Macaire ou la grande peur des censeurs', *Europe: revue littéraire mensuelle* 703–4 (Nov.–Dec. 1987): pp. 49–60 (p. 53).
[17] Adamowicz-Hariasz, 'From Opinion to Information', p. 177.
[18] On the threat of censorship and criticism for plays featuring violence and sex-related material in the period, see Oscar Méténier, *Les Voyous au théâtre* (Brussels: H. Kistemaeckers, 1891).

disquiet caused by the ever-popular appeal of criminality as a literary motif and source of mass entertainment.

Despite providing intellectual and ideological justification for the attempted suppression of popular crime narrative, authoritative discourses were often complicit with the contagion they condemned. Highlighting this irony in her study of fin-de-siècle female criminality, Ann-Louise Shapiro writes that 'while professionals saw their expertise compromised by popular accounts [...] [they] were in part responsible for both the seepage of this material into popular culture and for the slippage between popular and scientific writing'.[19] To support her vision of cultural contagion, Shapiro cites the increasing theatricality of trials held at the *cour d'assises*, memoirs published by former chiefs of police, and criminological studies:

> Seemingly oblivious to the paradox, criminological studies endlessly repeated the sordid details of sensational cases as they ritually condemned prurient interest in crime, soon producing a stock of familiar criminal lore and a long list of infamous *causes célèbres* that were so well known as to become reference points in both high and low cultural forms.[20]

To this list of complicit discourses, we can add the *Gazette des Tribunaux*, which disseminated summaries of criminal proceedings, offering writers a wealth of primary source material. Furthermore, while contributing to popular 'criminal lore', specialists in criminal anthropology and psychopathology regularly cited literary examples to support their analyses, and in some cases treated famous writers as case studies.[21] Writers with scientific pretensions, most famously Émile Zola, mirrored this practice when justifying their depiction of criminal and transgressive behaviour by claiming that their fictional works contributed productively to their contemporaries' understanding of these phenomena.[22] In this way, the interchangeability of crime-centred content blurred the boundaries separating a denigrated popular culture from the bastions of literary and scientific authority.

Writers were not oblivious to the ironies and complicities at play in the network of shared criminal references that criss-crossed generic boundaries, literary schools, and authoritative discourses. For although the theme of criminality was associated with mimetic and entertainment-driven popular literature on the one

---

[19] Shapiro, *Breaking the Codes*, p. 39.
[20] Shapiro, *Breaking the Codes*, p. 40.
[21] Notable examples include Cesare Lombroso's work *The Man of Genius* (*L'uomo di genio*), which was first published in 1888 and subsequently translated into French (1889) and English (1891). This work highly influenced Max Nordau, whose *Degeneration* (*Entartung*, 1892–3) was dedicated to Lombroso. Both works contributed to wider debates about literary bad influence in fin-de-siècle France.
[22] Zola did so most famously through the preface to the second edition of *Thérèse Raquin* (1868) and in his later essay 'Le Roman expérimental', first serialised in *Le Voltaire* between 16 and 20 October 1880. See Émile Zola, *Thérèse Raquin* (Paris: Gallimard, 2001), pp. 23–30, and *Le Roman expérimental*, 5th ed. (Paris: Charpentier, 1881), pp. 1–53.

hand, and with 'serious' scientific study on the other, this did not prevent authors from appropriating it for more satirical ends. Drawing on widespread interest in crime narratives, writers from across the literary spectrum raised questions about criminal responsibility, shared guilt, and injustice through fictional representations and discussions of murder. From plotting to enacting the crime, and dealing with its aftermath, fin-de-siècle murder fiction provides a rich source material for analysing literary complicity in one of its most clearly legally inspired forms. Referred to by one fin-de-siècle critic as 'murderer literature' ('la littérature des assassins'), this wide range of criminally inspired literary production included works that appeared, however ironically, to glorify criminal actions, while allying writers and readers with the murderer figure. Analysing both murder fiction and journalistic depictions of murder as an art form, this chapter demonstrates the meta-literary implications of criminal complicity across a range of fin-de-siècle texts.

## Complicit Narratives: *Nono*, *La Bête humaine*, and *Complices*

By thematising the transmissibility of guilt between fictional characters, fin-de-siècle writers satirised the judicial status quo while commenting self-reflexively on the implicating nature of witnessing, confessing, or judging a crime. This is apparent in three novels centred on complicity in the act of murder, penned by authors associated with Decadence, Naturalism, and popular fiction, respectively: Rachilde's *Nono* (1885), Émile Zola's *La Bête humaine* (1891), and Hector Malot's *Complices* (1893). The former appeared only a year after Rachilde's first *succès de scandale Monsieur Vénus* (1884). It recounts a tale of corrupted innocence, cold-blooded murder, and thwarted love. Rachilde's female protagonist Renée Fayor uses a suspended boulder in her father's garden to murder Victorien Barthelme, a penniless Don Juan figure who tries to blackmail her into marrying him, after having seduced and 'deflowered' her two years earlier. After initially fearing that her father's secretary, Bruno Maldas (the eponymous 'Nono'), may have witnessed the murder, Renée falls in love with him. Unable to confess her crime, for fear of making Bruno complicit with it, Renée attempts suicide, only to be rescued by a blasé duke, Edmond de Pluncey, whom she tricks into marriage. Bruno's subsequent flight from the Fayor family home is interpreted as proof of his guilt in the investigation surrounding Barthelme's disappearance. He is later arrested and faces trial for murder after Victorien's corpse is unearthed from General Fayor's garden. When informed of Renée's criminal responsibility, Bruno ensures that he is found guilty, in a gesture of amorous martyrdom that ends in his execution and Renée's sudden grief-stricken death. Like *Monsieur Vénus*, *Nono* recounts the story of a *femme fatale* whose idealised but impossible love for a socially inferior and feminised man catalyses a series of social and moral transgressions that ultimately lead to the destruction of the protagonist's beloved. However, unlike *Monsieur Vénus*, it includes motifs and techniques typically associated with popular romance, melodrama, and crime fiction. This unusual generic status helps to explain why, unlike its infamous predecessor, *Nono* was—and remains—largely neglected by critics.[23]

The same cannot be said for *La Bête humaine*, the seventeenth volume of Émile Zola's Rougon-Macquart cycle. The novel appeared serially in *La Vie populaire* between 1889 and 1890, when it was subsequently published in book format. Its plotline centres on the murder of Président Grandmorin by Roubaud and his wife Séverine, instigated by the latter's unwitting revelation that the victim (her patron and protector) had been sexually abusing her since she was sixteen. This first murder is witnessed by the novel's protagonist Jacques Lantier, who willingly helps to cover up the crime and becomes Séverine's lover. When Séverine recounts to Jacques her experience of murder, the latter's inherited flaw of pathological homicidal desire is reawakened, and their plan to murder Roubaud ends with Jacques killing Séverine instead, in a lust-induced frenzy. Through a combination of ineptitude and corruption, the criminal justice system is unable and unwilling to uncover the truth behind the murders, sentencing the half-guilty Roubaud alongside an innocent man, the marginal Cabuche, to life sentences of forced labour. Zola's murder story maintained the pseudo-scientific pretensions of the wider Rougon-Macquart cycle by appropriating elements of fin-de-siècle criminal anthropology. According to this vision, the primary characters, and notably Jacques Lantier, could be considered the fictional equivalent of real-life case studies. Yet alongside the work's pseudo-scientific pretensions we also find swathes of impressionistic detail and melodramatic plot devices, which demonstrate Zola's creative assimilation of a range of genres.

*Complices* was one of the final works published by the popular novelist Hector Malot (1830–1907).[24] Its narrative focuses on Hortense Courteheuse who, after years of marriage to a disagreeable solicitor, has an affair with one of her

---

[23] Very few Anglophone or Francophone Rachilde specialists have analysed *Nono* at length. When mentioned in their analyses, the novel usually only appears in passing. For example, Melanie Hawthorne offers a brief analysis of *Nono* as symbolising Rachilde's relationship to writing, in *Rachilde and French Women's Authorship: from Decadence to Modernism* (Lincoln, NE: University of Nebraska Press, 2001). While acknowledging that 'parts of *Nono* represent a carefully plotted murder story' (p. 126), Hawthorne dismisses the work's melodramatic style: 'Although certain twists of plot are indeed thriller material, many of the details of this long novel are hackneyed, and the ending exploits romantic cliché to full effect' (p. 128). For a recent analysis of *Nono*, on the topic of animality, see Arielle Verdelhan, 'L'Animal et l'animalité dans *Nono* (1885), avatars de la vérité' in *Rachilde ou les aléas de la postérité: de l'oubli au renouveau*, edited by Thierry Poyet, Minores XIX–XX, 5 (Paris: Lettres Modernes Minard, 2023), pp. 187–200.

[24] Born and raised in Normandy, Hector Malot studied law in Rouen and Paris before dedicating himself to a literary and journalistic career. He contributed to *Journal pour tous* and *L'Opinion nationale*, and published his debut novel in 1859 (*Les Amants*). Publishing over fifty novels in his lifetime, many of which were first serialised in newspapers, Malot is best known for *Sans famille* (1878) and *En famille* (1893), which told the story of an abandoned child and an orphaned child, respectively. His novels drew on popular topics and novelistic subgenres, including sentimental, historical, judicial, and

husband's legal clerks, La Vaupalière. Responding to various hindrances, including the installation of an electric alarm system at the marital home, Hortense drugs Courteheuse, initially to provoke illness and eventually to cause his death. She commits the murder with La Vaupalière's tacit, if fluctuating and begrudging, agreement. As in Zola's earlier murder novel *Thérèse Raquin* (1868), the accomplices' subsequent marriage is as unhappy as the first, due to the lack of an obstacle (and impetus) to desire, as well as the haunting effect of past crime and its cyclical repetition. Hortense's liaison with a second love interest, the younger legal clerk Médéric Artaut, is cut short by the local mayor Turlure's investigations, which lead to a trial against the eponymous accomplices. At trial, disagreements between medical experts reduces the persuasive power of Turlure's testimony and the traces of arsenic found in Courteheuse's exhumed body. Hortense subsequently wins over both jury and audience by confessing to adultery and making her husband sick, but not to murder. The novel ends with Hortense, the crime's primary instigator, being exonerated by the jury, while her (largely unwilling) accomplice La Vaupalière is sentenced to twenty years of hard labour.

Despite clear differences of style, position within their authors' wider oeuvre, and posterity in the canon, *Nono*, *La Bête humaine*, and *Complices* share a marked preoccupation with criminal responsibility and complicity. In particular, the plotlines of *Nono* and *La Bête humaine* rely on an integral association between murder and sexual transgression, with the former posited as a punishment for the latter. This process is twisted, even reversed, in *Complices*, where a murderess successfully avoids the legal consequences of her actions. Each novel highlights the structural and symbolic importance of murder scenes, the implicating power of confession, and the social injustice of criminal prejudice. Fictional representations of complicity in the novels' crime scenes, confession scenes, and trial scenes contributed to ongoing debates about criminal responsibility and raised metaliterary questions not only about the implication of writers and readers in the crimes depicted, but also about the perceived aesthetic debasement associated with popular literary forms.

## Locating Guilt: Crime Scenes

Setting and structure play an important role in fin-de-siècle murder fiction by heightening dramatic tension and contributing to the distribution of causality and guilt. Popular literary forms associated with criminality shared a proclivity

---

children's fiction, as well as the *roman personnel*. For further discussion of Malot's early career, see Myriam Kohnen, *Figures d'un polygraphe français. Hector Malot (1855–1881)* (Paris: Honoré Champion, 2016).

for theatricality,[25] and crime fiction frequently emphasised the importance of setting.[26] In fin-de-siècle murder fiction, 'setting the scene' becomes equivalent to 'setting up' or enabling the crime, and provides a locus for subsequent guilt via transference or narrative haunting. For example, *Nono*'s murder scene presents an eroticised and dramatised depiction of Victorien's demise beneath a falling boulder—an object which functions simultaneously as the murder weapon, crime scene, witness, and accomplice to Renée's crime. The novel's opening sequence depicts local labourers attempting to move the boulder to find a water source for the outside bathing space that Renée has had commissioned. Following this sequence, readers witness a night-time rendezvous between the former lovers, during which Victorien attempts to blackmail Renée into marrying him by threatening to reveal their amorous past. After Renée claims to hear someone approaching, Victorien hides beneath the now-suspended rock. Acting on impulse, Renée removes the architect's lever, causing the boulder to crush Victorien beneath its weight. The scene starts with an evocative description:

> Aux douces lueurs des étoiles, il voyait les cheveux de Renée se strier d'or [...] et, dans son visage levé, ses prunelles lui parurent rayonner comme rayonne le regard des fous qui se souviennent. [...] [Des] senteurs de verveines et des senteurs de roses se mariaient cavalièrement [...].
> Victorien [...] clignait les paupières, ayant des moiteurs dans les mains, et sans l'appeler, la voyait approcher malgré ses yeux fermés.[27]

> [By the gentle glimmer of starlight, he saw streaks of gold in Renée's hair [...] and, in her upturned face, eyes which seemed to glow like the dawning reminiscence in a madman's glance. [...] The scent of verbena and the scent of rose wedded unceremoniously together [...].
> Victorien's hands were clammy, and his eyes blinked shut, yet through his eyelids, and without calling her, he could see Renée approaching him.]

In this sequence, Rachilde builds up a sensual atmosphere, emphasising the impact of romanticised lighting effects—seen in the starlight, Renée's golden hair, and her gleaming eyes—alongside the heady floral perfume diffused in the night air. This atmosphere is suggestive of amorous union ('se mariaient cavalièrement') and were it not for hints of dramatic irony and foreshadowing, the reader might

---

[25] See Couégnas, *Introduction*, p. 138 and Queffélec-Dumasy, 'De quelques problèmes méthodologiques', p. 241.

[26] See Goulet, *Legacies of the Rue Morgue*, David Geherin, *Scene of the Crime: The Importance of Place in Crime and Mystery Fiction* (Jefferson: McFarland, 2008), and Dominique Kalifa, 'Les lieux du crime. Topographie criminelle et imaginaire social à Paris au XIXe siècle', *Sociétés & Représentations* 17, no. 1 (2004): pp. 131–50, doi:10.3917/sr.017.0131.

[27] Rachilde, *Nono* (Paris: Mercure de France, 1994), pp. 41–2. References will henceforth appear parenthetically in the text.

share Victorien's interpretation of the scene as initiating a sexual encounter. His reaction to Renée's approach displays erotic arousal: he has 'des moiteurs dans les mains'. However, Rachilde ensures that the reader predicts the crime Renée is about to commit, by describing Renée's glance, when she realises the fortuitous position that Victorien has taken beneath the rock, as 'le regard des fous qui se souviennent' ['the dawning reminiscence in a madman's glance']. In this way, readers are encouraged, via dramatic irony, to position themselves through Renée's viewpoint, even though the scene is, up until this moment, largely filtered indirectly through that of Victorien.

The narrative viewpoint shifts when Renée removes the architect's lever. In the preceding moments, Rachilde's description encourages mimetic absorption in the unfolding events. But immediately afterwards, the scene takes on a supernatural and theatrical atmosphere, which, combined with distancing effects, makes identification with the action more difficult. For example, when Renée knocks away the lever, the focus moves away from the characters: 'Alors, dans l'ombre, se passa un phénomène étrange qui fut rapide comme un truc de féerie' ['Then, in the darkness, something strange happened, as quickly as a magic trick']. In this sentence, the reader is invited to view the scene from afar, before being snapped back into the gruesome detail of Barthelme's body as it is crushed by the boulder: 'Cet homme jeune eut tout à coup le dos voûté, la tête enfoncée, le crâne élargi. Sa poitrine devint une masse, ses pieds disparurent, tandis que ses jambes rentrèrent dans son torse... puis deux jets brillants jaillirent de sa face disloquée... On ne distingua plus rien' ['All of a sudden, this young man had his back bent, his head staved in, his skull flattened. His chest turned into a lump and his feet disappeared, while his legs pushed up into his torso... two shining jets then gushed forth from his distorted face... It all disappeared from view'] (*Nono*, 42). The gruesome details appear alongside impersonal constructions, such as the reference to Victorien as '[cet] homme jeune' and the pronoun 'on'. This reduces readers' capacity to empathise with Renée's victim. The same can be said for Renée, who seems unable to accept complete responsibility for her actions: 'Renée Fayor resta là, devant son crime, ne sachant plus bien si elle venait de le commettre' ['Renée remained there, confronted with her crime, no longer entirely sure whether she had just committed it']. By describing events as if they were part of a stage production with special effects ('truc[s] de féerie'), Rachilde conveys Renée's self-positioning as a spectator of, rather than an actor in, the scene. The personification of the boulder, described as Renée's accomplice, further blurs the attribution of criminal responsibility: 'La roche avait repris son air entêté, sournois, et la morne immobilité d'une chose qui veut être complice' ['The rock had regained its stubborn, shifty appearance, and the dreary impassivity of something that wants to be complicit'] (*Nono*, 42). The adjectives 'entêté' and 'sournois' reflect elements of Renée's character, projected onto an inanimate object. This projection is ambiguous, since readers are reminded of the rock's non-human status, through the word 'chose', while the verb 'vouloir' clearly attributes agency to the boulder: a compliancy with and willingness to enable Renée's action. When considered within the sequence as a whole, it is as if the serendipity of the boulder's location, and Victorien's decision to hide beneath it, absolves the protagonist's crime, much like the earth underfoot absorbs the physical evidence of it.

Beyond the initial crime scene, the boulder gains symbolic meaning through its association with the *salle de bains* that Renée has built nearby. Later in the novel, a highly charged but unconsummated erotic encounter occurs here, when Nono chances upon Renée powdering herself after bathing. When they eventually kiss, the narrative notes their ironic positioning: '[le] canapé était près de la fenêtre donnant sur la roche. C'était adossée à son crime que Renée recevait les baisers de Brunos Maldas' ['the sofa was near the window looking out upon the rock. It was thus leaning up against her crime that Renée received Bruno Maldas's kisses'] (*Nono*, 165). Rachilde here aligns Renée's act of murder with erotic desire, while framing the latter as inevitably illicit. In what appears to be a form of punishment, the room's haunting presence disrupts their embrace:

> Nono colla ses lèvres au cou penché de la jeune femme... il y eut un suprême silence... les pierres écoutaient! Mais, brutalement, Renée s'arracha de l'étreinte ardente de Bruno, elle avait ouvert les yeux. Au sommet de la roche, dominant le vitrail et leur couche, un spectre s'était dressé; une ombre d'homme, gigantesque, interminable, s'allongeant toujours... (*Nono*, 166-7)

> [Nono pressed his lips against the young woman's inclined neck... there was complete silence... the stones were listening! But Renée suddenly tore herself away from Bruno's ardent embrace. She had opened her eyes. At the top of the rock, overlooking their bed beneath the stained glass window, a ghost had risen up; a gigantic, endless shadow of a man, that was spreading out ever further...]

The ghostly reminder of Renée's crime repeats the eroticised atmosphere of the earlier murder scene, which was also framed as a potential sex scene. Tension builds because the reader discovers the ghostly figure's identity at the same time as Rachilde's protagonist. Deprived of dramatic irony, the novel's readers are therefore encouraged to share Renée's fear in this sequence, which is rendered in highly melodramatic terms. In fact, Rachilde's contemporaries criticised the book's hyperbole, typical of melodrama and serial fiction, while deploring its hackneyed romanticism and *invraisemblance* ['implausibility'].[28] Nevertheless, the novel does

---

[28] Émile Goudeau (1849–1906) compared these elements of the novel to 'les plus mauvais jours de 1840' ['the worst days of 1840'], and Jules Boissière (1863–97) condemned the work's 'excentricité vieillotte' ['outdated eccentricity'], citing the unusual murder weapon as a prime example of its lack of verisimilitude. See Émile Goudeau, 'Impressions d'un lecteur', *L'Écho de Paris*, 20 Jan. 1885, and Jules Boissière, 'Notices bibliographiques', *La Presse*, 27 Jan. 1885.

not preclude a more ironic reading, for even Bruno acknowledges the absurdity of Renée's reaction to the shadow, by exclaiming 'Tu es folle!' ['You are mad!'] (167). Furthermore, the scene ends in bathos: the duke emerges from the ghost-like shadow and, unlike Bruno, initiates sex with Renée. In this way, the protagonist's displaced desire inadvertently reveals the implicit eroticism of her otherwise idealised chaste love, while re-enacting the seduction model of her first sexual encounter. The duke therefore symbolically, if not literally, becomes the ghost of Victorien Barthelme. Following the structural inevitability of this uncanny haunting, Renée's actions fail to counteract the novel's trajectory, which leads her further down the path of crime and enables Nono's execution.

The obsessive, cyclical structure of crime, where desire transfers onto an ambiguous 'other', against the backdrop of a recurring, haunting crime scene, also appears in *La Bête humaine*, through Zola's presentation of La Croix-de-Maufras: the central stage for most crimes depicted in the novel. The opening chapter reveals that the house at La Croix-de-Maufras served as the theatre to the female protagonist Séverine's lost innocence at the hands of her 'protector' and eventual abuser Grandmorin. In the subsequent chapter, the surrounding area becomes the backdrop to an attempted sex scene and almost-murder scene between Jacques and his chaste and proud cousin Flore.[29] To save Flore's life, Jacques flees into the barren countryside that reflects his psychological state: 'Ce pays désert, coupé de monticules, était comme un labyrinthe sans issue, où tournait sa folie, dans la morne désolation des terrains incultes' ['Criss-crossed by ridge upon ridge, this wilderness was like a labyrinth without an exit, in which his madness turned and turned upon itself amid the dreary desolation of this uncultivated land'].[30] The 'morne désolation' of La Croix-de-Maufras—much like the 'morne immobilité' of the boulder in *Nono*—adds to the scene's pathos and reflects the protagonist's destructive and guilty mental state. The image of the inescapable labyrinth symbolises Jacques's cycle of psychological stability and instability, while also implying the inevitability of the latter. This is confirmed by the fact that, after half an hour spent desperately fleeing across the countryside, Jacques returns serendipitously to the tunnel entrance just in time to witness Grandmorin's murder (*LBH*, 1046). The forceful sense of structural inevitability in Zola's depiction of La Croix-de-Maufras is suggestive of how narrative setting implicitly enables—or *sets up*—the crimes committed within it.

In a further analogy to the boulder in *Nono*, La Croix-de-Maufras and its environs return throughout Zola's novel as a form of structural haunting, through

---

[29] La Croix-de-Maufras is also the setting for Phasie's gradual poisoning at the hands of her husband Misard, and the train derailment caused by Flore's jealous revenge against Jacques and Séverine.

[30] Émile Zola, *La Bête humaine*, in *Les Rougon-Macquart: histoire naturelle et sociale d'une famille sous le Second Empire*, ed. Henri Mitterand, 5 vols (Paris: Gallimard, 1960–7), IV (1966), pp. 997–1331 (p. 1042). References to *La Bête humaine* are to this edition and are given in the text, preceded by the abbreviation *LBH*. For the English translation see Émile Zola, *La Bête humaine*, trans. Roger Pearson (Oxford: Oxford University Press, 2009), p. 51.

which sexual desire is aligned with violent crime. After witnessing Grandmorin's murder in a passing train, Jacques is eager to see the corpse. The narrative compares the crime scene, now situated alongside the train tracks bordering La Croix-de-Maufras, to an amorous rendezvous (*LBH*, 1049). Jacques's visceral excitement culminates in his confrontation with Grandmorin's corpse, described in a sequence of free indirect discourse, which concludes with the following lines: 'Ce qu'il rêvait, l'autre l'avait réalisé, et c'était ça. S'il tuait, il y aurait ça par terre. Son cœur battait à se rompre, son prurit de meurtre s'exaspérait comme une concupiscence, au spectacle de ce mort tragique. [...] Oui! il oserait, il oserait à son tour!' ['What he only dreamt about the other man had done, and there it was. If he were to kill, that's what would be lying on the ground. His pulse raced madly, and his violent itch to kill grew fiercer, like a sexual urge, at the sight of this sorry corpse. [...] Yes! He would dare, he too would dare!'] (*LBH*, 1050).[31] This section evokes Jacques's vicarious desire, identification, and self-denigration in comparison to the idealised murderer figure, while foreshadowing his copycat crime, displaced until Chapter Eleven, when he kills Séverine in the same way Roubaud killed Grandmorin.[32] In a moment of emphatic structural parallelism, Séverine's death hearkens back to that of her abuser: 'Ce corps délicat [...] c'était la même loque humaine, [...] qu'un coup de couteau fait d'une créature' ['This delicate body [...] was the same tatter of humanity, [...] to which a living creature is reduced by the simple stab of a knife'] (*LBH*, 1298).[33] The scene's mirroring effect appears through an overt reference to Grandmorin's corpse, but also through key verbs and phrases lifted from the earlier episode, such as: 'se contenter', 'faire ça', 'loque [...] pantin [...] chiffe', and 'qu'un coup de couteau fait d'une créature'. A sentence in the conditional, from Chapter Two: 'S'il tuait, il y aurait ça par terre' ['If he were to kill, that's what would be lying on the ground'] is transformed into an affirmative past tense: 'Il avait tué, et il y avait ça par terre' ['He had killed, and there it was on the ground'].[34] The use of repetition here exemplifies Calvin Brown's notion of 'the key passage', which Andrew Counter has more recently examined as a form of foreshadowing that works 'by strikingly enacting the necessity and inevitability of the plot's ultimate unfolding.'[35]

Zola's insistent use of repetition and foreshadowing leads to a hyperbolic association between La Croix-de-Maufras and the various crimes committed in the novel. Zola's contemporaries perceived the sheer number of these crimes to cross

---

[31] Zola, trans. Pearson, p. 60.

[32] Susan Blood also notes the importance of displacement to the novel's narrative structure and emphasises the mimetic logic of Jacques's crime, in 'The Precinematic Novel: Zola's *La Bête humaine*', *Representations* 93, no. 1 (Winter 2006): pp. 49–75 (pp. 53–6), https://www.jstor.org/stable/10.1525/rep.2006.93.1.49.

[33] Zola, trans. Pearson, p. 331.

[34] Zola, trans. Pearson, p. 60 and p. 331, respectively.

[35] Andrew J. Counter, 'Zola's Repetitions: On Repetition in Zola', *The Modern Language Review* 116, no. 1 (2021): pp. 42–64 (p. 45), doi:10.1353/mlr.2021.0073. Counter cites Calvin Brown on p. 44.

the limits of verisimilitude for the sake of dramatic appeal—a tendency associated with the denigrated serial novel. When reviewing Zola's novel for *Le Siècle*, the critic Charles Bigot (1840–93) wrote: 'Jamais on n'a tué plus, même dans un roman de M. Xavier de Montépin. [...] On le voit, la matière ne manque pas ici aux amateurs du genre "sensationnel". Six personnages: six crimes' ['There has never been so much killing, even in a novel by Mr Xavier de Montépin. [...] As you can see, there is plenty of material for "sensational" literature enthusiasts. Six characters: six crimes'].[36] Edmond Lepelletier expanded on this point by reminding *L'Écho de Paris*'s readers that 'tout cet ensemble dramatique est certainement entaché d'invraisemblance, mais il ne faut pas oublier que nous sommes en plein feuilleton criminel' ['all these dramatic events are certainly tainted with improbability, but we must not forget that we are in the middle of a crime series']. Furthermore, Lepelletier made explicit a prejudice only implied by other critics: that the sensationalist tendencies of serialised crime narratives were inextricably bound up in their appeal for a lower-class readership: 'Le crime est rendu avec une grande abondance d'effets d'horreur et tout se passe dans les conditions ordinaires de ces tableaux farouches destinés à être reproduits peinturlurés sur les murailles afin d'attirer la clientèle à un sou' ['The crime is described with an over-abundance of horror effects, and everything takes place in the same kind of conditions as those wild scenes intended to be garishly reproduced and plastered on walls, to attract the attention of penny paper readers'].[37] In fact, Zola had already faced criticism for the sensational poster published by *La Vie populaire* to advertise the novel's serialised publication.[38] By highlighting the belaboured dramatic effects in *La Bête humaine* and reminding readers of its status as a serial novel, critics accused Zola of pandering to, and cynically exploiting, vulgar tastes. This is comparable to the way in which Jean Lorrain and Octave Mirbeau accused Paul Bourget of pandering to the edulcorated tastes of upper-middle-class women, discussed in Chapter 2. Through this accusation, Zola's critics denied his writing literary merit while reaffirming the association between crime narrative and mass media culture.

While the structural and thematic *hantises* in Zola's novel are far from subtle, the dismissive tone adopted by many fin-de-siècle critics veils its more complex,

[36] Charles Bigot, 'Chronique littéraire. *La Bête humaine*', *Le Siècle*, 10 Mar. 1890. Xavier de Montépin (1823–1902) was a prolific writer of serialised fiction and popular plays. His bestseller *La Porteuse de pain*, serialised in *Le Petit journal* between 1884 and 1885, deployed the popular topos of the 'jeune fille persécutée' ['persecuted young woman'] (Angenot, 'La Littérature populaire', p. 324).

[37] Edmond Lepelletier, 'Chronique des Livres. *La Bête humaine* par Émile Zola', *L'Écho de Paris*, 11 Mar. 1890.

[38] In the 16 November 1889 issue of the *Journal des débats politiques et littéraires*, one journalist wrote: 'Personne n'est forcé de lire les livres de M. Zola. Mais tout le monde est forcé de voir un placard, surtout quand il prend les dimensions de celui dont nous parlons, et nous ne sommes pas convaincus que le droit de scandaliser les promeneurs fasse partie intégrante des conquêtes de 1789' ['No-one is forced to read books by Mr Zola. But everyone is forced to look at a poster, especially when it is as big as the one under discussion, and we are not convinced that the right to scandalise passers-by was really one of the major victories of 1789'].

unnerving elements (which may have provoked his contemporaries' vehemence in the first place). For it is undoubtedly an unsettling experience to read Jacques's jubilation as he contemplates the corpses of Grandmorin and Séverine, in episodes conveyed through vast swathes of free indirect discourse that prevent readers from orientating themselves morally in response to Jacques's experience of murder. Much like Lantier, whose homicidal desires receive the necessary spark of inspiration from witnessing another person's crime, Zola's readers take on the symbolic and moral weight of the novel's criminal obsession through the shared experience of witnessing its evocative representation. Fin-de-siècle readers acknowledged the complicitous position in which Zola's novel placed them by raising concerns about literary bad influence, whereby the act of witnessing illicit action through fictional representation was perceived to inspire copycat crimes. In *Le Siècle*, for example, Charles Bigot wrote: 'Si de telles pages tombaient sous les yeux de quelque détraqué glissant sur la même pente de l'obsession sanguinaire et n'ayant plus besoin que d'un léger coup dernier pour rompre ce qui, chez lui, résiste encore, l'effet pourrait être terrible' ['If such pages fell beneath the gaze of some madman falling down the same slippery slope of bloodthirsty obsession, and needing only one small, final push to break that which still resisted within him, the result could be dreadful'].[39] A month later, in the *Revue bleue*, he condemned Naturalist writers for denying their influence over, and moral responsibility towards, their readers.[40] For although Zola thematised the question of crime narrative's insidious effects within the novel itself, he failed to condemn these effects sufficiently to appease critics like Bigot.

Séverine's death is one of the only crimes to be depicted directly in the novel. By placing readers in the position of witness or bystander to Séverine's death, and by making them experience Lantier's murderous lust vicariously through sections of free indirect style, Zola establishes a form of complicity that is emphatically gendered and misogynistic. As Andrew Counter and Lisa Downing have noted, Jacques's destructive desires are presented as the logical extreme of widely accepted visions of masculine sexuality in patriarchal society: male supremacy ('la souveraineté du mâle') is reaffirmed by man's destruction of woman, and murder can be justified by masculine jealousy and possessiveness: 'elle ne serait jamais plus à personne' ['she would never belong to anyone now'] (*LBH*, 1298).[41] Indeed, both *La Bête humaine* and *Nono* dramatically stage the expectations and limitations of gender roles. Their narrative plotlines centre around the 'deflowering'

---

[39] Bigot, 'Chronique littéraire'.

[40] Charles Bigot, 'Psychologue naturaliste', *La Revue politique et littéraire*, 5 Apr. 1890, pp. 425–7 (p. 426).

[41] Zola, trans. Pearson, p. 331. See Andrew J. Counter, 'The Legacy of the Beast: Patrilinearity and Rupture in Zola's *La Bête humaine* and Freud's *Totem and Taboo*', *French Studies* 62, no. 1 (Jan. 2008): pp. 26–38 (p. 29), doi:10.1093/fs/knm237 and Lisa Downing, 'The Birth of the Beast: Death-Driven Masculinity in Monneret, Zola and Freud', *Dix-Neuf* 5, no. 1 (2013): pp. 28–46 (p. 35), doi: 10.1179/147873105790723321.

and sexual abuse of women, followed by revenge against the guilty male perpetrator. The vindicated protagonist in each novel meets a tragic end, which suggests an insidious form of victim-blaming against women who participate in their own revenge. Nonetheless, the novels differ significantly in the level of critical distance provided when depicting their female protagonist's death. Through its direct description of eroticised murder, *La Bête humaine* covertly assumes its implied reader to be a man capable of sharing Lantier's desires, and therefore obliges (actual) women readers to witness and be complicit with the misogynistic homosocial bonding between author, protagonist, and (implied) reader.[42] In contrast, *Nono* reports Renée's death indirectly, in the final pages of a story that foregrounds the heroine's complex personality and experience, ridicules many of the male characters, and presents her death not simply as a consequence of her sexual transgression or criminal guilt, but as the ultimate symbol of her tragic grief. Reader response in Rachilde's novel is less clearly gendered and facilitates a less fraught identification between women readers and the novel's heroine.

Whereas *La Bête humaine* and *Nono* present death as the consequence of female protagonists' involvement in murder, *Complices* depicts a canny but dislikeable heroine who successfully avoids penal retribution for murdering her first husband. It does so while critiquing the gendered norms which encouraged Hortense to commit the crime in the first place. The inequalities of marriage as an institution, the controlling behaviour of a loveless husband, and the desire to marry a younger, more attentive lover, provide the logic and justification for Courteheuse's murder. Unsurprisingly, the primary location and crime scene in *Complices* is the domestic interior of Hortense's marital home, which also serves as her husband's solicitor's office. Readers first encounter the house and its garden as a place of mystery and criminal detection, when Courteheuse finds a footprint in the soil of a recently raked flowerbed. Mistakenly interpreting the footprint as a sign of attempted burglary, Courteheuse fits out his home with an electric alarm system, thereby creating an obstacle for his adulterous wife and her lover. This action leads Hortense to drug her husband so that he is not disturbed by her interrupting the alarm system to continue her night-time assignations. The ensuing complications push Hortense to poison Courteheuse—initially to provoke illness, but subsequently to end his life, thereby facilitating her second marriage to La Vaupalière. With the obstacle to desire removed, the second marriage declines as quickly as the first, with the added threat of one spouse potentially informing on the other. As a crime scene, the house is therefore closely bound up in the stultifying

---

[42] In fictional depictions of rape and femicide, the threat of sexual violence can, according to Andrew Counter, function as a homosocial 'signifying structure' that 'reinscribes the female body as a sign which allows a certain communication for and between men'. Andrew Counter, 'Tough Love, Hard Bargains: Rape and Coercion in Balzac', *Nineteenth-Century French Studies* 36, nos. 1–2 (Fall–Winter 2007–8), pp. 61–71 (p. 68).

atmosphere of its owners' relationship, and with the oppressive inevitability of marital dissatisfaction, which seems to return regardless of the spouse's identity.

While reaffirming clichés about desire, love, and marriage, *Complices* reduces the reader's capacity to experience sympathy for Hortense's victim, in a gesture typical of the texts under study. Malot's novel makes it clear that Courteheuse cynically views marriage as a burden, which he only contemplates for personal financial gain.[43] He views his wife as a possession rather than as a person: '« Ma femme est un objet à mon usage », répétait-il à chaque instant devant elle, sans qu'un mot d'amour ou de tendresse corrigeât jamais cette parole caractéristique' ['Constantly and repeatedly, he would say in front of her: "my wife is an object made for my use", without a single word of love or tenderness to soften this characteristic remark'] (*Complices*, 80). Moreover, Courteheuse's greed prevents Hortense from experiencing the society lifestyle she had hoped to enjoy upon entering the marital state. Notably, he refuses to allow her to visit friends in Rouen and Elbeuf, due to the cost of train tickets, while hypocritically treating himself to a weekly trip to Rouen for a night of social drinking, gastronomic excess, and sexual pleasure (*Complices*, 80–3). Such flagrant evidence of the sexual double standard encourages sympathy towards Hortense's viewpoint, and is comparable to the unflattering descriptions of male murder victims in *Nono* and *La Bête humaine*. After dramatically revealing Séverine's childhood grooming, Zola's novel hints at Grandmorin's long history of sexual coercion and rape through the reported death of Louisette (Flore's younger sister and Cabuche's friend) and the testamentary gifts left in his will. The build-up of these references creates a pervading sense that Roubaud and Séverine's victim—like the administration he represents—should be punished for his hidden crimes. Likewise, it is difficult to feel sorry for a cynical philanderer and blackmailer, *Nono*'s Victorien Barthelme, who, like Grandmorin, is punished for his transgression. When discussing with Renée their earlier liaison, in the conversation immediately preceding his death, Victorien cynically rebuts her sexual idealism: 'Quel est le mari, quel est l'amant qui ne soit ou n'ait été un viveur? [...] Quelle est l'ingénue qui n'est charmée de cesser de l'être?' ['What husband or lover is not, or has never been, a philanderer? [...] What innocent young lady is not delighted to lose her innocence?'] (*Nono*, 37). While acknowledging that both men and women experience sexual curiosity, Victorien affirms the gendered inequality of such curiosity's consequences. He does so by confidently wielding the sexual double standard as a weapon to force Renée to marry him, in the name of preserving her reputation. Barthelme's final words, 'Tu seras bonne!' ['You will play along nicely!'], indicate his confidence and determination in seeking the most profitable outcome. By portraying unsympathetic victim characters whose sexual

---

[43] This chapter cites a modern reprint of the original 1893 text: Hector Malot, *Complices*, postface by Christian Millet (Darnetal: Petit à petit, 2001), p. 54 (references hereafter appear parenthetically in-text). Hortense, an illegitimate child, brought to the marriage a dowry of 120,000 francs, and the prospect of inheriting a further 300,000 francs from her bachelor uncle.

misdeeds provide mitigating circumstances for murder, Rachilde, Zola, and Malot express the difficulty of locating guilt in a specific action or individual. They appeal to the reader as witness and judge of both criminal and victim, in a process that mirrors confessional and courtroom scenarios within their respective narratives.

## Sharing and Displacing Guilt: Confession Scenes

Rachilde, Zola, and Malot's novels associate criminal complicity with erotic bonds. Both phenomena rely on shared illicit knowledge, transmitted in the medium of confessional dialogue. These exchanges displace blame onto the interlocutor or invite them to shoulder the burden of guilt. For example, in *La Bête humaine*, Séverine's relationship with Jacques elides criminal confession and sexual consummation. During the early stages of their acquaintance, Séverine ensures Jacques's complicitous silence through shared illicit knowledge and mutual possession: 'le lien était noué entre eux, indissoluble: elle le défiait bien de parler maintenant, il était à elle comme elle était à lui. L'aveu les avait unis' ['the bond had been tied between them, indissolubly: she defied him to talk now, he was hers as she was his. Her declaration had united them'] (*LBH*, 1122).[44] Confession here creates criminal complicity while acting as a forerunner to, and the equivalent of, sexual consummation. However, Séverine's confession is only a partial truth because she confesses through a form of denial and does not give any details about the crime itself. This half-truth mirrors Séverine's attempt to maintain her relationship with Jacques in platonic limbo. By doing so, she demonstrates fear that erotic and confessional desire are negative, destructive forces—a fear that is confirmed when the couple consummate their relationship:

> Lorsqu'elle le serrait d'une étreinte, il sentait bien qu'elle était gonflée et haletante de son secret, qu'elle ne voulait ainsi entrer en lui que pour se soulager de la chose dont elle étouffait. C'était un grand frisson qui lui partait des reins, qui soulevait sa gorge d'amoureuse, dans le flot confus de soupirs montant à ses lèvres. [...] Il flairait un danger, un frémissement le reprenait, à l'idée de remuer avec elle ces histoires de sang. (*LBH*, 1155)

> [When she held him, he could feel her all bursting, gasping, with her secret, as if she only wanted to fuse into one with him like this so that she could unburden herself of that which was suffocating her. A great tremor would spring from her loins, lifting her breasts in passion and rising to her lips in a mingling stream of

[44] Zola, trans. Pearson, p. 141.

sighs. [...] He sensed a danger, and his shuddering would return at the idea of going over these bloody deeds again.]⁴⁵

In this scene, Séverine's desire to confess mirrors her state of erotic arousal. Zola combines imagery of erection and ejaculation—seen by Séverine's desire to 'entrer en lui' and by the description of the past rising up within her, threatening to inundate Jacques in a 'flot confus'—with vaginal imagery, through displaced erotic attention to Séverine's mouth and lips. In this exchange, storytelling—particularly recounting stories about crime ('ces histoires de sang')—has the potential to encourage further crime through vicarious and mimetic desire. In a clear reworking of the 'bad influence' model, Jacques's fears regarding the repercussions of Séverine's full confession indicate the uncontrollable power of shared illicit knowledge, both within and beyond the written page.

The fatal unity of confession, sexual desire, and murder in *La Bête humaine* appears through two parallel scenes in mère Victoire's apartment. In the opening chapter, Séverine accidentally reveals the truth behind her relationship with Grandmorin, provoking Roubaud's violent jealousy (*LBH*, 1019). Knowledge *of* crime here leads to the desire to *commit* crime. Not only does this scene set up the murder that follows, but its haunting presence later in the novel leads to Séverine's full confession to Jacques in Chapter Eight. When Séverine finishes recounting her experience of murder, the couple engage in intense, almost bestial, sex: 'Ils se possédèrent [...] dans la même volupté douloureuse des bêtes qui s'éventrent pendant le rut' ['They possessed each other [...] with the same excruciating pleasure as animals that eviscerate one another while they mate'] (*LBH*, 1205).⁴⁶ This sequence clearly posits sexual desire as destructive, although this passion is experienced mutually and is not (in this instance) emphatically gendered. The scene's importance was evident to Zola's contemporaries, with critics such as Augustin Filon (1841–1916) and Paul Ginisty (1855–1932) praising its 'superb' and 'marvellous' rendering.⁴⁷ Jules Lemaître emphasised the visceral impact of reading Séverine's confession to Jacques, describing its pages as 'frissonnantes d'horreur et de mystère' ['trembling with horror and mystery'], and praising 'le je ne sais quoi de furieux et de désespéré que la confidence sanglante, chuchotée entre deux baisers, donne à leur bestial et sombre amour' ['the hint of fury and desperation that the bloody secret, whispered between two kisses, gives to their murky, bestial love'].⁴⁸ Even Charles Bigot—who, as previously mentioned, criticised *La Bête humaine* for its melodramatic appeal to popular audiences and its capacity to encourage real-life crime—cited the two confession scenes as some of the

---

[45] Zola, trans. Pearson, p. 176.
[46] Zola, trans. Pearson, p. 229.
[47] Paul Ginisty, 'Causerie littéraire', *Gil Blas*, 15 Mar. 1890, p. 3; Augustin Filon, 'Courrier littéraire', La Revue politique et littéraire, 22 Mar. 1890, pp. 378–81 (p. 379).
[48] Jules Lemaître, '« La Bête humaine »', *Le Figaro*, 8 Mar. 1890, p. 1.

novel's most stimulating chapters: 'des chapitres d'un intérêt palpitant, d'une force dramatique saisissante, d'un éclat de style incomparable' ['chapters that excite and thrill, with striking theatrical force, in an incomparable, dazzling style'].[49] Above all, the scene draws force from its structural significance as the turning point in the lovers' relationship. Séverine's full confession reawakens Jacques's murderous desires, leading him to try to kill a woman in the street during a post-coital pathological frenzy. It removes the layer of protection that the previously half-veiled hints had provided, and ultimately leads to Séverine's demise at Jacques's hands. In this way, the temptation to confess one's crimes in La Bête humaine creates a form of complicity that, rather than strengthening a relationship, leads to its bloody destruction.

Whereas Séverine manipulates the power of confession and sexual desire to maintain complicity with Jacques, Renée spends a large part of Nono's plotline trying to prevent sharing criminal knowledge with Bruno. Early in the novel, Rachilde's heroine intends to make Nono an accomplice in hiding her crime, by asking him to help wash off the blood she thinks has stained her shoes (Nono, 44). Renée later changes her mind when she perceives a budding (if doomed) romance between them: 'La moindre complicité avec Bruno ignorant devenait monstrueuse, puisque la fatalité le lui faisait aimer' ['Clueless as he was, the slightest complicity with Bruno became monstrous, since fate had made her love him'] (Nono, 90). She aims to maintain Bruno's innocence by refusing either to confess to him or to sleep with him. Unlike Séverine, Renée succeeds in maintaining their relationship in platonic limbo for the entire novel. Instead of implicating her beloved, Renée first reveals her crime to an upper-class philanderer, the Duc de Pluncey, with whom she orchestrates a marriage to benefit from the unspoken judicial protection afforded by a high social position. She confesses on their wedding night, after the following exchange:

—Que savez-vous de l'assassinat? Au moins répondez, puisque je dois aller plus loin sur le chemin de ce calvaire.
    —Vous m'aimeriez jusqu'au pardon?
    —Je te désire jusqu'à me faire complice de tes infamies! s'écria le duc ivre de rage en l'enlaçant éperdument. A peine eut-elle reçu le premier baiser de l'époux, qu'elle le repoussa, ses prunelles eurent des éclairs. (Nono, 249)

['What do you know about the murder? Tell me that at least, since I must go further with this ordeal'.
    'You would love me enough to forgive me?'
    Beside himself with rage and clasping her passionately, the duke exclaimed: 'I desire you enough to become the accomplice in your infamy!' No sooner

[49] Bigot, 'Chronique littéraire'.

had she received her husband's first kiss than she pushed him away, her eyes flashing with anger.]

The duke's desire to consummate their relationship pushes him to demand knowledge of Renée's illicit actions, which he presumes are sexual rather than murderous in nature. His use of the term 'complice' indicates a willingness to participate in any future cover-up. Rather than offering the couple a pathway towards greater union through complicity and sexual intercourse, as in *La Bête humaine*, confession provides Renée with the means to ensure disharmony in her marriage and to prevent her husband from claiming his conjugal 'rights'. By revealing the truth, Renée makes Edmond her accomplice in covering up the crime while asserting the impossibility of ever loving him. The crime stands in the way of their sexual union, and their relationship—like that between Séverine and Roubaud after Grandmorin's murder—remains sexless and mutually distrusting.[50]

By making the duke, rather than Bruno, her accomplice, Renée ends up condemning the latter instead of saving him. As a series of plot twists implicate the general's secretary, it becomes clear that Renée's plans to avoid judicial suspicion have endangered his life. Rachilde's protagonist subsequently tries to exonerate him through a series of attempted confessions. The first example occurs in Chapter Nine, when Renée escapes the marital home, only to chance upon the police discovering the crime scene and disinterring Barthelme's corpse. Tired of her ongoing pretence and hoping to clear Bruno's name, she intends to confess her crime once Victorien's corpse is revealed. The Duc de Pluncey, who has followed her, prevents her from doing so: 'Mais M. de Pluncey *n'était pas un bourreau*, il sauvait les gens malgré eux pour les abandonner plus tard à leur conscience' ['But Mr de Pluncey *was not an executioner*—he saved people against their will, to abandon them later to their own conscience'] (*Nono*, 292). Rachilde here plays with the dual meaning of 'bourreau' as executioner and torturer: Pluncey may wish to save Renée from the gallows, but only because he prefers that she torture *herself* with remorse. Not only this, but he is happy to let an innocent (and lower-class) man be executed in Renée's place, thereby saving the family name from public opprobrium. When Renée later visits Bruno's former sweetheart, the duke accompanies her, ostensibly for support—'Nous aurons la complicité qu'il vous plaira d'avoir madame' ['Madame, we will be as complicit as you wish us to be'] (*Nono*, 302)—but secretly to undermine her good intentions. In a melodramatic scene, Renée confesses to Amélie and asks her to hand over Bruno's love letters, which could help prove the duchess's guilt in court. Amélie lies about having kept the

---

[50] This pattern, of criminal complicity destroying a couple's harmony and sex life, can also be found in *Thérèse Raquin*, where Camille's ghost lies each night between the newly married (and formerly adulterous) couple.

letters and destroys them later that night.[51] Edmond then counteracts Renée's confession by passing her off as hysterical—an interpretation which Amélie and her husband are eager to accept, in order to avoid having any 'démêlés' ['problems'] with the police and to benefit from the bribe that buys their silence (*Nono*, 312). The episode concludes ambiguously: 'Le duc pouvait être content. Le résultat qu'il avait voulu obtenir en sacrifiant sa dignité devant un pharmacien était obtenu... et désormais la duchesse, sa femme, serait vraiment folle!...' ['The duke could feel satisfied. The result he had wished to achieve by sacrificing his dignity in front of a pharmacist had been obtained... and now the duchess, his wife, truly would be mad!...'] (*Nono*, 313). The word 'résultat' implies that the duke's actions constitute an active ploy to frame Renée's confessions as the ravings of a madwoman, thereby casting an ironic shadow over the word 'vraiment'. As Melanie Hawthorne notes, the principal drama in *Nono*'s final chapters 'rests on the irony that the murderer is unable to make her confessions credible', and it is Renée's decision to marry the duke that 'proves her undoing'.[52] By accepting Edmond's bribe and destroying Bruno's letters, Amélie and her husband become complicit with Edmond's plot to ensure a miscarriage of justice, in the name of honour-defending vengeance. Through these failed confession scenes, Rachilde emphasises the tragic inevitability of her lovers' fate and the ways in which shared knowledge can be manipulated to condemn an innocent man.

Unlike Séverine and Renée, Malot's heroine successfully uses confession to her own ends, to alleviate her guilty conscience and shift blame onto her accomplice. After initially having no qualms about poisoning her first husband to marry La Vaupalière, Hortense feels some remorse when she falls in love with Méderic (*Complices*, 263–4). To assuage her guilt, Hortense confesses to her childhood priest, Abbé Charles, who immediately sees through her act of contrition: 'c'était trop un plaidoyer, pas assez une confession' ['it was too much like a legal defence, and not enough like a confession'] (*Complices*, 278). Malot confirms the superficiality of Hortense's performance by describing the ease with which she lightens her conscience:

Bien que l'abbé Charles lui eût durement refusé l'absolution qu'elle espérait lui arracher, elle s'en revint très satisfaite de son voyage. [...] [Il] lui imposerait les pénitences les plus douloureuses qu'il pourrait inventer. Et après? Nous ne sommes plus au moyen âge où les pénitences étaient réellement des actes d'expiation. Elle accomplirait celles qu'il lui donnerait, et tout serait fini. (*Complices*, 280)

---

[51] In a similar gesture, Camy-Lamotte destroys the note that Séverine wrote to lure Grandmorin into Roubaud's trap, after initially keeping it as a safeguard. See *LBH*, pp. 1118 and 1317.
[52] Hawthorne, *Rachilde*, pp. 126 and 128.

[Although Father Charles had harshly refused to give her the absolution she was hoping to wrest from him, she came away incredibly satisfied with her trip. [...] [He] would make her undertake the most painful forms of penitence he could imagine. And afterwards? We are no longer in the Middle Ages, when religious punishments were true acts of expiation. She would complete the ones he gave her, and that would be that.]

This section of the narrative appears to adopt Hortense's voice through free indirect speech, while implicating the reader through the first-person plural ('Nous ne sommes plus [...]'). The brief question ('Et après?') and summarising statement ('et tout serait fini') simplify and banalise a serious crime. While there is an implicit indictment in Malot's depiction of Hortense's nonchalance, supposedly reflecting modern morality, there is also a degree of humour that offsets the novel's moralising gesture. This blend of criticism and mockery reappears in the trial against the two accomplices, when Hortense offers the jury and court audience a public confession on par with a theatrical performance: 'Quel spectacle avait jamais valu celui-là, en pleine chair palpitante?' ['What show had ever been as good as this one, thrillingly performed in the flesh?'] (*Complices*, 422). When performing at the witness stand, Hortense claims to be repeating in public the private confession to Abbé Charles, and cites this earlier action as proof of her honesty and contrition. Given the expedience of Hortense's earlier confession, she clearly manipulates appearances for the jury's benefit, while conveniently relying on the seal of confessional, which prevents priests from giving evidence in court. Through the structure of dramatic irony, Malot's readers perceive that the novel's fictional jury exonerate Hortense because she gives a better performance than La Vaupalière, re-writing the past and displacing the blame to avoid judicial punishment.

## Complicit with Injustice: Trial Scenes

Depictions of the justice system in fin-de-siècle murder fiction highlight the processes by which complicit silence and judicial know-how can shift blame away from the primary culprits and lead to miscarriages of justice. In *Nono* and *La Bête humaine*, this leads to the accusation and condemnation of innocent men in the murderer's stead. 'Innocent' in both the judicial and sexual sense, Nono and Cabuche experience a doomed, chaste romance that predates events in the novel, before falling in love with another, less sexually innocent, woman. They also provide the ideal scapegoat for a justice system unable (or unwilling) to uncover the truth behind the crimes being judged.[53] Each narrative depicts the characters' naivety with pathos and irony. Consider, for example, Rachilde's description of Nono's love for Amélie Nevasson: 'Nono n'avait pas de passion. Nono, adorable et naïf jusqu'au ridicule, ne connaissait pas les femmes. Nono aimait sa Lilie, Lilie en robe montante, voilà tout!' ['Nono did not experience passion. Nono, adorable and naïve to ridiculous extremes, knew nothing about women. Nono loved his Lilie, Lilie with her high-necked dresses, and that was it!'] (*Nono*, 53). By combining the adjectives 'adorable' and 'naïf' with the noun 'ridicule', Rachilde encourages an ironic reading of Nono's idealising approach to love. However, the narrative voice is ambiguous in the last sentence, where the exclamation 'voilà tout!' reads as free indirect discourse channelling Nono's uncomplicated vision of amorous relations. In a similar gesture, Zola describes Cabuche as a gentle giant, whose seeming savagery involves a simpler relation to desire than that experienced by Jacques Lantier: his face reveals 'un besoin de soumission tendre' ['an instinctive need to be submissive and loving'] (*LBH*, 1098).[54] Yet the characters' submissiveness to, and respect for, their idealised love objects works against them. We see this when Bruno fails to ignore Amélie's protestations about receiving more kisses from him (which she secretly desires but outwardly rejects),[55] and when Cabuche discovers Séverine's corpse and protects her modesty:

[Il] la saisit d'un élan fraternel, à pleins bras, la souleva, la posa sur le lit, dont il rejeta le drap, pour la couvrir. Mais, dans cette étreinte, l'unique tendresse entre eux, il s'était couvert de sang, les deux mains, la poitrine. Il ruisselait de son sang. (*LBH*, 1300)

[He] seized her in his arms as a brother might and lifted her on to the bed, folding back the sheet to cover her. But in the course of this embrace, this one moment of intimacy between them, he had got blood all over himself, on his chest and both his hands. He was streaming with her blood.][56]

By doing so, he is caught at the scene covered in Séverine's blood, thereby validating others' suspicions regarding his involvement in the crime.[57] Respecting

---

[53] Susan Blood considers René Girard's theory of the scapegoat as a means to maintain social order in 'The Precinematic Novel', noting that the irony present in *LBH* points more towards social disintegration than to social order (pp. 59–60).
[54] Zola, trans. Pearson, p. 114.
[55] See Rachilde, *Nono*, p. 56.
[56] Zola, trans. Pearson, p. 333.
[57] Cf. *Le Ventre de Paris*, where Florent is wrongly arrested for political agitation, after being found on the barricades with his hands covered in blood. This blood in fact came from the corpse of an anonymous woman, shot by soldiers on the rue Vivienne, as part of the violent suppression of opposition to the December 1851 coup. See Zola, *Les Rougon-Macquart*, I (1960), pp. 610–12.

Séverine's modesty gets Cabuche unjustly framed, tried, and condemned for murder. These narratives therefore suggest that male sexual innocence and chaste respect for women are self-defeating within a society whose predominant mode of masculine sexuality is one of aggression and possessiveness, as epitomised by Lantier's murderous desires. Although there is implicit critique of the sexual double standard and masculine sexuality in the novels, through the reader's awareness of the injustice of the trial scene outcomes, the ineluctable narrative logic of doomed male chastity seems to offer little room for alternative models of amorous union.

Nono and Cabuche show ignorance not only of sexual matters but also of judicial procedure. They are unable to explain or understand the murders of which they stand accused. Their lack of judicial expertise—which exists alongside, and is intertwined with, their sexual naivety—ultimately leads to their condemnation. In *Nono*, Bruno is repeatedly associated with verbs relating to ignorance. The novel's opening pages state that 'je ne sais pas' is his preferred response to most questions: 'C'était le mot de Bruno. Il ne savait jamais' ['That was Bruno's catchphrase. He never had a clue'] (*Nono*, 7). This seemingly irrelevant detail becomes significant later in the novel, when Bruno is unable to explain the presence of a letter, addressed to him, found in Victorien's remains. His only response is his catchphrase: 'Il lut la lettre, puis il la laissa tomber par terre.—Je ne sais pas! murmura-t-il. Ce fut tout. Nono avait compris qu'il était perdu' ['He read the letter, then let it fall to the ground. "I don't know!" he muttered. That was all. Nono had realised he was doomed'] (*Nono*, 298). Bruno's inability to explain the increasingly damning evidence contributes to his condemnation. Cabuche finds himself in a similar situation when he is interrogated about the gloves and handkerchiefs found in his woodland home. Too ashamed of his feelings for Séverine to explain his magpie-like hoarding, he can do nothing but repeat Bruno's phrase, 'je ne sais pas': 'il restait hébété, il répétait à chaque question qu'il ne savait pas. Pour les gants et les mouchoirs, il ne savait pas. Pour la montre, il ne savait pas. On l'embêtait, on n'avait qu'à le laisser tranquille et à le guillotiner tout de suite' ['he just sat there in a daze, repeatedly answering every question by saying that he didn't know. Gloves? Handkerchiefs? He didn't know. Watch? He didn't know. These people were getting on his nerves: why couldn't they just leave him alone and have him guillotined straightaway?'] (*LBH*, 1310).[58] The inability to explain events satisfactorily becomes a sign for criminal guilt. When faced with an overwhelming accumulation of uncanny and unfortunate coincidences Cabuche and Bruno can only respond with confusion to the events that have piled up against them.

It is not only unfortunate coincidence that condemns the innocent male characters in *Nono* and *La Bête humaine*, but judicial prejudice: they happen to fit into pre-existing models of criminality. For example, Cabuche is a 'repris de justice'

---

[58] Zola, trans. Pearson, p. 344.

['ex-convict'], having previously served a prison sentence for accidentally killing a man in a fight (*LBH*, 1091). Cabuche's status as an ex-convict renders him socially and criminally suspect by default, therefore justifying his mistreatment and false imprisonment.[59] Zola presents other characters' interpretations of Cabuche in narrative vignettes that are shot through with dramatic irony, including the first interrogation scene in Denizet's office: 'Saisi brutalement au fond de son trou, [...] il avait déjà, avec son effarement et sa blouse déchirée, l'air louche du prévenu, cet air de bandit sournois que la prison donne au plus honnête homme' ['Brutally seized from his lair [...] he had already assumed, with his torn smock and terrified demeanour, the shifty air of the accused man, that look of a cunning bandit which prison confers upon even the most upright of men'] (*LBH*, 1098).[60] The treatment Cabuche receives starkly contrasts with the polite and collusive atmosphere of the interrogations preceding his entrance, where Denizet ensures that the witness statements for the Lachesnaye couple and Mrs Bonnehon are purged of any incriminating evidence (*LBH*, 1093). It also reflects typical police procedure in the era, where suspects—particularly those of the lower classes—were considered guilty until proven innocent.[61] In this context, Cabuche's physical appearance—his 'blouse déchirée', 'air louche', and 'air de bandit sournois'—acts as unofficial evidence justifying Denizet's presumption of his guilt. Later in the novel, a similar prejudice frames the trial audience's interpretation of Cabuche: 'il était bien tel qu'on se l'imaginait, vêtu d'une longue blouse bleue, le type même de l'assassin, des poings énormes, des mâchoires de carnassier, enfin un de ces gaillards qu'il ne fait pas bon rencontrer au coin d'un bois' ['he was just as they had imagined him, dressed in a long, blue smock, the very picture of a murderer, with his enormous fists and great, carnivorous jaws, in short just the kind of person one would not wish to come upon in the middle of a dark wood'] (*LBH*, 1320).[62] Zola here satirises the criminological theory inspired by Lombroso's work on the 'born criminal', where certain physical traits express an individual's innate criminality. He also hints at the socially constructed nature of criminal typology. For example, the verb 'imaginer' situates the audience's viewpoint within the realm of a shared social, cultural, and moral imaginary, where appearances can be read according to pre-formed typologies. Similarly, the syntagm 'un de ces' is a marker of generalisation and *idées reçues* ['received wisdom']. Realist fiction abounds with these markers, because verisimilitude necessarily depends on the reader's recognition of normative types. The communal nature of received wisdom brings together ideas, discourses, and people, implicating the latter in the consequences of actions influenced by these shared preconceptions, in a form of cultural complicity.

---

[59] On nineteenth-century anxieties about recidivism, see Nye, *Crime, Madness and Politics*, pp. 49–96.
[60] Zola, trans. Pearson, p. 114.
[61] Cragin, *Murder in Parisian Streets*, p. 194.
[62] Zola, trans. Pearson, p. 355.

Shared cultural forms, notably the written word, transmit received wisdom. Cabuche's lack of education, his probable illiteracy, and his general lack of cultural know-how therefore place him at a distinct disadvantage when perceived through the lens of others' judgement. In this way he differs to Bruno Maldas, who, as General Fayor's secretary, takes on a position akin to a ghost writer by transcribing and editing his employer's memoirs and political speeches. He does so with a degree of success and flair that is commented on by other characters in the novel.[63] While Cabuche remains an unwitting scapegoat whose ignorance prevents him from mastering the justice system, Bruno, by the time he faces trial, actively manipulates criminological discourses and judicial preconceptions in order to ensure a guilty verdict. When addressing the jury, he uses knowledge of others' prejudices to achieve self-condemnation, by deliberately playing up to the role of an unrepentant criminal: 'Messieurs, dit-il d'un ton ferme, je suis un monstre; je le reconnais et m'en fais gloire! [...] Vous n'avez pas pitié d'un de vos semblables... je vous souhaite de n'avoir jamais rencontré votre rival à la portée d'une roche branlante' ['"Sirs," he said firmly: "I am a monster. I acknowledge it with pride! [...] You have no pity for your own kind... I hope that you never meet your rival within reach of a precariously balanced boulder"'] (*Nono*, 339). By proudly confessing to Victorien's murder, and by emphasising his lack of remorse, Bruno undermines any mitigating circumstances a crime of passion might otherwise have granted him. He also disables any argument in favour of his rehabilitation by asserting that, if pardoned or released, he will murder the first woman who falls in love with him (*Nono*, 339). At each stage of this self-implicating confession, Bruno evokes fin-de-siècle legal debates: crimes of passion, mitigating circumstances, Lombroso's 'born criminal', and recidivism.[64] Furthermore, in the phrase 'un de vos semblables', Bruno posits his audience as equally capable of, and therefore morally complicit in, his crime, while framing the jury's condemnation of him as hypocritical.

Bruno's ability to make this speech marks his sudden transition from 'le doux naïf' ['the sweet innocent'] to masterful manipulator and cynic (even if his cynical posturing is ultimately a mask). After the duke informs him of Renée's guilt, Nono adopts an interpretative role that manipulates both actual evidence and the 'proof' that goes without saying ('évidences'). Like Denizet in *La Bête humaine*, who rejects the possibility of Jacques as Séverine's murderer in favour of an 'assassin évident' ['obvious murderer'] (*LBH*, 1308),[65] Nono creates an explanatory vision of the murder that adheres to psychological, social, and judicial prejudices, which the audience and jury will accept as true, but which is ultimately false.

---

[63] During one of General Fayor's public speeches, an undercover police inspector, pretending to be a servant of Fayor's rival, Edmond de Pluncey, says to Nono: 'vous avez fièrement fait gloser votre général' ['you interpreted your general with remarkable boldness'] (*Nono*, p. 187).

[64] For further information about these legal debates, see Nye, *Crime, Madness and Politics*, pp. 49–131.

[65] Zola, trans. Pearson, p. 341.

But unlike Denizet, he manipulates these prejudices for altruistic ends, rather than perpetuating them unreflectingly. By learning this skill, Bruno becomes less like Zola's scapegoat than Malot's heroine, whose successful performance ensures her freedom. As part of a well-established comparison between criminal court proceedings and theatre, Hortense takes on the role of an actress who performs a melodramatic rendering of her own life: 'Quel spectacle avait jamais valu celui-là, en pleine chair palpitante?' ['What show had ever been as good as this one, thrillingly performed in the flesh?'] (*Complices*, 422). In addition to her acting skills, Hortense wields the creative power of a playwright. During the trial, La Vaupalière listens to his accomplice's 'récit' ['story'] and is astounded by 'l'art diabolique avec lequel la vérité était arrangée' ['the diabolical artistry with which the truth was laid out'] (*Complices*, 423). The character's implied critique of Hortense's capacity to manipulate the truth exists alongside his begrudging respect for her creativity and self-possession. In this way, Hortense, like Bruno, becomes a symbol for literary authorship: a profession that relies on a talent for creating convincing fictions that, when presented in the realist mode, are conveyed as 'truth'.

The comparison between legal courts and theatre has clear meta-literary implications, which work in tandem with references to the role of literature and press media in inspiring crime and facilitating injustice. In *Complices*, for example, Hortense draws inspiration from 'un livre de voyage sur l'Italie' ['a travel book about Italy'] for her initial plot to make her husband sleep soundly as she switches off the alarm system at night (*Complices*, 89). Similarly, in *La Bête humaine*, Séverine uses ideas found in novels when plotting Roubaud's murder with Jacques (*LBH*, 1289). Through *mise en abyme*, these references affirm fin-de-siècle fears about literature's capacity to incite, encourage, or enable crime, by providing instructional precedents for would-be criminals to follow. At the same time, the novels demonstrate the importance of journalism as a medium for debating courtroom dramas and influencing public opinion around crime. Preceding and during the trial in *Complices*, Médéric supports Hortense's case by courting newspapers to ensure that they report positively on her character: 'il avait compris bien vite de quelle importance il était pour elle qu'elle eût une bonne presse, surtout un bon public' ['he had quickly understood how important it was for her to have a good press, and above all a good audience'] (*Complices*, 379). Public debate and gossip clearly influence the legal outcomes in each work, by prejudicing the reaction of trial audience and jury members, whether that be in favour of Hortense's liberation or to condemn the innocent outcasts Bruno and Cabuche. For example, while Bruno is awaiting trial in *Nono*, the public assess his character according to cliché and hearsay rather than actual evidence: 'Les uns se représentaient Bruno comme un rustre sournois rempli de passions sauvages malgré son instruction. Les autres, comme un vicieux sadique tuant pour le simple plaisir de tuer, mais ayant l'esprit de cacher ses victimes et ses vices' ['Some people saw Bruno as a cunning ruffian full of wild passions, despite his education. Others imagined him as a perverted sadist who killed for the mere pleasure of it, but who had the presence of mind to hide his victims and his vices'] (*Nono*, 317). It is because of such prejudice that Bruno is able to play up to criminal typologies and claim to be a monster without having to substantiate his claims. He simply affirms their pre-existing prejudices, which ignore the lack of corroborating evidence.

By depicting the influence of literature and the press on unjust criminal trial outcomes, Rachilde, Zola, and Malot criticised the criminal justice system while implicating their own literary practice in such injustice. Parodying social discourses about criminality, they highlighted the ease with which responsibility and blame could be displaced onto innocent victims of cultural prejudice, and the extent to which literature was complicit with this process. As producers of crime fiction, the novelists participated in the phenomena they critiqued, and the metaliterary references peppered through their works offer a self-aware nod towards the genre's double bind. Such references also implicate the novels' readers, who inhabit a morally ambivalent position as witness, confessor, and judge of criminal actions that largely go unpunished. By combining moral uncertainty, social satire, and self-implication in their narratives, each of the three authors participated in a wider cultural phenomenon that aligned criminal complicity with artistic creation and performance. This comparison featured predominantly in works by avant-garde writers of the period, who, in a range of fiction and spoof journalism, celebrated the transgressive elements of criminality in a more open and deliberate manner. Playfully twisting the arguments of their more conservative, traditionalist contemporaries, marginal writers transformed the question of murder and criminal complicity into a source of literary solidarity and cross-media collaboration.

## 'Murderer Literature'

In the opening issue of *La Revue blanche*'s Parisian series, the writer-journalist Maurice Beaubourg remarked upon his contemporaries' growing obsession with murder.[66] Loosely disguised as a personal anecdote, the article functions as both literary criticism and self-promotion for its author's recently published work, *Contes pour les assassins* [*Tales for Murderers*] (1891). Adopting a faux-naif satirical tone, Beaubourg recounts having recently sat next to a flea-ridden ruffian on a

---

[66] *La Revue blanche* was first published in Belgium, from December 1889, before moving offices to Paris in 1891. Initially run by Auguste Jeunehomme, Joe Högge, and the brothers Paul and Charles Leclerq, in 1891 the Natanson brothers (Thadée, Louis-Alfred, and Alexandre) took over and remained in control until the final issue (April 1903). As a prominent 'little magazine' (*petite revue*), *La Revue blanche*'s content was eclectic and international in nature, combining literature, theatre, music, and the visual arts. It promoted young talent, expanded avant-garde artistic networks, and established its own publishing house in 1893. On the review's contributions to fin-de-siècle French culture, see Janet Bergman-Carton, '*La Revue Blanche*: Art, Commerce, and Culture in the French fin-de-siècle', *Nineteenth-Century Contexts* 30, no. 2 (2008): pp. 167–89, doi: 10.1080/08905490802212458.

park bench. Despite his appearance, Beaubourg's interlocutor reveals himself to be an educated man from a similar social milieu: 'Malgré les haillons qui le couvrait, il avait un esprit orné, paré' ['Despite the rags which covered him, his mind was embellished and well adorned']. The pair fall into conversation, discussing 'l'utilité non seulement physique mais moral du meurtre' ['the not only physical but moral utility of murder'] and the recent works of writers, including Zola and Rachilde, 'qui patronnaient l'assassinat dans des opuscules' ['who wrote short works in support of murder']. To refer to this phenomenon, Beaubourg's companion coins the term 'la Littérature des assassins' ['Murderer Literature'].[67] The word 'des' in the term 'littérature des assassins' is playfully ambiguous, since it could be interpreted as literature that is *about* murderers, *for* murderers, or *by* murderers. This ambiguity blurs the ethical boundaries between characters, readers, and writers. The term's expanded definition reads as follows:

> [Il] m'expliquait comme quoi M. *Zola*, le créateur du Lantier de la BÊTE HUMAINE, avait véritablement fondé l'école, en niant la responsabilité des individus, et en démontrant que les donneurs de coups de couteaux ne faisaient que remplir une des fonctions naturelles de leur existence [...].
> Mme *Rachilde*, dans un livre bien plus curieux encore [*La Sanglante Ironie*], [...] avait empiré sur la théorie du maître de Médan. [...] Si chez Mme Rachilde les meurtriers se montraient les seuls gens intéressants, ils apparaissaient dans le À L'ÉCART de MM. *Minhar* et *Vallette* les seuls vraiment artistes et philosophes. Il fallait absolument avoir assassiné quelqu'un, pensaient ces auteurs, pour pouvoir saisir et étudier le jeu de sa personnalité. (*LLA*, 39)

> [He explained to me how Mr Zola, the creator of Lantier in *La Bête humaine*, was the school's true founder, by denying individual responsibility and demonstrating that purveyors of stab wounds were merely fulfilling one of the natural functions of their existence [...].
> Mrs Rachilde, in an even more curious book [*La Sanglante Ironie*], [...] had taken Professor Medan's theory to worse extremes. [...] If, in Mrs Rachilde's works, murderers proved to be the only people worthy of interest, then in *À l'écart*, by Messrs. Minhar and Vallette, they appeared to be the only true artists and philosophers. It was absolutely necessary to have killed someone, these authors thought, to study and understand the inner workings of one's character.]

In this section, Beaubourg brings together writers working in difference schools and sub-genres—Naturalism, Decadence, and the *roman psychologique*, respectively—to form a literary family or network that valorises murder against

---

[67] Maurice Beaubourg, 'La Littérature des assassins', *La Revue blanche*, Oct. 1891, pp. 35–41 (p. 38). References will henceforth appear parenthetically in the text, preceded by the abbreviation: *LLA*.

the grain. Yet there is a clear hierarchy established between these literary schools: murder evolves from a natural impulse in Zola to an aesthetic object in Rachilde, before finally achieving the status of an artistic imperative in Minhar and Vallette.

Beaubourg's presentation of murderer literature creates a form of illicit solidarity between the writers he analyses, who are united by their family resemblance and shared tendency to valorise murder, regardless of their real-life sympathies or antipathies. This solidarity extends towards a 'knowing' targeted reader, who is expected to appreciate the article's irony and paradoxes. The article closes with a representation of such collusive literary relationships via *mise en abyme*, when the drinking companion expresses his regret at never having met Maurice Beaubourg, who, as the article's reader knows, is the very person to whom he is speaking. In an effusive exclamation, Beaubourg subsequently reveals his identity:

—Maurice Beaubourg!... m'écriai-je suffoqué, mais c'est moi!...
Et nous tombâmes dans les bras l'un de l'autre.
Depuis lors je me suis affligé d'un secrétaire, qui n'est au fond qu'un complice anticipé! (*LLA*, 40–1)

['Maurice Beaubourg!...' I exclaimed, astounded, 'but that's me!...'
And we fell into each other's arms.
Ever since then, I have been burdened with a secretary, who is basically nothing more than a future accomplice!]

The ending creates an important link between literary camaraderie and criminal complicity: a friend acting as a 'secrétaire' becomes '[un] complice anticipé'. Yet the tone of the final exclamation is undeniably ambivalent, since the verb 's'affliger' negatively contrasts with the affectionate embrace described in the preceding sentence. This off-note in the article's denouement hints at the ambiguity of complicit literary friendships and the burden of solidarity—a topic examined further in Chapter 4, which analyses a literary friendship network demonstrating the ambivalence suggested in Beaubourg's otherwise humorous and celebratory article.

In 'La Littérature des assassins', Beaubourg depicts a sliding scale of viewpoints, from murder considered as a natural impulse to murder considered as an aesthetic object and artistic imperative. Continuing a satirical tradition pioneered by Thomas de Quincey in 'On Murder Considered as One of the Fine Arts' (1827), the art-murder analogy appeared across an array of fin-de-siècle novels and newspaper articles penned by avant-garde writers.[68] As a taboo topic, murder facilitated a specific form of paradoxical literary position-taking, based on the valorisation

---

[68] On Decadent writers' adoption of De Quincey's art-murder analogy to parody authoritative discourses and to reformulate *l'art pour l'art* ['art for art's sake'], see Kalifa, *L'Encre et le sang*, p. 188 and Downing, *The Subject of Murder*, p. 10.

of illicit ethical and aesthetic values. This tendency is apparent in works by Octave Mirbeau that depicted murder as a natural urge from which society benefits while hypocritically condemning it. Throughout the late 1880s and 1890s, Mirbeau published a series of articles on the topic of murder, which he later amalgamated to create the 'Frontispiece' to *Le Jardin des supplices* (1899). An early example includes 'L'École de l'Assassinat', published in *Le Figaro* on 23 June 1889.[69] The article opens with a description of the public's pleasure in shooting human-like figures at local fairs. It subsequently argues that such amusements provide an outlet for innate murderous desires, which are encouraged by society and its institutions: 'Le besoin de tuer naît chez l'homme avec le besoin de manger, et se confond avec lui. Ce besoin instinctif qui est la base, le moteur de tous les organismes vivants, l'éducation le développe, au lieu de le réfréner' ['Man's urge to kill is born with his urge to eat, and merges with it. Rather than holding it back, education develops this instinctive urge, which is the foundation and driving force of all living organisms']. Mirbeau goes on to define war as 'la suprême synthèse de l'éternelle et universelle folie du meurtre' ['the ultimate synthesis of the timeless and universal obsession with murder'], concluding that society should not condemn murderers, since it encourages the so-called 'crime' for its own purposes. By reversing the widely held moral proscription of murder, the article adopts a paradoxical position while highlighting the contradictions between French society's apparent values (whether moral, religious, or political) and the actions committed or justified by its constituent members.

Mirbeau returns to this question in the post-prandial discussion between male intellectuals and politicians in the 'Frontispiece' to *Le Jardin des supplices*.[70] During the conversation, a member of the 'Académie des sciences morales et politiques' claims:

> S'il n'y avait plus de meurtre, il n'y aurait plus de gouvernements d'aucune sorte, par ce fait admirable que le crime en général, et le meurtre en particulier sont, non seulement leur excuse, mais leur unique raison d'être... Nous vivrions alors en pleine anarchie, ce qui ne peut se concevoir...[71]

> [If there were no murder, government of any sort would be inconceivable. For the admirable fact is that crime in general, and murder in particular, not simply

---

[69] Mirbeau re-published this text, with minor changes, as 'La Loi du Meurtre', in *L'Écho de Paris*, 24 May 1892.

[70] Published at the height of the Dreyfus affair, *Le Jardin des supplices* attacked bourgeois corruption and colonial violence, while offering an ambivalent moral position laced with violent eroticism. The central narrative describes the male protagonist's relationship with a mysterious *femme fatale* called Clara, who gives him a guided tour of the different forms of torture practised in a Chinese prison.

[71] Octave Mirbeau, *Le Jardin des supplices*, ed. Michel Delon (Paris: Gallimard, 1991), p. 44. References will henceforth appear parenthetically in the text, preceded by the abbreviation: *LJS*.

excuse it, but represents its only reason to exist... Otherwise we would live in complete anarchy, something we find unimaginable...']^72

In this opening section, Mirbeau subverts the social defence approach to criminal justice by suggesting that society is in fact best defended by encouraging crime rather than by preventing it. His *académicien* character goes on to affirm that 'natural' murderous instincts are given legal outlets ('exutoires légaux'), including colonial expansion, war, hunting, and antisemitism (*LJS*, 45). Above all, war epitomises 'l'éternelle et universelle folie du meurtre, du meurtre régularisé, enrégimenté, obligatoire, et qui est une fonction nationale' ['the eternal and universal folly of murder—murder regulated, registered and made compulsory as a national occupation'] (*LJS*, 53)[73]—a phrase lifted from Mirbeau's earlier newspaper articles. This view reappears later in the novel when a weapons designer associates social progress with homicidal efficiency: 'Nous vivons sous la loi de la guerre [...]. Pour la rendre de plus en plus meurtrière et expéditive il s'agit de trouver des engins de destructions de plus en plus formidables... C'est une question d'humanité... et c'est aussi le progrès moderne' ['We live subject to the laws of war [...]. To make it more murderous and expeditious you need to find more and more formidable engines of destruction. It's a matter of humanity... and modern progress'] (*LJS*, 121).[74] Mirbeau here ironises discourses surrounding scientific and technological progress, as well as the ethical language used to promote them ('humanité', 'progrès'). In so doing, he opposed traditional moral authority, while adopting a counter-discursive, paradoxical, and humorous literary position typical of the avant-garde.

While Mirbeau's works featured intellectual discussions among non-practising pro-murderers, Rachilde and Beaubourg depicted murderer characters who highlight society's hypocrisy in condemning murder and assert its societal value. Rachilde frequently explored morbid themes in her Decadent works, notably thematising criminal complicity in *Nono*. She returned to the topic of murder in *La Sanglante Ironie* (1891): a bildungsroman framed as an autobiographical confession by a convicted murderer awaiting execution. The opening frame text reveals the narrator-protagonist Sylvain d'Hauterac's glorification of murder, considered a natural human urge, and of murderers, referred to as 'philosophes opérants' ['philosophers in action'].[75] He reverses the logic of fin-de-siècle depopulation fears by asserting the social utility of murder through an extended medical analogy, claiming that '[le] sang habilement répandu fait la santé des corps, et trop de sang conservé mène à la pourriture' ['deftly spilt blood makes the body healthy,

---

[72] Octave Mirbeau, *Torture Garden*, trans. Michael Richardson (Sawtry: Dedalus, 2010), p. 18.
[73] Mirbeau, trans. Richardson, p. 26.
[74] Mirbeau, trans. Richardson, p. 84.
[75] Rachilde, *La Sanglante Ironie* (Paris: L. Genonceaux, 1891), p. 3. References will henceforth appear parenthetically in the text, with the abbreviation: *LSI*.

whereas retaining too much of it leads to corruption'] (*LSI*, 6). By evoking the notion of bloodletting—'cette si necessaire périodique saignée des peuples' ['this very necessary regular human bloodletting'] (*LSI*, 5)—Sylvain aligns historical medical practices with violent warfare, in a way that justifies the latter within a quasi-scientific framework, akin to social Darwinism. However, Sylvain's 'logic' weakens as a result of the hyperbolic, obsessive nature of his confession, which betrays the character's mental instability.[76] In this way, the narrative encourages its readers to question the validity of Sylvain's arguments, and thereby renders ambiguous the work's supposedly evident celebration of murder.

A similar ambiguity lies at the heart of Maurice Beaubourg's short fiction of the same period. Appearing in 1890 with a preface by Maurice Barrès, *Contes pour les assassins* contained a selection of short prose pieces depicting criminal association while satirising elements of criminal narrative.[77] As previously mentioned, Beaubourg indirectly promoted this work at the end of the 'murderer literature' article appearing in *La Revue blanche*. The longest story of the collection, 'Moi!', depicts the budding relationship and criminal association between the middle-aged protagonist-narrator Jérôme Polydor and a youth called Eloi Chandouillette, as well as their unsuccessful murder attempts.[78] After discussing their mutual hatred of police officers at a concert in Luxembourg garden, the pair join forces to commit a murder, much to Jérôme's delight:

L'espérance de devenir le complice d'un malfaiteur, but secret de mon existence altérieure, malfaiteur moi-même... c'est l'essence intime de mon individu,... et un peu de franchise, voyons,... de chaque... Parfaitement,... de chaque individu !... cette espérance effaçait tout à mes yeux !... (*Contes*, 24)

[The hope of becoming a criminal's accomplice, the secret ambition of my former life, and a criminal myself... it is the very essence of my character.... and, let's be honest, that of everyone... that's right,... everyone's character!... this hope eclipsed all else in my view!...]

---

[76] A bibliographical notice of *La Sanglante Ironie*, appearing in *L'Intransigeant* on 14 February 1891, confirms the contemporary perception of Sylvain's excessive character traits: 'C'est une bizarre étude de l'amour du néant chez un jeune homme sentimental, du pessimisme tournant à la manie du crime dans un cerveau exaspéré pas [sic] les mesquineries et les brutalités de l'existence' ['It is a peculiar study of a young sentimental man's love for nothingness, of pessimism turned to criminal insanity in a mind pushed beyond its limits by the mean and brutal nature of existence'].

[77] Maurice Beaubourg, *Contes pour les assassins* (Paris: Perrin, 1890). 'L'Intermédiaire' (pp. 127–40) ironises the role played by periodical culture in the dissemination of criminal stories by advertising a journal that acts as an intermediary between murderers and would-be victims. 'Célestin Gardanne' (pp. 143–207) satirises the overly analytical approaches of scientific discourse and psychological novels. 'Le Drame de la route de Tremuth' (pp. 245–61) parodies the crime fiction genre by reconstructing the potential events leading to a crime, before openly acknowledging the detective work to be pure fiction.

[78] Beaubourg, *Contes*, pp. 9–123. References will henceforth appear parenthetically in the text.

Beaubourg here depicts a character who claims to reveal the universal nature of murderous desire, while criticising the moral hypocrisy of those who condemn him for committing openly and 'sans rougir' ['without shame'] what they commit 'tout bas, en catimini' ['quietly, on the sly'] (*Contes*, 120). By centring his characters' opinions in the story, Beaubourg seems tacitly to endorse them. Having said that, Jérôme frequently appears unreliable and deranged. The frame text describes his seclusion in an asylum and the main text betrays the narrator's mental imbalance through the presence of hyperbole, self-absorption, and incoherent sentences punctuated liberally with ellipses and exclamations. Not only this, but the accomplices' murder attempt is a failure, and their association swiftly deteriorates as the narrative progresses. By depicting Jérôme's mental instability and failed criminal urges, Beaubourg maintains an ironic distance that offsets the character's hyperbolic and paradoxical claims.

While Jérome Polydor is clearly an unreliable narrator, he becomes the mouthpiece for Beaubourg's paradoxical position-taking on the topic of murder. Like Sylvain d'Hauterac in *La Sanglante Ironie*, Jérôme adopts politically charged and 'scientific' neo-Malthusian language to justify his destructive urges. First, he imagines a world where the weaker part of the population is killed, leaving the remaining one per cent to repopulate the planet (*Contes*, 40–1). After considering this scenario, he admits that he does not care about repopulating France, and that the top one per cent may not necessarily reinvigorate the population (*Contes*, 43). Instead, he confesses an underlying desire for the entire human race to be destroyed, concluding as follows: 'Si je l'avoue aussi ingénûment, c'est que mon égoïsme et le tour d'esprit agréablement malthusien que je possède, s'en accommodent volontiers. Cependant, je crois préférable de dissimuler encore ce but, et de débiter de nouvelles sornettes utilitaires, pour donner le change aux nigauds' ['If I am able to confess this so openly, it is because my selfish nature and my pleasantly Malthusian mindset can accommodate the idea quite nicely. However, I prefer to keep this goal hidden, and to reel off some fresh utilitarian twaddle, to pull the wool over these simpletons' eyes'] (*Contes*, 45–6). The protagonist's reasoning reveals not only the extreme ideologies to which social Darwinism and neo-Malthusianism could be put, but also their vague theoretical foundations and subsequent capacity to be wielded at cross-purposes to their ostensible aims of human progress. We see this in the flippant way with which Jérôme reduces neo-Malthusian thought to an individual mindset ('tour d'esprit'), aligns it with his own egotistic self-absorption ('égoïsme'), and adopts it out of misanthropic spite ('pour donner le change aux nigauds'). By mocking 'simpletons' willing to believe in utilitarian 'twaddle', Jérôme suggests that such arguments are faulty, while implying that the scientific and political figures who employ them are either as ignorant as their audience or as manipulative and hypocritical as himself. Neither interpretation leaves room for a naïve acceptance of the pro-murder stance depicted in Beaubourg's narrative, and this ambiguity highlights the self-implicating nature of avant-garde paradox, which mocks its own arguments as much as those it claims to refute.

A self-critical edge underlies the avant-garde's polemical assertion not only that murder is morally acceptable and socially useful, but also that it should be considered as an artistic medium. The vision of murder as an autotelic art form appears in the central narrative of *Le Jardin des supplices*, when an executioner discusses with Clara the art of killing well (which he juxtaposes with English colonialist mass murder):

> L'art, milady, consiste à savoir tuer [...]. C'est-à-dire travailler la chair humaine, comme un sculpteur sa glaise ou son morceau d'ivoire... [...] Mais, tout se perd aujourd'hui... [...] tout ce qui rend la mort collective, administrative et bureaucratique... toutes les saletés de votre progrès, enfin... détruisent peu à peu, nos belles traditions du passé... [...] Nous sommes vaincus par les médiocres... Et c'est l'esprit bourgeois qui triomphe partout... (*LJS*, 206–7)

> [Art, milady, consists in knowing how to kill [...]. That means to take the same care over human flesh as a sculptor does over his clay or piece of ivory [...]. But everything today is becoming lost. [...] Everything makes death collective, administrative and bureaucratic. What it amounts to is that all the indecency of your progress is gradually destroying our beautiful traditions of the past. [...] We are being conquered by mediocrity. And everywhere the bourgeois spirit triumphs...][79]

Mirbeau's depiction of the executioner as a maligned artist is clearly an attack against bourgeois culture shot through with serious moral indictment. Yet it also functions ironically, in a self-aware and self-implicating gesture. First, there is the fact that, in different sections of the text, Mirbeau aligns pro-murder positions with members of the bourgeois elite and yet also with the avant-garde rebelling against them. Then, through the executioner figure, Mirbeau satirises avant-garde snobbery that sets itself apart from the mainstream while relying on this mainstream as a source of oppositional self-definition. In this way, the analogy between artist and murderer enables Mirbeau to enact social critique while recognising the ambiguous complicity of his own polemical, avant-garde position.

Mirbeau's playful self-critique recurs in other avant-garde texts which question the value of art or suggest that literature, as an art form, is inferior to murder. In Beaubourg's 'Moi!', Eloi Chandouillette undermines Jérôme Polydor's assertion of murder's autotelic value by claiming that murder is best employed as a means to an end:

[79] Mirbeau, trans. Richardson, pp. 153–4.

On ne découpe pas par l'amour de l'art, et tu n'es qu'un artiste!... Artiste!... Qu'est-ce cela!... Illusoire!... Microzoaire!... Du nerf, voyons, du nerf!... Tue par métier!... Évite toute passion pour ou contre celui que tu assassines,... que le seul profit soit ton guide!... (*Contes*, 29)

[Nobody slits a throat for the love of art, and you are nothing more than an artist!... Artist!... What is an artist? An illusion!... A microscopic life form!... You need to put some welly into it!... Kill for professional reasons!... Avoid any feeling, whether positive or negative, towards the person you are killing... Let profit alone be your guide!]

By describing the artist's role as 'illusory' and 'microscopic', Eloi denigrates the artistic vocation and rejects the comparison between art and murder. Instead, he valorises a pragmatic, dispassionate, and financially driven approach to violent crime. The denigration of art returns towards the end of the narrative, when the protagonist is on the run from the police, after his failed murder attempt and Eloi's rejection. At this point, Jérôme considers alternative career paths, including literary art, which he swiftly rejects: 'L'art? Déchéance!... L'asile de nuit des idiots qui se plaignent sans savoir pourquoi.' ['Art? It's degeneracy!... A temporary shelter for idiots who complain without knowing why!'] (*Contes*, 119). By referring to artists as 'idiots', this quotation undermines the value of the text as a whole. Furthermore, the term 'asile' ['shelter'] indirectly evokes the asylum in which the narrator-protagonist has been forcibly placed. After having contemplated alternative careers, Jérôme concludes: 'Plus je réfléchis, plus je considère que l'assassinat est le seul métier qu'un être méthodique, logique, conscient de lui-même et de son époque, puisse accepter' ['The more I think about it, the more I view murder as the only job that a methodical and logical individual, conscious of himself and of his era, could accept'] (*Contes*, 119). By claiming that murder is a logical career superior to art, Jérôme redeploys Eloi's pragmatic approach, but without clearly delineating the ends to which murder should be put. The incoherence of Jérôme's arguments, taken alongside the frame text's assertion of his insanity, undermines the protagonist's theorising and ironises the murder-as-art analogy.

The meta-literary value of theorising about murder becomes, in its own right, the target of another avant-garde text: 'Théorie rationnelle de l'assassinat propre'. Penned by Romain Coolus in response to Beaubourg's 'La Littérature des assassins', the article ostensibly provides a defence of murder as a professional vocation worthy of unionisation. Nonetheless, throughout the article it becomes clear that Coolus's imagined spokesperson is not himself a member of the murdering profession, but speaks on behalf of practising murderers. He does so because the latter refuse to theorise about their craft, 'prétextant [...] leur inaptitude physique à faire usage de l'instrument des plumatifs, qui est rarement incisif et moins souvent contondant' ['claiming, as a pretext, their physical inability to use the wordsmith's instrument, which is rarely incisive and less frequently blunt'].[80] By describing the writer's pen as an ineffective instrument, Coolus derides a popular analogy between pen and sword, typically used to evoke a writer's capacity to attack enemies and right social wrongs. The implicit suggestion, that a murderer contributes more to society than a writer, parodies and destabilises the 'good influence' model of literature, while valorising murder as superior to literary art. However, the text undermines its own validity by depicting a writer ('plumatif') as the article's primary source, rather than an actual murderer. Following the text's own logic, the reader should be wary of any claims the pro-murder 'plumatif' makes to represent a profession from which he is, by essence, excluded.

## Murder: A Writer's Profession

Despite presenting an ambivalent approach to the art-murder analogy, Coolus's article extends Beaubourg's earlier arguments by promoting murderous associations that transcend a dyadic relationship between two individuals. From its opening, 'Théorie rationnelle' adopts the language of political solidarity by depicting murderers as demanding 'réparation[s]' for the way society treats them, and as considering syndicalisation in order to gain recognition for their working community or 'corporation' (TR, 575). The text subsequently lists a series of 'axiomes liminaires' ['preliminary axioms'] setting forward the guiding principles behind the murderers' syndicate, which range from the importance of a healthy diet to the value of attending classes in medical dissection (TR, 577). This structure parodies discourses related to workers' rights, but also specific genres such as the scientific treatise, etiquette manuals, and political tracts. The axioms numbered XI–XIII are particularly noteworthy, warning against romance, friendship, and accomplices: 'Ce sont les femmes qui ont la plupart du temps vendu les criminels de haute marque [...]. Tout ami est un dénonciateur possible. [...] Le complice [...] n'est pas seulement le dénonciateur possible, mais bien l'accusateur probable' ['It is women who have most often sold out high-end criminals [...]. Every friend is a possible informer. [...] The accomplice [...] is not only a possible informer, but a probable accuser'] (TR, 578). These axioms function ironically because they emphasise the dangers of criminal association in a tract that argues for greater solidarity between murderers. Yet by codifying murder according to a set of principles and practices, Coolus clearly attributes to it the status of a professional vocation. The article concludes with a proposal that murder should be considered a respectable career path, to be taught and recognised at a national level:

---

[80] Romain Coolus, 'Théorie rationnelle de l'assassinat propre', *La Grande Revue*, 25 Dec. 1891, pp. 575–83 (p. 576). References will henceforth appear parenthetically in the text, preceded by the abbreviation *TR*.

Nos assassins sont des artistes de décès: il est temps qu'on le reconnaisse et qu'on leur fasse jouer le rôle social auquel ils aspirent et ont droit. Quelqu'un ne proposait-il pas que l'État les enrégistrât [sic] et les prît à son service? Pourquoi en effet n'y aurait-il pas une école normale supérieure et nationale du meurtre? (*TR*, 582)

[Our murderers are artists of death: it is high time we recognise this and let them play the social role to which they aspire and rightly claim. Wasn't someone suggesting that the State should register them and take them into public service? In fact, why should there not be an *École normale supérieure* for murder?]

The rhetorical questions in this passage imply a faux-naif incredulity at the unappreciated status of murder in society and the 'obvious' solution of creating a state-supported professional structure dedicated to its development and expansion. Coolus explains that there would be examinations 'pour avantager ces fonctionnaires' ['for the benefit of these civil servants'], to provide them with a certificate that would protect them against the competition of 'les assassins amateurs' ['amateur murderers']. He further notes that '[il] y aurait naturellement des stagiaires, des chargés d'assassinat, des chourineurs à titre provisoire, des titulaires et des retraités' ['naturally, there would be trainee murderers, chief murderers, provisional murderers, tenured murderers, and retired murderers'] (*TR*, 583). The word 'naturellement' here functions in a similar way to the rhetorical questions noted above, by putting forward as 'natural' or 'obvious' a proposition that runs counter to the moral status quo. In this way, Coolus satirises the system of recognition he is parodying, namely: the state-sponsored education of civil servants via the *Grandes Écoles*. By mimicking the tenets of the *Grandes Écoles* system, and aligning it with a seemingly absurd suggestion, Coolus places some of the ridicule of the proposal at the pre-existing system's door.

Romain Coolus was not the first writer to parody the bureaucracy of professionalisation by proposing a means by which murderers could achieve official recognition. In 1884, a short-lived spoof weekly newspaper, the *Journal des assassins* [*Murderers' Paper*], claimed to publish articles and works by a secret network of infamous murderers. Naming their editor-in-chief as the long-dead, executed criminal Jean-Baptiste Troppmann ('Feu Troppmann' ['The Late Troppmann']), and listing the location for subscriptions as 'À minuit, aux coins des rues' ['At midnight, on street corners'], the *Journal des assassins* advertised its own fictionality while claiming to be an accurate representation of the criminal underworld. The review depicted murderers as providing a necessary and useful contribution to society:

Fléaux ou bienfaiteurs, les assassins sont nécessaires. Ils sont la manne des auteurs dramatiques, le pain quotidien des journalistes, l'existence assurée pour les gendarmes, les juges et les geôliers [...]. Utile et mystérieux, tel est l'assassin, et c'est pour cela que nous avons créé cet organe.[81]

[Whether champions of good or evil, murderers are necessary. For dramatists, they are a godsend; for journalists, their daily bread; for policemen, judges, and jailors, a guaranteed wage. [...] The murderer is both useful and mysterious, and this is why we have created this organisation.]

By highlighting the importance of murderers to literary production, the editor offers an ironic nod to the widespread interest in crime stories, and to the financial interest of writers and publishers in maintaining such interest. Keen to contribute to the pro-murder cause, the review asserted its desire to facilitate solidarity between actual and potential criminals, describing itself as an 'organe spécial à la corporation des assassins et des voleurs' ['institution dedicated to the corporation of murderers and thieves'] which provided representation for a marginalised group ('classe méconnue' ['little-known class']).[82] It also offered a range of services to its readership, including a small ad column, 'Demandes et offres d'emplois' ['Job Requests and Offers'], for would-be criminals and criminal groups to advertise and sell their services.[83] Most notably, the editorial board offered readers a murderer's certificate ('brevet d'assassin') as a supplement, announced in the eighth issue, which responded to a perceived need for the 'corporation' of murderers to be 'brevetée comme les autres industries' ['certified like other industries'] (see Figure 3.1).[84] While demonstrating a proclivity for tongue-in-cheek humour, these examples reflected avant-garde perceptions of their precarious position in the literary field. Presenting writers' need for solidarity through the lens of criminal association, they raised questions about the attribution of professional and cultural recognition, employing satire and parody to creative and polemical effect.

The *Journal des assassins* reveals the structural similarities between criminal associations and literary groups by highlighting their joint mediation via a burgeoning periodical culture. It suggests that the social and textual spaces through which criminal and literary accomplices might meet, exchange ideas, and plot together appear uncannily alike. This cross-media vision emerges through the multiple references to *Le Chat noir* in the *Journal des assassins*. *Le Chat noir* was a cabaret in Montmartre, which had an in-house review whose contributors frequented and performed at the eponymous drinking establishment. As well as achieving the status of a cultural icon, *Le Chat noir* brought together avant-garde,

---

[81] 'Notre programme', *Journal des assassins: organe officiel des chourineurs réunis*, 6 Apr. 1884, pp. 2–3.
[82] 'Abonnements de propagande', *Journal des assassins*, 6 Apr. 1884, p. 3.
[83] By offering advertising space to murderers, the *Journal des assassins* acted as a forerunner to the newspaper proposed in Beaubourg's 'L'Intermédiaire', *Contes pour les assassins*, pp. 127–40.
[84] 'Notre supplément', *Journal des assassins*, 18 May 1884, p. 2.

**Figure 3.1** 'Brevet d'assassin', *Journal des assassins*, 1 June 1884 (BnF).

working class, and criminal cultures in Montmartre. It is probable that editors of *Le Chat noir* also ran the *Journal des assassins*. Material reappeared across the reviews and the latter frequently mentioned Salis's cabaret.[85] For example, the first issue opens with a spoof article interviewing the murderer known as Michel Campi, who asks to speak with Léon Bloy, 'le fumiste qui écrit au *Figaro* et au *Chat Noir*' ['the charlatan who writes for *Le Figaro* and *Le Chat Noir*'].[86] Two pages later, a small ad reads: 'Un jeune homme, 30 ans, fort et robuste, demande un emploi dans une bande d'escarpes.—S'adresser à M. Salis, au cabaret du *Chat Noir*' [Young man, aged 30, strong and sturdy, looking for work in a gang of murderous thieves.—Send enquiries to Mr Salis, at the *Chat Noir* cabaret'].[87] The subsequent issue promoted the cabaret by listing its famous clientele:

> Le cabaret du *Chat noir* [...] est quotidiennement hanté par une foule de meurtriers de haut lieu et par les gens de lettres les plus en renom de la capitale. Victor Hugo, Juliette Lamber, Catulle Mendès, Emile Zola, Paul Alexis, Théodore de Banville, Fernand Xau, Armand Silvestre, François Coppée et Léon Collignon y prennent tous les soirs leur absinthe.
> 
> M. Alfred R..., l'un des plus grands assassins de l'avenir, celui-là même qui doit tuer trois vieillards de la rue des Mauvais-Garçons le 15 juillet prochain, y vient aussi tous les soirs pour y lire la prose ébaudissante de Léon Bloy, de Rodolphe Salis, de Niversac et de George Auriol.[88]
> 
> [The *Chat noir* cabaret [...] is haunted on a daily basis by a mass of high-class murderers and by the most renowned writers in the capital. Victor Hugo, Juliette Lamber, Catulle Mendès, Emile Zola, Paul Alexis, Théodore de Banville, Fernand Xau, Armand Silvestre, François Coppée, and Léon Collignon all consume their nightly absinthe there.
> 
> Mr Alfred R..., one of the greatest up-and-coming murderers, who plans to kill three elderly people on the rue des Mauvais-Garçons on 15 July, also comes there every evening to read the entertaining prose of Léon Bloy, Rodolphe Salis, Niversac, and George Auriol.]

By aligning famous writers with infamous murderers, this article reaffirms the art-murder analogy while advertising the cabaret as an exclusive and exciting place to

---

[85] 'La Revanche du guillotiné', first serialised in *Le Chat Noir* between 26 May and 15 September 1883, partially reappeared in *Journal des assassins* between 30 March and 20 April 1884. Signed 'Ponchon du Terrail' in *Le Chat noir*, it parodied works by Ponson du Terrail and mocked Émile Zola, who features as a central character. For an analysis of this work, see Catherine Dousteyssier-Khoze, 'Rodolphe Salis et Émile Zola: rencontres chatnoiresques', in *Le Rire moderne*, edited by Alain Vaillant and Roselyne de Villeneuve (Nanterre: Presses Universitaires de Paris Ouest, 2013), pp. 217–31 (pp. 222–30).
[86] Anon., 'Campi a parlé', *Journal des assassins*, p. 1.
[87] 'Demandes et offres d'emplois', *Journal des assassins*, p. 3.
[88] Anon., 'Tout le monde', *Journal des assassins*, 6 Apr. 1884, p. 4.

visit. The hyperbolic accumulation of names juxtaposes the anonymous would-be murderer ('M. Alfred R...'), whose future crimes are predicted by the review. While adding a sense of mystery, this reference increased the review's criminal credentials, by implying that its editors were somehow 'in on it'. The review confirms its management's collusive atmosphere by announcing its own criminal plans in a later issue: 'La rédaction du *Journal des Assassins*, afin de satisfaire la curiosité de ses nombreux lecteurs a pris toutes ses dispositions pour commettre une série d'assassinats, vols et crimes divers' ['In order to satisfy the curiosity of the *Journal des assassins*' many readers, the editorial staff have made all the necessary preparations to commit a series of murders, thefts, and a range of other crimes'].[89] Such declarations clearly played up to fin-de-siècle legal definitions of complicity as incitement and collaboration. First, by promoting the crimes of infamous murderers and proclaiming knowledge of future misdeeds, the review portrayed itself as encouraging and enabling criminal activity. Second, by providing a means of communication between criminals (notably through the small ad column) and aligning crime with literary production, the *Journal des assassins* reaffirmed the illicit potential of collaborative press practices. In this way, the valorisation of murder provided marginal writers a means for expressing literary solidarity, premised on the transgression of socio-cultural norms and the collusive creativity facilitated by fin-de-siècle press culture.

Writers across the literary spectrum appropriated the appeal of crime narrative in fin-de-siècle France. Debates about criminal and moral responsibility intersected with a widespread morbid interest in tales of violence and transgression, which frequently ended with a reassuring return to moral order. Rachilde, Zola, and Malot each refused their readers this reassurance, in stories that, with varying degrees of irony and satire, conclude with further crime and injustice. Instead, their stories highlight the ambiguities of criminal responsibility in ways that implicate readers, who, like the novels' characters, witness the crimes depicted and receive the murderers' confessions. It is clear from the play of identification and focalisation in these novels that the reader's desire is not—or is not supposed to be—for the criminals to be brought to justice. By describing the fatal role played by cultural prejudice and received wisdom in the condemnation of innocent men, Rachilde and Zola highlighted the ways in which scientific, judicial, and political discourses around crime parallel literary typologies, ultimately creating criminal fictions that work against the justice they claim to support. It is precisely these intersecting layers of complicity that avant-garde writers such as Mirbeau, Beaubourg, and Coolus manipulated when they presented the murderer as a figurehead for their

---

[89] 'Le Crime de demain', *Journal des assassins*, 13 Apr. 1884, p. 2.

counter-discursive positioning and controversial solidarity. Far from taking themselves too seriously, however, marginal authors explored the value of criminality with a tongue-in-cheek attitude that poked fun not only at the moralising discourses they parodied, but also at their own identification with aestheticised crime and collusion. By engaging with murder as a taboo topic, avant-garde writers created new forms of identification and collaboration between their peers, premised on a shared (if consistently ironised) valorisation of the illicit.

# 4
# Scandal and Collusion in Avant-Garde Media

In a literary marketplace increasingly dominated by mass consumerism, sensationalism, and celebrity culture, avant-garde writers manipulated the appeal of the illicit by adopting self-promotional marketing strategies that played up to the frameworks of criminality and immorality used, by friends and critics alike, to condone and condemn them respectively. Unlike their mainstream peers, they actively co-opted illicit themes and collusive relationships in order to establish their subversive aesthetic. Members of literary groups such as the *Hydropathes*, Decadents, and Symbolists, took up a bohemian, anti-bourgeois stance that blended youth culture, popular culture, and an aestheticised criminality. Their sense of group identity depended on a rejection of normative models of acceptable behaviour, moral codes, and aesthetic tradition.[1] Transgressive identities and behaviour were an integral part of the public image cultivated by avant-garde writers, who actively promoted a risqué image of themselves and their peers in the press. These strategies forged literary complicity through collusive and collaborative relationships, which, if not overtly illicit, often involved a degree of secrecy or mystery.[2] Avant-garde writers and their readers could therefore become metaphorical accomplices with one another by identifying with an exclusive and transgressive literary in-crowd, whose inner workings and secrets are made available to those 'in the know'.

Writers' choices regarding their self-presentation and position in relation to pre-existing socio-cultural groups undergird their strategic 'position-taking' in the literary field.[3] In order to build and maintain their respective position, authors need to convince their readers and fellow writers to accept and perpetuate their self-image. Referred to by recent Francophone critics as 'ethos' or 'posture', a writer's self-image relies on social networks and media strategies. As a means of conveying authority and credibility, 'ethos' is constructed both within an author's works—their content, style, etc.—and through shared knowledge that is external

---

[1] See Bénédite Didier, *Petites revues et esprit bohème à la fin du XIXe siècle (1878–1889)* (Paris: L'Harmattan, 2009).

[2] Pierre Larousse, *Grand dictionnaire universel du XIXe siècle*, 17 vols (Paris: Administration du Grand Dictionnaire universel, 1866–77), IV (1869), pp. 784–5.

[3] Pierre Bourdieu, *Les Règles de l'art: genèse et structure du champ littéraire* (Paris: Seuil, 1992).

to their written production.[4] In a similar way, a 'posture' is a 'soi construit'[5] ['constructed self'] established through an author's rhetoric and real-life actions, as well as by the public and media who receive and perpetuate it.[6] Avant-garde writers in fin-de-siècle France regularly encouraged readers to participate in the construction and dissemination of risqué authorial 'postures'. They wielded collaborative press practices to perpetuate transgressive identities with which readers could feel illicit solidarity, thereby mirroring the incitement and collaboration models of literary complicity. These strategies involved a degree of risk-taking, since readers of a given work might refuse to become willing accomplices in the creation of an author or group's self-image.[7] Conversely, an author's readers (including other writers) may go too far in their appropriation and dissemination of a risqué persona, such that the former loses control over their self-image and potentially suffers undesirable consequences.

The mediatised staging of public personae, and its attendant risks, played an integral part in nineteenth-century French literary culture. By the 1880s, veiled depictions of celebrity writers, journalists, and performers—such as Félicien Champsaur's *Dinah Samuel* (1882) and Marie Colombier's *Les Mémoires de Sarah Barnum* (1883)—abounded in the publishing marketplace, eliciting widespread interest and controversy. Such books revealed the inner mechanisms of literary and artistic networks that provided writers of the period survival strategies and pathways to success in the cultural marketplace. A notable example of this phenomenon was the literary *cénacle*, which Anthony Glinoer and Vincent Laisney define as 'un cercle restreint d'écrivains et de peintres animés par des liens d'amitié réciproques et par des convictions esthétiques convergentes, qui se retrouvaient périodiquement au domicile de l'un d'entre eux pour confronter leurs idées, unifier leurs vues et raffermir leur volonté' ['a restricted circle of writers and painters motivated by their reciprocal friendship bonds and by shared aesthetic convictions, who would regularly meet up at one another's homes in order to compare their ideas, to consolidate their plans, and to strengthen their resolve'].[8] Throughout the century, such groups existed historically, while

---

[4] See Ruth Amossy, 'La double nature de l'image d'auteur', *Argumentation et Analyse du Discours* 3 (2009), doi:10.4000/aad.662, paragraph 22, and Melliandro Mendes Gallinari, 'La "clause auteur": l'écrivain, l'*ethos* et le discours littéraire', *Argumentation et Analyse du Discours* 3 (2009), doi:10.4000/aad.663, paragraph 26.

[5] Jérôme Meizoz, *Postures littéraires. Mises en scène modernes de l'auteur* (Geneva: Slaktine Érudition, 2007), p. 28.

[6] Laurence van Nuijis, 'Postures journalistiques et littéraires', *Interférences littéraires* 6 (May 2011): pp. 7–17 (p. 12), http://www.interferenceslitteraires.be/index.php/illi/article/view/573/444.

[7] This refusal would amount to a rejection of what Melliandro Mendes Gallinari has called the 'clause auteur' ['author clause'] implicit in the textual 'contract'. Gallinari describes authorship as a 'clause' in the contract proposed (consciously or not) by an author to their readership, which constitutes a risk or wager, betting on the cooperation of the writer's interlocutors. See Gallinari, 'La "clause auteur"', paragraph 19.

[8] See Anthony Glinoer and Vincent Laisney, *L'Âge des cénacles. Confraternités littéraires et artistiques au XIXe siècle* (Paris: Fayard, 2013), p. 10. See also pp. 25–6.

also appearing in fictional works known as *romans cénaculaires*.[9] Beyond this genre, *cénacles* asserted their influence in many ways, across different media. At the textual level, the collusive 'échange de bons procédés' ['quid pro quo'] typical of *cénacle* culture included the exchange of epigraphs, dedications, and laudatory reviews.[10] These textual strategies created a sense of plotting or conniving behaviour between members of literary groups whose apparent secrecy increased public curiosity and cultivated readers' desire to be 'in on it'.[11] The construction of literary images or 'brands', at both an individual and collective level, therefore relied on maintaining a degree of tension between secrecy and publicity.[12]

Combining the commodification of literary culture and collective promotional strategies, nineteenth-century literary camaraderie has been considered as a form of 'cross-marketing' *avant la lettre*.[13] Although such terms might seem anachronistic, nineteenth-century French writers were already employing the lens of mass media advertising to conceptualise literary self-promotion.[14] They did so by using the trade term 'réclame', which, according to the *Dictionnaire de l'Académie française*, refers to a specific form of veiled advertising: '[se] dit, dans le Journalisme, d'Un petit article inséré dans le corps d'un journal, et qui a pour objet d'attirer l'attention sur un livre, une marchandise, un médicament, etc., plus sûrement que par une annonce ostensiblement payée' ['in journalism, refers to a short article inserted in the main body of a newspaper, which aims to attract attention on a book, product, medicine, etc., more efficiently than with an openly

---

[9] Examples of the *roman cénaculaire* include: Henry Murger's *Scènes de la vie de bohème* (1851) and *Buveurs d'eau* (1855), Champfleury's *Amis de la nature* (1859), the Goncourt brothers' *Charles Demailly* (1860) and *Manette Salomon* (1867), Émile Zola's *L'Œuvre* (1886), Alphonse Daudet's *Le Petit chose* (1868), Jean Arène's *Jean-des-figues* (1868), Jules Vallès's *Le Bachelier* (1881), Rosny aîné's *Le Termite* (1890), and Camille Mauclair's *Le Soleil des morts* (1898). See Anthony Glinoer and Vincent Laisney, 'Les illusios perdues, ou les romans cénaculaires', in *Romans à clés: Les ambivalences du réel*, edited by Anthony Glinoer and Michel Lacroix (Liège: Presses Universitaires de Liège, 2014), pp. 66–85 (p. 71).

[10] On the use of dedications in avant-garde periodicals, see Solenn Dupas, 'Pratiques fumistes de la dédicace dans *Le Chat noir*. Formes et enjeux d'une poétique en réseaux', in *Vie de bohème et petite presse du XIXe siècle. Sociabilité littéraire ou solidarité journalistique?*, edited by Alain Vaillant and Yoan Vérilhac (Nanterre: Presses universitaires de Paris Nanterre, 2018), pp. 241–63.

[11] Glinoer and Laisney, *L'Âge des cénacles*, pp. 441–51. Cf. Vincent Laisney, 'Une "franc-maçonnerie de la réclame": le cénacle à l'âge de la littérature industrielle', in *L'Auteur et ses stratégies publicitaires*, edited by Brigitte Diaz (Caen: Presses universitaires de Caen, 2019), pp.145–53 (p. 152).

[12] See Marie-Ève Thérenty and Adeline Wrona, 'Introduction', in *L'Écrivain comme marque*, edited by Marie-Ève Thérenty and Adeline Wrona (Paris: Sorbonne Université Presses, 2020), pp. 7–29 (p. 20).

[13] Brigitte Diaz, 'Du *puff* au *buzz*: naissance de la publicité littéraire', in *L'Auteur et ses stratégies publicitaires*, edited by B. Diaz, pp. 9–19 (p. 18) and José Luis Diaz, 'Les écrivains en vitrine ou la "réclame personnelle" à l'œuvre (1830–1865)', in *L'Auteur et ses stratégies publicitaires*, edited by B. Diaz, pp. 37–50 (p. 49).

[14] For a historical overview of this tendency, see José-Luis Diaz, 'Et la littérature tomba dans la réclame...', in *Portraits de l'écrivain en publicitaire*, edited by Myriam Boucharenc and Laurence Guellec (Rennes: Presses Universitaires de Rennes, 2018), pp. 19–37.

paid-for advert']. [15] As this definition suggests, the practice of 'réclame' was viewed with suspicion, since it blurred the aesthetic and ethical boundary between paid advertising and main copy. [16] Understood figuratively, the term also evoked promotional strategies more generally: '*Faire de la réclame*, Faire des appels bruyants à la publicité, chercher par tous les moyens à attirer l'attention du public' ['*Faire de la réclame*. To make an ostentatious use of publicity, to seek to attract public attention by any means possible']. [17] Writers' complicity with advertising strategies, widely denigrated in the era, can be interpreted as a necessary evil in the financially driven market of cultural consumerism. But it also begs the question: to what extent were writers in control of their self-image? Relying on stereotypes and simplified traits, a writer's media persona is limited in complexity and easily appropriated for other agendas. [18] To explore the precarious balancing act between a successful literary reputation and its restrictive, reductive counterpart, this chapter analyses the self-promotional and collusive media practices employed by two infamous avant-garde writers.

## Partners in Crime: Rachilde and Jean Lorrain

Rachilde and Jean Lorrain were key players in a group of media-savvy avant-garde writers who collaboratively traded on scandal in order to build and maintain their literary infamy. In the mid-1880s, they constructed their reputations as innovative Decadent writers and adopted self-promotion strategies that co-opted the titillating appeal of taboos surrounding gender and sexuality. [19] The overtly gender-bending protagonists of Rachilde's early novels, her decision to wear men's clothing, and her highly contested 'perverse virgin' persona, parallel the homo-eroticism and Decadent themes found in Lorrain's early poetry, his interest in

[15] *Dictionnaire de l'Académie française*, 7th ed., 2 vols (Paris: Librairie de Firmin-Didot & cie, 1878), II, p. 585.
[16] On the wider cultural phenomenon of 'réclame' in nineteenth-century France, see Marie-Ève Thérenty, 'La réclame de librairie dans le journal quotidien au XIXe siècle: autopsie d'un objet textuel non identifié', *Romantisme* 155, no. 1 (2012): pp. 91–103, doi:10.3917/rom.155.0091.
[17] *Dictionnaire*, II, p. 585.
[18] See J.-L. Diaz, 'Les écrivains en vitrine', p. 46, and Ruth Amossy, '*Ethos*, image d'auteur, marque', in *L'Écrivain comme marque*, edited by Thérenty and Wrona, pp. 165–74 (p. 169).
[19] On Rachilde's self-promotional strategies, see Jennifer Birkett, *The Sins of the Fathers: Decadence in France, 1870–1914* (London: Quartet Books Limited, 1986), Melanie Hawthorne, *Rachilde and French Women's Authorship: From Decadence to Modernism* (Lincoln: University of Nebraska Press, 2001), and Diana Holmes, *Rachilde: Decadence, Gender and the Woman Writer* (Oxford: Berg, 2001). For Lorrain, see Thibault d'Anthonay, *Jean Lorrain: miroir de la Belle Époque* (Paris: Fayard, 2005), Philippe Jullian, *Jean Lorrain ou Le Satiricon 1900* (Paris: Fayard, 1974), Robert Ziegler, 'The Author of Public Opinion in Jean Lorrain's "Les Lépillier"', *Dalhousie French Studies* 26 (Spring 1994): pp. 39–47, https://www.jstor.org/stable/40799306, Sébastien Paré, 'Les avatars du Littéraire chez Jean Lorrain', *Loxias* 18 (2007), doi:10670/1.1hmvhm, and Alexandre Burin, '« Monsieur, JE JOUE MON PERSONNAGE » Jean Lorrain, construire sa propre légende', *Savoirs en prisme* 12 (Sept. 2020): pp. 235–52, doi:10.34929/sep.vi12.115.

criminal and lower-class social *milieux*, as well as his dandified posturing and 'open secret' homosexuality.[20] It was also in the mid-1880s that Rachilde and Lorrain became friends.[21] They frequented similar haunts of the avant-garde literary scene, such as the Café de l'Avenir and the Soleil d'Or in Paris.[22] Throughout their respective careers, the pair produced *romans à clef* and other biographically revealing fictional works.[23] By doing so, they courted controversy and provoked retaliation, including duels and legal action in Lorrain's case.[24] They also contributed to little magazines such as *Panurge* (1882–3), *Le Zig-Zag* (1882–6) and *Le Décadent littéraire et artistique* (1886–9), before acquiring more stable literary and journalistic positions.[25] Through these media, the pair supported and promoted one another in the early stages of their careers, enacting forms of avant-garde sociability based on provocative self-promotion.

The mediatised relationship between Rachilde, Lorrain, and their peers demonstrates that the perceived benefits of 'réclame' for writers in search of notoriety were often counterbalanced by the strategy's negative associations with conniving behaviour. The pair expressed a conflicted attitude regarding their personal 'brand' and their colleagues' role in disseminating it. Lorrain scholars have noted the author's ambivalence towards his scandalous persona, which had negative repercussions on his life, while also providing additional fodder for strategic recuperation.[26] Recent Rachilde scholarship further highlights the reductiveness involved in perpetuating controversial literary personae, from the dual perspective of fin-de-siècle writers and their modern critics (the latter of whom risk both diminishing and over-glorifying their object of study). In *Before Trans*

---

[20] I use the terms 'homosexuality' and 'same-sex desire' interchangeably throughout this chapter, while acknowledging the former's historical anachronism.

[21] On the pair's interconnecting friendships, see Anthonay, *Jean Lorrain*, Hawthorne, *Rachilde*, and Michael Finn, *Hysteria, Hypnotism, the Spirits, and Pornography: Fin-de-Siècle Cultural Discourses in the Decadent Rachilde* (Newark: University of Delaware Press, 2009).

[22] Anthonay, *Jean Lorrain*, pp. 171–7.

[23] Several of Rachilde's novels, such as *Nono* (1885), the preface to *À mort* (1886), and *La Marquise de Sade* (1887), contain autobiographical details about the author's childhood and adolescence. She later published *Le Mordu, mœurs littéraires* (1889): a *roman à clef* depicting various figures from the avant-garde literary scene. Lorrain also published novels with à-clef elements, including but not limited to: *Très Russe* (1886), *Monsieur de Bougrelon* (1897), *Monsieur de Phocas* (1901), *Les Noronsoff* (1902), and *Le Tréteau* (1906).

[24] A thinly veiled and scathing portrait in Lorrain's 1886 novel *Très Russe* led its target, Guy de Maupassant, to challenge the author to a duel (which Lorrain avoided, thereby damaging his reputation). Lorrain would later face a defamation trial, instigated by the artist Jeanne Jacquemin, for an article, 'Victime', published in *Le Journal* on 11 January 1903. See Éric Walbecq, 'Le procès de Jeanne Jacquemin contre Jean Lorrain en mai 1903*l*, in *Jean Lorrain, produit d'extrême civilisation*, edited by Éric Walbecq and others (Mont-Saint-Aignan: Publications des Universités de Rouen et du Havre, 2009), doi:10.4000/books.purh.125.

[25] Rachilde became a regular contributor to the *Mercure de France*, whose weekly salon she hosted as the wife of its founding member and director, Alfred Vallette (1858–1935). Lorrain contributed to a variety of newspapers during his lifetime, including *Le Courrier français*, *L'Événement*, and *L'Écho de Paris*.

[26] See Paré, 'Les avatars du Littéraire', and Alexandre Burin, 'The Harlequin Poetics: Fragmentation, Performance, and Scandal in Jean Lorrain' (PhD dissertation, Durham University, 2020), pp. 174–5.

(2020), Rachel Mesch takes issue with modern visions of Rachilde as a 'savvy self-promoter who cultivated shocking behavior in the interest of publicity and fortune'.[27] Instead, she proposes to study the more 'human' side to Rachilde, with a critical viewpoint that acknowledges the existence of vulnerability alongside audacity.[28] Rather than choosing between the two extremes of savvy self-promotion and heartfelt self-expression, this chapter seeks to demonstrate that playfulness and affect are not mutually exclusive, but in fact mutually imbricated.[29] Charting the fine line between collusive and compromising literary relationships, I suggest that without vulnerability, there would be no audacity in the first place.

## Collusive Genres: *Romans à clef* and Little Magazines

The rhetoric of complicity and collusion, based on shared insider knowledge and a sense of being 'in on it', is prevalent in two genres favoured by fin-de-siècle avant-garde writers: the *roman à clef* and the *petite revue*. Melissa Boyde defines the former as 'fictional works in which actual people or events can be identified by a knowing reader, typically a member of a coterie'.[30] Originating in French salon culture of the seventeenth century, and finding a new lease of life in the nineteenth-century *roman cénaculaire*, the *roman à clef* became a genre favoured by exclusive literary groups who traded on readers' vicarious pleasure by partially revealing the group's inner workings and secrets. In essence, *romans à clef* offer fictional representations of thinly veiled (but recognisable) literary, artistic, or society figures. They posit the existence of a knowing reader who can unlock the work's keys by recognising and understanding the veiled references. The *roman à clef* therefore relies on the appeal of speculation and mystery. Referential clues hint that there is something veiled or hidden—that is, something *to be known*—which in turn prompts the reader's desire to uncover and know it. The genre also perpetuates a sense of elitism and 'us vs. them', since not all readers are able to unlock the work's secrets.

The inevitable exclusiveness of *romans à clef* means that they have not tended to age well, nor have they been celebrated in the literary canon. Often lacking the

---

[27] Rachel Mesch, *Before Trans: Three Gender Stories from Nineteenth-Century France* (Stanford: Stanford University Press, 2020), p. 127.

[28] Mesch, *Before Trans*, pp. 127 and 152.

[29] Recent analyses of writers' self-promotion strategies acknowledge the role of affect alongside literary playfulness. See Thérenty and Wrona, 'Introduction', pp. 19–20 and Yoan Vérilhac, '*Hoc signo vinces*: le pur poète symboliste comme marque?', in *L'Écrivain comme marque*, edited by Thérenty and Wrona, pp. 175–86 (p. 185).

[30] Melissa Boyde, 'The Modernist Roman à Clef and Cultural Secrets, or, I Know that You Know that I Know that You Know', *Australian Literary Studies* 24, nos. 3–4 (2009): pp. 155–66 (p. 156), doi:10.20314/als.dfae519805.

contextual and intertextual knowledge required to unravel a novel's clues, modern readers come up against the genre's seeming opacity. Because of its historical situated-ness, and despite the prevalence of à-clef literary structures in elite and avant-garde literary circles, the pleasures associated with reading *romans à clef* have often been posited as culturally illegitimate. Sean Latham notes that the genre is typically perceived as a 'guilty pleasure', because it fails to live up to an ideal of literature as a purely aesthetic object, divorced from historical and biographical referentiality.[31] He questions the validity of this demarcation by highlighting the fact that Modernist writers, who ostensibly idealised formal innovation over concerns of realism, frequently published works that depended on a presumption of referentiality and of biographical knowledge in their readers. According to Latham, modern critics have too frequently dismissed the *roman à clef* as glorified gossip, without appreciating its potentially disruptive and innovative power. This power is located in the 'infectious' or 'viral' quality of the genre's 'conditional fictionality', whereby any fictional text can potentially be transformed into a factual narrative, and implicate its readers in the process.[32] Moreover, *romans à clef* shift the creative impetus away from writers and towards readers by relying on acts of recognition and interpretation.[33]

The act of partially revealing hidden or veiled meanings to a select, knowing readership extended beyond the generic limitations of the *roman à clef* and featured heavily in avant-garde journalism. A range of journalistic sub-genres employed à-clef literary structures, including gossip columns, interviews, and literary portraits.[34] Furthermore, there was a telling crossover between the *roman à clef* and the *petite revue* ['little magazine'], which avant-garde writers such as Rachilde and Lorrain exploited to great effect. Like the *roman à clef*, the *petite revue* was a culturally marginal literary phenomenon that reflected the interests of a specific coterie, addressed a knowing reader, and relied on the appeal of spectacle and of the illicit. *Petites revues* were an eclectic range of literary and artistic reviews that varied significantly in format, periodicity, and durability. They supported lesser-known writers by providing a medium for publication and self-promotion. Through them, aspiring authors could disseminate their public image through polemical debate, portraits, and *mises en scène* of their wider social and literary circles. The genre flourished and fluctuated in the mid-1880s and became increasingly professionalised in the 1890s: a decade that witnessed the foundation of notable titles such as *Le Mercure de France* (1890–1965), *La Revue blanche* (Belgian series: 1889–91, Parisian series: 1891–1903), and *La Plume*

---

[31] Sean Latham, *The Art of Scandal: Modernism, Libel Law, and the Roman à Clef* (New York: Oxford University Press, 2009), p. 16.
[32] Latham, *The Art of Scandal*, p.15.
[33] Latham, *The Art of Scandal*, p. 44.
[34] See Glinoer and Lacroix, eds., *Romans à clés*.

(1889–1914).[35] Amounting to more than a literary genre, however, the culture of *petites revues* was also a social phenomenon that blended real-life friendships with media-friendly performance. In many cases, members of the reviews' editorial board hosted literary salons, dinners, or parties that brought contributors and their extended social network together on a regular basis. The depiction of these gatherings in the periodicals' pages involved a rhetoric of exclusive company keeping, since the events were frequently organised on a 'by invitation only' basis.[36] That said, through descriptions of otherwise closed-off social gatherings, *petites revues* expanded their impact by encouraging readers to participate vicariously in the group's socio-literary enterprise.[37]

Associated with café and cabaret culture, *petites revues* blended a polemical, bohemian spirit with bawdy humour, in-jokes, and witty jibes. These stylistic tendencies frequently subverted mainstream norms of moral acceptability and good taste. Bénédicte Didier refers to the subversive positioning of little magazines as 'la bohème des contrebandiers' ['smugglers' bohemia']:

> Le terme de contrebande implique détournement de la loi, stratégies secrètes, mise en place d'une société parasite qui profiterait des ressorts de la société (publicité, mentalité de la 'clientèle' bourgeoise, industrialisation de l'art, succès de l'image du bohème) mais en refuserait paradoxalement les principes.[38]
>
> [The term 'contraband' [or 'smuggling'] implies bending the law, employing secret strategies, and establishing a parasitic organisation that profits from the inner workings of society—including: advertising, a bourgeois 'clientele' mindset, and a popular image of the bohemian lifestyle—but which paradoxically refuses that society's principles.]

Didier's comments are useful because they evoke the avant-garde gesture of appropriating and subverting commercial advertising strategies and bourgeois consumerism. This gesture of appropriation can be considered ethically and aesthetically dubious, since the avant-garde risked undermining their own anti-establishment ideals by being caught up in mainstream practices. Indeed, the

---

[35] See Yoan Vérilhac, 'Petites revues', in *La Civilisation du journal: histoire culturelle et littéraire de la presse française au XIXe siècle*, edited by Dominique Kalifa and others (Paris: Nouveau Monde éditions, 2011), pp. 359–73.

[36] On the varying levels of 'openness' of avant-garde social gatherings, see Philippe Leu, '« La diffusion par le verbe ». La forme revuiste comme matrice du réseau de sociabilités de *La Plume*', in *Vie de bohème et petite presse du XIXe siècle. Sociabilité littéraire ou solidarité journalistique?*, edited by Alain Vaillant and Yoan Vérilhac (Nanterre: Presses universitaires de Paris Nanterre, 2018), pp. 291–305.

[37] See Julien Schuh, 'Les Dîners de la Plume', *Romantisme* 137, no. 3 (2007): pp. 79–101, doi:10.3917/rom.137.0079.

[38] Didier, *Petites revues*, p. 208.

language used by modern critics to examine little magazines confirms its ambiguous status. For example, Yoan Vérilhac describes avant-garde promotional techniques as an 'échange de bons procédés' ['quid pro quo'] bordering on 'copinage' ['cronyism'],[39] while Didier compares little magazines to a 'société parasite' ['parasitic organisation'] and to freemasonry.[40] Such language highlights the complicit nature of the literary relationships Vérilhac and Didier analyse, while implying that readers may feel excluded, rather than included, by such practices.

This chapter argues that by wielding the *petite revue* and the *roman à clef*, the literary 'partners in crime' Rachilde and Lorrain manipulated scandal and subversion for the purposes of self-promotion, while creating alternative—if problematic—forms of solidarity based on the mutual construction of illicit media personae. It analyses a series of intertextual and journalistic exchanges from the mid-1880s, including a debate about women writers or *bas bleus* ['bluestockings'] in a little magazine called *Le Zig-Zag*, and two à-clef novellas by Rachilde and Lorrain's mutual friend, Oscar Méténier. Playing up to the ambiguities of their gender identity and sexuality, the pair adopted revealing promotional strategies associated with the bluestocking figure they claimed to revile—strategies which earned them vituperative critique in turn. Mirroring Latham's vision of the *roman à clef* as a viral, contagious genre, this cycle of opposition and implication involved an element of risk, because the public revelation of private information, however playful or theatrical, inevitably exposes the vulnerability of those involved.

## Avant-Garde Polemic in *Le Zig-Zag* (1885)

*Le Zig-Zag* was a weekly illustrated review originally published in Lyon. Its first series ran from 24 December 1882 to 25 October 1885, and its second series from 16 May 1886 to 26 December 1886. During the hiatus between the two, the review briefly changed its name to *Gil Blague*, for a single specimen issue dated December 1885.[41] The editor-in-chief, Aymé Delyon, worked alongside an administrator, Erüal, and later a series of *directeurs*.[42] *Le Zig-Zag* framed itself from the opening issue as a literary, artistic, and humorous review, with the tagline: 'Tous les genres sont bons, hors le genre ennuyeux' ['All genres are good, except boring ones']. It was part of a wider community of burgeoning (if frequently short-lived) avant-garde little magazines—such as *Le Chat noir* (1882–97) and *La Nouvelle Rive Gauche/Lutèce* (1882–6)—that valorised novelty, diversity, and youthful

---

[39] Yoan Vérilhac, 'Petites revues', p. 367.
[40] Didier, *Petites revues*, pp. 209–12.
[41] The title *Gil Blague* puns with the well-known newspaper *Gil Blas* (1879–1940).
[42] Little is known about Aymé Delyon beyond brief descriptions found in the review itself. In 1884, she published a novel, *Mademoiselle Éliane*, first serialised in *Le Zig-Zag* (23 Mar. 1884–4 May 1884). 'Aymé Delyon' may also be a pseudonym, since phonetically it reads like 'Aimé de Lyon' ['Beloved of Lyon'].

exuberance. This avant-garde approach solidified as Le Zig-Zag gained offices in Paris, which it held from December 1884 to the end of its print run, but then waned during its second series.[43] The writer-journalist Léo d'Orfer (1859–1924) contributed a regular column, 'La Chronique Parisienne', from March to October 1885, and became the review's *directeur* in May 1885.[44] By this point d'Orfer was infamous for setting up a series of short-lived reviews throughout the early 1880s. In spite of these failed enterprises, he retained enough influence in Parisian avant-garde circles to encourage the collaboration of up-and-coming writers: Rachilde, Jean Lorrain, and Jules Renard (1864–1910). While enhancing the review's literary credentials through his friendship network, d'Orfer encouraged contributions foregrounding gossip and scandal, thereby appeasing the review's supposedly frivolous readership.[45]

On 4 October 1885, Le Zig-Zag published a special issue on women writers, or *bas bleus*, which provided Rachilde and Lorrain a springboard to promote their controversial public personae (No. 146). In the opening article, 'Chronique raisonnable', Léo d'Orfer frames the debate and summarises key contributions. Rachilde, in 'Un fois pour toutes! [sic]', depicts bluestockings as hypocritical man-haters with a proclivity for over-sharing intimate secrets in public.[46] Lorrain, under the pseudonym Jack Stick, offers a vituperative attack on his female counterparts, whom he associates with eroticised self-promotion. In the subsequent issue (No. 147), d'Orfer publishes responses to the debate in an article entitled 'Guichet de réclamations', including those penned by Camille Delaville and Rachilde.[47] It is probable that these responses were mostly, if not entirely, fabricated, in order to increase the humorous appeal and polemical impact of the debate. Rachilde

---

[43] During its second series, with the sub-title 'Journal de la Maison', Le Zig-Zag took on a format more typical of women's magazines, with columns on fashion, recipes, health, and beauty.

[44] Léo d'Orfer (1859–1924), pseudonym for Marius Pouget, undertook military service in the colonies before living and working in Paris from the early 1880s onwards. He founded and ran a series of short-lived reviews, including: La Jeunesse, Le Molière, Le Capitan, and La Revue de Paris. D'Orfer and Rachilde were probably lovers for a period during the 1880s. See Hawthorne, Rachilde, pp. 120–1 and Finn, Hysteria, pp. 51–64.

[45] '[C]es furieux [les lecteurs] me demandent de l'actualité, des racontars, des cancans de boulevards et de coulisses, toute sorte de piment pour désaffadir [sic] cette pauvre littérature trop saine pour leurs estomacs blasés.' ['These maniacs [readers] demand news, gossip, and backstage tattle, any bit of spice to make this wretched and overly healthy literature more appetising for their jaded stomachs.'] 'Chronique Parisienne. Projets', Le Zig-Zag, 21 June 1885.

[46] The initial misspelling in the title is clearly a typographical error. Henceforth I refer to Rachilde's article as 'Une fois pour toutes!'

[47] Françoise Couteau (née Chartier), writing under the pseudonym Camille Delaville (1838–88), was a proto-feminist writer and journalist. Unhappily married, Delaville came to Paris to separate from her husband, before obtaining a divorce in 1885. She wrote for L'Événement, L'Opinion Nationale, Le Gaulois, La Presse, and Le Grand Journal. She founded and ran two smaller reviews: Le Passant and La Revue verte. Known for hosting parties and receptions, she was involved in Jeanne Thilda's 'dîners des bas-bleu', discussed below. Despite disagreeing on female emancipation, Delaville and Rachilde were good friends. See Lettres de Camille Delaville à Georges de Peyrebrune 1884–1888, ed. Nelly Sanchez (Brest: Publications du Centre d'étude des correspondances et journaux intimes des XIXe et XXe siècles, 2010), pp. 24–74 and Finn, Hysteria, pp. 41–3.

then starts a new column, 'Zig-Zag Parade', which opens the 18 October issue (No. 148). In a meta-literary *mise en scène*, Rachilde depicts herself performing on an upturned barrel, promoting *Le Zig-Zag* to potential readers, and defending it from potential detractors. The audience heckles her with questions, and Jack Stick appears dressed in drag, before revealing his identity. In the same issue, Lorrain contributes an article, 'Encore les réclamations', structured as a bipartite letter addressed to Léo d'Orfer. The first part, signed 'Lorrain', refers to Jack Stick as a friend for whose antics he is apologising. The second part, signed 'Jack Stick', offers a tongue-in-cheek 'amende honorable' ['public apology'] to the offended *bas bleus*. Finally, in the 25 October issue (No. 149), Rachilde offers portraits of her fellow contributors in the second and final 'Zig-Zag Parade' article, 'Auteurs et décors', which includes a positive appraisal of Lorrain.

The polemical charge and transgressive implications of Rachilde and Lorrain's contributions to *Le Zig-Zag* stem from the divisive topic of women writers' position in fin-de-siècle literary culture. By the late nineteenth century, the figure of the *bas bleu* had been a longstanding source of contention, satire, and polemic across Britain and France. First used in 1653 to evoke the plain clothes worn by puritans under Cromwell, the term 'bluestocking' came to refer to 'witty or learned people of both sexes' by the eighteenth century. From mid-eighteenth century onwards, a group of British women writers—including Hannah More (1745–1833), Elizabeth Montagu (1718–1800), and Hester Thrale (1740–1821)—appropriated the term to refer to themselves and to the coterie who would attend their respective literary salons.[48] As a group, the bluestockings cultivated public personae 'built around intellectual accomplishment [...], female friendship, an Anglican-centred piety, and social responsibility'.[49] By 1782 the neutral or complimentary aspect of the term was lost and replaced by a predominantly pejorative one, evoking 'a learned, pedantic lady'.[50] Moyra Haslett associates this negative shift with the evolution of anti-feminist satire in the late eighteenth century, when the bluestocking was as much 'a figure in satiric discourse' as a historical group of individuals.[51] At this point, a French equivalent emerged: *bas bleu*, which primarily translated the negative version of 'bluestocking' and retained little association with the historical

---

[48] Arnold Anthony Schmidt, 'Review: Bluestockings, George Eliot, and Nineteenth-Century Sociability', *Nineteenth Century Studies* 25, no. 1 (2011): pp. 271–8 (p. 273), doi:10.5325/ninecentstud.25.2011.0271.

[49] Betty A. Schellenberg, 'Bluestocking Women and the Negotiation of Oral, Manuscript, and Print Cultures', in *The History of British Women's Writing, 1750–1830*, edited by Jacqueline M. Labbe (Basingstoke: Palgrave Macmillan, 2010), pp. 63–83 (pp. 64–5).

[50] Evelyn Gordon Bodek, 'Salonières and Bluestockings: Educated Obsolescence and Germinating Feminism', *Feminist Studies* 3, nos. 3–4 (Spring–Summer 1976): pp. 185–99 (p. 188), https://www.jstor.org/stable/3177736.

[51] Moyra Haslett, 'Bluestocking Feminism Revisited: The Satirical Figure of the Bluestocking', *Women's Writing* 17, no. 3 (2010): pp. 432–45 (p. 433), doi:10.1080/09699082.2010.508927.

English bluestocking group.[52] The term circulated in dictionaries, panoramic literature, and caricature during the July Monarchy, notably Honoré Daumier's *Le Charivari* caricatures and Frédéric Soulié's *Physiologies du bas-bleu* (1841). Satire turned to vitriol in the second half of the nineteenth century, when the figure was increasingly perceived to be a threat to society by rejecting maternal and domestic responsibilities. In a collection of critical essays entitled *Les Bas-bleus* (1878), Jules Barbey d'Aurevilly depicted professional female writers as a threat to conventional femininity and social order.[53]

By the time Rachilde and Lorrain became published authors and journalists, the *bas bleu* had therefore come to represent a longstanding polemical tradition, bound up in socio-political concerns about gender roles and the literary marketplace. This tradition resurfaced in July 1884 when Jeanne Thilda (aka Mathilde Kindt, 1833–86) announced a series of bluestocking dinners in the newspaper *Gil Blas*. According to Thilda, the dinners were attended by leading female writers, including Camille Delaville, Georges de Peyrebrune (1841–1917), and Olympe Audouard (1832–90). In the article, Thilda situates her peers within a respected lineage of women writers, citing the *précieuses* as literary forebears. Rather than completely rejecting feminine stereotypes, she plays up to an eroticised image of the woman writer: 'si nous avons les bas de couleur bleue, ils sont si transparents qu'on voie la jambe rose au travers' ['our stockings might be blue in colour, but they are transparent enough for pink-hued legs to be seen through them'].[54] Furthermore, Thilda's monthly dinners capitalised on the French tradition of literary *salons*, where women actively participated in, and had tangible influence over, intellectual exchanges.[55] Long regarded as 'antechambers of the academy', *salons* offered networking opportunities and publicity to a select coterie.[56] By framing the dinners as an extension of aristocratic practices, and by insisting on the *bas bleus*' acceptable femininity, Thilda implicitly responded to the criticism of Jules Barbey d'Aurevilly, who had politely but wittily rejected an invitation to attend the event.[57]

Thilda's efforts to reframe and counteract criticism of the *bas bleu* demonstrate the challenges of the status quo: women writers in fin-de-siècle France faced an ambivalent audience at the best of times, and a vitriolic one at the worst. This range appeared in the *Zig-Zag* special issue, which used the bluestocking's controversial

---

[52] Karen L. Humphreys, '*Bas-bleus, filles publiques*, and the Literary Marketplace in the Work of Jules Barbey d'Aurevilly', *French Studies* 66, no. 1 (2012): pp. 26–40 (p. 29), doi:10.1093/fs/knr204.

[53] See Sharon Larson, '"Elle n'est pas un "bas-bleu", mais un écrivain": Georges de Peyrebrune's Woman Writer', *Nineteenth-Century Contexts* 40, no. 1 (2018): pp. 19–31 (pp. 21-2), doi:10.1080/08905495.2018.1393734.

[54] Jeanne Thilda, 'Le Dîner des bas-bleus', *Gil Blas*, 10 July 1884.

[55] Schmidt, 'Review: Bluestockings', p. 273.

[56] Bodek, 'Salonières and Bluestockings', p. 191.

[57] Thilda published Barbey's rejection letter in her article, without his permission.

status to promote the review as an arena for avant-garde discussion. It framed the *bas bleu* debate as a polemic, attracting a series of responses that continue beyond the initial special issue. This structure creates an atmosphere of controversy, which enables a combative form of social identification. Léo d'Orfer highlights the power of polemic to divide and unite in the special issue's leading article: 'Je commence par déclarer ici que, d'une part, je prends la responsabilité des articles de mes rédacteurs et que, d'autre part, je ne suis aucunement de leur avis' ['I'll start here by declaring that, on the one hand, I take responsibility for my authors' articles, while on the other, I share none of their opinions'].[58] The manager's opening comments set the tone for polemical diversity and present *Le Zig-Zag* as a forum for debate. By taking responsibility for the special issue, d'Orfer implicates himself and his colleagues in its titillating contents and controversial spirit. He also hints at the legal responsibility held by editors, directors, and publishers in the period. As discussed in Chapter 1, it was the act of publishing—and not simply writing—illicit or provocative material that was punishable by law.[59] Before summarising and responding to the issue's primary articles, d'Orfer defends bluestockings from their critics. He asserts the appeal of women writers as lovers and muses, exclaiming: 'Qu'importe que le bas soit bleu, pourvu que la jambe soit rose et blanche!' ['Who cares if the stockings are blue, provided that the legs beneath are rosy white!'] In a similar gesture to Jeanne Thilda in *Gil Blas*, d'Orfer appeals to the sensuality of female nudity and implied sexual availability to underscore the *bas bleu*'s essential femininity.

Following d'Orfer's opening comments, the editor-in-chief Aymé Delyon offers a typological study of the much-contested figure in 'Paris-Bas-bleu'. In a nod to the literary tradition of *physiologies*, she defines sub-genres of the *bas bleu* according to their financial, social, and artistic means, as well as their attitude towards literary production.[60] Examples include the *bas bleu* 'riche', 'humanitaire', 'amateur', 'sérieux et bon', 'prud'homme', 'genre pion', 'docteur', and 'incompris' ['rich', 'humanitarian', 'amateur', 'serious and good', 'wise', 'prefect-like', 'doctor', and 'misunderstood'].[61] Rachilde takes Delyon's light satire towards polemical critique in the subsequent article 'Une fois pour toutes!' Opening her contribution with a complaint regarding the topic's unoriginality, Rachilde goes on to depict bluestockings as hypocritically idolising the men they would undermine: 'Cette lutte de la femme de lettre [sic] contre la suprématie du mâle qu'elle adore ressemble assez

---

[58] Léo d'Orfer, 'Chronique raisonnable', *Le Zig-Zag*, 4 Oct. 1885.
[59] On fin-de-siècle authors and publishers' legal responsibility, see Yvan Leclerc, *Crimes écrits: la littérature en procès au XIX$^e$ siècle* (Paris: Plon, 1991), pp. 13–128, and Gisèle Sapiro, *La Responsabilité de l'écrivain: littérature, droit et morale en France (XIXe–XXIe siècle)* (Paris: Éditions du Seuil, 2011), pp. 323–518.
[60] The *physiologie* had gained popularity earlier in the century, partly in response to Louis-Philippe's 1835 censorship laws, which prevented journalists from satirising the king and his ministers. See Humphreys, '*Bas-bleus, filles publiques*', p. 28.
[61] Aymé Delyon, 'Paris-Bas-Bleu', *Le Zig-Zag*, 4 Oct. 1885.

à la lutte de Monsieur Léo Taxil contre le cléricalisme: un beau jour on se retourne et on s'agenouille!' ['This conflict between women writers and the supremacy of men they adore is like Mr Léo Taxil's fight against clericalism: one day you switch sides and kneel down before it!']⁶² She attacks her female contemporaries' moral hypocrisy and compares their rise in numbers to Egypt's plague of locusts. After criticising male writers such as Guy de Maupassant, René Maizeroy, and Jean Richepin for becoming romantically or sexually involved with pretentious female writers, Rachilde suggests that prostitutes' love letters have more artistry than *bas bleus*' published works. In a rhetorical flourish at the end of 'Une fois pour toutes!', the Decadent writer acknowledges her own hypocrisy in attacking bluestockings by writing: 'Après cela, Monsieur, je suis femme de lettres, vous savez!...' [And after that, Sir, I'm a woman writer, you know!...]⁶³

Appearing alongside Rachilde's text is the most polemical contribution to the *bas bleu* special issue: Lorrain's 'Le Troisième Sexe', published under the pseudonym 'Jack Stick'. In this article, Lorrain/Stick throws critical vitriol on his female counterparts, described as 'un flot montant de vieilles gardes, une marée de mondaines rancies' ['a rising flood of old guards, a tide of rancid society women'] who turn the domain of literary production into 'le camp des invalidées de l'alcôve et des refusées de la galanterie' ['the camp filled with intimacy's castoffs and gallantry's rejects'].⁶⁴ Contrasting d'Orfer's hints at the *bas bleus*' sexual availability, Lorrain here emphasises their sexual obsolescence. He subsequently depicts Jeanne Thilda's monthly *bas bleu* dinners, employing a lexis of visceral disgust and citing Rachilde as the only praiseworthy exception to the general rule of female incompetence. Following Lorrain's vitriolic criticism, while offering a stance in direct opposition to it, Léo d'Orfer places a letter he claims to have received from Camille Delaville. In this letter, Delaville attributes to men an underlying fear of female rivals in the intellectual and artistic domains. She also decries the social injustice of men insisting that women hide their talents or offset them by investing time in more traditional feminine roles: '[les] hommes sérieux vous prendront en grippe à moins que vous ne soyez jolie [...]. Même parmi celles qui ont un réel talent aucunes ne sont supportées ou appréciées qui n'ont pas effacé le côté littéraire de leur existence par autre chose' ['serious men will take a strong dislike

---

[62] Rachilde, 'Une fois pour toutes!', *Le Zig-Zag*, 4 Oct. 1885. Léo Taxil (1851–1907) was an anticlerical writer who ostensibly converted to Catholicism in 1885, only to reveal a decade later that this conversion was part of a series of hoaxes targeting Freemasonry.

[63] Rachilde's approach to gender identity is a recurrent topic in Rachilde studies, analysed through various critical lenses: feminist, queer, and—more recently—trans. Rachel Mesch provides a critical overview of these trends in 'Trans Rachilde: A Roadmap for Recovering the Gender Creative Past and Rehumanizing the Nineteenth Century', *Dix-Neuf* 25, nos. 3–4 (2021): pp. 242–59, doi:10.1080/14,787,318.2021.2017562. While acknowledging the role played by recent scholarly developments in nuancing modern readers' appreciation of a noteworthy literary figure, I adopt the approach Mesch used in *Before Trans* by using she/her to refer to Rachilde, who here describes herself as a woman writer.

[64] Jack Stick (pseud. Jean Lorrain), 'Le Troisième Sexe', *Le Zig-Zag*, 4 Oct. 1885.

to you unless you are pretty [...]. Even amongst those women with real talent, no-one receives support or appreciation unless they have covered up the literary side of their existence with something else'].[65] Throughout her letter—the only proto-feminist viewpoint in the issue—Delaville suggests that this 'autre chose' equates to domestic and sexual subservience to male prerogatives.

The range of opinions expressed within the *Zig-Zag* special issue incited further debate, encouraged by the structure of collaborative reader response built into the review's format. In the subsequent issue, d'Orfer highlights the force of polemic in uniting opposing individuals by emphasising the quantity and vehemence of letters responding to the *bas bleu* issue:

> Nous recevons une pluie de réclamations au sujet de notre numéro des Bas-Bleus et nous ne pouvons pas insérer les plus jolies malheureusement!... Les femmes sont dans un état de fureur inexprimable: lire plutôt les lettres de Rachilde qui ne s'attendait pas à être malmenée par nous et de Madame Camille Delaville [...] qui a vraiment tort de tant se défendre d'avoir du talent etc....

> [We're receiving a torrent of complaints about our Bluestocking issue and unfortunately we can't include the best ones!... The women are in a fit of inexpressible outrage: you should read the letters from Rachilde, who didn't expect us to pan her, and from Mrs Camille Delaville [...] who is wrong to protest so much about not having any talent...]

The article's controversial tone perpetuates a logic of outrage and defensiveness. It depicts well-known literary personalities defending their reputations and opinions from the criticism and mockery aired in the special issue. The responses attributed to Rachilde and Camille Delaville are indicative in this regard, since both writers complain about being placed alongside Jack Stick's 'Le Troisième Sexe'. Delaville employs a vocabulary of moral outrage to distance herself from Stick's vulgarity: 'Il m'a été fort désagréable de trouver une lettre de moi absolument intime, installée dans le *Zig-Zag*, [...] parce que j'ai horreur de me trouver avec des gens mal élevés, [...] et il m'a été odieux de voir mon nom à côté de cet article ordurier' ['I found it very unpleasant to find an entirely private letter of mine placed in *Le Zig-Zag*, [...] because I cannot stand being amongst ill-mannered people, [...] and I was appalled to see my name next to that foul article']. The physical proximity of their respective texts is seen to enable Delaville's unintentional complicity with Stick's more controversial viewpoints. Rachilde's response, placed immediately after Delaville's, reveals a similar concern: 'J'éprouve le besoin d'expliquer ma boutade: *Une fois pour toutes*, car, placée à côté des effroyables élucubrations de Jacques Stick (Paul Bonnetain, dit-on), elle semble devoir être

---

[65] Camille Delaville, 'Une lettre', *Le Zig-Zag*, 4 Oct. 1885.

pris au pied de la lettre' ['I feel the need to explain my little joke, *Une fois pour toutes* because, being placed next to the frightful ravings of Jacques Stick (Paul Bonnetain, apparently), it seems to have been taken at face value'].[66] By rejecting certain interpretations of her writing as too literal, in the phrase 'être pris au pied de la lettre', Rachilde maintains deniability through an implicit *mise en page* metaphor. Both writers share a desire for self-justification in the face of potential misinterpretation. At the same time, they recognise—and indeed highlight—the fact that their articles are read *alongside* ('à côté de', 'au pied de') and *in correlation* with those produced by fellow contributors. Even if their articles differ in opinion or tone, the periodical's structure therefore creates complicity through proximity. Yet by highlighting this process of guilt through association, Delaville and Rachilde paradoxically—and perhaps deliberately—emphasise and valorise the controversy in which they find themselves implicated.

## *Réclame* and *réclamation*

To explain this seeming paradox, I would highlight the relationship between 'réclamation' ['complaint'] and 'réclame' ['promotion'] in *Le Zig-Zag*. The former features prominently in the review's article titles, notably in the collective 'Guichet de réclamations' and in Lorrain's later piece: 'Encore les réclamations'. The noun 'réclamation' is derived from the verb 'réclamer'. According to the *Dictionnaire de l'Académie française*, the meanings of 'réclamer' include: putting forward an insistent request or demand, acting on someone's behalf to defend or protect them, and protesting against something.[67] In the context of the *Zig-Zag* exchanges, the word suggests a reaction involving emphatic disagreement with, and defensiveness against, the object of complaint. Through the verb 'réclamer', 'réclamation' is related to another noun, 'réclame'. Both words share a root in the Latin verb *reclamare* (to cry out/call back/protest against), while 'réclame' also borrows from the later Italian verb *richiamere* (to remind/recall).[68] Historically, 'réclame' was a term used in the printing domain, where it evoked the practice of placing the first word of the following page beneath the final word of the page that precedes it. In the theatre, it referred to the final words of a couplet that prompted other actors to reply. This meaning has suggestive parallels with the term's use in journalism, where it denoted indirect forms of advertising and publicity strategies.[69] Like the actors' couplets, advertising strategies attract the reader-audience's

[66] 'Guichet de réclamations', *Le Zig-Zag*, 11 Oct. 1885.
[67] *Dictionnaire*, II, p. 585.
[68] See 'Réclame, subst. fém' in *Trésor de la Langue Française informatisé*, ATIL: CNRS and Université de Lorraine, http://www.atilf.fr/tlfi, accessed 29 Jan. 2023, and Pierre Larousse, *Grand dictionnaire universel du XIXe siècle*, 17 vols (Paris: Administration du Grand Dictionnaire universel, 1866–77), XIII (1875), p. 781.
[69] Larousse, XIII (1875), pp. 781–3. See also Thérenty, 'La réclame de librairie'.

attention and prompt a programmed response: their interest in, and subsequent decision to purchase, the advertised product. In this context, 'réclame' therefore implies promotion, support, and sympathy, whereas 'réclamation' evokes rejection, denial, and antipathy. Despite their seeming juxtaposition, the two concepts are closely intertwined, as d'Orfer's opening lines in the 'Guichet de réclamations' suggest. By viewing 'réclame' and 'réclamation' as two sides of the same coin, we can see the correlation between the mutual self-promotion typical of sympathetic, collusive relationships and the self-defence mechanisms of polemical antipathy.

In the October 1885 issues of *Le Zig-Zag*, the *bas bleu*'s ambiguous gender status provided Rachilde and Lorrain with a whipping boy against which they could situate themselves, as well as a springboard for expressing and promoting their own non-normative approaches to gender and sexual identity. Polemical *réclamation* therefore united with and paved the way for mutual *réclame*. This process can be seen in 'Le Troisième Sexe' and in the responses it provoked. In the former, Lorrain portrays *bas bleus* as 'une marée de mondaines rancies [qui] bat lamentablement, désespérément le seuil des éditeurs et l'escalier des bureaux de rédaction' ['a tide of rancid society women [who], in a desperate, dismal flood, crash down upon publishers' doorsteps and editorial office stairways']. The term 'marée' perpetuates fin-de-siècle anxieties about the increasing number of female writers in the literary marketplace. The language of abjection reflects the article's polemical nature and the debate's underlying misogyny. Describing older, upper-class women writers as 'rancid' aligns literary worth with stereotyped visions of youthful charm and feminine sexual availability, by implying that women can only be good writers if they are sufficiently young and (therefore) desirable. Any other type of female authorship is therefore scandalous, because it gives visibility and voice to women who are culturally compelled to remain invisible in the heteronormative system of gendered sexual expectations. The scandal of female authorship undergirds Lorrain presentation of *bas bleus* as an army of old, fat, and bitter women whose appetite for celebrity is only rivalled by their ridiculous attempts at erotic seduction: 'des roueries de vieux dromadaires à dessiller les yeux peints du plus maquillé des poètes parnassiens' ['ruses of old laced mutton sufficient to open the painted eyes of the most makeup-laden Parnassian poets']. By aligning female writers' love affairs with bestiality, Lorrain channels a form of misogynistic disgust that is shot through with transgressive sexuality, including homoeroticism. The latter appears through references to effeminate 'poètes parnassiens' and the article's title, since '[le] troisième sexe' ['the third sex'] was a code word for non-normative sexuality throughout the nineteenth century. Lorrain appropriates the term's culturally loaded negative connotations and applies them to *bas bleus*, suggesting that they are even more culturally, morally, and physically abject than male and female homosexuals: 'Il y avait Sodome, il y avait Lesbos, nous avons les Bas-Bleus, le troisième sexe; ni hommes ni femmes, Bas-Bleus. Les Bas-Bleus, c'est-à-dire le clan des Tétonnières hors d'âge, bedonnantes, ventrues, gorgiasées, velues' ['We've had Sodom, we've had Lesbos, and now we have the Bluestockings, who, as the Third Sex, are neither men nor women. The Bluestockings: that is, the clan of hairy, shapely women with bulging bellies and bosoms, who are long past their sell-by date'].[70]

Lorrain's adoption of homophobic discourses in his attack on the *bas bleu* was ironic and hypocritical, and would have been read as such by fin-de-siècle readers 'in the know'. By the time Lorrain contributed to *Le Zig-Zag*, he already had a reputation for depicting same-sex desire. His early poetry treated topics typically associated with the burgeoning Decadent literary school, including a notable thematic obsession with 'perverse' sexual identities and behaviours. In *Modernités*, published a few months before the *bas bleu* debate, Lorrain celebrated the morally ambiguous appeal of figures associated with a performance-centred and thrill-seeking vision of modernity: dancers, circus performers, fairground boxers, and prostitutes.[71] In the circus spectacle of the modern world, both men and women sold sex appeal to an avid public: 'Sous l'éclatant maillot de soie, | Mettant les yeux de femmes en joie, | Les reins vigoureux des lutteurs | Confondent leurs âcres senteurs | Avec les parfums de vanille, | Montant des seins nus de la fille | Qui songe, accoudant au rebord | Des loges son bras cerclé d'or' ['Beneath dazzling silk costumes, | Sparking joy in women's eyes, | The fighters' vigorous loins | Blend their pungent scent | With the fragrant vanilla | Rising from the bare breasts of a harlot | Who daydreams, with a gold-ringed arm | Leaning upon the box's edge'].[72] This stanza, taken from the collection's eponymous poem, blends feminine and masculine forms of eroticism in a heady celebration of sexual performance, exchange, and changeability. Male nudity, particularly that of the 'lutteur' ['fighter'], repeatedly attracts the male poetic gaze, in a way that decentres the female body from being the primary source of erotic attraction. As well as these indirect hints of homoeroticism, there are overt references to male and female homosexuality in poems throughout the collection, including: 'Coquines', 'Little Boy', 'Darling', 'Athénienne', and 'Copailles'.[73] By October 1885, the association between Jean Lorrain and homoeroticism was therefore firmly established in the minds of readers who had access to his poetic production.

It is with this prior association in mind that we can appreciate the layers of irony Lorrain employs in 'Le Troisième Sexe'. In his comparison of the *bas bleu* to the culturally abject figure of the homosexual, Lorrain offers a hierarchy of monstrosity by suggesting that bluestockings are simultaneously *too* monstrous and *not monstrous enough*:

---

[70] Jack Stick, 'Le Troisième Sexe'.
[71] It is noteworthy that Léo d'Orfer reviews *Modernités* in 'Causerie littéraire', *Le Zig-Zag*, 14 June 1885.
[72] Jean Lorrain, *Modernités* (Paris: E. Giraud & Cie, 1885), p. 10.
[73] Lorrain, *Modernités*, pp. 22–3, 82, 90, 93, and 105, respectively.

> Classons les sexes, bon Dieu! Je leur ai assigné le troisième déjà si encombré depuis Héliogabale et Sapho; mais, monstres pour monstres, Ganymède, Héphestion, Patrocle, Antinoüs chez les anciens, le duc d'Epernon, le marquis d'O, et la chevalière d'Eon sous nos rois bien-aimés étaient de jolis monstres [...]. Or, parmi les monstresses de la littérature, où est-il, le joli monstre?[74]

> [For God's sake, let's delineate the sexes! I assigned them the third sex, already over-crowded since Heliogabalus and Sappho. But, if we can choose between monsters, Ganymede, Hephaestion, Patroclus, Antinous in ancient times, as well as the Duke of Epernon, Marquis d'O, and Chevalière d'Éon under the reign of our beloved kings, were beautiful fiends. [...] Now, among our literary monstresses, where can we find the beautiful fiend?]

In this diatribe, Lorrain seemingly calls for a return to traditional gender roles ('Classons les sexes, bon Dieu!'). He does so while glorifying figures such as Heliogabalus and Sappho, whose sexual ambiguity earns them the appreciative and oxymoronic epithet 'jolis monstres'. On one level, Lorrain appears to reproach the *bas bleus* for their failure to adhere to sexual norms. The irony of this approach would have been plain to readers 'in the know' regarding Lorrain's sexual preferences. Even those not already part of *Le Zig-Zag*'s knowing readership can infer, from the presence of hyperbole, oxymoron, and paradox, that not all is as it seems. While offering this faux naïf critique of bluestockings' sexual impropriety, Lorrain seems to bemoan the bluestockings' inability to subvert gender norms with sufficient panache, when compared to their younger, more avant-garde contemporaries (the 'jolis monstres'). We can see that Lorrain flips the negative cultural stigma attached to sexual deviance by valorising the subversive 'monstrosity' of non-normative sexual identities. However, this reversal relies on a misogynistic rejection of women who exist outside specific gender norms (feminine desirability and sexual availability), in favour of 'jolis monstres' who reverse key aspects of these norms while perpetuating others. In this way, gender subversion retains elements of misogyny and sexual subversion reproduces homophobia, by connecting a series of parallels between seemingly divergent approaches.

The lexis of perversity and monstrosity in 'Le Troisième sexe' recurs throughout the October *Zig-Zag* issues, as part of the contributors' banter-filled exchanges. In this context, Lorrain's vision of the sexually ambiguous 'joli monstre' works not only to support his own controversial persona in opposition to the *bas bleu*, but also to promote Rachilde's provocative media image via collaborative *réclame*. In the special issue, both Lorrain and d'Orfer perpetuate an already popular vision of Rachilde as an androgynous, perverse writer of risqué Decadent novels. Based on a biographical reading of her early works, this image dominated

---

[74] Jack Stick, 'Le Troisième Sexe'.

media representations of Rachilde throughout the 1880s, and only started to shift once she married Alfred Vallette in 1889. In 'Le Troisième Sexe', Lorrain indirectly applies the term 'joli monstre' to Rachilde by affirming her status as an exception to the norm:

> Un ami qui lit par-dessus mon épaule me demande grâce pour Rachilde et Jacques Vincent. Mademoiselle Rachilde est, paraît-il jeune, vierge et jolie personne. Cela fait d'autant plus son éloge que *Monsieur Vénus*, le seul de ses livres qu'il m'ait été donné de lire, est d'une corticante dépravation. Tous mes compliments à la stupéfiante précocité de son cerveau.[75]

> [A friend reading over my shoulder asks me to spare Rachilde and Jacques Vincent. Miss Rachilde is a virginal and pretty young lady, it seems. It is all the more to her credit that *Monsieur Vénus*, which is the only one of her books that I've been given to read, contains deep-rooted depravity. All my compliments to her mind's astounding precocity.]

In a gesture of collusive—if somewhat ambivalent—friendship, Lorrain offers an appraisal of Rachilde's perversity, while doing so through the lens of a homosocial exchange between men about the limited value of women writers. It is noteworthy that Rachilde receives recognition only after a male colleague speaks on her behalf ('Un ami [...] me demande grâce'), in a discussion that relies on her absence. Furthermore, Lorrain and his male colleague place Rachilde in a double bind by valorising her difference to other women, while ironically praising her desirable 'feminine' traits: youth, virginity, and beauty.

Lorrain's use of hyperbole, seen in the terms 'corticante dépravation' and 'stupéfiante précocité', highlights the back-handed nature of his compliments and conveys a tongue-in-cheek tone suggestive of the article's light-hearted provocation. This tone is congruent with the issue as a whole, and mirrors that of Léo d'Orfer's leading article, which playfully condemns Rachilde's hypocritical attack on bluestockings:

> Et vous, Rachilde, jeune Éphèbe mal sexué, dit-on, vous qui avez trop de talent pour être une femme, et pas assez de raison pour être un homme... selon la grammaire, pourquoi bouderiez-vous vos compagnes au sujet de leurs passions? C'est bien plutôt contre des jolis monstres de votre espèce que je voudrais m'élever.[76]

> [And you, Rachilde—a sexless young ephebe, or so they say—you who are too talented to be a woman, but too illogical to be a man... following grammatical

---

[75] Jack Stick, 'Le Troisième Sexe'.
[76] D'Orfer, 'Chronique raisonnable'.

logic, why would you take issue with your female peers on the topic of their passions? It is beautiful fiends such as yourself that I would much rather stand up against.']

D'Orfer highlights the ambiguity of Rachilde's gender status and sexuality by using the word 'Éphèbe', which was typically used in literature of the period to refer to effeminate male homosexuals. He also pre-emptively lifts Lorrain's term 'joli monstre' ['beautiful fiend'] in a way that combines mock-moralising reproach with playful appreciation. By doing so, he adds to the homosocial atmosphere of men-talking-about-women, while claiming to defend the latter from others' critique. In these instances, both men play a part in collaboratively staging Rachilde's illicit literary persona. Even so, they mitigate their appraisal of her perversity with references to hearsay: 'dit-on' and 'paraît-il'. Rachilde's status as a 'jeune Éphèbe mal sexué' or a 'jeune, vierge, et jolie personne' is therefore ironically questioned while being implicitly promulgated.

The back-and-forth between mockery and support, hinted at in the review's very title, is part of a wider phenomenon of provocative banter between literary *camarades* in *Le Zig-Zag*. After all, Rachilde does not leave her colleagues' comments unanswered. She responds to them directly in the 'Guichet de réclamations' of the subsequent issue, thereby contributing to an otherwise male-centred discussion.[77] In the 'Guichet', Rachilde addresses d'Orfer the following witticism: 'je tiens à déclarer *une fois pour toutes* à votre directeur, Monsieur Léo d'Orfer, que les mots *jeune Éphèbe mal sexué* ne peuvent m'atteindre, venant de sa part' ['To your manager, Mr Léo d'Orfer, I really wish to declare, *once and for all*, that the words "sexless young ephebe" cannot harm me, coming from him']. Rachilde here implicates her critic in the sexual perversity he mock-condemned, according to the logic that it takes one to know one.[78] She then contradicts Jack Stick, initially misidentified as the Naturalist writer Paul Bonnetain (1858–99),[79] by distancing herself from his vision of her as a perverse virgin: 'Quant à Monsieur Jacques Stick [sic] (autrement dit Monsieur Paul Bonnetain), le brevet de virginité qu'il me délivre me paraît inutile. Je vous en conjure, mes chers amies [sic], ne posons pas trop pour les vierges, tout le monde se moquerait de nous' ['As for Mr Jack Stick (aka Mr Paul Bonnetain), the virginity certificate he grants me seems unnecessary. I beseech you, my dear friends, let's not over-play the virgin role, for

[77] Although some of the 'Guichet' responses seem to have been fabricated for comic effect, it is unlikely that prose with Rachilde's signature would have been printed without her knowledge, due to her position as a minor celebrity and friend to the *directeur* Léo d'Orfer. Furthermore, Rachilde mentions her 'Guichet' response in the later article 'Zig-Zag Parade', thereby acknowledging its content.
[78] This comment can also be interpreted as a veiled reference to their rumoured relationship.
[79] It is significant that Rachilde hypothesises that 'Jack Stick' might be Paul Bonnetain, who was equally adept at appropriating moralising discourses and manipulating controversy for self-promotion. His recently published Naturalist novel about masturbation, *Charlot s'amuse* (1883), depicted a different but relatedly scandalous deviation from heteronormativity. On the novel's obscenity trial and Bonnetain's subsequent acquittal, in late December 1884, see Leclerc, *Crimes écrits*, pp. 395–401.

everyone would laugh at us if we did'].[80] In this section, Rachilde places herself in an authoritative position, dispensing advice to fellow writers. The appellation 'mes chers amies' may simply be a typographical error, implying that *bas bleus* are her primary interlocutors. Conversely, it is also possible to read this grammatical mis-gendering as a deliberate *clin d'oeil* ['knowing wink'] to fellow Decadent writers, such as Lorrain, who cultivated public personae associated with subversive gender identities or non-normative sexualities. Rachilde's advice, 'ne posons pas trop pour les vierges', therefore functions not only as a gender-specific critique, but also as a broader warning against the risks of constructing a scandalous media identity. Nonetheless, this advice appears disingenuous, because Rachilde would continue to play up to the 'perverse virgin' persona throughout the 1880s, most notably in the autobiographical preface of *À mort* (1886). This work provoked a series of vitriolic critical responses, including an à-clef polemical pamphlet by Gisèle d'Estoc, entitled *La Vierge-réclame*.[81] In the pamphlet, d'Estoc aligns the self-promotional strategies employed by Decadent writers like Rachilde with exhibitionism: 'vous exhibez vos personnes comme des acteurs de trétaux' ['you flaunt yourselves like actors on a stage']. She refutes Rachilde's virginal status and accuses her of tricking readers (and fellow writers) into maintaining a gimmicky illusion: 'vous trichez avec le public, vous avez recours à la mise en scène et aux *trucs*' ['you play around with the public, resorting to deception and *stage tricks*'].[82]

D'Estoc's critique, however vitriolic it may be, offers a perceptive account of writers' mutual *réclame* as a form of complicit performance. Her appeal to theatrical imagery negatively reflects that which appears throughout the October 1885 *Zig-Zag* issues. For example, in 'Zig-Zag Parade', Rachilde repays the favour of her colleagues' promotional *réclame* through a staged *mise en scène* of the review and its contributors. She centres questions of gender identity by addressing the audience: 'Mesdames, Messieurs et les autres, s'il s'en trouve!...' ['Ladies, Gentlemen, and others, if there are any!...'] By acknowledging—however tentatively and playfully—the presence of individuals outside the gender binary, Rachilde extends the equivocal celebration of sexual deviance expressed in the *bas bleu* special issue. The character Jack Stick represents such deviance in 'Zig-Zag Parade' through his drag persona, described in a stage direction: '(*Une grosse femme très belle qui doit être Jacques Stik* [sic] *déguisé pour nous faire peur*)' ['(*A heavy-set and very beautiful woman, who must by Jacques Stik* [sic] *dressed in disguise to scare us off*)']. The chaos greeting Rachilde's 'performance' culminates in Stick revealing his identity to be Jean Lorrain:

[80] 'Guichet de réclamations'.
[81] This chapter's analysis of Gisèle d'Estoc is indebted to the work of Melanie Hawthorne and Michael Finn.
[82] Gisèle d'Estoc, *Les Gloires malsaines: La Vierge réclame* (Paris: Librairie Richelieu, 1887), pp. 114 and 126.

A ce moment Jacques Stik [sic] saute sur le tonneau après avoir enlevé sa robe de femme. On reconnaît... qui ça? Ce drôle de Jean Lorrain (que je prenais pour Paul Bonnetain). Armé d'une cravache, il profite du désordre pour régler de vieux comptes [...] et nous tombons tous dans le petit tonneau.[83]

[At this moment Jack Stick leaps upon the barrel after having taken off his lady's dress. It turns out to be.... Who? That queer old Jean Lorrain (who I thought was Paul Bonnetain). Armed with a riding crop, he makes the most of the confusion to settle some old scores [...] and we all end up falling into the little barrel.]

Rachilde here aligns Lorrain's use of a pseudonym with gender-bending disguise and its subsequent unveiling.[84] Her vision of Lorrain as a provocative transvestite settling scores with his enemies works alongside, and intersects with, Lorrain's own combative *mise en scène*. In 'Encore les réclamations', which appeared in the same issue as 'Zig-Zag Parade', Lorrain offers a mock-apology to the *bas bleus* in a bipartite letter addressed to Léo d'Orfer. The article highlights (implicitly autobiographical) gender ambiguity and homoeroticism from the opening lines: 'En ma qualité de poète des Ephèbes, [...] je comprends un peu l'horreur de Jack Stick pour les grosses poitrines ['In my role as poet of ephebes, [...] I somewhat understand Jack Stick's loathing of large bosoms']. The word 'Éphèbe'—used earlier by d'Orfer to describe Rachilde—is not gratuitous, since it was frequently used in the nineteenth century as a code word for sexual and amorous relations between men. Lorrain confirms the homoerotic implications of the term by referring to four *bas bleus* dedicatees as 'quatre jolis hommes' ['four pretty men'] and citing Shakespeare as a justificatory precedent for homoerotic verse.[85] Through these playful references to gender ambiguity and homoeroticism, Rachilde and Lorrain's articles in number 148 of *Le Zig-Zag* contribute to the ongoing polemic and benefit from the *réclame* it enabled.

As well as combining polemic with *réclame*, Lorrain used 'Encore les réclamations' to respond to criticism he had recently received in the press. Much like Rachilde's perverse virgin status, Lorrain's dandified and homoerotic media

---

[83] Rachilde, 'Zig-Zag Parade', *Le Zig-Zag*, 18 Oct. 1885.
[84] On the relationship between pseudonyms and transvestism in Decadent literature, notably in the works of Rachilde and Jean Lorrain, see Leonard Koos, 'Improper Names: Pseudonyms and Transvestites in Decadent Prose', in *Perennial Decay: On the Aesthetics and Politics of Decadance*, edited by Liz Constable and others (Philadelphia: University of Pennsylvania Press, 1999), pp. 198-214.
[85] Jean Lorrain, 'Encore les réclamations', *Le Zig-Zag*, 18 Oct. 1885.

persona attracted accusations of Decadent posturing. The day preceding *Le Zig-Zag*'s special issue on the *bas bleu*, the writer-journalist Félicien Champsaur (1858–1934) had published an article entitled 'Poètes décadenticulets' ['Decadentista Poets'] in the literary supplement of *Le Figaro*. In it, he criticised Decadent writers such as Lorrain for playing up to sexual ambiguity, suggesting that their homoeroticism was nothing but attention-seeking farce:

> Touchant la trentaine ou frôlant la cinquantaine, [...] ils racontent qu'un tel est "collé" avec tel autre [...]. Et, l'hiver, à l'époque des bals masqués, ils se déguisent en mignons.
> Mais c'est un simple genre, une attitude de décadenticulets. Ils sont réservés, ingénus, d'une complète respectabilité [...]. "Nous confessons bien des péchés que nous n'avons pas commis".
> Quelqu'un a dû dire cela.
> Le vice?
> Ils n'en sont pas capables.[86]

> [Coming up to their thirties or verging on their fifties, [...] they say that one man is 'shacked up' with another [...] And, in winter, during the period of masked balls, they dress up as dainty darlings.
> But it's only an act, a posture adopted by Decadentistas. They are reserved, naïve, and completely respectable. [...] 'We confess to many sins that we have not committed'.
> Someone must have said that.
> Vice?
> They aren't capable of it.]

Champsaur seems to criticise writers less for experiencing same-sex desire than for *playing up to* homoeroticism for the ends of self-promotion. This approach towards non-normative sexual identity was not uncommon in the period. Andrew Counter has shown that, at the fin de siècle, while homosexuality per se was denounced as perversion, the homosexual proclivities of specific individuals tended instead to be dismissed as mere posturing.[87]

Lorrain responds to Champsaur's attack in 'Encore les réclamations' by ironically confirming its accusations through repeated references to homosexuality. As previously mentioned, Lorrain promotes his status as a 'poète des Ephèbes'

---

[86] Félicien Champsaur, 'Poètes décadenticulets', *Le Figaro, supplément littéraire*, 3 Oct. 1885.

[87] Andrew J. Counter, 'One of Them: Homosexuality and Anarchism in Wilde and Zola', *Comparative Literature* 63, no. 4 (2011): pp. 345–65, doi:10.1215/00104124-1444419.

in the first half of the letter. In the second half, 'Jack Stick' cites Champsaur directly by referring back to Lorrain as a 'poète décadent, sacré décadenticulet par Félicien Champsaur, teneur de *massacre* à la grande foire permanente du Figaro' ['Decadent poet, anointed as a "decadentista" by Félicien Champsaur, the head *slaughterer* at *Le Figaro*'s great non-stop fairground']. Lorrain's use of two pseudonyms in this article suggests precisely the kind of personality-splitting posturing for which he was criticised. In a similar way, his 'apology' to the *bas bleus* simply further enacts the mocking behaviour for which he is supposedly apologising. Not only this, but Lorrain implicates Champsaur in the very performance-driven media tactics his critic denigrates by describing *Le Figaro* as a 'grande foire permanente' ['great non-stop fairground'].[88] Once again, readers find the schoolyard logic that it 'takes one to know one' at work here. By playing up to his critic's accusations and highlighting Champsaur's complicity with what he critiques, Lorrain unravels his opponent's logic while repurposing *réclame* for the purposes of *réclamation*.[89] In a parallel gesture, Rachilde contributes to this process in her portrait of Lorrain in the second 'Zig-Zag Parade' article: 'Un bon zig!... Excellent poète, superbe lutteur, vigoureux chroniqueur. (Voir le n° des Bas-Bleus.) [...] Accablé de tous les vices qu'il porte d'ailleurs crânement (n'en ayant d'ailleurs aucun, mais si heureux de passer pour un horrible monstre)' ['A great bloke!... An excellent poet, superb fighter, and hard-hitting columnist. (See the number on bluestockings.) [...] Condemned for all manner of vices, which he boldly carries off (although he doesn't actually have any of them, he's very happy to pass for a horrible monster)'].[90] Rachilde here celebrates Lorrain's deliberate but ambivalent adoption of a perverse persona, which she suggests is projected by detractors who accuse him of vices that are not in fact his own. Lorrain wears or carries these accusations off with panache ('porte[r] [...] crânement'), choosing to 'pass' as a monster and to re-deploy others' criticism to his own ends. The phrase 'si heureux de passer pour un horrible monstre' indirectly evokes Champsaur's description of Decadent posturing, while positively reframing it as a clever way to disarm criticism through ironic appropriation. As the ongoing *Zig-Zag* debate demonstrates, *réclame* has a parasitic or infectious quality, whereby criticism of self-promotional strategies becomes implicated in, and is appropriated by, those very strategies. By collaboratively manipulating this quality through their media exchanges, Rachilde and Lorrain implicate one another in strategies of mutual self-promotion, while re-appropriating and subverting the discourses used by their detractors.

---

[88] Lorrain, 'Encore les réclamations'.
[89] It is worth noting that only two years before writing 'Poètes décadenticulets', Félicien Champsaur had published an infamous *roman à clef* about the actress Sarah Bernhardt, entitled *Dinah Samuel* (1883). He was therefore equally guilty of pandering to the widespread interest in biographically revealing fiction.
[90] Rachilde, 'Zig-Zag Parade. Auteurs et décors', *Le Zig-Zag*, 25 Oct. 1885.

## *Déshabillage*, or Public Striptease

Rachilde and Lorrain's *réclame* relies on a process of staged autobiographical unveiling. This media strategy involves the indirect but deliberate revelation of personal anecdotes and secrets (whether real or fictionalised) in order to arouse readers' curiosity. I refer to this phenomenon, which is synonymous with à-clef literary structures, as *déshabillage* ['undressing'] due to the insistent way it is associated with exhibitionism and striptease. As previously noted, critics attributed this approach not only to bluestockings, but also to Decadent writers, who were accused of playing titillating identity games in order to gain notoriety. Although Rachilde and Lorrain were objects of criticism in this regard, they shared their critics' suspicion of *déshabillage* when it was practised by others. As with their position on gender, Rachilde and Lorrain took an ambiguous, hypocritical position on the question of *déshabillage*, criticising *bas bleus* for engaging in partially veiled or fictionalised acts of self-revelation, while promulgating the tendencies they condemned and implicating their readers in the process.[91]

Throughout the *Zig-Zag* exchanges, the pair lampoon bluestockings for using scandalous anecdotal references to pique their readers' interest in illicit (i.e. sexual) secrets. Rachilde criticises female writers for hypocritically combining moralising pretensions with titillating self-revelation: 'les femmes de lettres ont l'absurdité [...] de dire tout ce qu'elles font entre leur repas du soir et celui du matin... de la perturbation dans nos mœurs' ['women writers are absurd enough [...] to speak about what they do between their evening and morning meals... for the disruption of our morals'].[92] The eroticised self-revelation Rachilde claims is rife in female-authored literary production matches the sexualised self-display found in Lorrain's satirical description of Thilda's monthly dinner:

> [Un] dîner-parade, dîner-réclame, dont les comptes-rendus rédigés et publiés par d'anonymes *Mitaines de soie* et d'insinuantes *Pattes de velours* pétillaient d'affriolantes et savoureuses indiscrétions [...]. Et qu'y avons-nous [les journalistes] vu? [...] [T]outes ces horreurs, toutes ces chairs *fumées*, apoplectiques et vineuses, exhibées, débordantes, étalées avec une complaisance, une effronterie, une telle bonne volonté et un tel désir de plaire qu'ils en devenaient touchants d'inconscience.[93]

> [A] parade dinner or publicity-stunt dinner, reviewed in articles written and published by anonymous *Silk Mittens* and obsequious *Velvet Paws*, frothing over with

---

[91] On Lorrain's broader tendency to condemn media practices he himself used, see Paré, 'Les avatars du Littéraire'.
[92] Rachilde, 'Une fois pour toutes!'
[93] Jack Stick, 'Le Troisième Sexe'.

alluring and juicy indiscretions [...]. And what did we [journalists] see there? [...] All these ghastly horrors, all this *smoked* flesh—wine-red and haemorrhaging—exhibited, over-flowing, and flaunted with such indulgence, such impudence, such willingness, and such a desire to please that their very thoughtlessness made them touching.]

Lorrain's critique emphasises the close association between the deliberately staged visual availability of female nudity ('toutes ces chairs [...] exhibées, débordantes, étalées') and titillating journalistic forms. By evoking 'comptes rendus' ['reviews' or 'reports'] signed under feminised and fetishistic pseudonyms ('Mitaine de soie' and 'Patte de velours'), Lorrain targets the widespread practice of recounting social events in gossip columns.[94] He depicts the *bas bleu* dinners and their mediation through gossip-hungry reviews as a public striptease. This comparison aligns the *bas bleu* with prostitution and thereby implicitly devalues her work. In a similar gesture, Lorrain's postscript lampoons the well-known writer and journalist Gyp (pseud. Comtesse de Martel de Janville, 1849–1932):

> P.S. Je n'ai pas fait à Gyp l'outrage de la citer parmi les bas-bleus [...]. [D]ans *Autour du mariage*, dans le *Monde à côté*, dans *Bob* et ses autres livres, Mme de Martel s'est toujours si complaisamment et si gracieusement déshabillée en public, qu'on ne peut l'accuser d'avoir jamais fait du roman.[95]

> [P.S. I have not done Gyp the dishonour of citing her amongst the bluestockings. [...] In *Autour du mariage*, in *Le Monde à côté*, in *Bob* and her other works, Madame de Martel has always stripped off so indulgently and so graciously in public, that she could never be accused of having written a novel.]

Lorrain's mock-compliment ostensibly suggests that the act of writing novels ('faire du roman') is more compromising than indecent exposure ('[se déshabiller] en public'), while implying that the distinction is irrelevant in Gyp's case. The adverb 'complaisamment' targets Gyp's complicity with a morally and aesthetically suspect media strategy. In this way, women writers who engage in autobiographical self-revelation—whether in public social displays or in published novels—are stripped of value and consideration, thereby typifying the widespread denigration of *romans à clef* as a genre.

Despite criticising *bas bleus* for their proclivity for titillating self-revelation, both Rachilde and Lorrain were equally guilty of manipulating the appeal of

---

[94] Clara Sadoun-Édouard reads the practice of men writing under feminised pseudonyms in society newspapers less as a sign of subversion than of voyeurism, fetishism, and mythification, in *Le Roman de* La Vie parisienne *(1863–1914): Presse, genre, littérature et mondanité* (Paris: Honoré Champion, 2018), pp. 296–7.

[95] Sadoun-Édouard, *Le Roman de* La Vie Parisienne, pp. 296–7.

illicit autobiographical references in order to gain readerly interest. This ambiguity appears in 'Zig-Zag Parade', where Rachilde playfully shifts the blame for literary *déshabillage* onto the reader. She suggests that writers are burdened with the voyeuristic desires that readers project onto them, by depicting audience members interrupting her presentation of *Le Zig-Zag* with questions such as: 'peut-on monter quand les réd-actrices s'habillent?' ['can you go upstairs when the copywriter women are getting dressed?'] and 'A-t-on du vice, derrière le Rideau? Se vend t'on bien? Il est entendu que je ne parle pas de la feuille... mais des rédac!... [sic]' ['Is there vice behind the curtain? Do you sell well? Of course, I'm not talking about the paper... but about the writers!']96 A voyeuristic desire to watch female contributors (un)dressing is rendered synonymous with the desire for titillating anecdotes. The emphasis on individual contributors' sexual proclivities—seen in the references to nudity, vice, performance ('réd-actrices'), and prostitution ('se vendre')—suggests that readers are more interested in the review's 'behind the scenes' action than in its actual content. While implicitly criticising this tendency, Rachilde also plays up to it. She depicts herself performing in a tight-fitting 'maillot' ['costume'] and uses the article to reveal Lorrain's authorship of 'Le Troisième Sexe' by *undressing* his drag persona. Similarly, in the second 'Zig-Zag Parade' article, she offers readers a tantalising glimpse inside the review's offices, thereby drawing on the popular journalistic subgenre of visiting and interviewing writers in their own homes.97 The description includes voyeuristic references to Aymé Delyon's bedroom: 'La chambre à coucher de la rédactrice en chef... N'entrez pas, Messieurs et Mesdames... n'entrez pas!...' ['The editor-in-chief's bedroom... Do not enter, Ladies and Gentlemen... do not enter!...']98 Throughout Rachilde's articles, the relationship between supply and demand becomes blurred, and it is unclear who is to blame for the widespread literary tendency of *déshabillage*.

Lorrain also contributes to this dilemma in 'Encore les réclamations', not only by filling his bipartite mock-apology with the homoeroticism analysed above, but also by describing Jack Stick as 'nu comme un ver' ['buck-naked'] when offering his versified mock-apology to the *bas bleus*. Stick's nudity suggests an act of self-humiliation, for the purposes of 'amende honorable' ['making amends'], while simultaneously creating a relationship of compromising implication between himself and the reader. Lorrain hints at this ambiguity in the closing lines of the first section: 'Suis-je assez compromis! Que l'homme qui n'a jamais péché me jette la dernière pierre' [Have I been sufficiently compromised? Let the man who's never

---

[96] Rachilde, 'Zig-Zag Parade'.
[97] On this practice, see Olivier Nora, 'La Visite au grand écrivain', in *Lieux de mémoire*, edited by Pierre Nora, 3 vols (1984–92), II (1986), pp. 563–87, and Marielle Gubelmann, 'La Visite à l'écrivain (1870–1940). Variations autour de la figure d'auteur sous la Troisième République' (Master's dissertation, University of Lausanne, 2007).
[98] Rachilde, 'Zig-Zag Parade. Auteurs et décors'.

sinned cast the last stone']'.[99] Through an ironic reformulation of Scripture, he acknowledges the compromising nature of his own writing, while implicating the reader in the homoerotic desire it depicts. When readers unravel and comprehend hints at homoerotic self-revelation, there is a risk that they might recognise themselves in the 'perverse' desires they discover. Or, as Latham puts it: 'the secrets we unlock might be our own'.[100] Much like Rachilde's *mise en scène* of the audience's curiosity in 'Zig-Zag Parade', the underlying homoeroticism in Lorrain's evocation of compromising nudity encourages his reader to recognise suggestive *clins d'œil*, in a way that depends upon the desire it simultaneously creates and reveals.

## Compromising Revelations in *Romans à Clef*

Rachilde and Lorrain's contributions to *Le Zig-Zag* highlight an ambiguous association between self-revelation, self-promotion, and self-humiliation, thereby hinting at the risks of self-exposure on the public stage. These associations incite further debate about the relationship between audacity and vulnerability in avant-garde media strategies. To what extent were fin-de-siècle writers in control of their public image? Where did the distinction lie between savvy self-promotion and the genuine—if indirect and playful—expression of identity and affective experience? What happened when a writer went too far in exposing a friend or colleague on the public stage? Two contemporary à-clef novellas written by Oscar Méténier, one of the pair's mutual friends, help provide answers to these questions. Méténier worked as a police clerk in Paris before entering the avant-garde literary scene in the 1880s, befriending Lorrain in 1883.[101] He published articles, novels, and plays, and founded the Grand Guignol theatre in 1897. Frequenting the social and literary circles associated with Decadence, Méténier attended parties and balls with Lorrain and Rachilde by his side.[102] Drawing on a detailed knowledge of Parisian criminal and lower-class *milieux*, Méténier's works fed the popular obsession with criminality and social transgression at the fin de siècle. Modern critics affirm that Méténier shared Lorrain's same-sex desire.[103] Like his Decadent colleagues, he regularly created literary *mises en scène* of non-normative gender identities and sexualities. Revealing an array of personal and scandalous anecdotes about Lorrain and Rachilde respectively, 'L'Aventure de Marius Dauriat' (1885) and 'Décadence' (1886) explored the close relationship between *réclame* and *déshabillage* at a thematic and meta-textual level. Analysing Méténier's novellas

---

[99] Lorrain, 'Encore les réclamations'.
[100] Latham, *The Art of Scandal*, p. 62.
[101] Anthonay, *Jean Lorrain*, p. 165.
[102] See Hawthorne, *Rachilde*, pp. 100–1.
[103] See Finn, *Hysteria*, p. 49, and Mesch, *Before Trans*, p. 148.

alongside their reception by the texts' veiled protagonists shows how the boundary between collusive and compromising literary relationships was as narrow as it was fluid, and that these relationships involved real risk for, and required adroit negotiation from, those implicated in them.

Published in *La Chair* (1885), 'L'Aventure de Marius Dauriat' recounted an anecdote circulating at the time about Lorrain's sexual proclivities. The story went that Lorrain's liaison with a circus strongman ended in the former's being left humiliated, without any clothes, in a disreputable hotel room. The anecdote, later confirmed by Rachilde in *Portraits d'hommes*, is thinly veiled in Méténier's novella.[104] It depicts the relationship between a Decadent poet (the eponymous 'Marius Dauriat') and a circus strongman ('Nicolas le Boucher'), which breaks down due to the former's insatiable search for an increasingly gender-bending— if not gender-transcendent—relationship. After being unceremoniously jilted in favour of a female lover, Nicolas le Boucher conspires to take vengeance on Dauriat, with the help of one of his petty criminal friends, nicknamed Napoléon. Nicolas and Napoléon trick Dauriat into thinking they will help to procure him a young girl with masculine traits. They lure the poet into Napoléon's apartment, strip him naked—supposedly in preparation for the promised sexual escapades— before revealing their disgust at his 'dépravations', assaulting him, and escaping. After coming round, Dauriat is forced to leave the apartment partially clothed in a mismatching wardrobe, which raises the suspicions of two local police officers. Unable to denounce Nicolas and Napoléon, for fear that they will comment on his sexual preferences in court, Dauriat flees the scene in a hired carriage before the police have a chance to arrest him.

A year after *La Chair*, Méténier published a second trilogy of novellas: *La Grâce* (1886), containing another à-clef story. 'Décadence' describes an androgynous and virginal actress, Mary Staub, who, with the help of her witty and aloof friend Le Rozay, takes vengeance on a former suitor, Arsène Meunier, who had recently jilted her in favour of a more feminine lover: Mary's fellow actress and rival Jane Normand. After a successful performance of Le Rozay's new play, Mary attends a party organised by a mutual acquaintance. Dressed in men's clothing, she exchanges barbed witticisms with Arsène and wagers that she can seduce Jane Normand *as a man*. Mary's androgynous charm, and a few glasses of champagne, suffice to pique Jane's desire. In a dramatic climax, Jane offers herself to Mary in the hostess's boudoir, revealing her breasts by ripping off her own bodice and passionately kissing Mary. In a heady embrace laced with a hint of sadistic pleasure, Mary bites Jane's lips and neck, before pushing her through a doorway leading back into the ballroom, for everyone to witness her humiliation. The protagonist has clear similarities with Rachilde, whose androgynous gender presentation and

---

[104] Rachilde, *Portraits d'hommes*, 6th ed. (Paris: Mercure de France, 1930), pp. 79–92.

'perverse virgin' persona was widely discussed in the mid-1880s. Other biographical details add to the à-clef status of the novella. It is highly probable that Arsène Meunier, described in the story as a womanising journalist known for writing frothy erotic fiction, stands in for Catulle Mendès—a writer with whom Rachilde had a brief and intense erotic (but apparently non-sexual) relationship.[105] Furthermore, the figure of Le Rozay has traits similar to Jean Lorrain, and it is possible that Jane Normand represents Rachilde's supposed admirer-turned-enemy Gisèle d'Estoc.[106] In both novellas, Méténier explores the sexual ambiguity of his friends' relationships in a way that plays up to the curiosity such relationships provoked. Each story contains a vengeance plot concocted by a jilted, betrayed lover and their friend-accomplice, which results in public humiliation for their target. In these instances, public humiliation involves nudity or *déshabillage*, which functions as a productive metaphor for the compromising revelations at the heart of *romans à clef.*

In 'L'Aventure', the sexually ambiguous and implicitly homoerotic nature of Marius Dauriat's relationship with Nicolas le Boucher emerges indirectly through a double-layered description—first from Nicolas's viewpoint, then from an impersonal narrator. The story opens *in media res* with a description of a Parisian dive bar and a strongman performing for its seedy clientele. Another strongman, Nicolas le Boucher, enters the bar and recounts his woes to Napoléon, a well-known pimp and thief ('un barbe fameux [...] pour son audace et ses condamnations' ['a pimp well known for his audacity and criminal convictions']).[107] In an extended scene of dialogue written in turn-of-the-century popular slang, Nicolas describes having been stood up by 'une copaille' who owes him money. Akin to its modern equivalent 'pédé' ['poof' or 'faggot'], the homophobic slur 'copaille' defines the eponymous character according to his non-normative sexual desire and behaviour before he enters the scene. However, the precise nature of Nicolas's relationship with Marius is only hinted at in the story, and never fully revealed, such as when Nicolas reminisces about their boxing lessons and bemoans Marius's flightiness:

Un gars bath, pas vrai? Avec sa moustache blonde et bien frisée, ses douilles toujours peignées, ses mirette bleues… Il avait du nerf, c'gringalet-là! [...] Je l'adorais, c'môme-là! Ah! c'qu'on a fait des noces ensemble! [...] C'était trop beau! Ça pouvait pas durer! D'puis un moment, m'sieur avait des caprices, des lubies… Moi, j'endurais ça! quand on aime, est-ce pas?… Puis, tout d'un coup, ni vu, ni connu, je t'embrouille, disparu! (*LC*, 201)

---

[105] On Rachilde and Mendès's relationship, see Finn, *Hysteria*, pp. 47–51.
[106] On Rachilde and d'Estoc's relationship, see Hawthorne, *Rachilde*, pp. 121–4.
[107] Oscar Méténier, *La Chair* (Brussels: Henry Kistemaeckers, 1885), p. 199. References will hereafter appear parenthetically in the text, preceded by the abbreviation *LC*.

[A nice-looking bloke, isn't he? With his blond, curly moustache, his well-combed locks and blue peepers... He had guts, for a puny little guy! [...] I adored that little flower! Man, we had some fun together! [...] But it was too good to be true, it couldn't last! For some time, he had sudden fads and passing fancies!... And I endured it, because that's what love does to you, right?... Then, all of a sudden, no word from him, no contact—I'm not kidding you, he completely disappeared!]

After admiring the poet's appearance ('bath' = bien/beau) and vigour ('du nerf'), Nicolas employs a romantic lexis to describe his feelings for Marius ('adorer' and 'aimer'). He goes on to explain that he lost his job at the Neuilly circus after getting into a fight with someone who mocked his misfortune and claimed to have seen Marius in the arms of a young woman. Unfortunately, the accusation turns out to be true: 'Au bout de deux jours, qui que je dégote? Mon Marius avec une gonzesse! Penses-tu qu'il faut avoir du vice!!' ['Two days go by, and what do I find? My Marius with some hussy! What a crafty little pervert!!'] (*LC*, 203). The term 'vice' is loaded with irony, through a displacement of the social stigma attached to homoerotic desire, here applied to its apparently 'normal' heterosexual counterpart.

Despite this seemingly incomprehensible move from same-sex to heterosexual desire, Marius's choice of sexual partner involves—and indeed seems to require—a degree of gender ambiguity that retains a homoerotic element. The narrative confirms the shifting nature of Marius's desire when retelling the story of Nicolas and Marius's relationship in more traditional literary language. After presenting Marius as a 'poète décadent' [decadent poet'] and 'névros[é]' ['neurotic'], the narrator describes his sudden attraction to Nicolas: 'Un jour, à la foire de Neuilly, il était tombé en extase devant le torse élégant et musculeux de Nicolas-le-Boucher, chez Marseille' ['One day, in Marseille's fighting ring at the Neuilly Fair, he became entranced at the sight of Nicholas-the-Butcher's graceful, muscular chest']. Marius's enthusiasm for Nicolas and his boxing lessons lasts for several months, until he meets 'un être singulier, une sorte de fille-garçon à qui il eût été difficile d'assigner un âge et un sexe' ['a strange person, a kind of girl-boy to whom it would have been difficult to assign an age or a sex'] (*LC*, 206). Breaking off his relationship with Nicolas, Marius soon tires with his 'nouvelle conquête' ['new conquest'] by the end of one week. Having received Nicolas's invitation to meet him at the dive bar, Marius decides to go along, 'non pour renouer, mais toujours en quête d'un idéal parfois entrevu, jamais atteint' ['not to rekindle their affair, but constantly on the lookout for an ideal he had occasionally glimpsed but never achieved'] (*LC*, 207). The narrative retelling of Nicolas's story poeticises the relationship by describing it as part of Marius's journey towards an unattainable ideal that blends aestheticism with eroticism. It employs Decadent tropes of gender ambiguity and sexual perversion in a mystifying, almost obtuse way. This mystification juxtaposes the brutal clarity of the term 'copaille', used by Nicolas and Napoléon in the opening sequence. By opposing two versions of the story, Méténier provides a self-aware nod to the obtuse extremes to which Decadent literature could go in its valorisation of perversity, while at the same time contributing to this obfuscation by emphasising sexual ambiguity in his own stories.

'Décadence' employs a similar technique of narrative bifurcation in order to highlight its protagonist's ambiguous sexual identity. Like 'L'Aventure', Méténier's 1886 novella opens *in media res*, with a conversation between male audience members attending Le Rozay's most recent play, starring Rachilde's avatar Mary Staub. The men discuss the nature of Staub's relationship with Meunier and watch avidly to see the actress's reaction when Meunier enters with Jane Normand. Their conversation helps to situate the story's principal characters, including Le Rozay, who is presumed to be privy to his protégée's secrets, 'dans les secrets des dieux' ['in the know', or 'in cahoots with the gods'].[108] It also provides the backstory to the actresses' rivalry, describing how Jane encouraged her journalist friends to use gossip and speculation to attack Mary:

> On fit des allusions malveillantes. On épilogua sur les goûts de Mary Staub, sur son habitude de se vêtir en homme, en affectant des allures garçonnières [...]. Ce qu'on lui pardonnait le moins, c'était sa retenue. [...] C'était indécent. Alors des insinuations avaient été lâchées, perfidement. Des doutes avaient été émis sur son sexe; on avait parlé d'un vice de conformation, de maladie. (*LG*, 74–5)

> [People dropped malicious hints. They talked endlessly about Mary Staub's tastes, her tendency to wear men's clothing and to affect a boyish appearance [...]. What they found most unforgiveable was her self-control. [...] It was obscene. So they let slip some deceitful insinuations. Doubts had been expressed regarding her sex; people spoke of deformity and illness.]

The malicious nature of this gossip affirms the widespread sense of frustration with Mary's lack of romantic interest in her male 'camarades'. By pathologising her difference, the journalists attempt to offset her uncanny rejection of normative gender roles and sexual identity. But these attacks lose their edge when Staub's relationship with Meunier is made public—something which 'dérouta absolument les médisants' ['had the slanderers completely baffled.']. The details surrounding the rise and fall of this unexpected relationship remain a closely guarded secret, which only increases people's curiosity:

> Lui qui, si volontiers, ouvrait à deux battants les portes de son alcôve, ne laissa jamais échapper un mot sur la nature de sa nouvelle liaison. [...] Derrière les

---

[108] Oscar Méténier, *La Grâce* (Paris: E. Giraud, 1886), p. 71. References will henceforth appear parenthetically in the text, preceded by the abbreviation *LG*.

réticences du journaliste, on devina une comédie, dont personne n'avait trahi le secret, mais qui eut le don d'exciter au plus haut point la curiosité. Que s'était-il donc passé? Comment Mary Staub, l'indéchiffrable, allait-elle accepter le lâchage du premier homme auquel elle eût accordé ses faveurs? (*LG*, 76–7)

[The man who was usually so willing to open his bedroom doors wide to the world, did not let a single word slip about the nature of his new relationship. [...] Behind the journalist's reticence, people could sense a secret drama being played out, which nobody could penetrate, but which had the knack for arousing everyone's curiosity until it reached fever pitch. So, what had happened? How would the inscrutable Mary Staub react to being discarded by the first man to whom she had granted her favours?]

In this series of questions, the narrative brings readers up to speed on the backstory before returning to the ongoing play and the much-awaited arrival of Arsène and Jane. Its structural build-up functions as a *mise en abyme* of the curiosity aroused by *romans à clef*, and of the performance-driven nature of artistic and literary personae.[109] In particular, the two questions reaffirm the audience's curiosity, which has escalated in anticipation of the climactic performance—not Le Rozay's play, but Meunier's public display of his new relationship.

The presentation of backstory in both 'Décadence' and 'L'Aventure' foregrounds the initial act of betrayal that provokes the main vengeance plot of each novella. The vengeance 'plot' can be understood in two ways: (1) as the sequence of events depicted in the story, and (2) as a secret plan concocted by a group of people to commit an illegal or harmful action. In Méténier's novellas, the second type of plot, or *complot*, is devised by two accomplices: the injured party, or victim of the initial betrayal, and one of their friends. The accomplices have traits associated with masculinity (assertiveness, violence, and honour), whereas the plot's victims display maligned 'feminine' characteristics (passivity, sensuality, and inconstancy). Nicolas and Napoléon's conversation in 'L'Aventure' culminates in the pair plotting an unknown form of vengeance. After a lengthy and detailed dialogue, the narrative silences the plot's details, describing their conversation at a distance: 'Il [Napoléon] lui parla à l'oreille, longuement' ['He [Napoléon] whispered at length in his ear']. In this sentence, the adverb 'longuement' hints at an elaborate plan, arousing the reader's curiosity while refusing to satisfy it straightaway. Similarly, by retelling Nicolas's story through a more 'literary' lens, the narrative further defers the reader's satisfaction. Despite this ambiguity, the reader can infer that the plan

---

[109] This scene is reminiscent of the opening sequence in Émile Zola's novel *Nana* (1880). See Émile Zola, *Les Rougon-Macquart: histoire naturelle et sociale d'une famille sous le Second Empire*, ed. Henri Mitterand, 5 vols (Paris: Gallimard, 1960–67), II (1961), pp. 1095–108.

will involve a degree of criminal activity. For example, Napoléon's interest in Marius's expensive clothing ('des diamants à sa limace et du jonc plein des poches' ['with diamonds on his shirt and gold in his pockets']) suggests that the plan will involve theft—a crime for which Napoléon assures Nicolas they will suffer no consequences: 'Pas de danger! C'est une copaille! Il jaspinera au quart, pour la forme, mais y aura pas de pet pour toi!' [No danger involved! He's a poof. He'll go yapping to the police for form's sake, but nothing for you to worry about!'] (*LC*, 204). Even though Napoléon's assurances prove to be well-founded, Nicolas's concerns resurface when the men trick Marius into their trap. After helping Marius to undress, Nicolas experiences a faltering reserve and twinge of guilt: 'Il se demanda s'il ne devait pas rester et le défendre quand même contre Napoléon' ['All the same, he wondered whether he should stay and defend him from Napoleon']. In response to Nicolas's suggestion that they leave Dauriat in the flat without carrying out their plan, Napoléon goads him on by questioning his strength of character: 'T'as donc pas de cœur?' ['Are you completely spineless?'] (*LC*, 213). In this way, Napoléon plays a dual role of accomplice and primary instigator in the vengeance plot of 'L'Aventure'.

The criminal conspiracy between Nicolas and Napoléon in 'L'Aventure' parallels a more loosely complicit relationship between Mary Staub and Pierre Le Rozay in 'Décadence'. The pair are presented as artistic colleagues and 'partners in crime', much like their real-life equivalents Rachilde and Lorrain. In the entr'acte following Meunier and Jane's scandalous entrance, Le Rozay rebukes Mary for being overwhelmed by emotion and refusing to continue with the performance: 'Je te croyais plus élégamment vicieuse, plus froidement perverse, incapable de tout sentiment' ['I thought you were more exquisitely depraved and dispassionately perverse, incapable of any emotion'] (*LG*, 83–4). These reprimands successfully shake the actress out of her stupor and goad her into action. Le Rozay encourages her to carry on with the performance and to take the opportunity for vengeance that he will help arrange. Although the playwright leaves the specific form of revenge up to Mary, he participates in the witty sparring between Meunier and Staub over dinner. In this section, Le Rozay exchanges occasional glances with Mary, much to Meunier's chagrin: 'La tacite complicité de Pierre Le Rozay le gênait visiblement. Il avait affaire à trop forte partie' ['Pierre Le Rozay's tacit complicity made him visibly uncomfortable. He was dealing with too great a match'] (*LG*, 104). The tacit complicity Meunier evokes here implies a relationship of mutual support, as well as a sense of collusion or conspiracy. Le Rozay later extends his conspirational role by acting as a witness to Jane Normand's 'defeat' in the boudoir. As third wheel to Mary's tryst, Le Rozay sees Jane ripping off her corset as a passionate demonstration of her desire. Mary rejects her advances before offering them sarcastically to Pierre, who politely declines (*LG*, 110). This refusal reverses the logic of triangulated desire typical of homosocial bonding, presuming that Mary, as the text suggests, adopts a masculine position in relation to Jane. Pierre's cold detachment juxtaposes with, highlights, while also undercutting, the erotic violence of the scene. His dual role as enabler and witness contributes to the success of Mary's vengeance, which punishes Jane's homoerotic advances with nudity and public humiliation.

The association between nudity, public humiliation, and homoerotic desire propels the revenge plots in both of Méténier's novellas. In 'L'Aventure', Nicolas' vengeance involves stripping Marius, who is then is forced to exit Napoléon's apartment in a bizarre accoutrement of mismatching clothing. As he tentatively leaves the building, Marius is described as having 'des allures de Robert Macaire' ['something of Robert Macaire about him'] (*LC*, 216). Robert Macaire was a popular fictional figure associated with petty crime and unscrupulous swindling.[110] The elegant, dandified poet's sudden forced transformation is so convincing that two police officers in the area follow him because they suspect he is a criminal. One of them refers to Marius as 'Quelqu' échappé de Charenton' ['some escaped lunatic from Bedlam'], while the other remarks 'Il n'a pas l'air bien catholique!' ['He doesn't seem very Catholic!'] (*LC*, 217). By stealing Marius's clothes, Nicolas and Napoléon take away the sartorial veneer of social respectability, placing the poet in a highly compromising position in which *he* is the suspected criminal, not them. When Marius later sees his aggressors on the street, the irony of this role reversal becomes evident. Nonchalantly smoking cigarettes, Nicolas and Napoléon call out to him: 'Bonjour, copaille!' ['Hey, faggot!'] Faced with this homophobic slur, Marius realises he cannot risk denouncing their crime to the nearby police officers:

C'était leur défense que ces hommes venaient de lui jeter à la face. Une arrestation, un jugement, c'était le nom de Dauriat traîné dans la boue!...

Bonjour, copaille!... Il entrevit la police correctionnelle avec son public de bons petits journalistes, venant voir l'affaire de ce pauvre ami Dauriat! [...] Bonjour copaille!... Il entendait déjà dans les rues les camelots clamer:—Demandez la scandaleuse affaire Marius Dauriat! derniers détails! cinq centimes! (*LC*, 218–19)

[It was their defence strategy that these men had just thrown in his face. An arrest, a judgement... this would drag the Dauriat name through the mud!... Hey, faggot!... He saw the correctional court with its audience of good little journalists, coming to see the trial of their poor friend Dauriat! [...]

Hey, faggot!... Already he could hear the newspaper pedlars hawking loudly in the streets: 'Marius Dauriat's scandalous trial: read all about it! Find out the latest details, for five cents!']

In this extended sequence of free indirect style, Méténier depicts Marius's frustrated realisation about his compromised position. The homophobic slur

---

[110] See Marion Lemaire, *Robert Macaire: la construction d'un mythe. Du personnage théâtral au type social, 1823–1848* (Paris: Honoré Champion, 2018).

becomes a repetitive refrain that evokes the future consequences of any denunciation on his part. The words surrounding each repetition of the name 'Dauriat' reaffirm the importance of reputation and a related fear of public scandal: 'traîné dans la boue', 'ce pauvre ami', and 'la scandaleuse affaire'. Furthermore, the police force and justice system are shown to be complicit with a scandal-mongering press. Although Marius ostensibly shifts the responsibility for scandal onto fellow writers and journalists, this section constitutes an indirect avowal of guilt. When faced with the prospect of being judged morally and legally by a wider public, Marius is keenly aware that his homosexual preferences and regular frequentation of lower-class and criminal *milieux* would be interpreted as proof of wrongdoing by many of his peers. In this way, Marius's silence and embarrassing escape hint at the very real threat of publicly revealing non-normative sexual identities, which ran the risk of reducing a writer to becoming the object of gossip and mockery rather than a respected figure in the literary scene.

The representation of same-sex sexualities in nineteenth-century French culture frequently implied a loss of social distinction or 'encanaillement' ['slumming'].[111] Compared to the identity-forming strategies of Colette, Proust, and Gide, writers such as Rachilde and Jean Lorrain marked the limit of what could be acceptably written at the fin de siècle.[112] As Michael Lucey demonstrates in *Never Say I* (2006), fin-de-siècle writers sought to achieve an equilibrium between transgression and acceptability, due to their desire to express a particular identity or position without losing face. He suggests that most first-person identities are 'produced out of the need to assume a countenance, to keep face, to save face, within whatever social situation one finds oneself and at the same time out of a desire to bring to literary expression forms of experience that can be avowed only with difficulty'.[113] The idea of 'saving face' helps to mitigate modern critics' propensity to glorify transgressive authorial personae without considering the nuances and risks involved in their elaboration. It also helps to account for the inevitable conflict between forms of position-taking that 'pass' public approval and those which bring shame or humiliation upon those undertaking more risqué experiments with self-expression.

## Collaborative Exposure: Vulnerability and Risk

The centrality of humiliation to Méténier's à-clef stories begs the question: how did Rachilde and Lorrain respond to the potentially compromising material he published? This question is particularly interesting in the case of Lorrain, whose

---

[111] For an extensive analysis of this topic, see Michael Lucey, *Never Say I: Sexuality and the First Person in Colette, Gide, and Proust* (Durham, NC: Duke University Press, 2006).
[112] Lucey, *Never Say I*, p. 86.
[113] Lucey, *Never Say I*, p. 164.

avatar Marius Dauriat is left in a more embarrassing and compromising position than Mary Staub. As previously mentioned, the plotline of 'L'Aventure' was based on an anecdote circulating at the time, regarding Lorrain's involvement with a circus strongman. Although Rachilde later confirmed the story's veracity in her memoir *Portraits d'hommes*, it is difficult to know for certain whether the details of the anecdote were fabricated in order to endorse Lorrain's scandalous reputation. What is clear, however, is that the pair's avant-garde peers easily recognised Lorrain behind Marius Dauriat. For example, Léo d'Orfer comments on the thinly veiled nature of Méténier's à-clef story when reviewing *La Chair* for *Le Zig-Zag*. In the 'Causerie littéraire' column of number 147, which appeared between the *bas bleu* special issue and the number containing Rachilde and Lorrain's *mises en scène*, d'Orfer cites 'L'Aventure de Marius Dauriat' as '[son] morceau de prédilection' ['[his] favourite section']. When summarising the story's plot, he hints at its à-clef status—'Un poète, dont le nom est à peine voilé, s'est épris d'un hercule de la baraque de Marseille' ['A poet, whose name is scarcely hidden, fell for a fighter at Marseille's ring']—and reveals its embarrassing denouement: 'Nicolas dépouille Marius de ses habits, se sauve, et ce dernier est obligé, avec force terreurs, de regagner son domicile à moitié nu' ['Nicolas strips Marius of his clothes, runs away, and the latter, in a state of absolute terror, is forced to return home half naked'].[114] Elements of Marius's character, including his status as a world-weary Decadent poet and his proclivity for wrestling with burly men, would have been recognisable to Lorrain's friends and peers.[115] If these references were insufficient, Méténier dedicates the story overtly to Lorrain, thereby handing readers the key before they even start reading the text. By highlighting this story in his review of the collection, d'Orfer further spreads the rumours surrounding Lorrain's sexual activities, encouraging readers in the know to unravel Méténier's poorly veiled references.

The strongman anecdote in 'L'Aventure' was in fact part of a broader intertextual exchange between Lorrain and Méténier. Through their references to strongmen in writings published in 1885, the pair contributed to a collective literary myth and collaboratively constructed media personae. Several strongmen characters appeared in Lorrain's poetry collection, *Modernités*, which was published only a few months before Méténier's à-clef novella. The eponymous poem

---

[114] Léo d'Orfer, 'Causerie littéraire', *Le Zig-Zag*, 11 Oct. 1885.
[115] 'Marius Dauriat était un vrai poète, poète décadent par exemple. D'une vieille famille bretonne. Les effluves salées [sic] de la plage natale n'avaient pu vivifier son sang appauvri et anémié. Comme tous les névrosés de cette fin de siècle, il avait conscience de son délabrement physique et moral.' Méténier, *La Chair*, p. 205. ['Marius Dauriat was a true poet—a Decadent poet, well I never! From an old Breton family. The salted fragrance from his native beaches had failed to invigorate his depleted and weakening bloodline. Like all these fin-de-siècle neurotics, he was fully aware of his physical and moral deterioration.'] Lorrain was from Normandy, not Brittany, but the northern, coastal backdrop remains an important 'key' to understanding the story's veiled references.

notably evokes the erotic appeal of 'les reins vigoureux des lutteurs' ['the fighters' vigorous loins']. Another poem, 'Nostalgie', describes the reminiscences of a former strongman: 'Jadis, en casquette à trois ponts, | Il faisait des poids aux barrières | Chez Marseille, et les chiffonnières | Aimaient son beau torse aux poils blonds' ['Long ago, wearing a mack's hat, | He'd lift weights on the outskirts | At Marseille's, and the rag-and-bone women | Loved his beautiful gold-haired chest'].[116] Like the character Nicolas le Boucher in 'L'Aventure', the strongman in 'Nostalgie' worked at Marseille's fighting ring ('Chez Marseille'). By including this reference, Lorrain hinted at the anecdote that Méténier would later reveal. Furthermore, by dedicating the poem to Méténier, Lorrain pre-empted the latter's reciprocating gesture of dedicating 'L'Aventure' to him. Through these shared references and dedications, Lorrain and Méténier formulated the strongman anecdote as a secret between friends 'in the know'. Above all, it was a secret shared *publicly* in a way that strengthened the collusive nature of their media relationship.

As a figure, the strongman combines strength and audacity with eroticised self-display and risk-taking performance. His career, like that of other circus performers, notably acrobats, was fast-paced and short-lived.[117] Because of these factors, the strongman symbolises avant-garde writers' media strategies and their awareness of such strategies' limitations. Lorrain employs this symbolism in 'Nostalgie' by depicting the former fighter, who is now 'gras, bouffi, maussade' ['fat, bloated, sullen'], reminiscing about his glory days amidst the 'éclatant brouhaha des foires' ['fairgrounds' resounding din'].[118] By evoking the deleterious influence of ageing on the strongman's career, Lorrain associates successful performance—both physical and artistic—with an intense, and sexually vigorous, youth. As an ageing bar worker, the former fighter has lost access to his previous lifestyle, and relies on the sale of 'vin fade' ['tasteless wine'] to make a living. Viewed as a metaphor for artistic or literary creation, the 'vin fade' denotes an impoverished, but reliably lucrative, product that the fighter/artist sells after losing his former talent. In a similar way, Rachilde's self-depiction as a circus performer in 'Zig-Zag Parade' expresses an equally ambivalent vision of literary commerce, through the article's emphasis on sexualised performance, audience heckling, and the bathetic climax of the reviews' collaborators falling into an upturned barrel. By conveying such ambivalence, Lorrain and Rachilde enacted what Jennifer Forrest has called the 'double duty' of artists/writers who identified with circus performers, namely: avowal and derision. First, the pair acknowledged their place in the commercial literary marketplace, restricted by the need to please a certain public. At the same time, they mocked themselves and others in a gesture of empowerment

---

[116] Lorrain, *Modernités*, p. 47.
[117] On the association between acrobats and artists in the nineteenth century, see Jean Starobinski, *Portrait de l'artiste en saltimbanque* (Geneva: Albert Skira, 1970).
[118] Lorrain, *Modernités*, p. 47.

that '[set] the stage for the creation of original work'.[119] What is more, circus performance, like artistic or literary creation, was frequently collaborative in nature.[120] The same can be said for Méténier's accomplice characters—whether strongman and pimp ('L'Aventure') or actress and playwright ('Décadence')—as well as the collusive collaborators portrayed in the October 1885 *Zig-Zag* articles.

The references to attractive strong men in Lorrain and Méténier's texts provoke curiosity through a covert *clin d'œil* to shared knowledge and secrets. Tantalising hints at homoerotic desire and relationships create collusion between the author(s) and the knowing reader. As with Rachilde and Lorrain, these shared references also contributed to a relationship of collaborative *réclame*. Rather than bemoaning the anecdote's revelation, Lorrain actively orchestrated it with Méténier, showing a canny appreciation of the promotional potential of its scandalous content. In a letter sent on 16 January 1885, Lorrain confirms that he has read, and enjoyed, a passage of one of Méténier's works in progress—a passage that, although unnamed, is clearly from 'L'Aventure':

> J'ai lu le passage. Beaucoup trop flatteur, mon cher! [...] Comme je l'ai écrit à Fénéon, je suis né fatigué, et de cette fatigue l'horreur de l'amour physique et les curiosités étranges, tout le malsain d'une nature qui n'éprouve qu'à travers les sensations des autres [...]. Enfin, vous me flattez. C'est très aimable à vous. Un mot pourtant: à la place du *Rempart de Belleville* (bien roman du boulevard), mettez *Nicolas le Boucher* ou *l'Assassin de la Bastille*.[121]

> [I read the extract. Much too flattering, my dear! [...] Like I said in my letter to Fénéon, I was born world-weary, with a world weariness that loathes physical love and perverse curiosity. Mine is the unhealthy sort of nature that only experiences feelings through the sensations of others [...]. Well, you flatter me. And it's very kind of you. But just a few remarks: instead of 'Rempart de Belleville' (a bit too pulp fiction), put 'Nicholas the Butcher' or 'the Bastille Murderer'.]

The published version of 'L'Aventure' includes the phrase 'être né fatigué', and Méténier clearly followed Lorrain's advice about changing the lover's name to Nicolas le Boucher. By sending the story to Lorrain in advance of its publication, Méténier actively sought approval for its content. Then, by praising the piece and

---

[119] Jennifer Forrest, *Decadent Aesthetics and the Acrobat in Fin-de-siècle France* (New York: Routledge, 2020), pp. 42–3.
[120] When analysing Edmond Goncourt's novel *Les Frères Zemganno* (1879), Forrest notes that acrobats provided 'a very serviceable model for depicting collaboration'. See Forrest, *Decadent Aesthetics*, p. 102.
[121] Jean Lorrain, *Correspondance. Lettres à Barbey d'Aurevilly, François Coppée, Oscar Méténier, Catulle Mendès, Edmond Deschaumes, Mecislas Golberg, etc., suivies des articles condamnés*, ed. George Normandy (Paris: Éditions Baudinière, 1929), p. 69.

suggesting changes, Lorrain collaborated in the text's construction and became complicit in the revelation of a risqué anecdote.

This type of collusion was not unusual for their friendship circle. Like Lorrain, Rachilde actively collaborated with Méténier in the fictionalised revelation of compromising details about her private life in 'Décadence', whether that be her early infatuation with Catulle Mendès or her potentially bisexual love interests. She did so by approving a draft of the text, and by announcing her approval publicly in a review of the published trilogy:

> L'histoire m'étant dédiée, et déjà offerte *sur épreuves*, je remercie en passant Méténier, le rassurant tout à fait au sujet de l'opinion du public, lequel trouve souvent mauvaises des choses qu'il n'est pas capable de juger.
> (... Dis donc, Méténier, nous nous la serrons à sa barbe, n'est-ce pas ?) [...] Oscar Méténier [...] est un excellent camarade, n'oubliant pas plus les services que les injures. [...] Bref, un homme.
> Va faire paraitre prochainement: *La Bohème Bourgeoise*.[122]

> [Having dedicated the story to me, and after sending me a draft copy, I would like to thank Méténier in passing, while offering him complete reassurance regarding public opinion, which often takes issue with things it cannot understand.
> (... And hey, Méténier, we're doing it at their expense, right?) [...] Oscar Méténier [...] is an excellent friend, who never forgets to return a favour or an insult. [...] All in all, a good fellow.
> Will soon be publishing *La Bohème bourgeoise*.]

Rachilde's article, published in *Le Décadent*, is an extended public display of literary camaraderie, which functions explicitly through the exchange of promotional favours ('services'). These favours include: hinting at à-clef structures, exchanging written drafts, offering positive critical reviews, publicly valorising their friendship, and promoting upcoming material. Michael Finn has suggested that the similarities between the revenge sequences in 'Décadence' and *La Marquise de Sade* indicate that Rachilde reciprocated Méténier's gesture by sending him part (if not all) of the drafted manuscript for her 1887 novel, elements of which he subsequently incorporated—with her permission—into his à-clef novella, as a form of pre-emptive *réclame*.[123] Although Finn's suggestion is difficult to prove, it matches the spirit of Rachilde's *Le Décadent* article, which acts like a *roman à clef* by

---

[122] Rachilde, 'L'auteur de *La Grâce*', *Le Décadent littéraire et artistique*, 11 Sept. 1886.
[123] Michael Finn, 'Imagining Rachilde: Decadence and the *roman à clefs*', *French Forum* 30, no. 1 (Winter 2005): 81–96 (pp. 84–5), https://www.jstor.org/stable/40552371. Finn highlights the similarities between Jane Normand's humiliation in 'Décadence' to that of the Comtesse de Liol in the fire-poker scene from *La Marquise de Sade*. Both works share the plot device of a homoerotic

offering readers a chance to witness the pair's friendship unfold in the pages of the review. In the parenthetical aside addressing Meténier—'(... Dis donc, Meténier, nous nous la serrons à sa barbe, n'est-ce pas?)'—Rachilde posits the general reader, representing 'l'opinion du public', as both a witness to and victim of their mockery. As the examples of 'L'Aventure de Marius Dauriat' and 'Décadence' demonstrate, Rachilde, Lorrain, and Meténier manipulated structures of titillating revelation and (self-)exposure in *romans à clef*, while actively orchestrating their publication and reception in ways that contributed not only to the elaboration of their individual public personae, but also to a discourse of company keeping and avant-garde camaraderie.

However, mediatised relationships of literary complicity were not all fun and games: misunderstandings could occur, trust be broken, and reputations compromised. It is no coincidence that Meténier's novellas centre thematically and structurally on acts of public exposure and humiliation, since the *roman à clef* constantly bordered on compromising the individuals whose personal lives they partially revealed. This was notably the case for Lorrain, because—unlike Mary Staub in 'Décadence', who successfully takes vengeance on her former lover—his character occupies a humiliated, undressed position at the end of 'L'Aventure'. After initially thanking Meténier for his supposedly 'flatteur' and 'aimable' depiction in the drafted version of the story, Lorrain's enthusiasm waned once the anecdote became public. In a letter dated 28 September 1885—after the publication of *La Chair* and just before the *Zig-Zag* exchanges—Lorrain reveals an ambivalent relationship to the otherwise consensual and collaborative revelation of his scandalous sex life. He clearly identifies with Meténier's character, referring to his youthful existence as 'le passé de Marius Dauriat' ['the past of Marius Dauriat']. He also offers to provide 'réclame' for *La Chair* in a review called *La Suisse romande*.[124] Nonetheless, he adds an ambivalent postscript: 'M'as-tu assez compromis avec ton Marius Dauriat?' ['Have you compromised me enough with your Marius Dauriat?'][125] The addition seems incongruous—indicating irony, a change of heart, or perhaps a combination of the two. It is of course possible that Lorrain only received a short section of 'L'Aventure' before publication, rather than the whole story. After all, Lorrain refers to having read a 'passage', which was not necessarily a completed draft.

---

rendezvous serving as a cover for vengeance against a denigrated female rival and would-be lover. Furthermore, in each story the spurned rival bares her breasts to an indifferent protagonist, before being pushed into the arms of the man who is the original source of rivalry between them. The primary difference is that Jane's humiliation happens publicly, in front of her entire social circle, whereas the only other witness to the Comtesse de Liol's degradation and branding is Mary's husband, Louis de Caumont.

[124] Lorrain, *Correspondance*, p. 84.
[125] Lorrain, *Correspondance*, p. 86.

What is clear, however, is that by 6 January 1886, Lorrain was eager to tone down the scandalous element of their *réclame*, when he asked Méténier not to emphasise his non-normative sexuality in an upcoming article:

> Je n'ai jamais douté de toi, *mio caro*, je me suis rappelé à ton bon souvenir et voilà. [...] Si cela ne t'est pas trop pénible, n'insiste pas, je t'en prie, dans l'étude que tu veux bien me consacrer, sur quelques bizarreries de ma vie privée. Ces bizarreries sont bien communes et n'inquiètent que quelques pourris de littérature comme toi et moi. J'aime à croire que j'ai des côtés plus intéressants que le boulet de mes vices, bien effacés d'ailleurs, bien passés à l'état de fantômes et d'évocations...[126]

> [I never doubted you, *mon cher*, I'm simply reminding you of past favours and nothing more. [...] If it's not too much of a trouble, please can I ask you, in the study you are kind enough to devote to me, not to insist too much on the quirks of my private life? These quirks are very common and only interest literary swine such as you and me. I like to think that I have a more interesting side to me than the burden of my vices, which have truly faded and passed on to the form of ghost-like recollections...]

The co-existence of reproach and gratitude in Lorrain's letter shows the precarious balance involved in relationships of literary complicity. In this instance, it seems that Méténier took his role too far. By revealing more information than necessary, and by depicting his friend in an unflattering light, Méténier's contribution to their media relationship was more compromising than constructive. Lorrain's desire to avoid the topic of sexuality marks a shift in tone from the outwardly playful and celebratory *Zig-Zag* articles. He airs fears that the publication of controversial but intimate information risked reducing writers to biographical quirks, preventing them from being appreciated for their literary production: 'J'aime à croire que j'ai des côtés plus intéressants que le boulet de mes vices.' Publicly revealing Lorrain's past sexual exploits amounts to imprisoning him ('boulet') and holding him back from being appreciated fully as a writer. As this epistolary exchange demonstrates, the publication of *La Chair* became as much a source of conflict between Lorrain and Méténier as it was of collusive unity.

The precarious balance between promotional and compromising public exposure also affected Rachilde and Lorrain's relationship. In 1888, Lorrain republished an earlier laudatory article 'Mlle Salamandre' in *Dans l'oratoire*. He adds a postscript condemning the autobiographical preface to *À mort* (1886) and the episode where Rachilde slapped Paul Devaux at a public lecture, for criticising her friend Léonide Leblanc. He also refers to rumours that Maurice Barrès, the

---

[126] Lorrain, *Correspondance*, pp. 89–90.

dedicatee of *À mort*, had been Rachilde's lover: 'nous avons également appris que M. Maurice Barrès [...] aurait posé devant elle pour le Maxime de Bryon de son livre *A mort* et qu'elle aurait... subi le charme très réel de ce délicat entre les délicats' ['we have also learned that Mr Maurice Barrès [...] apparently posed for her as the Maxime de Bryon from her book *À mort*, and that she apparently... endured the very real charm of this most discerning of refined men'].[127] Lorrain's use of ellipsis ensures that the reader interprets the phrase 'subi le charme' as an erotic innuendo. In a subsequent letter to Barrès himself, dated 16 July 1888, Rachilde criticises her colleague's lack of subtlety:

> Lorrain a des délicatesses de charretier qui se trouve pour la première fois dans une alcôve de satin bleu... Et dans celle de la Publicité il commet sottise sur sottise. Ce qu'il y a de bête c'est que je l'aime bien, le défends toujours et que nous avons l'air de nous entendre pour certain monde.[128]

> [Lorrain has as much tact as a sailor who finds himself for the first time in an alcove lined with blue satin.... And in publicity's intimate alcove he commits folly after folly. The stupid thing is: I like and support him, and we seem, to certain people, to get along.]

Rachilde perceives her relationship with Lorrain to be fundamentally ambivalent: outwardly complicit ('nous avons l'air de nous entendre') but problematically compromising. She refutes Lorrain's accusation of 'ridicule' with her own perception of his 'sottise', according to the perennial logic that it takes one to know one. As in Lorrain's correspondence with Méténier, Rachilde's letter to Barrès demonstrates that there is a fine line between acceptable and unacceptable ways of revealing potentially compromising information.

Much like the brief dispute between Lorrain and Méténier—which was only temporarily alleviated by the publication of Méténier's long-awaited article[129]— this unstable moment in Rachilde and Lorrain's friendship highlights the vulnerability at the heart of relationships of collusive and revealing *réclame*. Rather than undermining the processes of literary complicity found in *Le Zig-Zag*, Lorrain and Rachilde's correspondence sheds light on the stakes involved. Publicity through staged biographical unveiling can function productively in relationships

---

[127] Jean Lorrain, *Dans l'oratoire* (Paris: C. Dalou, 1888), p. 215.

[128] Rachilde and Maurice Barrès, *Correspondance inédite, 1885–1914*, ed. Michael Finn (Brest: Publications du Centre d'étude des correspondances et journaux intimes des XIXe et XXe siècles, 2002), p. 121. The word 'charretier' here functions like 'sailor' in the expression 'to swear like a sailor' ('jurer comme un charretier')—that is, to describe an uncouth individual.

[129] Oscar Méténier, 'Ceux de demain. Jean Lorrain', *La Revue moderne*, 20 Sept. 1886, pp. 580–8. On 6 Oct. 1886, Lorrain thanks Méténier for the article, noting his intention to re-print the article in other reviews: 'Quand on a une bonne réclame, comme la tienne, on l'use jusqu'à la corde' ['When you have some good publicity, like what you've written, you use it until it's worn out']. Lorrain, *Correspondance*, p. 103.

of mutual promotion between literary *camarades,* but the consequences are potentially compromising. Indeed, these kinds of relationship, however dynamic and playful, often rely on pre-existing vulnerability: being a female writer in the male-dominated literary field, or being a homosexual in heteronormative society. This vulnerability is not merely a consequence of the self-exposure involved in these strategies. Rather, it is at the strategies' origin. Complicity and 'réclame' can in these instances even be understood as coping tactics or defence mechanisms that are playfully, and somewhat perversely, channelled into the creation of irreverent public personae.

With this in mind, I suggest that playfulness and sincerity are not mutually exclusive, and that the audacity expressed by writers like Rachilde, Lorrain, and Méténier could not exist without the vulnerability underlying their positions. This view nuances modern readings of the group's self-promotion strategies. As noted earlier, Rachel Mesch has distanced herself from earlier accounts of Rachilde's self-fashioned identity displays as 'striptease' or 'crafty manipulation', asserting that it would be better to understand these displays as choices 'made out of necessity'.[130] In many ways, Mesch's interpretation reflects Lucey's vision of the inevitable balancing act between self-expression and saving face by fin-de-siècle writers with non-normative sexual identities. Exemplifying such balancing acts, Rachilde and Lorrain's media relationships confirm that 'there is vulnerability alongside audacity', and that the authors' facetious self-depictions contained their own kernel of truth.[131] Having said that, the moments of vulnerability and self-expression in these texts do not offset completely the disconcerting, even antipathetic, power of avant-garde writers' obfuscations. Whether viewed positively, as a source of community-producing collusion, or negatively, as an off-putting 'in-crowd' aesthetic that promotes transgression chiefly for its promotional potential, it is clear that performative mystification was a recognisable shared trait among marginal writers who expressed non-normative identities through their public personae. It seems logical, after all, that a literary movement premised on rejecting mainstream literary practices should be populated largely by individuals who felt alienated by, or disconnected from, normative identities.[132] In this context, form united with content: alternative or maligned literary genres such as the *petite revue* and *roman*

---

[130] Mesch, *Before Trans,* p. 172.
[131] Mesch, *Before Trans,* pp. 152, 190, and 199.
[132] Stéphane Gougelmann notes that 'écrivains en peine avec leur siècle' ['writers at loggerheads with their century'] are more likely to reject normative gender ideology and genre-based hierarchies, in '« En littérature, ils ont le sexe changeant. » Jean Lorrain et l'émancipation des catégories de genre', *Romantisme* 179, no. 1 (2018): pp. 70–84 (p. 71), doi:10.3917/rom.179.0070.

*à clef* offered an 'oppositional space' through which writers could express and explore complex identities and solidarities.[133]

Rachilde and Lorrain's media relationships offer a rich source for understanding the dynamic, if often ambivalent, forms of literary complicity that were integral to avant-garde sociability at the fin de siècle. By revealing and valorising non-normative gender identities and sexual orientations, the pair capitalised on the appeal of illicit topics as well as the bonds created via shared secrets and the sense of being 'in on it'. Demonstrating the close links between vulnerability and audacity, they navigated the fine line dividing collusive and compromising literary relationships. Intertextual exchanges in Rachilde, Lorrain, and Méténier's works highlight the importance of media networks for the production of authorial personae, the reception of specific works, and the literary field's wider functioning. Their interconnected friendships reveal the close association between non-normative gender or sexual identities, and alternative solidarities in avant-garde literary culture. Not only this, but by combining textual striptease with subversive forms of solidarity, Rachilde and Lorrain adopted textual strategies popularised across a range of other marginal press formats, which include the fascinating (and as yet largely uncharted) realm of saucy magazines: the erotic network par excellence.

---

[133] Michael Lucey refers to journalism and the music-hall as collaboratively establishing a similar 'oppositional space' against the discourses of doctors, lawyers, and politicians (*Never Say I*, p. 131). Alexandre Burin makes a similar point when discussing 'queer heterotopias' in 'The Harlequin Poetics', pp. 148–55.

# 5

# Saucy Magazines

## An Erotic Network

Eroticism played a central role in fin-de-siècle French mass media and popular entertainment. Titillating forms of spectacle, such as the Moulin Rouge and Folies Bergère, sold sex appeal and arousal to an avid public. Bookshops and kiosks abounded with sensational novels and newspapers recounting the latest scandals. Posters and advertisements featured eye-catching sensual imagery to sell their wares. Although this playful eroticism is frequently eclipsed in accounts of the era by more familiar pathologising discourses of decadence and degeneration, it nonetheless lives on in the popular imagination and in the Parisian tourism industry.[1] The sexually suggestive media formats that flourished in the period created an ambiguous erotic realm, hovering somewhere between phantasmatic representation and real-world practices and possibilities. Nowhere is this tendency clearer than in 'revues légères' ['saucy magazines']: literary and artistic reviews whose tone and content were defined by titillation, gossip, and risqué humour. The genre is notable for using eroticism to create bonds between texts, writers, and readers. Drawing on the incitement and collaboration models of complicity discussed in Chapter 1, saucy magazines depicted illicit desire and behaviour without moral censure, appealed to a shared prurient humour, recounted their readers' sex lives, and forged solidarity between writers and publishers condemned for obscenity. To analyse such forms of erotic complicity, this chapter adopts a broad vision of literature that includes journalism, advertising, and visual culture. By examining phenomena associated with mass media, consumer culture, and popular entertainment, I suggest that ephemeral production, the flotsam of the canon, offers flashes of light—many-hued, sometimes garish—onto fin-de-siècle French culture.

### The 'revue légère' *Don Juan* (1895–1900)

The fin-de-siècle boom in French periodical production, enabled by improving print technologies and increased press freedom, led to the proliferation of cheaper,

---

[1] Traditional accounts of fin-de-siècle eroticism include Bram Dijkstra, *Idols of Perversity: Fantasies of Feminine Evil in Fin-de-Siècle Culture* (Oxford: Oxford University Press, 1986) and Vernon Rosario, *The Erotic Imagination: French Histories of Perversity* (Oxford: Oxford University Press, 1997). For a more recent popular history, see Dominique Kalifa, *Paris: Une histoire érotique d'Offenbach aux sixties* (Paris: Payot, 2018).

more ephemeral literary and artistic reviews. These were often illustrated and aimed at a wide range of readerships, from the popular to the avant-garde. A notable emerging genre was the 'revue légère', associated with erotic titillation and gossip. The most well known of these reviews is La Vie parisienne, which was founded under the Second Empire and lasted well into the twentieth century (1863–1970).[2] Other notable examples include: Le Courrier français (1884–1914), Le Fin de Siècle (1891–1909), and Le Frou-Frou (1900–23). There are also many less well-known titles, such as: Paris-Gaîté (1891), Beautés parisiennes (1891–2), La Grisette (1894–7), Folichonneries (1896–7), and La Vie amoureuse (1897). This range of titles varied in format, publication frequency, paper quality, and price— which are all key factors when considering a periodical's potential readership and posterity.[3] Despite these differences, 'revues légères' shared key characteristics: (1) they were illustrated, containing drawings that centred on eroticised female bodies; (2) they were humorous: satire, irony, word play, and jokes appeared throughout their visual and textual content; and (3) they published similar types of column, presented in similar ways: opinion pieces, gossip columns, literary and artistic reviews, serialised fiction, advice/agony aunt columns, readers' correspondence, alongside marketing texts such as small ads and *réclame*. The latter, in this context, refers to a specific form of advertising strategy, where an advert's promotional text is disguised to pass as main copy. By definition, this strategy tends to blur generic boundaries, offering reviews such as *Don Juan* an opportunity for collusive literary creativity.[4]

*Don Juan* was an illustrated literary and artistic review published between 1895 and 1900. It was founded by Alfred Hippolyte Bonnet and run by René Emery. Although these names are not well known, Emery in particular is worthy of greater critical attention. He not only ran a series of 'revues légères' but was also on friendly terms with key figures of the literary avant-garde, such as Aurélien Scholl (1833–1902) and Rachilde.[5] From 1891–2, he was the editor-in-chief of

---

[2] For a recent study of *La Vie parisienne*, see Clara Sadoun-Édouard, *Le Roman de* La Vie parisienne *(1863–1914): Presse, genre, littérature et mondanité* (Paris: Honoré Champion, 2018).

[3] *La Vie parisienne* was the most expensive, at 35 centimes per issue. *Le Courrier français* and *Le Frou-Frou* cost 20 centimes per issue. *Le Fin-de-Siècle*, *Don Juan*, and *La Grisette* cost 10 centimes per issue, and *Les Folichonneries* only 5 centimes. For comparison, an issue of a daily newspaper such as *Le Figaro* cost around 15 centimes. Price often reflects physical and symbolic posterity: the more expensive reviews were printed on higher quality paper, attracted more well-known writers, and were aimed at a readership from higher social strata than their less expensive and more ephemeral counterparts. They were published in a format destined for album binding, and therefore were more likely to be preserved in complete collections.

[4] As noted in Chapter 4, the term 'réclame' refers to a specific form of veiled advertising, where businesses pay to have material inserted into the paper's main copy, and to publicity strategies more generally. See Marc Martin, *Trois siècles de publicité en France* (Paris: Éditions Odilie Jacob, 1992) and Marie-Ève Thérenty, 'La réclame de librairie dans le journal quotidien au xixe siècle: autopsie d'un objet textuel non identifié', *Romantisme* 155, no. 1 (2012): pp. 91–103, doi:10.3917/rom.155.0091.

[5] See *Lettre de René Emery à Rachilde* (Paris: Bibliothèque Littéraire Jacques Doucet, LT Ms 10207, [ND]), [NP], and two letters from René Emery to Aurélien Scholl, dated 27 Dec. 1890 and 27 Feb. 1898 (author's private collection).

*Le Fin de Siècle*, which was *Don Juan*'s predecessor and precursor.[6] During this short time, Emery accumulated several charges for 'outrages aux bonnes mœurs' ['affront to public decency']. He was condemned alongside co-contributors of *Le Fin de Siècle* on 30 December 1891 (one-month prison sentence, 3,000-franc fine), on 20 January 1892 for having published 'La Pieuvre' by Georges Brandimbourg (one-month prison sentence, 1,000-franc fine), and on 27 January 1892 for one of his 'Sapho' articles, entitled 'Filles de Lesbos' (three-month prison sentence, 3,000-franc fine).[7] These details are listed in the procedural documents to another trial, dated 25 May 1892, where he was tried once more, for an article entitled 'Gorges à l'air' ['Bare Breasts']. Demonstrating repeated recidivism, Emery received a harsher punishment for this offence: thirteen months in prison and a 3,000-franc fine.[8] To avoid serving his prison sentences, Emery took voluntary exile in Belgium, in the latter half of 1892.[9] According to a letter that Emery wrote to Rachilde, by mid-1893 he had got back onto the bandwagon, publishing from Belgium the first issue of a 'revue morte-née' ['still-born review'] called... *Don Juan*. This issue was swiftly seized by the authorities and appears to have left little or no other trace.[10] Between mid-1893 and mid-1895, Emery returned to Paris and became the editor-in-chief of Bonnet's journal. The first issue of the Parisian *Don Juan* appeared on 8 June 1895. Within five months of its initial publication, the review claimed to have reached a circulation figure ('tirage justifié') of around 40,000 copies per issue.[11] This reflects similar figures cited by *Le Fin de Siècle* in 1896.[12] These figures, which might be exaggerated, are four times the circulation rate of the more expensive and fashionable 'revue légère' *La Vie parisienne*—estimated between 8,000 and 10,000 copies by Clara Sadoun-Édouard[13]—and approximately half that of *Le Figaro* in the same period.[14] In response to this sign of popularity, *Don Juan*—which initially appeared weekly on Saturdays—became a bi-weekly (appearing twice a week) from 11 January 1896.

---

[6] On the link between *Don Juan* and *Le Fin de Siècle*, see Jean Watelet, *La Presse illustrée en France, 1814–1914*, 2 vols (Lille: Atelier national de reproduction de thèses, 1998), II, pp. 653–6.

[7] See Paris, Archives de Paris (AP), série D1U6, Jugements, Rôles, Répertoires, Audiences: D1U6 413, 30.12.1891—CHARDON, Hippolyte and others, D1U6 415, 20.01.1892—EMERY, René Marie and others, D1U6 416, and 27.01.1892—CHARDON, Hippolyte and EMERY, René Marie.

[8] See AP, D1U6 428, 25.05.1892—JULIEN, Henry Alexandre and EMERY, René Marie, and série D2U6, Tribunal Correctionnel de la Seine, Dossiers de Procédure (1828–1940): D2U6 95, 25.05.1892—JULIEN, Henry, Alexandre and EMERY, René, Marie.

[9] On Emery's self-imposed exile, see Rodolphe Bringer, *Trente ans d'humour* (Paris: France-Édition, 1924), p. 33. My chronology is necessarily approximate due to the lack of specific dates in the sources available.

[10] *Lettre de René Emery à Rachilde*.

[11] *Don Juan*, 19 Oct. 1895. References to *Don Juan* hereafter appear parenthetically in the text, cited by date.

[12] '[Notre tirage] atteint aujourd'hui 37.5000, et les commandes que nous avons déjà reçues pour le mois de mai vont le porter à plus de 40.000,—tous chiffres constatés officiellement par procès-verbaux d'huissier.'['Today our print run has reached 37,500 copies, and the orders we have received for the month of May will bring it up to over 40,000 copies. All figures officially certified by a bailiff's report.'] *Le Fin de Siècle*, 16 Apr. 1896.

[13] Sadoun-Édouard, *Le Roman de* La Vie parisienne, p. 62.

[14] See Martin, *Trois siècles*, p. 95.

However, by mid-1898, the review's success started to wane, as is suggested by its gradual reduction in size, content, and frequency. In 1900, its publication became increasingly erratic, before ceasing entirely.

During its five-year print run, the review's content was incredibly eclectic. It published a wide range of literary contributions, from up-and-coming avant-garde writers to popular authors of titillating fiction. These texts appeared alongside society gossip columns, reader-response competitions, and satirical illustrations. The first page hosted the review's most notable regular columns: a charismatic comment-section-cum-agony-aunt column ('La Chronique de Sapho'), a gossip column ('La Vie parisienne'), and satirical pieces—initially in verse, then increasingly in prose—by 'Des Esquintes'.[15] The pseudonym 'Des Esquintes' is an example of the review's proclivity for word play. It is a pun on the verb 'esquinter'—in this context 'to pan' or 'to slate'—and a playful reformulation of Huysmans's protagonist in À rebours, Des Esseintes. The review here aligns itself with, while playfully ironising, avant-garde literary culture, by appealing to readers' shared knowledge (however rudimentary) of a landmark Decadent text, and by adopting the critical practice of 'éreintement' ['slating'] typical of avant-garde little magazines.[16] The two internal pages of the review featured a selection of short prose pieces, poems, serialised novels, and more sporadically recurring columns, such as a reader-response column, 'Nos Cours d'amour', and a literary review column, 'La Vie littéraire'. Notable contributors included: Remy de Gourmont (1858–1915), Alfred Jarry (1873–1907), Camille Lemonnier (1844–1913), and Léo Trézenik (1855–1902). The three writers analysed in Chapter 4—Rachilde, Jean Lorrain, and Oscar Méténier—were also regular contributors. This list of avant-garde authors reveals the porous boundaries between different forms of marginal press publication. The final page of each issue was adorned with a humorous and saucy drawing, by artists and caricaturists such as Édouard Couturier (1871–1903) and Paul Balluriau (1860–1917), who contributed to several satirical journals, including L'Assiette au beurre (1901–36), Le Rire (1894–1971), Le Fin de Siècle (1891–1909), Le Courrier français (1884–1914), and Gil Blas illustré (1891–1903).[17] Like their more titillating counterparts, satirical illustrated reviews demonstrated the broad marketability of transgression by offering a similar blend of anti-establishment critique, risqué topics, and popular entertainment.[18] The frothy eroticism and

---

[15] 'La Chronique de Sapho' was probably penned by René Emery. An earlier version, entitled 'Chroniques perverses' and signed under the same pseudonym, appeared in Le Fin de Siècle during Emery's editorship.

[16] On the practice of 'éreintement', see Yoan Vérilhac, La Jeune critique des petites revues symbolistes (Saint-Etienne: Publications de l'Université de Saint-Etienne, 2010), pp. 89–96.

[17] It is noteworthy that in 1896, the 'Éditions du Don Juan' published a collection of Couturier's drawings, Des femmes en chemise, with a preface by René Emery.

[18] On the presence of erotic topics in satirical illustrated reviews—some of which can also be classified as 'revues légères'—see Daniel Grojnowski and Mireille Dottin-Orsini, 'La prostitution dans la presse parisienne à la fin du xix$^e$ siècle', Littératures 69 (2013): pp. 187–211, doi:10.4000/litteratures.159 and Gabriel P. Weisberg, 'Louis Legrand's Battle over Prostitution: The Uneasy Censoring of Le Courrier Français', Art Journal 51, no. 1 (1992): pp. 45–50, doi:10.1080/00043249.1992.10791551.

polemical humour of these drawings pushed the limits of moral acceptability, attracting censorship to the review in July 1896, when Bonnet was condemned for outraging public decency. These larger images usually appeared above half a page of advertisements selling various products, including books, cough medicine, and sex toys.

Like many other reviews and newspapers of the period, *Don Juan* valorised the interaction between textual production and reception, creating 'fictions d'interlocution' ['dialogic fictions'] centred on readers' voices, both real and imagined.[19] Valérie Stiénon has stressed the importance of dialogism to periodical formats and its links with earlier forms of *salon* culture, discussing the ways in which readers' voices were used to define and promote a review, while distinguishing it from competitors.[20] To examine the dialogic construction of targeted readerships in *Don Juan*, this chapter analyses the collusive forms of address and response employed throughout the magazine's pages. From the first issue, *Don Juan*'s editorial team framed the reading experience as a form of erotic exchange between reciprocally desiring partners. By idealising readers' discerning taste and offering opportunities for them to publish copy via competitions and questionnaires, *Don Juan* gave its readers a sense of control over, and collaboration with, the review's content. This content frequently crossed into illicit territory, pushing the boundaries of 'acceptable' frothy eroticism by treating risqué topics—such as female sexual pleasure, birth control, and abortion—and by publishing works deemed 'obscene' by Parisian correctional courts. Implicating readers in such material created a complicit bond existing within a broader network of illicit solidarity between writers, publishers, and sex-related commerce. Understood as a form of 'proxénétisme' ['procuring'] or 'pimp journalism', *Don Juan*'s literary, artistic, and economic enterprise encouraged and enabled readers to engage in both imagined and actual erotic relations. Analysing the culturally promiscuous saucy magazine format, where original contributions from avant-garde elites rubbed shoulders with titillating titbits and sex toy adverts, I argue for a more nuanced appreciation of genres that might otherwise be dismissed as sordid ephemera.

## Seduction, Solicitation, and Collaboration

Seduction was at the heart of *Don Juan*'s literary and artistic agenda. The review defined its targeted readers by their capacity for desire, and their willingness to have this desire solicited by the periodical's content. This reader-text relation

---

[19] Elina Absalyamova and Valérie Stiénon, 'Introduction. Pour une étude des voix du lecteur en régime médiatique', in *Les Voix du lecteur dans la presse française au XIXe siècle*, edited by Elina Absalyamova and Valérie Stiénon (Limoges: Pulim, 2018), pp. 7–42 (p. 21).

[20] Valérie Stiénon, 'Lecteurs truqués: sur la fabrique médiatique du lectorat au XIXe siècle', in *Les Voix du lecteur*, edited by Absalyamova and Stiénon, pp. 171–89.

implies a reciprocal form of collaboration, situated ambiguously between gallantry and prostitution. Through a series of 'Aux Lecteurs' ['To the Readers'] articles, *Don Juan* plays out its own eroticised reception. Reformulating traditions of courtly love and *galanterie*, the review depicts itself as a *soupirant* ['suitor'] striving to attract the attention and favours of the reader.[21] By placing its readers in a position of discernment, akin to that of the courtly lady, *Don Juan* moves beyond a one-sided seduction model of reading, towards a form of imagined erotic sociability, where readers are encouraged to desire, identify with, and contribute towards the review's titillating contents. In the opening column of *Don Juan*'s first issue, the review claims to supplement and improve amorous relations, by feeding the imaginations of lonely singletons ('[*Don Juan*] peuplera ta solitude des mille et une adorées que tu désires' ['[*Don Juan*] will populate your solitude with a thousand and one adorable, desirable women']), and by uniting couples through repeated acts of shared reading ('vous lirez ensemble les belles histoires d'amour' ['you will read wonderful love stories together']). The relationship between the review and its readers resembles a reciprocally desiring embrace:

> A vous toutes, les chères souveraines, [...] c'est à vous que *Don Juan* lance son clair et triomphal salut. [...] Et vous viendrez à lui, sous sa nouvelle et si moderne incarnation, le journal, qui lui permettra de se trouver à la fois dans les mains de cent mille [...]. O femmes, o chères aimées [*sic*], toutes, toutes, je vous aime, je vous adore... Je suis à vous... Venez à moi! (8 June 1895)

> [It is to each and every one of you, dearest queens of my heart, [...] that *Don Juan* launches his clear and triumphant salute. [...] And you will come to him, in his new and most modern incarnation: the newspaper, which will allow him to be held in the hands of hundreds of thousands of women, simultaneously [...]. Oh my dear and beloved ladies! I love and adore every single one of you... I am yours... Come to me!]

*Don Juan*'s self-created role of a courtly or gallant lover ('Je suis à vous') returns at the end of the article, which insists on the importance of novelty to attract readers' attention: '*Don Juan* [...] sera sans cesse en quête d'attractions et de nouveautés. Il aura enfin la sollicitude, l'éveil, l'inquiétude d'un amoureux qui veut plaire, découvrir chaque jour des fleurs nouvelles et rares, pour les offrir à ses bien-aimées' ['*Don Juan* [...] will consistently seek novelty and appeal. He will have the attentiveness, alertness, and concern of a lover who wishes to please, each day finding new and rare flowers, so he can offer them to his beloved women readers']. This vision of amorous attentiveness, emphasised by the lover's 'sollicitude' and

---

[21] On the tradition of *galanterie*, see Alain Viala, *La France galante: Essai historique sur une catégorie culturelle, de ses origines jusqu'à la Révolution* (Paris: Presses Universitaires de France, 2008).

'inquiétude', places the imagined reader's taste, judgement, and pleasure at the centre of the review's agenda. It therefore gives actual readers a sense—however constructed it may be—of having real influence over *Don Juan*'s content and evolution, since their pleasure or displeasure is rendered synonymous with the success or failure of the review.

*Don Juan* maintained this image of readers' influence across all moments of address from the editorial team, particularly when highlighting the review's successes or announcing significant format changes. For example, the review increased its frequency from weekly to bi-weekly publication within only a few months of its existence. The advance announcement of this change appeared just after a declaration of the week's notably high print run: 'Tirage justifié de ce numéro: 40,000 exemplaires. Nous remercions de tout notre cœur nos lectrices, nos lecteurs, nos correspondants, tous nos amis qui ont contribué au si rapide et si merveilleux succès de notre journal' ['This issue's official print run: 40,000 copies. From the bottom of our hearts, we thank our readers of both sexes, our reporters, and all of our friends who have contributed to our paper's incredibly swift and extraordinary success'] (19 Oct. 1895). The notice interprets the number of issues printed as a direct reflection of readers' approbation of the review's contents, and subsequently a desire for *more* of this content. When the review finally became a bi-weekly, three months after the initial announcement, a notice placed distinct emphasis on readers' desire, pleasure, and discernment:

> Pour répondre aux sollicitations pressantes qui nous étaient faites, nous avons décidé que ce journal paraîtrait deux fois par semaine. Cette périodicité nous permettra d'introduire des éléments nouveaux dans notre rédaction. Le lecteur capricieux exige sans cesse de la variété, du nouveau. *Don Juan* a compris ce désir; il s'efforcera de toutes ses forces à le satisfaire, comme il l'a fait jusqu'à ce jour. (11 Jan. 1896)

> [To respond to the insistent requests the paper has received, we have decided that it should appear twice a week. This frequency will allow us to introduce new elements into our writing. The capricious reader constantly demands variety and novelty. *Don Juan* has understood this desire; he will strive with all his might to satisfy it, as he has done to this day.]

Vocabulary relating to the issuing and satisfaction of demands ('sollicit[er]', 'exige[r]', 'satisfaire') emphasises the seemingly impossible task of satisfying the reader, who in this case appears under the generic masculine ('le lecteur'). (Whereas the review's vision of eroticised literary discernment is elsewhere overtly feminised.) On *Don Juan*'s third anniversary, the editorial team announced '[u]ne nouvelle organisation financière' ['a new financial organisation'] that would enable the review to continue to satisfy its readers' demands for novelty:

'Cette transformation comporte tout un programme nouveau, qui comportera des gaspillages, des folies; mais *Don Juan* est un prodigue: il jette l'or à pleines mains, pour cueillir un sourire de ses lectrices' ['This transformation includes an entirely different programme, which will bring with it wasteful and extravagant spending—but *Don Juan* is a generous man: he spends gold in abundance to catch a smile from his [female] readers' lips'] (9 Dec. 1897).[22] At this point, a new address (34 rue de Lille) appears alongside '18, rue Feydeau' on the review's header, whose style noticeably changes.[23] In addition to the half-page drawing located on the fourth page, an increased number of smaller drawings appeared on the periodical's other pages. The larger number of drawings would have contributed to the 'gaspillage' mentioned above, due to increased printing costs.

*Don Juan*'s self-styled image as a 'prodigue' evokes relationships between wealthy men and courtesans, thereby marking a subtle shift from the review's earlier emphasis on the supposedly disinterested figure of the courtly lover. In 1898, *Don Juan* announced more radical changes: to reduce in format size but increase in page number. To justify the increased financial burden of changing print format, the management cited their desire to please the courtesan-reader:

On nous demandait d'adopter le type des grands journaux illustrés, tels que la VIE PARISIENNE, l'ILLUSTRATION, etc. [...] [N]ous avons étudié attentivement la question et en avons atteint enfin la solution. Notre prochain numéro aura huit pages de dessins et de textes. Ainsi transformé, DON JUAN, plus coquet, plus élégant que jamais, aura donné une fois de plus à ses lectrices et à ses lecteurs la preuve que sa seule ambition est de leur plaire, à tout prix, et toujours. (31 March 1898)

[We were asked to adopt the style of large illustrated newspapers, such as *La Vie parisienne*, *L'Illustration*, etc. [...] We studied the question attentively and finally reached a solution. Our next issue will have eight pages of images and text. Through this transformation, becoming more stylish and more elegant than ever, *Don Juan* will once again have given his readers (men and women alike) proof that his only ambition is to keep on pleasing them, no matter the cost.]

---

[22] On 1 December 1897, *Don Juan*'s shareholders sold the property of the review, 18 rue Feydeau. See *Journal des papetiers*, 1 Dec. 1897, p. 565.

[23] This change in header style appeared from 12 December 1897 onwards. The review's first header, from June 1895 to April 1896, depicted a cluster of women's faces in front of a quill. The second header, from April 1896 to Dec. 1896 and April 1897 to Dec. 1897, framed this original image with two topless women, holding a quill and reading a piece of paper, respectively. From Dec. 1897 to May 1898, the header depicted a cherub beside an extended floral motif. From Dec. 1896 to April 1897 and from June 1898 onwards, the header featured the review's title against a plain backdrop.

The vocabulary of 'coquetterie' and finance ('à tout prix') hints at courtesan culture, because the reader's favours are no longer being *won* through courtly feats, but rather *bought* through the review's prodigality. Furthermore, the decision to change format also reflects a shift in the review's status and reception. By adopting a similar format to that of popular rival papers *La Vie parisienne* and *L'Illustration*, *Don Juan* was adapting to a shifting market. But these changes did not seem to bring the review further success, since its decline occurred soon after (between May and June 1898). At this point it reverted to weekly publication, and contained only four sides of the smaller format, with fewer images. The changes described above therefore prefigured, and perhaps contributed towards, the review's eventual demise in 1900.[24] In this way, potential failure continually haunted the celebratory announcements in *Don Juan*'s 'Aux Lecteurs' articles. Readers' desires, much like the whims of their courtesan cousins, were perceived to be constantly shifting, with their positive reception, and continuing loyalty, always threatening to wane.

Through explicit address in the 'Aux Lecteurs' articles, *Don Juan* appealed to readers' desire, pleasure, and approbation, in a reader-text relation aligned with courtly love traditions, but implicitly akin to prostitution. It depicted itself as soliciting positive responses from its readership, who were, in turn, framed as contributing indirectly to the creative process of the review. However, *Don Juan*'s creation of a reader-centred literary and artistic programme was not limited to 'response' in the sense of 'reception', but also involved structures of *textual* responses, with the reader collaborating in the production of journalistic content. From the beginning of its existence, *Don Juan* appealed for contributions through a column entitled 'Nos Cours d'amour' ['Our Courts of Love'], where readers could respond creatively to specific questions, usually oriented around erotic and amorous themes. The review published texts it received, judged them in a competition, and awarded prizes for the best submissions. The series was later replaced by quasi-scientific surveys and questionnaires, which were a common feature of fin-de-siècle newspapers and reviews across the cultural spectrum.[25] Highlighting the saucy magazine's specificity, the topics featured in *Don Juan* encouraged solidarity between collaborators, readers, and editors, while feeding off the erotic—and potentially illicit—appeal of intimate stories and confessions.

The editorial team announced the 'Nos Cours d'amour' column in *Don Juan*'s second issue. Presented as a modern version of courtly *jeux floraux* traditions, the column replicated poetic competitions in which men's literary contributions would be judged by a jury of noblewomen whose favour(s) they sought:

---

[24] The BnF has some gaps in its holdings of *Don Juan*'s later issues. It is therefore difficult to date precisely the moment the review returned to weekly publication.

[25] On the culture of 'enquêtes' ['surveys' or 'investigations'] in the period, see Dominique Kalifa, 'Enquête et « culture de l'enquête » au XIXe siècle', *Romantisme* 149, no. 3 (2010): pp. 3–23, doi:10.3917/rom.149.0003.

Aux temps joyeux où la galanterie et l'amour resplendissaient en France, du plus pur et du plus brillant éclat, de nobles dames avaient institué ces fameuses *Cours d'amour* qui étaient les plus poétiques de toutes les fêtes. [...]

Un jury composé de jolies femmes soumettait aux poètes une question subtile et délicate de controverse passionnelle. [...]

Les nobles dames décernaient à celui dont la chanson ou le discours leur semblait digne de leur élection, une fleur, une simple fleur;—mais on dit que la nuit venue, si le poète se présentait, cette fleur à la main, sous les fenêtres des jolies dames, une échelle de soie se déroulait sur la muraille, une plus chère fleur à recueillir.

*Don Juan* va tenter de renouveler ces jeux, en instituant des *Cours d'amour*, las! moins brillantes que celles d'antan [...]. (15 June 1895)

[In the happy days of yore, when France radiated with love and gallantry, of the purest and most brilliant lustre, some noble women established those famous 'Courts of Love', which were the most poetic of all celebrations. [...]

A panel of beautiful women would put forward a subtle and delicate topic for the poets to debate, on affairs of the heart. [...]

The noble ladies would offer an award—a flower, a simple flower—to the poet whose song or speech seemed worthy of their election. But they say that, when night fell, if the poet presented himself beneath the pretty ladies' window, with their flower in his hand, a silken ladder would unfurl upon the wall, providing an even more valuable flower for him to reap.

*Don Juan* is going to attempt to reinvent these games, by establishing a new form of 'Courts of Love', which—alas!—are less brilliant than those of yesteryear.]

A sense of nostalgia, experienced in response to the loss of past traditions, dominates the first half of the announcements ('Au temps joyeux'). The text reinforces this sentiment through hyperbole ('du plus pur et du plus brillant éclat', 'les plus poétiques de toutes les fêtes'), and vocabulary evoking 'feminine' delicacy ('subtile', 'délicate', 'douce'). The 'nobles dames' organising and judging medieval poetry competitions align metonymically with the flower they offer to their chosen winner. The erotic value of this symbolic gesture is not left to the imagination: the 'simple fleur' represents a promise or token to be exchanged for sexual favours: 'une plus chère fleur à recueillir'. By emphasising the exchange value of the poetry prize, where literary merit could buy sexual favours, *Don Juan* increased the correlation between literature, sex, and prostitution appearing elsewhere in the review. After all, in *Don Juan*'s version of the 'cours d'amour', the prize offered is emphatically material and financial: 'UNE FLEUR EN OR ou une somme de CENT FRANCS' ['A GOLDEN FLOWER or a sum of ONE HUNDRED FRANCS'].

Due to the lack of archival sources, it is difficult to confirm whether *Don Juan*'s competition submissions were genuine, and whether the prize was ever actually awarded. Nevertheless, it is clear that the 'Nos Cours d'amour' column perpetuated an image of readerly collaboration, both in its promise to publish readers' written contributions, and in its appeal to female readers to identify with, and enact the role of, the 'nobles dames' on the judging panel. With these caveats in mind, it is worth noting that competition submissions were signed under both masculine and feminine names, which suggests that *Don Juan* offered women readers imaginative and textual space to contribute to the review's collaborative enterprise. Although the predominant forms of eroticism appearing in *Don Juan* seem chiefly aimed at heterosexual men, these columns hint at a wider readership, including women who were comfortable with the levels of transgression and titillation connoted by the review's content. Indeed, the existence of a female readership is implied across various columns—notably 'La Chronique de Sapho'—and is supported by the presence of female-targeted advertisements on the fourth page. That said, the blurring of gender in *Don Juan*'s competitions also facilitates a triangular, homosocial structure in which male authors and readers bond through their prurient interest in—and competitive desire to channel or manipulate—the sexual preferences and behaviour of others (especially women).[26] In this process, the mock-nostalgic depiction of a medieval courtly tradition flatters the review's readers and encourages them to share their romantic and erotic secrets ('faites-nous de chers aveux') in a public forum.

As the word 'aveux' suggests, the anecdotes *Don Juan* solicited from its readers were potentially illicit or immoral in nature. By encouraging readers to share their erotic secrets, 'Nos Cours d'amour' engaged not only with early literary traditions such as *fin'amors* and *galanterie*, but also with contemporaneous cultural phenomena—most notably the rise in quasi-scientific discourses surrounding sexuality and pathology.[27] It is therefore significant that the column was occasionally replaced by different formats, more obviously inspired by scientific, medical, and journalistic uses of the survey or questionnaire format. In number 88, an article entitled 'Notre enquête sur l'amour' ['Our Survey on Love'] announces a new form of reader-response column, which diverges from the nostalgic medievalism of the first series of 'Nos Cours d'amour'. Notably, it evokes fin-de-siècle depopulation fears and socio-political discourses about 'degeneration', which announced a decline in socially sanctioned amorous desire, in turn attributed to the blurring of traditional gender roles.[28] The article notes

---

[26] A comparable homosocial triangle, combining erotic interest in and rivalry over a feminine 'other', existed in the hyper-masculine realm of fin-de-siècle book collecting. See Willa Z. Silverman, *The New Bibliopolis: French Book Collectors and the Culture of Print, 1880–1914* (Toronto: University of Toronto Press, 2008), p. 167.

[27] On this topic, see Rosario, Rachel Mesch, *The Hysteric's Revenge: French Women Writers at the fin-de-siècle* (Nashville: Vanderbilt University Press, 2006), and Robert Nye, *Crime, Madness and Politics in Modern France: The Medical Concept of National Decline* (Princeton: Princeton University Press, 2014).

[28] See Francis Ronsin, *La Grève des ventres: propaganda néo-malthusienne et baisse de la natalité française (XIX—XXe siècles)* (Paris: Éditions Aubier Montaigne, 1980), and Nye, *Crime, Madness and Politics*.

how doctors, psychologists, and statisticians are concerned about women's sexual behaviour and willingness to procreate: 'S'il faut les en croire, la femme surtout ressent de moins en moins les sollicitations du sexe, et perd complètement le sentiment de la maternité' ['If these men [of science] are to be believed, women in particular are feeling less and less tempted by sexual urges, and are losing their maternal feeling completely']. To assess and alleviate such concerns, the review solicits its female readers to respond to a questionnaire created by 'Dr Stary' ('le docteur Stary'), who plans to analyse their responses in a wider study:

1° A quel âge avez-vous aimé pour la première fois?
2° Votre premier amour fut-il purement sentimental ou sensuel?
3° Vers quel âge la sensualité s'est-elle éveillée en vous?
4° Avez-vous eu plusieurs amours en même temps?
5° Avez-vous des enfants? Le sentiment de la maternité est-il en vous violent, faible, ou nul? A-t-il quelque influence sur vos amours? (25 July 1896)

[1. How old were you when you first experienced love?
2. Was your first love purely sentimental or sensual?
3. At what age did you first discover sensual feelings?
4. Have you had several liaisons at the same time?
5. Do you have children? Is maternal feeling strong, weak, or non-existent in you? Does it have any impact on your love life?]

The shift in column format, towards an 'enquête' or 'questionnaire', reflects a shift in the type of imaginary relationship created between the reader-contributors and the column organisers. Rather than exemplifying a reciprocal bond between courtly ladies and their would-be suitors, the column depicts a more hierarchised and gendered doctor-patient relationship. It solicits only female readers for responses, and seeks their amorous experiences not for the artistic merit of their rendering, but for the scientific value of their content. This clearly restricts the creativity of potential reader-collaborators, and pathologises—or at least mystifies—female experience. However, much like the nostalgic medievalism of 'Nos Cours d'amour', the quasi-scientific claims of the 'Enquête' are recognisably clichéd tropes, acting above all as pretexts for borderline erotic material. Indeed, the evidently sexual nature of the response column's questions confirms such a reading.[29] Both frameworks facilitated the act of sharing titillating anecdotes

---

[29] After the first question, 'Quelle est la meilleure caresse?' ['What is the best caress?'], 'Nos Cours d'amour' asked readers: 'Quelle différence y-t-il entre l'amour d'une blonde et l'amour d'une brune?' ['What difference is there between the love of a blond and that of a brunette?'] (8 Feb. 1896), 'Que préférez-vous: aimer sans être aimé ou être aimé sans aimer?' ['Do you prefer to love without reciprocation, or to be loved without reciprocating?'] (4 Mar. 1896), 'Quelle est la meilleure heure du jour pour aimer et pourquoi?' ["What is the best hour in the day to make love, and why?'] (26 Aug. 1896), and 'La femme se donne-t-elle plus souvent par curiosité, par ennui or par amour?' ['Do women give themselves most frequently out of curiosity, boredom, or love?'] (7 Oct. 1896).

in the public domain and encouraged readers to collaborate in this material through their written contributions and imagined participation in the review's erotic sociabilities.

The frame texts introducing *Don Juan*'s reader-response columns highlight the slippage between artistic and scientific pretexts for erotic content, as well as the threat of crossing into illegitimate, obscene territory. From as early as the eighth issue, *Don Juan* confirms the presence of pornographic contributions by announcing their necessary elimination: 'Beaucoup de réponses ont été éliminées, parce qu'elles étaient d'un... décolleté à faire frémir une demi-vierge' ['Many responses have been eliminated, because they were... revealing enough to make a *demi-vierge* tremble'] (29 July 1895). The editorial decision to censor responses is less interesting than the way the column announces it. By using ellipsis and evoking the figure of the *demi-vierge* ['half-virgin'][30]—here trembling with shame, pleasure, or a combination of the two—the frame text arouses readers' curiosity regarding the eliminated texts, and their suspicions about the column's supposedly moral and artistic justifications. In the latter half of 1896, 'Nos Cours d'amour' returns, after a brief interlude filled by Dr Stary's survey. The new signatory of the column, 'Clisson',[31] frequently reminds readers to keep their contributions as 'clean' as possible:

> Je dois tout d'abord avertir ici mes correspondants que nos *Cours d'Amour* devant constituer une sorte de traité psychologique, je n'insérerai que les lettres dont la teneur sera d'une parfaite correction. Mes lectrices et mes lecteurs me sauront gré de sauvegarder des sentiments respectables, et d'essayer de faire une œuvre intéressante, curieuse, mais non pas égrillarde. (16 Sept. 1896)

> [First of all, I must warn my correspondents that since our 'Courts of Love' are meant to form a kind of psychological treatise, I will insert only those letters which demonstrate the utmost propriety. My readers of both sexes will be grateful to me for upholding a sense of respectability, and for trying to create a work that is interesting and curious, but not lewd.]

And:

> Ai-je besoin de recommander à nos correspondants, de conserver dans leurs lettres la jolie et sérieuse tenue qu'ils ont eue jusqu'à aujourd'hui. N'oublions pas que nos *cours d'amour* ne doivent prêter à aucune critique. (4 Nov. 1896)

---

[30] 'A woman (esp. a young woman) of doubtful reputation or suspected unchastity, who is not a virgin except in the strict physiological sense of the word'. See 'demi-vierge, n.', *OED Online*, Oxford University Press, Dec. 2022, www.oed.com/view/Entry/49744, accessed 3 Jan. 2023. Marcel Prévost popularised the term in his novel *Les Demi-vierges* (1894), which offered an extended (mock-)castigation of sexually provocative, if ultimately reserved, women.

[31] The first series of 'Nos Cours d'amour' were unsigned.

[Do I need to instruct our correspondents once more that their letters should retain the lovely, thoughtful manner that they have shown up until now? Let us not forget that our *Courts of Love* must not give rise to a single criticism.]

These reminders can be read literally, as an honest assessment of contributions the review actually received, or more ironically as a ploy intended to titillate readers by reminding them of the social and moral sanctions *Don Juan* frequently disrupts and subverts. In fact, the column doubly emphasises the obscenity it supposedly condemns. First, the repeated reminders suggest that readers ignored Clisson's injunctions, and that their contributions remained consistently on the verge of offering illicit or obscene content. Second, the references to external criticism ('N'oublions que nos *cours d'amour* ne doivent prêter à aucune critique'), simultaneously evoke—and yet diffuse, via ironic humour—the real-life threat of censorship experienced by the review.[32] Moreover, the qualifying adjectival phrasing—'une *sorte* de traité psychologique', '[une] *parfaite* correction', and 'la *jolie et sérieuse* tenue' (my emphasis)—combines ambivalence, hyperbole, and oxymoron in a way that encourages an ironic reading. These frame text examples highlight the slippage between 'acceptable' erotic content and obscenity while ostensibly condemning the latter, in a gesture of complicit mutual understanding, or 'clin d'œil', between the review and its readership. By facilitating the public dissemination of titillating material while ostensibly censoring readers' sexual excess, the review shifted some of the blame for risqué material onto its readers, as part of a self-defensive (if playful) ruse, which responded ironically to the very real threat of punishment from Paris's correctional courts.

## Titillation, Polemics, and Obscenity

As the predominant theme and style, erotic titillation appeared throughout *Don Juan*'s eclectic pages. Like other forms of public entertainment in Belle Époque Paris, the review frequently extolled the sensual appeal of female nudity.[33] In centring this theme, it relied on an explicitly prurient and shared male gaze, which—according to the logic of homosociality—largely excludes the desired female object from responding or contributing to the process. The prurient male gaze underlies many of *Don Juan*'s drawings and texts. For example, in the gossip column 'La Vie parisienne', the bodies of actresses and *demi-mondaines* become

---

[32] Bonnet was condemned for 'outrage aux bonnes mœurs' in July 1896. The second series of 'Nos Cours d'amour', including these mock-moralising reminders, started only a month after the trial judgement (No. 97, 26 Aug. 1896). Such 'moral' reminders therefore indirectly responded to, and mocked, judicial censorship.

[33] On the widespread but controversial appeal of female nudity in the period, see Lela F. Kerley, *Uncovering Paris: Scandals and Nude Spectacles in the Belle Époque* (Baton Rouge: Louisiana State University Press, 2017).

the source of endless titillating anecdotes.[34] Consider, for example, the description of Jane Derval's performance in *Peur des coups*, at the Théâtre Pompadour:

> C'est un spectacle à recommander, et très artiste, parce que les jambes de Jane Derval sont superbement modelées, et toutes ses courbes, toutes ses lignes pleines et harmonieuses.
> Et quand elle se penche—oh! la charitable!—sa gorge tout entière se révèle; je vous assure que ça n'a rien de désagréable pour les rétines: au contraire!
> Quels apéritifs, avant minuit! (28 Nov. 1896)

> [It's a show to write home about, and very artistic, because Jane Derval's legs are shaped superbly, her curves and lines are all harmonious and well-drawn.
> And when she bends over—oh, what a charitable lady!—her entire bosom is unveiled. I assure you that it does not leave an unpleasant impression upon the retina: quite the contrary!
> Enough to whet the appetite, before midnight!]

The article's *mise-en-scène* of female nudity places a thin veil of artistic value ('un spectacle [...] très artiste') to a performance that is evidently geared towards erotic arousal. It depicts Derval as complicit with her visual objectification by the audience, as she offers herself to their hungry gaze ('oh! la charitable!'). By adopting a playful and conversational tone, the segment conveys the ambiguous homosociality of the gossip column as a genre, where female nudity acts as visually stimulating and tactile fodder for the male-centred erotic imagination.[35] *Don Juan* encouraged this form of communal voyeurism elsewhere in the column. For example, a series of short articles, entitled 'Leurs seins' ['Their Bosoms'], combined *demi-mondaine* sociabilities with blatant eroticism:

> Pour voir un coin de chair de femme, rouler une tête sur ces blancheurs si douces, aspirer les senteurs qui s'en dégagent, je donnerais volontiers mon esprit à Brunetière et mon âme à Satan; ne vous étonnez donc pas si, avec des ruses d'Apache, une patience de serpent, [...] je me suis glissé furtivement dans les boudoirs de nos agenouillées les plus connues pour les croquer dans leur déshabillage et vous dire comment elles les ont: en poire, en pomme, en courge ou en calebasse.
> Je transcris fidèlement les notes prises dans cette enquête amoureuse. (9 May 1897)

---

[34] The *OED* defines 'demi-monde' as: 'The class of women of doubtful reputation and social standing, upon the outskirts of "society." (Sometimes, though improperly, extended to include courtesans in general.)' *OED Online*. Dec. 2022. Oxford University Press, https://www.oed.com/view/Entry/49696, accessed 3 Jan. 2023.

[35] In *Le Roman de La Vie parisienne*, Sadoun-Édouard also notes the importance of orality to *La Vie parisienne* (pp. 103–4), suggesting that such reviews use the tone of 'causerie' in order to 'créer une communauté imaginée et participative' ['to create an imaginary, participatory community'] (p. 107).

[To catch a glimpse of the female body, to roll one's head upon such soft white skin, to breathe in the scent it emanates, I would happily give my mind to Brunetière and my soul to Satan. So don't be surprised that, with the cunning of a bandit and the patience of a serpent, [...] I slipped furtively into the boudoirs of our most famous courtesans in order to sketch them in a state of undress, and to tell you what kind of pair they've got: whether they're shaped like apples, pears, squashes, or gourds.

I offer a faithful transcription of my notes taken during this amorous investigation.]

The author here frames the mini-series as an ode to female beauty, encouraging the reader to experience the sensual pleasure aroused by the sight, smell, feel, and taste of women's breasts. Implicit or explicit address, seen in the use of 'nous' and 'vous', encourages identification and unites the author and reader through shared desires and experiences. Indeed, it is in the name of a shared, implicitly masculine, erotic curiosity that the author offers a furtive glimpse of *demi-mondaines*' naked bodies. At the same time, the text claims to channel academically credible scientific interests. The word 'enquête' implies a quasi-scientific justification for erotic intrusion, which matches poorly with the titillating tone of the article as a whole. Shared voyeuristic desire establishes readers' complicity with an invasion of women's personal lives, as does the text's playful—if somewhat disconcerting—humour. The latter ranges from literary satire to smutty jokes, as seen in the parallels made between Brunetière and Satan, as well as the fruit- and vegetable-based sexual innuendos. By turning the voyeuristic, invasive appreciation of non-consensual female nudity into a joke shared between men, 'La Vie parisienne' contributes towards the mostly unquestioned sexism of the review.

In 'La Vie parisienne', sexualised gossip about women is clearly a source of misogynistic homosocial desire. As Alistaire Tallent notes, recounting stories about sexually available women creates an 'intimate imaginary connection' between men, particularly when they are enclosed within male-to-male dialogic frame texts.[36] By addressing an implicitly male reader, the journalist-narrator of 'Leurs seins' creates precisely this kind of complicit bond, which tacitly justifies voyeurism and sexual harassment. After all, his furtive forays into demi-mondaines' boudoirs contain a poorly veiled threat of sexual violence that functions as a homosocial 'signifying structure' that 'reinscribes the female body as a sign which allows a certain communication for and between men'.[37] However, the disquieting implications of articles like 'Leurs seins' do not tell the whole story of the relationships between eroticism and gender in *Don Juan*. For, as Sharon Marcus has convincingly demonstrated, erotic interest in women was not a purely

---

[36] Alistaire Tallent, 'Intimate Exchanges: The Courtesan Narrative and Male Homosocial Desire in *La Dame aux camélias*', *French Forum* 39, no. 1 (2014): pp. 19–31 (p. 28), doi:10.1353/frf.2014.0001.

[37] Andrew Counter, 'Tough Love, Hard Bargains: Rape and Coercion in Balzac', *Nineteenth-Century French Studies* 36, nos. 1–2 (Fall–Winter 2007–8): pp. 61–71 (p. 68), https://www.jstor.org/stable/23538479.

masculine experience during the nineteenth century. In fact, different types of cultural production in the period 'solicited a female gaze for images that put women, their bodies, and the objects that adorned them on display'.[38] This is born out even in *Don Juan*'s most sexualised gossip, to the extent that descriptions of actresses and other female celebrities featured heavily in more culturally legitimate women's magazines, such as *Femina* and *La Vie heureuse*.[39] The smutty humour found in 'Leurs seins' is but one end of a spectrum of eroticised femininity that appealed to both a male and female gaze.

A better way of assessing *Don Juan*'s gendered eroticism is therefore to consider the broader feminisation of the review, its readers, and its contributors. For although *Don Juan* frequently relied on male-to-male homosocial complicity, it also appealed to a feminised equivalent by positing its readers as women. The *rédaction* often addressed its comments and questions to a feminised readership ('nos lectrices'), and the back page regularly featured drawings that depicted women reading *Don Juan* (see Figure 5.1). In a gesture of self-promotional *mise en abyme*, such images invited all readers to identify with the redolent women absorbed in the review's pages. Furthermore, the review's overarching feminisation applied not only to readers, but also to the review and its contributors. Despite promoting a masculine self-image as the eponymous seducer in many of its 'Aux Lecteurs' articles, *Don Juan* also adopted feminised self-images and voices. For example, Édouard Couturier contributed a series of polemical drawings between December 1897 and January 1898, in which the review—personified as a female Don Juan wearing a costume and plumed hat—admonished political figures for their failings. The review's tendency to play up to femininity, typical of saucy magazines of the period, also took the form of male journalists signing articles under feminine pseudonyms. This gesture can be read as a sign of subversion, but also as a conduit for voyeurism, fetishism, and mythification.[40]

A striking example of this practice was 'La Chronique de Sapho': a recurring opinion piece column that doubled up as an agony aunt column. Signed 'Sapho', the column was in fact written by the editor-in-chief René Emery. Appearing as the leading article in almost every issue, it acted as a *fil conducteur* ['guiding thread'] to the review's wider aesthetic, political, social, and ethical positioning. Blending opinion pieces, personal stories, and agony-aunt-style advice, the column discussed erotic and amorous topics not only as a personal or private matter, but also as a reflection of wider social and political debates. These included: virginity, romance, adultery, divorce, sexual freedom, the double standard, and

---

[38] Sharon Marcus, *Between Women: Friendship, Desire, and Marriage in Victorian England* (Princeton: Princeton University Press, 2009), p. 119.

[39] For analysis of *Femina* and *La Vie heureuse*, see Rachel Mesch, *Having It All in the Belle Époque: How French Women's Magazines Invented the Modern Woman* (Stanford: Stanford University Press, 2013).

[40] Sadoun-Édouard, *Le Roman de* La Vie parisienne, pp. 296–7.

**Figure 5.1** E. Cros, 'Petit lever', *Don Juan*, 18 November 1896 (BnF).

neo-Malthusianism.[41] In the Sapho articles, social critique frequently intersected with titillating striptease, especially when they treated topics such as love, marriage, and the wedding night.[42] For example, 'Nuit de noces' ['Wedding Night'] (22 Jan. 1896) was framed as an agony aunt response to correspondence sent by predominantly female readers. Its opening lines blended mockery with subversive moral guidance: 'Comme je vous méprise et comme en même temps je vous plains, mes bonnes petites amies, qui venez me dire vos désillusions et vos nostalgies du rêve qui hantait vos nuits virginales, avant le mariage' ['How I disdain and yet also pity you, my dear little friends, as you come to tell me about your disappointments and about the nostalgic reveries that haunted your virginal dreams, before marriage']. Sapho's ambivalent reaction, blending pity with disdain, paves the way for a lengthy appeal to women's shared experience of the 'fall' from visions of marital bliss to the disappointing experience of sexual consummation:

> Pauvres amies, je vous ai vues alors, désabusées, pleurant, regrettant le beau rêve, maudissant l'amour, accusant la vie. Et j'ai compris de suite que le mariage était [...] la geôle plus affreuse jusqu'à l'heure où la fenêtre s'ouvrirait, sur les décors de l'adultère.
> Je vous ai, combien de fois, entendu accuser votre mari, lui reprocher son inexpérience, comme si vous n'étiez pas, vous, les vraies coupables, les petites sottes, les impuissantes!
> Avez-vous jamais songé, une minute avant le mariage, à vous préparer au mystère de la première nuit?

[Dear friends, I saw you at that moment, disillusioned, crying, lamenting that beautiful dream, cursing love, reeling from life's blows. And I understood immediately that marriage would be [...] the most dreadful jail until the moment a window opened upon the backdrop of adultery.
So many times, I have heard you blame your husband, reproaching him for his inexperience, as if you yourselves had not been silly little fools, the truly guilty and impotent ones!
At any point preceding your marriage, did you ever consider preparing yourself for the mystery of that first night?]

From an initial attack on social institutions (through the marriage-as-prison metaphor), Sapho shifts towards a form of victim-blaming, condemning her

---

[41] Indicative titles from 'La Chronique de Sapho' include: 'Amour nature' (15 June 1895), 'Contre le divorce' (27 July 1895), 'La Culotte et l'amour' (7 Sept. 1895), 'Péchons, mes sœurs!' (25 Mar. 1896), 'Sensuelles' (9 Sept. 1896), 'La Liberté de l'Amour' (28 Oct. 1896), 'Le Duel des Sexes' (21 Mar. 1897), and 'Les Malthusiennes' (1 May 1898).

[42] As Clara Sadoun-Édouard notes, the wedding night was a privileged (and always potentially subversive) topic in saucy magazines. Sadoun-Édouard, *Le Roman de La Vie parisienne*, pp. 296–7 and p. 302.

readers for failing to supplement and subvert these inadequacies through their own 'preparations'.

The idea of *preparing oneself* for sexual relations, metonymically represented by the wedding night, becomes the pretext for an erotic sequence in the second half of the article. After gently berating her readers, Sapho offers her own experience as an exemplary alternative narrative. Starting with the confession 'J'ai failli me marier' ['I almost got married'], Sapho mentions the details of her engagement to a young man, before describing at length her wedding 'preparations'—a series of intimate scenes where Sapho rehearses the act of undressing and simulates erotic embraces:

J'appris à me déshabiller coquettement [...]. Dans une psyché, je me voyais, et je m'aimais un peu, à m'apercevoir ainsi, frissonnante, comme une fleur à l'instant épanouie... Et je me disais que mon petit mari, tel un fou, accourrait, me voudrait embrasser [...]. Je fermais les yeux, et je m'inclinais sur le divan, très doucement, m'abandonnant à ses adorations, à ses caresses très tendres, encore respectueuses, mais très peu...

Et mes lèvres simulaient le baiser que je lui rendrais. [...]

Et cette comédie m'affolait... Je désirais la caresse simulée; j'appelais mon bien-aimé; j'aurais voulu le voir apparaître tout à coup, par quelque sortilège... avec joie, je me serais donnée...

[I learned to undress myself coquettishly [...]. I would look at myself in the mirror, admiring and adoring the sight of myself standing there, quivering like a flower that has just opened up in full bloom... And I would tell myself that my darling husband, mad with passion, would run towards me and want to kiss me [...] So I would shut my eyes and lie down very slowly upon the settee, giving myself over to his adoration, to his very tender caresses, which were still respectful, but only somewhat...

And my lips practised the kiss that I would give him in return. [...]

And this playacting drove me wild... I desired the caress I was simulating; I called out my beloved's name; I would have wanted him to appear before me, all of a sudden, by some magic spell... I would have given myself to him with great pleasure...]

The scene enacts a titillating striptease that incorporates the desiring male gaze into its performance. The desire and pleasure Sapho experiences by watching her performance in the mirror re-enacts structures of alienation—whereby women are obliged to view themselves as sexual objects—while paradoxically enabling the autotelic realisation of an active subject position. There are also homoerotic and homophobic undercurrents, when lesbian desire appears indirectly as an offshoot of, and extension to, female vanity ('je m'aimais un peu').[43]

The twist in 'Nuit de noces' comes when Sapho explains why she brought an end to her engagement: two weeks before the wedding, she finds out that her fiancé has visited a prostitute—a form of 'preparation' she finds unacceptable, and inferior to her own. This narrative 'chute' ['fall'] highlights the sexual double standard of society's valorisation of pre-marital female virginity. However, Sapho's disappointment is framed not only as an ethical question, but also as an aesthetic one. By spending the night with a prostitute, her fiancé relegates sex to something banal and commercial, whereas Sapho constructs it as a performance, a work of art. Her ideal is premised on its unattainability. After all, although her experience parallels the trajectory of her readers' disappointment, evoked in the first half of the article, Sapho's wedding night—unlike theirs—*never actually happens*. Sapho escapes her readers' fate and is left free to explore her desires via extra-marital means. Not only this, but, on a symbolic level, Sapho's *mise en scène* surpasses the reality that it represents and supplements. The most erotic moment of the story is when men are emphatically absent. By highlighting male absence, the text reverses the traditional male-centred homosocial bond, and enables a form of homosociality between women. Indeed, the column's agony aunt structure clearly offers women readers a forum for identification, shared experience, and mutual education. Even so, 'La Chronique de Sapho' retains traces of a male-centred homosocial bond, since it is a series of articles penned by a man, who employs a feminised signature and encourages an objectifying form of voyeurism. While evoking female-centred pleasure and appealing to solidarity between women, the topics under discussion continue to serve as titillating pretexts for a prurient male gaze.

Beyond titillation, 'La Chronique de Sapho' provided space for more polemical standpoints on the intersecting phenomena of politics, sex, and art. In the column, Emery actively contributed to contemporaneous debates surrounding sexual liberty, marriage, and—most controversially—abortion rights. He defended, and implicitly encouraged, sexual practices and family planning methods that were not only considered immoral, but were punishable by law. In an early Sapho article, 'L'Amour en herbe', Emery unambiguously reveals the illicit potential of the advice column:

> [Je] suis désolée de ne pouvoir à toutes, à tous, tendre une main secourable; amener à un mendiant d'amour une jolie fille, prête à le consoler de ses cruelles attentes; verser à la misérable, qui demain peut-être maudira l'amour et la

---

[43] This is reminiscent of a scene in Zola's *Nana* (1880), where Nana admires herself undressing in front of a mirror, with Muffat looking on. See Émile Zola, *Les Rougon-Macquart: histoire naturelle et sociale d'une famille sous le Second Empire*, ed. Henri Mitterand, 5 vols (Paris: Gallimard, 1960–7), II (1961), pp. 1269–71.

maternité, les breuvages meurtriers qui transforment le sein de la femme en un sépulcre flétri. (3 Aug. 1895)

[[I] am sorry not to be able to give a helping hand to all my readers, both men and women: to offer men seeking love a beautiful girl, willing to provide consolation for all that time spent cruelly waiting; to pour out a glass to unfortunate women, who may soon curse both love and maternity, a glass filled with murderous potions to transform their wombs into withered tombs.]

The primary two forms of assistance requested by Sapho's readers effectively amount to sexual procuration and complicity in abortion. Sapho's apologetic refusal to grant such requests confirms their taboo status, while hinting at the column's possible role as a 'bad influence' on its readers. Indeed, by apologising for her incapacities, and by emphatically *not* condemning the validity of their desires, the agony aunt figure implicitly condones—or at least excuses—the actions in question.

Despite refusing to facilitate sexual liaisons and abortions, Emery repeatedly promoted female sexual liberty in the Sapho column, arguing in favour of birth control and decriminalising abortion. By doing so, he contributed to a broader social movement referred to as neo-Malthusianism. This movement drew inspiration from Thomas Malthus's warnings, in *An Essay on the Principle of Population* (1798), about uncontrolled population growth leading to decreased living standards and eventual population decline. Unlike Malthus, who proposed delayed marriage and chastity as 'moral' solutions to overpopulation, neo-Malthusian thinkers advocated the use of contraception—and, if necessary, abortion—to control population growth.[44] One of the leading French neo-Malthusians was Paul Robin (1837–1912), an anarchist and pedagogue who—after spending several years of political exile in England throughout the 1870s—supervised the Prevost Orphanage from 1880 to 1894.[45] Robin first encountered neo-Malthusian thinking during his exile in England and subsequently wrote a series of pamphlets supporting population limitation. In 1896, he founded the Ligue de la régénération humaine, which published articles and propaganda promoting birth control in its newspaper *Régénération*. Largely financed through the sale of contraceptive devices, the Ligue gradually gained wider support, establishing four branches in Paris, and another twenty across France.[46] The fin-de-siècle birth control movement drew most of its support from the libertarian left, including

---

[44] On the link between Malthus' political and economic thought and neo-Malthusianism, see Ronsin, *La Grève des ventres*, pp. 28–31.

[45] Robin lost this position due to the controversy surrounding his innovative methods, which included co-education. This reaction was part of an upsurge of conservative criticism associated with the anti-anarchist backlash experienced in France throughout 1893–4.

[46] Ronsin, *La Grève des ventres*, pp. 46–61.

anarchist individualists, syndicalists, and radical feminists, but it was shunned by socialists and Marxists. Notable feminist sympathisers included Marie Huot (1846-1930, the antivivisectionist who coined the term 'grève des ventres' ['womb strike']), Madeleine Pelletier (1874-1939, the first French female psychiatric doctor), the activist Nelly Roussel (1878-1922), and the journalists Gabrielle Petit (1860-1952) and Marguerite Durand (1864-1936). These feminists wrote and spoke in favour of women's right to sexual freedom and to control over their bodies through contraception and legalised abortion.[47] In doing so, they diverged from the large majority of conservative, bourgeois feminists who valorised maternity and concentrated on women's suffrage rather than sexual freedom.[48]

Despite its underlying sexism, *Don Juan* drew on the intersecting trends of neo-Malthusianism, individualism, and radical feminism in its approach to sexual politics. In 'Couveuses' (24 Aug. 1895), an article from the Sapho column, René Emery discussed a paper that Robin presented to the Société d'anthropologie de Paris on 20 June 1895.[49] Highlighting the debate's gendered nature and the importance of birth control to increasing women's freedom, Emery praises Robin for his depiction of women's prescribed role in society as 'absurde, ridicule, [et] ignoble' ['absurd, ridiculous, [and] vile']. He describes how women, according to Robin's argument, are caught in a double bind between two forms of 'esclavage' ['slavery']: either they can follow the socially prescribed role of virtuous mothers, condemned to 'corvées conjugales' ['conjugal duties'] and 'enfantements répétés' ['repeated childbirth'], or they can dedicate their lives to the 'joies stériles' ['sterile joy'] of sexual liberty, equated with prostitution. After noting the hypocrisy of the widespread but unspoken use of family planning methods ('les fraudes et les supercheries' ['frauds and deception']), Sapho/Emery rejects the pronatalist tendency to relegate women to their reproductive capacities: '[La] Terre est trop peuplée. Et cela suffit pour réclamer, au nom des femmes, une liberté que l'on nous refuse: celle d'êtres femmes: non plus femelles couveuses ['The Earth is overpopulated. And this fact is enough to claim, in the name of women, a right we are refused: the right to be women, and not female incubators']. By using the word 'nous' here, Emery

---

[47] In the period, the primary form of birth control was coitus interruptus. Barrier methods—including condoms, diaphragms, sponges, pessaries, and caps—were regularly advertised in newspapers, alongside pharmaceutical products claiming spermicidal properties, vaginal syringes, and douches. Such products were relatively expensive and often ineffective unless they were employed in combination. The lack of accessible, affordable, and effective birth control led many women to have recourse to abortion, which was criminalised by article 317 of the penal code. See Angus McLaren, *A History of Contraception: From Antiquity to the Present Day* (Oxford: Basil Blackwell, 1990), pp. 178-214, Hera Cook, *The Long Sexual Revolution: English Women, Sex, and Contraception 1800-1975* (Oxford: Oxford University Press, 2004), pp. 122-42, and Jean-Yves Le Naour and Catherine Valenti, *Histoire de l'avortement. XIXe-XXe siècle* (Paris: Éditions du Seuil, 2003).

[48] See Ronsin, *La Grève des ventres*, pp. 157-161, Angus McLaren, *Sexuality and Social Order: The Debate Over the Fertility of Women and Workers in France, 1770-1920* (New York: Holmes & Meier, 1983), pp. 164-5, and Le Naour and Valenti, *Histoire de l'avortement*, pp. 69-75.

[49] Paul Robin, 'Dégénérescence de l'espèce humaine; causes et remèdes', *Bulletins et mémoires de la Société d'Anthropologie de Paris*, Series 4, Vol. 6 (1895), pp. 426-33.

aligns the figure of Sapho with her readers in a way that he did not do in 'Nuit de noces', which used 'vous' more frequently than 'nous'. The tone also changes, from the patronising titillation of 'Nuit de noces', to a more forceful socio-political call to arms. The article's concluding comments, discussing degeneration theories and racial regeneration, swiftly head towards a more disturbing vision of ethnic cleansing ('laver la race' ['to purify the race']), which is uncomfortable reading for modern critics. Neo-Malthusians often employed eugenicist arguments, citing the benefits of birth control (or, if necessary, abortion) in preventing the transmission of inherited diseases and disabilities. Some critics have viewed this approach as a ploy to get conservatives and medical practitioners on board by re-working the social utility argument employed by natalists concerned about depopulation.[50] The line between adoption and re-appropriation in such cases is difficult to draw, so it is important to acknowledge this more disquieting tendency when analysing the movement.

As well as promoting the acceptability of birth control, Emery defended abortion as part of a socially conscious response to the gendered inequalities of fin-de-siècle French society. In 'Ventres honteux' ['Ashamed/Shameful Wombs'], he attacked traditional moral norms that circumscribe and punish women's sexuality in the name of 'honour', claiming that:

> [Elle] n'est pas coupable celle qui veut aujourd'hui dépouiller son ventre de la flétrissure et de la honte—puisque l'être germé des semences de l'amour, sans le goupillon du prêtre ou l'écharpe du maire, ne sera que bâtard, méprisé, sans nom, sans héritage, sans droits, et que sa naissance comme une souillure jaillira sur la mère aussi! (12 Dec. 1896)

> [A woman is not guilty if she wishes to cleanse her womb of all tarnish and shame, since the creature that germinates from the seeds of love, without the priest's blessing or the mayor's sanction, will be nothing but a bastard—despised, nameless, without legacy or rights—whose birth will rebound upon the mother and taint her, too!]

Emery here emphasises the hypocrisy of religious and political institutions who condemn women for wanting to abort illegitimate children. He insists that the status of 'bastard' is only made possible through the moral and civil codes created by these institutions, which promote the sexual double standard for their own self-serving interests. Such arguments regularly featured in both neo-Malthusian and feminist writing of the period. They appeared in the pages of *Gil Blas*, in an article by Séverine (pseud. Caroline Rémy, 1855–1929), as well as in Marguerite Durand's

---

[50] McLaren, *Sexuality and Social Order*, p. 101; Le Naour and Valenti, *Histoire de l'avortement*, p. 56.

feminist paper *La Fronde*.[51] By expressing these viewpoints in the Sapho column, Emery enhanced the review's controversial self-image, in a gesture that combined the subversive scandal-mongering of avant-garde little magazines and the political commitment of feminist periodicals. That said, *Don Juan*'s politics of sexual liberation cannot be completely untangled from its aesthetics of frivolity or lightness ('légèreté'). On the one hand, Emery's arguments in favour of abortion rights and greater sexual freedom can be interpreted as an attempt to justify or ennoble the review's erotically titillating and taboo content. On the other hand, this frothy content can also be seen to function as a cover for *Don Juan*'s underlying political radicalism. These readings are not mutually exclusive. The review clearly encouraged its readers to identify with voyeuristic and vicarious forms of desire and pleasure, while simultaneously offering them polemical social critique and subversive sexual politics. Titillation and polemic were thus interconnected phenomena that contributed to the illicit and rebellious nature of *Don Juan*'s sexual and textual networks.

The complicit bonds created within the review's pages were transgressive in both the symbolic and the judicial realms. In July 1896, Alfred Hippolyte Bonnet faced trial for 'outrages aux bonnes mœurs', after publishing content in *Don Juan* that was considered obscene by the correctional courts. The ninth chamber cited a series of images published between April and May 1896, alongside an article entitled 'Les Sœurs Barrisson' (25 April 1896), as evidence of the crime, defined by the law of 2 August 1882.[52] The inculpated images included two drawings by Léon Roze, 'Printemps sérieux!' (18 April 1896) and 'Avant le salon' (25 April 1896), and three by Édouard Couturier: 'Photographie exécutée place de la Bourse' (29 April 1896), 'La Fête de madame' (6 May 1896), and 'Le Maillot trop étroit' (13 May 1896). The trial judgement reads as follows:

> [Il] résulte de l'instruction et des débats [...] [que] Bonnet [...] a commis le délit d'outrage aux bonnes mœurs, par la vente, l'offre, l'exposition et la distribution sur la voie publique et dans les lieux publics des numéros de ce journal, [...] lesquels contiennent [...] une série de dessins présentant un caractère manifestement

---

[51] See Jacqueline (pseud. Caroline Rémy), 'Le droit à l'avortement', *Gil Blas*, 4 Nov. 1890, Marcelle Tinayre, 'Lettre de la mère Gigogne à quelques intellectuels', *La Fronde*, 24 Apr. 1898, and Jeanne Caruchet, 'Avortées et avorteuses', *La Fronde*, 24 Jan. 1903.

[52] Article 1 of the 2 Aug. 1882 law reads: 'Est puni d'un emprisonnement d'un mois à deux ans et d'une amende de 16 francs à 3.000 francs quiconque aura commis le délit d'outrage aux bonnes mœurs, par la vente, l'offre, l'exposition, l'affichage ou la distribution gratuite sur la voie publique et dans les lieux publics, d'écrits, d'imprimés autres que le livre, d'affiches, dessins, gravures, peintures, emblèmes ou images obscènes' ['The punishment for whomever commits the crime of outraging public decency, through the sale, supply, exhibition, display, or free distribution in public thoroughfares and in public places of obscene works—including: texts, printed material other than books, posters, drawings, engravings, paintings, emblems, and images—is a prison sentence lasting between one month to two years and a fine ranging from 16 to 3,000 francs']. *Lois annotées ou Lois, décrets, ordonnances, avis du Conseil d'Etat, etc., avec notes historiques, de concordance et de jurisprudence*, IX (Paris: Recueil Sirey, 1881–5), p. 376.

obscène en raison non seulement de la nudité partielle, mais aussi des attitudes et des gestes des personnages, caractère accentué par les légendes qui se trouvent au bas de chacun de ces dessins, que Bonnet a vainement au cours des débats, allégué le caractère artistique de ces dessins; que le délit, résultant d'après la loi, de haute publication d'images obscènes, ne saurait être effacé ni atténué par l'habileté de l'exécution.[53]

[The result of the inquiry and debate is that Bonnet [...] has committed the offence of outraging public decency, through the sale, supply, exhibition, and distribution in public thoroughfares and in public places, of journal issues, [...] containing [...] a series of drawings which have a manifestly obscene nature, not only due to the presence of partial nudity, but also because of the characters' demeanour and gestures. The drawings' obscene nature is further emphasised by the captions located beneath each of them. While Bonnet vainly sought, throughout the debate, to argue for the drawings' artistic nature, it is judged, in accordance with the law, that the criminal offence of publishing large numbers of obscene images can neither be effaced nor mitigated by their skilful execution.]

There is a marked appreciation here for the ways in which text and image functioned subversively in illustrated reviews. Visual obscenity—defined by the presence of nudity alongside undescribed 'attitudes' and 'gestes'—could, according to this judgement, be made even more illicit by the presence of humorous captions. The definition of 'obscenity' remains flexible, however, because sexual innuendo alone was not always sufficient to attract censorship. An unsubtle reference to female genitalia ('chats') in the description of a can-can performance, in 'Les Sœurs Barrisson', attracted the censor's condemnation. At the same time, the court considered the phallic symbolism of an illustration depicting asparagus spears insufficiently obscene to count as evidence, and discounted it from the trial.[54] 'Les Asperges', by Vato, depicts a young boy emerging from a cracked egg to sell asparagus to a group of half-naked women, who beckon him with eager and lustful glances. It is unclear why this drawing escaped censorship while the others were condemned. Perhaps its erotic playfulness was sufficiently subtle to reduce its subversive potential, or perhaps indirect evocations of male genitalia were considered less threatening than the female equivalent. Either way, this judgement confirms the view that criminal categories such as 'outrage aux bonnes mœurs'

---

[53] AP, D1U6 577, 16.07.1896—BONNET, Auguste Hippolyte.

[54] On this question, the judgement reads: 'En ce qui concerne le numéro portant la date du neuf mai 1896, lequel contient à la quatrième page, un dessin intitulé "Les asperges", attendu que ce dessin ne revêt pas un caractère obscène qui permette de le retenir à la charge de Bonnet comme constituent un élément de la prévention, le renvoie des fins de la poursuite sur ce chef' ['With regards to the issue dated 9 May 1896, the fourth page of which contains a drawing entitled "Asparagus": the court finds that this drawing has an insufficiently obscene nature for it to be a cognisable element of the charges against Bonnet, and dismisses it from consideration in the proceedings']. AP, D1U6 577.

were highly flexible and often contradictory.[55] It also demonstrates the courts' critical awareness of structures of textual reception, and the complicit relationships it created.

In response to Bonnet's trial, and eventual condemnation, the review's editors penned a series of articles defending their aesthetic stance and their manager's moral probity.[56] The content and title of 'Pour l'art' (20 May 1896) are clearly inscribed in the tradition of using *l'art pour l'art* as a legal defence.[57] In the article, the review declares its pure intentions, attacks its critics' hypocrisy, and compares obscenity debates to France's wars of religion:

> [Nous] tenons à déclarer hautement—et les lecteurs qui depuis un an sont fidèles à *Don Juan* le savent—que ce journal est purement artistique et littéraire, qu'il n'a jamais cherché à exciter ni à flatter les passions malsaines. [...] *Don Juan* chante l'amour, la beauté, l'art, la joie de vivre...
>
> Cette œuvre [...] ne vaut-elle pas mieux que [...] le cri de guerre poussé par des Français contre d'autres Français, sous prétexte qu'ils ne sont pas de la même religion?—La Direction.
>
> [We are keen to declare openly—and the readers who have been loyal to *Don Juan* for the past year know it well—that this paper is purely artistic and literary. It has never sought to arouse or encourage unhealthy passions. [...]. *Don Juan* sings the praises of love, beauty, art, and joie de vivre...
>
> Is this endeavour [...] not worth more than [...] the battle cry exclaimed by French people against other French people, under the pretext that they are not of the same religion?—The Management.]

The hyperbolic tone of the final question alerts the reader to its rhetorical and tongue-in-cheek nature. The parenthetical appeal to readers' knowledge of the review's content further contributed to the article's ironic tone by functioning as a knowing wink (or 'clin d'œil') to its own transgression. Therefore, the editors' claims to moral probity, when considered against the backdrop of the review's predominant 'légèreté', are clearly meant to be taken with a pinch of salt.

After the trial's verdict was announced, *Don Juan* published a second 'Pour l'art' article. It criticised the hypocrisy of people belonging to 'ligues pudibondes' ['prudish pressure groups'], who enact their zeal through negative attacks on others' actions, rather than by setting a good example (25 July 1896). The term 'ligues pudibondes' here refers to organisations such as La Ligue pour le relèvement de

---

[55] On the ambiguity and flexibility of obscenity, and of the structures of censorship that define and regulate it, see Nicholas Harrison, *Circles of Censorship: Censorship and its Metaphors in French History, Literature, and Theory* (Oxford: Clarendon Press, 1995) and Elisabeth Ladenson, *Dirt for Art's Sake: Books on Trial from Madame Bovary to Lolita* (Ithaca: Cornell University Press, 2007).

[56] Bonnet was condemned to pay a 1,000 franc fine, in addition to court fees. AP, D1U6 577.

[57] See Ladenson, *Dirt for Art's Sake*.

la moralité publique and the Société centrale de protestation contre la licence des rues.[58] The latter was presided by René Bérenger, popularly nicknamed 'Père la Pudeur' (a derogative term for 'prude', like 'bluenose'), who becomes a recurring *bête noire* in the review's pages. A later 'Chronique de Sapho' article entitled 'Vive l'Amour et Zut à Bérenger!' (18 April 1897), depicts Bérenger's moralising standpoint as mere posturing ('C'est une pose, rien de plus' ['It's a pose, and nothing more']). This vision of Bérenger recurs in a series of texts by Emery, 'Bérenger au Salon', published from 29 April to 16 May 1897. The faux-anecdotal serial describes Bérenger trying to cover artistic nudes with fig leaves. The writer-protagonist debates with the senator, highlighting the unnecessary extremity, and ultimate hypocrisy, of the latter's viewpoints. While implicitly attacking well-known zealots with satire, the *rédaction*'s response to the July 1896 trial also contained a celebratory element that aligned artistic merit with controversy. In a short text immediately following the second 'Pour l'art' article, *Don Juan* published a biography of Bonnet, which affirmed the latter's moral virtue. While ostensibly pandering to the moralising framework of the review's detractors, Emery's opening lines suggest a more subversive appropriation: 'A la liste glorieuse des *Condamnés de la Neuvième*, après J.-L. Forain, Raoul Ponchon, Jean Lorrain, Oscar Méténier, Jules Roques, Zo d'Axa, Léon Maillard, Vignola, etc., il faut ajouter désormais le nom de notre excellent et cher ami: A. H. Bonnet' ['To the glorious list of "Those Condemned by the Ninth Chamber", after J.-L. Forain, Raoul Ponchon, Jean Lorrain, Oscar Méténier, Jules Roques, Zo d'Axa, Léon Maillard, Vignola, etc, we must now add the name of our excellent and dear friend: A. H. Bonnet']. By attributing glory to criminally inculpated artists, writers, journalists, and review directors, Emery's article establishes a community whose artistic and literary value increases when they attract moral condemnation and censorship. The list creates ties of illicit solidarity between individuals, typically associated with avant-garde circles, whose published works were perceived to incite 'immoral' sexual desires and behaviour, for the purposes of notoriety and financial gain.

### Selling Sex: Periodicals as *Proxénètes*

Periodicals like *Don Juan* encourage, enable, and profit from erotic relations, whether these take place in the reader's imagination, through vicarious identification, or in actual sexual practices. By doing so, they enact a form of *proxénétisme* ['procuring'], or 'pimp journalism', playing the role of sexual go-between. The term 'proxénétisme' reframes the metaphor of literature as prostitution, which evolved and strengthened throughout the nineteenth century. According to Éléonore Reverzy, writers who published in the century's later decades differed from their

---

[58] See Ronsin, *La Grève des ventres*, pp. 121–9.

predecessors by overtly identifying with and appropriating the metaphor, rather than criticising and rejecting it.[59] The analogy took centre stage in fictional depictions of journalism in the era, most famously in Balzac's *Illusions perdues* (1837–43), the Goncourt brothers' *Charles Demailly* (1860), and Maupassant's *Bel-Ami* (1885).[60] Beyond fictional representation, reviews such as *Don Juan* pushed the metaphor closer to reality by intersecting text and imagery with material culture, through the medium of advertising. This tendency is particularly visible in the fourth page of the review, which featured humorous and titillating drawings (the most obvious target for censorship), and half a page of advertisements. A large proportion of the adverts in *Don Juan* promote sex-related products: condoms, aphrodisiacs, and sex toys. Supported by morally questionable sources of income, 'revues légères' participated in wider erotic networks that contributed to the real-life sexual experiences of fin-de-siècle readers. Through its creative manipulation of advertising formats, *Don Juan* reveals the productive intersection between commerce and art made possible by the saucy magazine format.

*Don Juan* financially profited from the sale of sexual products and services. Its advertising columns contain a plethora of adverts that, in half-veiled language, sell condoms, aphrodisiacs, erotica, and sex toys. One example is a recurring advert for 'Maison A. Claverie', a shop that sold a range of medical products—including hernia belts, feminine hygiene products, and prosthetic limbs—alongside sexual paraphernalia such as condoms, lubricant ('crème de Vénus'), and sex toys. By the start of the twentieth century, the shop had gained renown and approbation for its range of corsets, which were regularly advertised in *Femina* and *La Vie heureuse*: women's magazines with greater social legitimacy and cultural cachet than *Don Juan*.[61] The business had a fabric factory at Romilly-sur-Seine, and its financial success enabled the owner, Charles Auguste Claverie, to purchase the château des Milandes in 1900. Claverie then sold his business in 1905 to the entrepreneur Georges Bos, who would later be awarded the legion of honour for his contribution to French commerce.[62] Claverie's range of products highlighted suggestive analogies between forms of medical, sexual, and sartorial intimacy. It was precisely the intimate nature of these products that created practical issues for those selling them, due to fin-de-siècle sexual taboos and laws on public decency. Consider an example of the Maison Claverie advert's usual format in *Don Juan* (see Figure 5.2).

---

[59] Éléonore Reverzy, *Portrait de l'artiste en fille de joie: la littérature publique* (Paris: CNRS Éditions, 2016), p. 180.

[60] Edmund Birch analyses these works in *Fictions of the Press in Nineteenth-Century France* (London: Palgrave Macmillan, 2018).

[61] Rachel Mesch notes how *Femina* and *La Vie heureuse* cultivated 'identification between readers and subject matter' by blending advertising and main copy and by promoting special offers on products such as Claverie's 'Liane' corset. *Having It All*, pp. 42–3.

[62] See Agnès Chauvin, 'Auguste Claverie, le parcours remarquable du propriétaire du château des Milandes en 1900', *Bulletin de la Société Historique et Archéologique du Périgord* 140, no. 3 (2013): pp. 357–62.

**Figure 5.2** Maison Claverie advert in *Don Juan*, 18 November 1896 (BnF).

The advert employs a vocabulary of security and discretion—'Prudence', 'Sureté', 'Sécurité absolue', and 'Complète discrètion' ['Caution', 'Reliability', 'Absolute Security', and 'Complete discretion']—that metonymically signifies the type of products sold (most notably contraceptive devices), while confirming their taboo or illicit nature. In Claverie's market, there was a tension between the need for publicity and the need for secrecy: to avoid clients' embarrassment and legal complications, the shop needed to offer a clandestine service. This explains the advert's self-contradiction: the half-veiled language used to refer to condoms ('ARTICLES SECRETS [...] garantis incassables' ['SECRET ITEMS [...] guaranteed to be unbreakable']) and sex toys ('APPAREILS SPÉCIAUX pour L'USAGE INTIME de l'Homme et de la Femme' ['SPECIAL DEVICES for INTIMATE USE by Men and Women']) juxtaposes the advert's use of capitalisation and bold typeface, which draw attention to these seemingly veiled terms. Through a process of unveiling, the reader/client makes the imaginative leap to 'uncover' the advert's open secret. However shallow these covering gestures may seem, they were necessary in an era where the lines between licit and illicit sexual behaviours were routinely scrutinised and enforced through judicial mechanisms that could contribute to a business's ruin, if its owners were found guilty of outraging public decency.

Despite the shop's prudent marketing manoeuvres, Maison A. Claverie was not immune to the censoring forces of the correctional courts. On 15 February 1897, only a few months after Bonnet's trial, Charles Delbret (1862–1914), known as Charles Auguste Claverie, was accused of 'outrages aux bonnes mœurs'.[63] Condemned on 24 March 1897, he joined Emery's 'liste glorieuse des *Condamnés de la Neuvième*'.[64] The official 'réquisitoire définitif' ['final indictment'], reprimands Claverie not only for the obscene nature of the products he sells, but also for the way he displays and advertises them. The document exemplifies how judicial mechanisms regulated sexual morality and gender roles at the fin de siècle. First, there is clear sexist gender ideology at work in the court's appraisal of Claverie's 'obscene' products:

---

[63] For the procedural documents from Claverie's trial, see AP D2U6 110, 24.03.1897—DELBRET, Charles (dit A. CLAVERIE Charles-Auguste).

[64] Claverie was condemned to a one-month prison sentence and a fine covering the trial's court fees. Because it was his first condemnation, the court gave him a suspended sentence, with five years' probation. AP, D1U6 602, 24.03.1897—DELBRET, Charles (dit CLAVERIE).

Il y a d'abord des 'préservatifs pour hommes', qui pouvant avoir pour objet de protéger les parties sexuelles de l'homme contre la contagion des maladies ou syphilitiques ou vénériennes, sont d'un certain usage au point de vue médical. Mais on n'en peut pas dire des 'préservatifs pour dames', des éponges de sûreté et de l'appareil d'un médecin allemand, nommé Hartmann, [...] tous ces instruments ont pour but et pour utilité exclusive d'empêcher le coït d'être fécond; ils ne répondent à aucun but avouable ni ne peuvent être conseillés par aucun médecin.[65]

[First there are 'male condoms', which have a certain practical usage from the medical point of view, since they can be used to protect the male sexual organs from contagious illnesses, whether syphilitic or venereal. But the same cannot be said for 'female condoms', contraceptive sponges, and the device made by a German doctor, named Hartmann, [...] since all of these instruments are intended and used only to prevent reproductive coitus. They do not serve a respectable purpose and no doctor should recommend them.]

The logic distinguishing between male and female contraception here seems dubious, since male condoms were also created with the aim to prevent pregnancies.[66] But the double standard is clear: men can have non-procreative sex for fun and can feel justified in wanting to avoid any unpleasant consequences, but women can *only* (want to) have sex for procreative purposes. This restrictive vision of female sexuality reappears in the court's condemnation of sex toys created for female pleasure. A series of items, including a form of ribbed condom ('le parisien dentelé'), a cock ring designed for clitoral stimulation ('l'anneau dentelé'), and fingering toys ('doigtiers') are cited as obscene due to the immorality of their usage: '[ils] n'ont pour but que de procurer à la femme par leur introduction dans le vagin, des sensations voluptueuses, et de concourir ainsi à des pratiques contre-nature' ['their sole purpose is to bring about voluptuous sensations in women through their insertion into the vagina, thereby contributing to unnatural practices']. The phrase 'pratiques contre-nature' is particularly loaded, due to its association with other non-reproductive sexual practices considered 'perverse' at the fin de siècle—most notably, homosexuality. Female sexual freedom and female pleasure are not only morally condemned, but indirectly criminalised, by the French correctional courts' punishing the act of selling products that enable and encourage either of them.

The illicit power of sex shops can be productively compared to the role played by the 'revues légères' advertising them. While benefiting financially from advertising

---

[65] AP, D2U6 110.

[66] A similar distinction between male and female contraception was made in the 'Loi du 31 juillet 1920 réprimant la provocation à l'avortement et à la propagande anticonceptionne'. See Ronsin, *La Grève des ventres*, pp. 146–7.

revenue paid by businesses like Claverie's shop, *Don Juan* contributed to a wider commercial network that facilitated pleasure-centred and non-procreative sexual activity between real-life individuals. Furthermore, the review represented, validated, and promoted female pleasure and agency in ways that, although riddled with sexist tropes, mirrored the threat to moral order posed by Claverie's shop. The fact that both businesses were punished by the correctional courts strengthens this comparison. In both examples it is difficult to draw a line between subversion and financial gain. By offering space for female agency and pleasure in their relative businesses, Claverie and Bonnet were being financially canny: they saw a market and exploited it. Furthermore, *Don Juan*'s advertising pages played a similar role to the physical space of Claverie's shop, in a way that reveals further similarities between literary and erotic commerce. In the 'réquisitoire définitif' for Claverie's trial, the shop's display cabinets, shop window, and catalogues become the site for judicial scrutiny:

> Non seulement Claverie tenait ces objets dans son magasin à la disposition des acheteurs, mais il en exposait quelques uns [sic] dans sa vitrine, de façon à tirer l'attention des passants [...]. Il faisait mieux: ces appareils étaient décrits avec figures à l'appui et avec des indications tant sur leur objet que sur la manière de s'en servir, dans un catalogue-prospectus qui était remis sur simple demande à tout client dans le magasin.[67]

> [Not only did Claverie keep these objects available to customers in his shop, but he displayed some of them in his shop window, to attract the attention of passers-by [...]. He went even further: these devices were described with supporting illustrations and with information regarding both their purpose and how to use them, in a brochure-catalogue that was handed over to any customer in the shop upon request.]

Above all, the court condemned the sex objects' accessibility and visibility to the public, in accordance with the emphasis on publicity found in legal definitions of 'outrage aux bonnes mœurs'. The question of ease of access—with the objects 'à la disposition des acheteurs' and catalogues 'remis sur simple demande à tout client'—evokes concerns about the potential 'public' of clients present in the shop. This reflects fin-de-siècle debates about the appropriateness of literary material for readerships defined by overdetermined social, moral, and political anxieties: women, children, and the working classes.[68]

Much like Claverie's shop window, *Don Juan*'s pages sold 'obscene' erotic products to an anonymous readership. The concerns raised in Claverie's trial

---

[67] AP, D2U6 110.
[68] On the question of 'suitable' reading and its relation to periodical culture, see Kate Flint, 'Reading in the Periodical Press' in *The Woman Reader, 1837–1914* (Oxford: Clarendon Press, 1993), pp. 136–83.

regarding accessibility and publicity of sex-related products (particularly to women) therefore also applied to *Don Juan*'s readers, because they could see Claverie's adverts regularly featured on the review's back page. These adverts presume, or at least hope, that *Don Juan*'s readers will become, if they are not already, a part of Claverie's clientele. It might seem logical to assume that *Don Juan* had a predominantly male readership, because the presence of such adverts was irreconcilable with traditional femininity and the sexual double standard.[69] Even so, the review repeatedly addressed 'nos lectrices' and appropriated the erotic appeal of femininity for both male and female readers. Moreover, its back page included adverts aimed specifically at women, from breast-enhancing products ('Farine Egyptienne') to children's toys ('Bébé jumeau'), which further attest to a perceived female readership. After all, it seems unlikely that businesses selling such products would pay to place adverts in a paper whose readership did not include their target audience (see Figure 5.3). It is therefore noteworthy that in March 1898, only a year after Claverie's judgement, French politicians and jurists targeted newspapers' advertising pages (alongside correspondence columns and postal delivery services) with a 'Loi contre la licence des rues' ['Law against public licentiousness'].[70] If providing women with easy access to condoms and sex toys was, according to French jurists, a way of encouraging 'des pratiques contre nature' ['unnatural practices'], any means of restricting their dissemination would be a boon for acceptable morality. Conversely, by selling and advertising these products in their respective businesses, Claverie and Bonnet created financially and libidinally productive—if tacitly illicit—spaces for a diverse range of customers.

While offering readers the ability to purchase condoms and sex toys, *Don Juan* also facilitated creative forms of erotic textual exchange. In the 'petites annonces' ['small ad' or 'classified ad'] column, the review listed personal ads featuring messages between supposed lovers, requests for saucy correspondence, and other avowals of desire.[71] Examples of messages between lovers published in this column include rendezvous planning: '*Lovely*. Tout est prêt... L'échelle est posée... T'attend. ch. soir à 10 h. à partir jeudi prochain' ['*Lovely*. Everything is ready... The ladder is in place... Waiting for you, every evening at 10pm, from next Thursday'] (24 June 1896), post-coital reminders: 'L. X. 42, J'ai trouvé ton corset sous mon divan. Viens le chercher' ['I found your corset beneath my settee. Come find it'] (14 Nov. 1896), and separations '*Pierrot*: Le Carnaval est fini. L'amour aussi.

---

[69] This assumption appears briefly in Martin, *Trois siècles*, p. 65, and Reverzy, *Portrait de l'artiste*, p. 156.

[70] See *Contre la licence des rues (loi du 16 mars 1898)* (Orléans: Auguste Gout et Cie, 1906), p. 6.

[71] For a recent study of the personal ad in Third Republic French journalism, see Hannah Frydman and Claire-Lise Gaillard, '"Les dessous des petites annonces": quand les intimités se marchandent à la quatrième page des journaux (IIIe République)', in *Les Petites annonces personnelles dans la presse française (XVIIIe–XXe siècles)*, edited by Hannah Frydman and Claire-Lise Gaillard (= *Histoire, économie et société* 39, no. 3, 2020): pp. 45–66, doi:10.3917/hes.203.0045. This special issue offers interpretations that parallel my own analysis.

**Figure 5.3** Advertising Page, *Don Juan*, 18 November 1896 (BnF).

Inutile me revoir. Tu perds ton temps' ['*Pierrot*: Carnival is over. And love with it. No use seeing me again. You're wasting your time'] (29 Feb. 1896). By charting various stages in erotic relationships, these messages tap into the imaginative appeal of love stories and adultery novels, while taking a short format more akin to *faits divers*.[72] They encourage readers to fill in the gaps, creating potentially endless romantic and erotic narratives from very few details. Where the message format encourages *Don Juan*'s general reader to posit themselves as an outsider looking in on the relationships of others, thereby gaining a vicarious, voyeuristic form of pleasure, the offer/request format places the reader in the role of a potential recipient of amorous attention. The titillating appeal of the small ad here becomes intertwined with actual—and not just implicit—appeals to reader response. In the review, there are numerous and recurrent requests for marriage, love affairs, and the exchange of correspondence. Many of the advertised relationships were illicit, due to their implicitly extra-marital, pleasure-centred, and non-procreative nature.[73] The messages function as sexual solicitation, and the columns as a form of dating service *avant la lettre*.[74] Consider, for example, the following two adverts: 'Jeune dame qui s'ennuie, désir corresp. gaie pour distraire' ['Young lady, getting bored, seeks fun correspondence for her amusement'] (18 Jan. 1896) and: 'Dame libre après-midi et 2 jours par semaine, serait recon. à M. très bien, qui voudr. procurer distract' ['Lady, free two days a week in the afternoon, would be grateful to find Mr. Dashing, who would seek to provide entertainment'] (29 Feb. 1896). 'Distraction' and 'distraire' here have clear—if implicit—sexual connotations, thereby exemplifying the kind of veiled advertising that French correctional courts struggled to penalise throughout the fin-de-siècle period.[75] In these examples, adverts solicit readers both as potential lovers and as voyeurs, through their imaginative implication in the future relations between the person making erotic requests, and those fulfilling them. By implicating the reader's desires and vicarious pleasure, while offering space for extratextual erotic connections and relationships to blossom, *Don Juan* takes on the role of a *proxénète* or sexual go-between, blurring the boundary between imagined and actual sexual activity.

---

[72] The term 'fait divers' refers to a short, often sensational, news item.

[73] On the perceived dangers of small ads facilitating (especially female) non-procreative sexual freedom, see Hannah Frydman, 'Freedom's Sex Problem: Classified Advertising, Law, and the Politics of Reading in Third Republic France', *French Historical Studies* 44, no. 4 (2021): pp. 675–709, doi:10.1215/00161071-9248720.

[74] For a history of the 'matchmaking' market in France from the nineteenth to twentieth centuries, see Claire-Lise Gaillard, *Pas sérieux s'abstenir. Histoire du marché de la rencontre. XIXe–XXe siècles* (Paris: CNRS Éditions, 2024).

[75] Charting the evolution of legal responses to sex-related classifieds in late nineteenth- and early twentieth-century France, Frydman notes that it was only in the 1920s that a legal precedent of 'surface' reading, when dealing with obscene or immoral material, shifted towards an approach that punished 'any ad facilitating autonomy from sexual norms, no matter how coded it might be'. See 'Freedom's Sex Problem', pp. 697–700.

The review confirmed the correlation between small ads, prostitution, and *proxénétisme* through *mises en scène* of personal ads that emphasised the complexity of readers' relationship to the advertising format. In a series of fictional correspondence, 'Lettres à Maud', René Emery charted a passionate but doomed romance that began with an epistolary exchange via *petites annonces*.[76] The first two instalments, entitled 'Petites annonces' and 'Poste restante', describe the protagonist's decision to use small ad columns as a means of finding his ideal beloved (who turns out to be Maud, the fictional letters' recipient). At the start of the series, Emery's protagonist offers an ambivalent analysis of small ads as a medium for erotic exchange:

En ces listes, souvent grotesques, de demandes et d'offres galantes qui s'étalent audacieusement aux petites annonces des journaux mondains, je n'ai vu [...] qu'une sorte de Bourse de l'amour, et de quel amour? celui qui rôde sur les boulevards, vagabonde par les rues, affamé, glouton, se repaissant des plus médiocres régals et buvant l'ivresse à n'importe quels flacons. [...] Cependant, [...] je découvris, dans le tas, des appels à l'amour, des cris d'espoir, des sanglots de passion qui se trahissent par je ne sais quelles paroles plus sincères, [...]. [Je] reconnaissais encore l'inquiétude et la révolte des âmes altières, captives des bagnes et des galères contemporaines, condamnés [sic] à la vie bête, rêvant malgré tout l'affranchissement sentimental par la grâce de romanesques et poignantes aventures... (30 May 1896)

[In these (often ludicrous) lists of gallant requests and offers, which are splashed throughout the small ad columns in society newspapers, I have only ever seen [...] a sort of Lovers' Stock Exchange—and what kind of love is at stake? The kind that roams the boulevards and prowls the streets, starving and gluttonous, feasting on the most mediocre delights and seeking intoxication from any available bottle. [...] However, [...] I discovered, amongst the heap, calls for love, cries of hope, tears of passion, given away by words somehow sincerer than the rest, [...]. And again, I could recognise the anxious revolt of proud and superior souls, imprisoned in modern-day galleys and penal servitude, condemned to a brutish existence, and dreaming, in spite of everything, of a sentimental liberation granted by the grace of romantic and poignant love affairs...]

The opening lines of this quotation combine vocabularies of sex, money, and prostitution, evoking both visceral desire and disgust. Nonetheless, this initial sense of abjection gives way to an aestheticised passion attributed to 'des âmes altières' fighting against the restrictive bonds of social acceptability. The

---

[76] 'Lettres à Maud' was published as the review's opening article, in alternation with 'La Chronique de Sapho', between 30 May and 25 July 1896.

story's protagonist then successfully finds his ideal lover, thereby vindicating an otherwise questionable and debased medium. While offering a thematic discussion of classified advertising, Emery's presentation of the genre in 'Lettres à Maud' also indirectly promotes *Don Juan*'s own small ad column. It does so by encouraging readers to consider it as a potential source of passionate love affairs, however fictionalised. The potentially anecdotal (but probably fictional) nature of the letters also hints at the ambiguous status of *petites annonces* as a genre, which—like Emery's story—combine unverifiable referentiality with creative re-appropriation and *réclame*. In this way, 'Lettres à Maud' depicts small ads, via *mise en abyme*, as an enabling textual space in which readers can actively participate.

As well as offering readers a space for sexual exchange, the small ad format facilitated playful textual appropriations that can be understood in literary and artistic terms. There are many examples of readers (or perhaps members of the *rédaction*) creatively manipulating the genre through *clins d'œil* and ironic humour: 'Il commence à faire froid. Qui me veut réchauffer' ['It's starting to get cold. Who wants to warm me up'] (5 Dec. 1896), 'Je suis myope; les laides me paraissent jolies. Avis aux laides' ['I'm shortsighted; ugly women look beautiful to me. Ugly women, be advised'] (24 June 1896), and 'Un fou, qui a été traité durant 3 ans dans une maison d'aliénés et qui se croit guéri, désire union avec j. femme, jolie, élég. un peu toquée.' ['A madman, who was treated in a madhouse for 3 years and now thinks he's cured, seeks union with a young, elegant woman who's a bit loony'] (4 July 1896). The tongue-in-cheek humour apparent in these examples fits in well with the tone of the review, while demonstrating the creativity with which an otherwise seemingly banal or purely lucrative literary form can be appropriated. Furthermore, it was not only anonymous readers or members of the *rédaction* who injected creativity into the genre. Businesses also frequently used the small ad message format to advertise their products via indirect (if not particularly subtle) forms of *réclame*. This confirms that the *petites annonces* column was widely perceived as something that people bothered to read. A noteworthy example of businesses placing veiled small ads can be found in a series of messages referring to 'Farine Egyptienne'— a product that supposedly encouraged breast growth.[77] The small ads promoting this product replicate the lovers' messages analysed above, while swiftly revealing their status as *réclame*:

> Adèle. T'es belle, mais j'aime les gros nichons! Ecris donc à M. Laurent, 17, rue Saint-Joseph, Paris et dem.-lui une boîte de sa merveill. farine égyptienne à 3 fr. 50 la boîte franco. En un mois tu auras une gorge divine. Anatole. (10 June 1896)

> [Adèle. You're beautiful, but I like big tits! So write to Mr Laurent, at 17 Rue Saint-Joseph, Paris, and ask him for a box of his marvellous Egyptian Flour, at 3.50 francs a box (postage included). Within a month you'll have an exquisite bosom.]

[77] This product was also promoted through regular inserted advertisements. See Figure 5.3.

And:

*Paulette.* Je ne te reverrai que le jour où tu auras développé ta poitrine, ce que tu obtiendras en un mois par l'usage de la farine Egyptienne de Laurent, 17, rue St-Joseph. Paris. 3 fr. 50 la boîte franco. (20 June 1896)

[*Paulette.* I will only see you again once your chest has developed in size— something you can achieve in a month by using Laurent's Egyptian Flour, from 17 Rue Saint-Joseph, Paris. 3.50 francs a box (postage included).]

The businesses paying for small ads of this type could, with the implicit if not overt collusion of the review's *rédaction*, sell their wares with enhanced appeal to readers. This enhanced appeal stemmed from the adverts' similarity with, and physical proximity to, the titillating content of 'real' personal ads. Of course, the supposedly disguised nature of the advertising strategy is far from convincing. In fact, a large part of the pleasure offered by *réclame* relies on the reader's ability to spot—however easily—the attempted advertising 'ploy'. In a strangely productive yet cyclical logic, readers are encouraged to congratulate themselves on not having been duped, while effectively being 'metaduped' into this self-congratulatory mode. These examples of self-aware, playful, and titillating reformulation hint at the perceived financial benefits of wielding the small ads' influence, while demonstrating their creative potential as a genre.

*Don Juan*'s advertising was, like much of its content, emphatically eroticised. It aligned sexual vigour with literary creation, further blurring the boundaries between adverts and art. Indeed, selling sex and selling art become interdependent and reciprocal gestures. For example, the review had an in-house book catalogue, the 'Bibliothèque du *Don Juan*' ['*Don Juan*'s Collection/Series'], which offered a range of products, from quasi-scientific treatises on sexual topics, to contemporary fiction with predominantly erotic themes.[78] Other saucy magazines had similar catalogues that sold near-identical products. This is not surprising, since many titles were set up and run by an interdependent network of editors and contributors.[79] Such books provided taboo or illicit forms of knowledge to a vast and

---

[78] The 'Bibliothèque du *Don Juan*' included works by: Camille Lemonnier, Catulle Mendès, Pierre Louÿs, Rachilde, Émile Zola, and René Maizeroy. Examples of 'scientific' treatises regularly advertised in the catalogue include Dr Michel Villemont's *L'Amour conjugal*, Krafft-Ebing's *Psychopathie sexuelle*, and a selection of works by Dr Pierre Garnier, discussing marital hygiene, impotence, sterility, and masturbation.

[79] *Folichonneries* (1896-7) regularly advertised the 'Bibliothèque du *Don Juan*' and for a time listed its offices at the same address as *Don Juan* (18 rue Feydeau). René Emery wrote the opening article in the first issue of *Folichonneries* (18 Apr. 1896), and the two reviews occasionally republished each other's content. *Le Fin de Siècle* also had an in-house 'Bibliothèque', offering a similar selection of books to the *Don Juan* catalogue. René Emery was the editor-in-chief at *Le Fin de Siècle* in its early years (1891-2), and it is probable that he maintained links with the review while he was in charge of *Don Juan*.

potentially 'unprotected' readership—much broader in scope than the scholarly or bibliophile collector of earlier (and less accessible) 'libertine' works.[80] By doing so, they fed contemporaneous concerns about the socially or morally harmful pedagogical function of texts. Saucy magazine catalogues sold 'scientific' books on sexual topics, whose thinly veiled erotic content could arouse readers' libido, thereby acting as glorified aphrodisiacs.[81] The comparison also appeared visually, through the review's *mise en page*. *Don Juan*'s book catalogue frequently appeared above or alongside adverts for aphrodisiac sweets called 'Bonbons Vert-Galant' (see Figure 5.3).[82] In this way, the vicarious erotic stimulation offered by the books sold in the 'Bibliothèque' existed side-by-side with their chemical counterparts, in a visual agglomeration of literature, desire, and sex.

The literature-as-aphrodisiac analogy became a source of creative appropriation in a series of indirect adverts or *réclame* found in the main body of the review. This gesture blurred the textual boundaries between dedicated advertising space and the review's main content. In May 1896, an article called 'Pour plaire aux femmes' appeared in 'La Vie parisienne':

Chacun connaît le refrain qu'a illustré un chanteur à la mode; cependant il paraît que plaire aux femmes est chose fort difficile. [...]

Notre génération est anémiée et débilitée par les excès et fatigues de toutes sortes: pour la régénérer, un savant a trouvé un produit qui augmente la vigueur morale, intellectuelle et physique, et régularise le jeu des principales fonctions de l'organisme.

C'est surtout sur l'acte de la génération que ce produit agit: il réveille les organes engourdis ou surmenés. (30 May 1896)

[Everyone knows that tune sung by a famous singer... But it seems that pleasing a woman is a difficult thing indeed. [...]

Our generation is anaemic and debilitated by all sorts of excessive and stressful activity. For its regeneration, a scientist has found a product which heightens one's moral, intellectual, and physical vigour, and regulates the balance between the principal bodily functions.

Above all, it is upon the progenitive act that this product takes effect: it reawakens organs that are fatigued or over-worked.]

---

[80] On the presence of erotic works in the libraries of fin-de-siècle bibliophiles, see Silverman, *The New Bibliopolis*, pp. 178–9.

[81] For a discussion of the dual nature of books as 'commodities and sexual stimulants', and of the sexually charged language used to refer to books in fin-de-siècle bibliophilic circles, see Silverman, *The New Bibliopolis*, p. 173.

[82] The term 'vert galant' refers to an 'Homme vif, ardent en amour' ['A vivacious man and passionate lover']. Pierre Larousse, *Grand dictionnaire universel du XIXe siècle*, 17 vols (Paris: Administration du Grand Dictionnaire universel, 1866–77), XV (1876), p. 740. It can be used to refer to men who retain sexual vigour regardless of their age, and is typically associated with the French King Henry IV, who is the figure depicted in the 'Bonbons Vert-Galant' advert (see Figure 5.3, centre).

The text co-opts the critical authority of 'Masque Rose', the general signatory for the column, for the purposes of unsubtle *réclame*. This lack of subtlety attracts the reader's attention in a deliberate way, as part of the review's wider constellation of intertextual meanings surrounding the aphrodisiac sweets. Articles in newspapers, journals, and magazines do not appear in isolation, but are linked visually with one another through editorial choices regarding *mise en page*. It is therefore noteworthy that 'Pour plaire aux femmes' appears just after the 'Le Boulevard' sub-section of 'La Vie parisienne'. The 'Boulevard' article in this issue puts forward an anti-natalist stance, typical of the review's wider sexual politics. The signatory 'X...' mocks the dominant class's depopulation fears, justifying abortion as a way of alleviating lower-class suffering: 'N'y a-t-il pas assez de victimes de l'égoïsme, de l'avarice, de la lâcheté?... D'autres? Pourquoi. Foutez d'abord du pain à ceux qui existent...' ['Are there not already enough victims of selfishness, avarice, and cowardice?... More people? Why? First of all, toss a bit of food to those who exist already...'] When read alongside, or just after, such a polemical and political affirmation of anti-natalist sentiment, the vocabulary of decline ('anémiée', 'débilitée') and vigour ('régénérer', 'vigueur') in 'Pour plaire aux femmes' can be read more ironically than if the *réclame* were analysed without any reference to its textual situation or *mise en page*. The blatant juxtaposition between the two subsections of 'La Vie parisienne' draws attention to itself, encouraging the reader to align degeneration discourses and depopulation fears not only with the perceived moral hypocrisy of the ruling classes, but also with the manipulative and unsubtle marketing techniques of *réclame*.

The veiled adverts for 'Bonbons Vert-Galant' accrued intertextual meanings over time, which demonstrate an editorial stance and advertising strategy that involved a playful form of irony. An article entitled 'Témoignage probant' appeared in *Don Juan*'s 'La Vie parisienne' gossip column on 29 August 1896. It posed as a letter from an ageing aristocratic client testifying to the efficacity of the sweets. On the review's front page, the article appears after a 'Le Boulevard' article attacking the Roman Catholic Church for putting Zola's *Rome* on the Index. It precedes a 'Chronique rimée' by Des Esquintes, entitled 'Histoire d'un crime', which depicts the fateful demise of a man in his eighties who continues to frequent prostitutes despite his old age. The satirical verse opens with the same first line as La Fontaine's fable 'Le Vieillard et les Trois Jeunes Hommes': 'Un octogénaire plantait'.[83] It offers a sexualised parody of the fable's message about old age and youth, which draws on the slang meanings of 'planter' and 'planteur': 'to fuck', and 'fucker', respectively.[84] In Des Esquintes's version, the elderly man

---

[83] In La Fontaine's fable, three young men mock an old man who is planting a tree, because he will not live long enough to see the fruits of his labour. The old man asserts the value of forward-thinking, regardless of age, and notes the fragility of life for all of humankind. He outlives the three younger men, who meet early deaths.
[84] A slang dictionary published the same year as 'Histoire d'un crime' offers one definition of 'planter' as: '(obsc.) coïter' ['(obsc.) to copulate'], and defines 'planteur' as: '(obsc.) s.m. —Paillard.

vaunts his wealth (and stamina) to the prostitutes and is subsequently killed. One of the women's pimps is arrested for the crime. The 'moral' of the story is less a condemnation of the murder than a critique of the old man's ridiculousness: 'Voilà comment un vieux planteur | Qui ne veut pas quitter sa bêche, | Peut dans une nuit de malheur | Malgré lui faire tête-bêche' ['And that's how an old shafter | Who is too attached to his spade, | Can, in one unfortunate night, | Inadvertently fall arse over elbow'].[85] When read after the 'Témoignage probant' vaunting the *bonbons* for their ability to make men sexually vigorous ('Je suis redevenu aussi ardent et vigoureux qu'à vingt ans'), the poem's dark humour adds further irony and contradiction to *Don Juan*'s use of *réclame*. The desire to maintain an active sex life in old age—with or without the assistance of aphrodisiacs—appears not only as ridiculous, but also potentially fatal. As these examples show, fin-de-siècle advertising strategies were frequently self-aware. Editorial choices, particularly regarding *mise en page*, created complex intertextual meanings that accrued over time. Combining pecuniary interest with an ironic shared humour, which is set up through satirical *clins d'œil* peppered throughout its pages, reviews such as *Don Juan* manipulated the creative potential of advertising to encourage their readership to invest financially and libidinally in its endeavours.

Despite their marginality as a genre, saucy magazines encapsulate how the fin-de-siècle reading experience was frequently structured according to a shared eroticism that was criticised for its supposed immorality, its 'obscenity', and—perhaps its most unforgivable attribute—its frivolity. By inviting readers to collaborate imaginatively and actually in the review's frothy and quasi-illicit content, *Don Juan* created a unique cultural space that blended literature and sex, frivolity and polemic, the avant-garde and the popular. Exemplifying both the 'incitement' and the 'collaboration' models of complicity, the saucy magazine sat precariously on the boundary separating acceptable and unacceptable forms of eroticism in the period. The forms of complicity constructed through its pages offer a window onto the sexual and textual networks of fin-de-siècle French literary culture, where playful eroticism, sexual libertarianism, and legal transgression combined and colluded under the censors' watchful—sometimes repressive, sometimes impotent—gaze.

---

—Libertin.—Vaillant en amour.' ['(obsc.) masc. noun.—Debauched man.—Libertine.—Sexual stallion.'] See Georges Delasalle, *Dictionnaire argot-français et français-argot*, pref. by Jean Richepin (Paris: Paul Ollendorff, 1896).

[85] The verb 'faire tête-bêche' is another sexualised pun, because it is a slang term for the '69' sex position.

# Epilogue

Questions of complicity and collusion recurred throughout fin-de-siècle French literature, cutting across differences of style, genre, and school. The concept defined writers' legal status, shaped their careers, and haunted their fictions. From adultery novels to murder fiction, *romans à clef* to *petites revues*, spoof newspapers to saucy magazines, it emerged as a way of thinking about bonds between writers, readers, and critics. By analysing complicity across a broad range of literary genres, this book has sought to answer the question posed on its first page: what happens to our understanding of literary culture when we view reading not only as a seductive or transgressive activity, but as a fundamentally *complicit* one? Having examined the implications of this question in close analytical detail throughout previous chapters, the book's epilogue offers a broader, synthesising response as its conclusion.

To define reading as a complicit activity is to re-assess literature on several interconnecting levels: moral, thematic, social, and cultural. On the first of these levels, literature represents a body of published written material that is limited, to a greater or lesser degree, by shared moral norms and the legal frameworks that regulate them. Whether expressed through peers' criticism or jurists' indictment, moral judgements limit the boundaries of what can or cannot be published with impunity in any given period. A writer can choose to accept or refute these boundaries, but—short of living in a vacuum—they cannot ignore them. For example, Paul Bourget questioned literature's formative role and crossed the boundaries of acceptable morality by publishing romanticised depictions of adultery early in his career. However, he adapted his position in response to the critique of others, and later penned a thesis novel condemning literature's immoral influence. Émile Zola took a slightly different approach. He refuted moralising criticism by claiming that his novels contributed to scientific understandings of human psychology and society by depicting illicit actions. Avant-garde writers went one step further. Rather than providing justifications for 'immoral' content, they flipped the moralising logic by valorising the 'bad influence' model against the grain. Literature was to be celebrated, these writers suggested, precisely *because* of its morally transgressive influence, and those caught pandering to acceptable morality were undoubtedly hypocrites. A writer's willingness or unwillingness to accept shared responsibility for literature's perceived negative effects was therefore a defining feature of their literary position. Similarly, a reader's standpoint had moral consequences, due to their perceived capacity to become willing accomplices in a work's transgression.

Thematic choices, as well as moral outlook, had an important role in placing and maintaining writers—and, by extension, their readers—in a specific literary position. Representing illicit actions and relationships allowed fin-de-siècle writers to situate themselves in relation to prevailing moral, social, and literary norms. It also allowed authors to question these norms, or to highlight the inequalities of their application. With this in mind, the notion of complicity goes a long way to explaining the predominance (and enduring popularity) of crime fictions, adultery stories, media scandals, and smut. Each of these genres describes something illicit to its readers, while presuming a shared interest in the phenomenon or a desire to experience it vicariously. By treating topics like murder and adultery, fin-de-siècle authors could engage with contemporaneous debates on legal responsibility and criminal justice, while manipulating the titillating appeal of transgression. By writing about scandal and smut, they could express non-normative identities and celebrate sexual pleasure in ways that were unacceptable in mainstream literature portraying less risqué subjects. Rather than treating these themes separately, the notion of complicity highlights their similarities and facilitates their comparison. Above all, it testifies to a shared cultural interest in illicit forms of individual and collective identity in the period.

To think of reading as a complicit activity is to elaborate upon literature's communal or inter-relational nature. It brings to the foreground the fact that literature is a sociological phenomenon that involves real-life individuals—whether they be writers, readers, publishers, or critics—and establishes bonds between them. One of the greatest contributions Pierre Bourdieu made to literary study was the idea that literature can be productively analysed in a relational way. His approach encourages literary scholars to pay attention to paratextual and extra-textual sources—such as dedications, newspaper articles, and correspondence—alongside 'primary' literary content, but also to re-think definitions of primary and periphery. Testifying to the importance of paratext is the fact that fin-de-siècle writers used dedications to create a sense of collusion between their friends and wider literary networks. As a part of writers' publicly mediatised relationships, such techniques appealed to readers' desire to be 'in on it'. Moreover, writers published articles praising and lampooning one another in the press, both to create complicity and to accuse each other of it. They exchanged letters testifying to the active collaboration required to establish literary personae, as well as to the risks involved in pushing a reputation too far. While providing a means of analysing such phenomena, a sociological approach reminds scholars of their inevitable complicity with the texts, authors, and ideas they study. Were avant-garde writers really transgressive, or do scholars like to see them as such? If a large majority of fin-de-siècle texts stayed within acceptable moral boundaries, why emphasise those which did not? How do scholars relate to, and move beyond, inherited formulations of cultural interest or worth?

To respond to such questions, the complicit reading model opens up a broad view of literature and its relation to other cultural artefacts. According to this vision, literature does not exist independently, but rather through its embeddedness in different media and institutions. Journalism, advertising, commerce, and the entertainment industry were but some of the many interrelated phenomena that shaped the production and reception of literary works in fin-de-siècle France. To examine the intersection of different types and different levels of cultural production, this book has analysed journalistic material alongside (and in conversation with) novels, short stories, and a range of ephemera. Its inclusive approach to textual production, some of which is not typically 'literary', sheds light on uncharted areas of the cultural map and levels out some—if not all—of its implicit hierarchies. Emerging from this process is an understanding that literature is an active and ongoing collaboration between its various 'accomplices': writers, readers, critics... and literary scholars.

# Bibliography

## Primary Sources

### 1) Newspapers and other periodicals

*L'Assiette au beurre* (Paris: 1901–36)
*Le Chat noir* (Paris: 1882–97)
*Le Courrier français* (Paris: 1884–1914)
*Le Décadent littéraire et artistique* (Paris: 1886–9)
*Don Juan* (Paris: 1895–1900)
*L'Écho de Paris* (Paris: 1884–1938)
*Le Figaro* (Paris: 1826–)
*Le Figaro, supplément littéraire* (Paris: 1873–1929)
*Le Fin de Siècle* (Paris: 1891–1909)
*Le Français* (Paris: 1868–98)
*La France: politique, scientifique et littéraire* (Paris: 1862–1937)
*La Fronde* (Paris: 1897–1929)
*Le Gaulois* (Paris:1868–1929)
*Gil Blas* (Paris: 1879–1940)
*La Grande Revue. Paris et Saint Petersbourg* (Paris: 1888–93)
*Le Journal* (Paris: 1892–1944)
*Journal de la Beauté* (Paris: 1897–1933)
*Journal des assassins: organe officiel des chourineurs réunis* (Paris: 1884)
*Journal des débats politiques et littéraires* (Paris: 1814–1944)
*Journal des papetiers en gros et en détail, des imprimeurs et des libraires, des relieurs et des cartonniers* (Paris: 1892–1914)
*La Justice* (Paris: 1880–1940)
*Les Lettres et les arts* (Paris: Boussod, Valadon et Cie, 1886–9)
*Le Petit parisien* (Paris: 1876–1944)
*La Presse* (Paris: 1836–1952)
*La République française* (Paris: 1871–1933)
*La Revue blanche* (Paris: 1891–1903)
*Revue chrétienne. Recueil mensuel* (Paris: 1854–1926)
*Revue des deux mondes* (Paris: 1829–1971)
*La Revue générale: littéraire, politique et artistique* (Paris: 1883–91)
*La Revue moderne: littéraire, artistique, philosophique* (Marseille: 1884–94)
*La Revue politique et littéraire* (Paris: 1871–1933)
*Revue scientifique* (Paris: 1884–1954)
*Le Siècle* (Paris: 1836–1932)
*Le Signal* (Paris: 1879–1914)
*Le Soir* (Paris: 1869–1932)
*Le Temps* (Paris: 1861–1942)
*La Vie parisienne* (Paris: 1963–1970)

## 2) Judicial and archive sources

Archives de Paris, Série D1U6: Jugements, Rôles, Répertoires, Audiences:
D1U6 413, 30.12.1891—CHARDON, Hippolyte; ROQUES, Hippolyte Jules; EMERY, Rene Marie; BRANDIMBOURG, Georges Charles; ALBERT, Joseph François Vicoire Agathe Sixte; LEROUX, Henri Auguste Gabriel
D1U6 415, 20.01.1892—EMERY, René Marie; MARTIN –; ERARD, Pierre Lefievre; MAINGUY, Emile Félix Edouard; BALLURIAU, Jean Baptiste (dit Paul)
D1U6 416, 27.01.1892—CHARDON, Hippolyte; EMERY, René Marie
D1U6 428, 25.05.1892—JULIEN, Henry Alexandre; EMERY, René, Marie
D1U6 577, 16.07.1896—BONNET, Auguste Hippolyte
D1U6 602, 24.03.1897—DELBRET, Charles (dit CLAVERIE)
Archives de Paris, Série D2U6: Tribunal Correctionnel de la Seine, Dossiers de Procédure (1828–1940):
D2U6 93, 15.07.1891—HEURTIER, Urbain; BESSE, Louis Octave
D2U6 95, 25.05.1892—JULIEN, Henry, Alexandre; EMERY, René, Marie
D2U6 110, 24.03.1897—DELBRET, Charles (dit A. CLAVERIE Charles-Auguste)
*Code pénal de l'empire français. Edition conforme à celle de l'imprimerie impériale* (Paris: Prieur, Belin fils, Merlin, and Rondonneau, 1810)
*Contre la licence des rues (loi du 16 mars 1898)* (Orléans: Auguste Gout et Cie, 1906)
*Journal officiel de la République française*
Letters from René Emery to Aurélien Scholl, 27 Dec. 1890 and 27 Feb. 1898 (author's private collection)
*Lettre de René Emery à Rachilde*. Paris, Bibliothèque Littéraire Jacques Doucet, LT Ms 10207
*Lois annotées ou Lois, décrets, ordonnances, avis du Conseil d'Etat, etc., avec notes historiques, de concordance et de jurisprudence*, IX (Paris: Recueil Sirey, 1881–5)
*Loi sur la liberté de la presse du 29 juillet 1881* (Paris: Dubuisson, 1881)

## 3) Published nineteenth-century sources

Balzac, Honoré de. *Œuvres complètes*, 24 vols (Paris: Michel Lévy Frères, 1869–76), I (1869)
Balzac, Honoré de. *The Complete Works of Honoré de Balzac*, ed. George Saintsbury, 36 vols, I: *The Magic Skin* (Boston: Colonial Press Company, 1901)
Bataille, Albert. *Causes criminelles et mondaines de 1888* (Paris: E. Dentu, 1889)
Beaubourg, Maurice. *Contes pour les assassins* (Paris: Perrin, 1890)
Bourget, Paul. *Essais de psychologie contemporaine: Baudelaire, M. Renan, Flaubert, M. Taine, Stendhal*, 3rd ed. (Paris: A. Lemerre, 1885)
Bourget, Paul. *Le Disciple* (Paris: Alphonse Lemerre, 1889)
Bourget, Paul. *Œuvres complètes. Romans I. Cruelle énigme, Un crime d'amour, André Cornélis* (Paris: Plon, 1900)
Bourget, Paul. *Essais de psychologie contemporaine. Études littéraires*, ed. André Guyaux (Paris: Gallimard, 1993)
Bourget, Paul. *Le Disciple*, ed. Antoine Compagnon (Paris: Éditions de Poche, 2010)
Delasalle, Georges. *Dictionnaire argot-français et français-argot*, preface by Jean Richepin (Paris: Paul Ollendorff, 1896)
De Quincey, Thomas. *On Murder*, ed. Robert Morrison (Oxford: Oxford University Press, 2009)
*Dictionnaire de l'Académie française*, 7th ed., 2 vols (Paris: Librairie de Firmin-Didot & cie, 1878)
Estoc, Gisèle d'. *Les Gloires malsaines: La Vierge réclame* (Paris: Librairie Richelieu, 1887)
Gautier, Théophile. *Mademoiselle de Maupin, double amour*, 2 vols (Paris: Eugène Renduel, 1836), I
Gide, André. *L'Immoraliste. Roman* (Paris: Mercure de France, 1902)
Gide, André. *The Immoralist*, trans. Alan Sheridan (London: Penguin, 2000)

Janet, Paul. 'De la responsabilité philosophique, à propos du "Disciple" d M. Paul Bourget', in *Principes de métaphysique et de psychologie: leçons professées à la Faculté des lettres de Paris, 1888-1894*, 2 vols (Paris: Librairie Ch. Delagrave, 1897), I, pp. 305-27
Larousse, Pierre. *Grand dictionnaire universel du XIXe siècle*, 17 vols (Paris: Administration du Grand Dictionnaire universel, 1866-77)
*Lettres de Camille Delaville à Georges de Peyrebrune 1884-1888*, ed. Nelly Sanchez (Brest: Publications du Centre d'étude des correspondances et journaux intimes des XIXe et XXe siècles, 2010)
Lorrain, Jean. *Modernités* (Paris: E. Giraud & Cie, 1885)
Lorrain, Jean. *Dans l'oratoire* (Paris: C. Dalou, 1888)
Lorrain, Jean. *Correspondance. Lettres à Barbey d'Aurevilly, François Coppée, Oscar Méténier, Catulle Mendès, Edmond Deschaumes, Mecislas Golberg, etc., suivies des articles condamnés*, ed. George Normandy (Paris: Éditions Baudinière, 1929)
Malot, Hector. *Complices*, postface by Christian Millet (Darnetal: Petit à petit, 2001)
Méténier, Oscar. *La Chair* (Brussels: Henry Kistemaeckers, 1885)
Méténier, Oscar. *La Grâce* (Paris: E. Giraud, 1886)
Méténier, Oscar. *Les Voyous au théâtre* (Brussels: H. Kistemaeckers, 1891)
Michelet, Jules. *Du prêtre, de la femme, de la famille*, 2nd ed. (Paris: Hachette, 1845)
Mirbeau, Octave. *Le Jardin des supplices*, ed. Michel Delon (Paris: Gallimard, 1991)
Mirbeau, Octave. *Combats littéraires*, ed. Pierre Michel and Jean-François Nivet (Lausanne: Éditions L'Âge d'Homme, 2006)
Mirbeau, Octave. *Torture Garden*, trans. Michael Richardson (Sawtry: Dedalus, 2010)
Murray, James, ed. *A New English Dictionary on Historical Principles: founded mainly on the materials collected by the Philological Society*, 11 vols (Oxford: Clarendon Press, 1888-1933), II (1893)
Pressens, Francis de, and Émile Pouget. *Les Lois scélérates de 1893-4* (Paris: Éditions de la Revue blanche, 1899)
Rachilde. *La Sanglante Ironie* (Paris: L. Genonceaux, 1891)
Rachilde. *Portraits d'hommes*, 6th ed. (Paris: Mercure de France, 1930)
Rachilde. *Nono* (Paris: Mercure de France, 1994)
Rachilde and Maurice Barrès. *Correspondance inédite, 1885-1914*, ed. Michael Finn (Brest: Publications du Centre d'étude des correspondances et journaux intimes des XIXe et XXe siècles, 2002)
Robin, Paul. 'Dégénérescence de l'espèce humaine; causes et remèdes', *Bulletins et mémoires de la Société d'Anthropologie de Paris*, Series 4, Vol. 6 (1895), pp. 426-33
Rod, Édouard. *Les Idées morales du temps présent* (Paris: Perrin, 1891)
Zola, Émile. *Le Roman expérimental*, 5th ed. (Paris: Charpentier, 1881)
Zola, Émile. *The Experimental Novel, and other essays*, trans. Belle M. Sherman (New York: The Cassell Publishing Co., 1894)
Zola, Émile. *Les Rougon-Macquart: histoire naturelle et sociale d'une famille sous le Second Empire*, ed. Henri Mitterand, 5 vols (Paris: Gallimard, 1960-7)
Zola, Émile. *Thérèse Raquin* (Paris: Gallimard, 2001)
Zola, Émile. *La Bête humaine*, trans. Roger Pearson (Oxford: Oxford Univerity Press, 2009)

## Critical Sources

Absalyamova, Elina, and Valérie Stiénon, eds. *Les Voix du lecteur dans la presse française au XIXe siècle* (Limoges: Pulim, 2018)
Adamowicz-Hariasz, Maria. 'From Opinion to Information: The *Roman-Feuilleton* and the Transformation of the Nineteenth-Century French Press'. In *Making the News: Modernity and the Mass Press in Nineteenth-Century France*, edited by Jean de la Motte and Jeannene M. Przyblyski (Amherst: University of Massachusetts Press, 1999), pp. 160-84
Amossy, Ruth. 'La double nature de l'image d'auteur', *Argumentation et Analyse du Discours* 3 (2009), doi: 10.4000/aad.662

Angenot, Marc. 'La Littérature populaire française au dix-neuvième siècle', *Canadian Review of Comparative Literature/Revue Canadienne de Littérature Comparée* 9, no. 3 (Sept. 1982): pp. 307–33

Angenot, Marc. 'On est toujours le disciple de quelqu'un, ou le Mystère du pousse-au-crime', *Littérature* 49 (1983): pp. 50–6, doi:10.3406/litt.1983.2185

Anthonay, Thibault d'. *Jean Lorrain: miroir de la Belle Époque* (Paris: Fayard, 2005)

Applegate, Debby. 'Roman à clef', *American Literary History* 7, no. 1 (Spring 1995), 151–160, doi:10.1093/alh/7.1.151

Artiaga, Loïc. *Des torrents de papier. Catholicisme et lectures populaires au XIXe siècle* (Limoges: PULIM, 2007)

Bayle, Ariane and others, eds. *L'Âge de la connivence: lire entre les mots à l'époque moderne* (Geneva: Droz, 2015)

Becker, Colette. 'Zola et Lombroso: A propos de *La Bête humaine*', *Les Cahiers Naturalistes* 80 (2006): pp. 37–49, https://gallica.bnf.fr/ark:/12148/bpt6k9788451w/f39.item

Bergman-Carton, Janet. '*La Revue Blanche*: Art, Commerce, and Culture in the French fin-de-siècle', *Nineteenth-Century Contexts* 30, no. 2 (2008): pp. 167–89, doi: 10.1080/08905490802212458

Bernheimer, Charles. *Figures of Ill Repute: Representing Prostitution in Nineteenth-Century France* (Durham and London: Duke University Press, 1997)

Birch, Edmund. *Fictions of the Press in Nineteenth-Century France* (London: Palgrave Macmillan, 2018)

Birch, Edmund. 'Keys: Press and Privacy in the Goncourts' Charles Demailly', *Nineteenth-Century French Studies* 42, nos. 3–4 (Spring–Summer 2014): pp. 206–20, https://www.jstor.org/stable/44122760

Birkett, Jennifer. *The Sins of the Fathers: Decadence in France, 1870–1914* (London: Quartet Books Limited, 1986)

Birnbaum, Pierre. *The Antisemitic Moment*, trans. Jane Marie Todd (Chicago: University of Chicago Press, 2003)

Blood, Susan. 'The Precinematic Novel: Zola's *La Bête humaine*', *Representations* 93, no. 1 (Winter 2006): pp. 49–75, https://www.jstor.org/stable/10.1525/rep.2006.93.1.49

Bodek, Evelyn Gordon. 'Salonières and Bluestockings: Educated Obsolescence and Germinating Feminism', *Feminist Studies* 3, nos. 3–4 (Spring–Summer 1976): pp. 185–99, https://www.jstor.org/stable/3177736

Boltanski, Luc. *Énigmes et complots: une enquête à propos d'enquêtes* (Paris: Gallimard, 2012)

Boucharenc, Myriam, and Laurence Guellec, eds. *Portraits de l'écrivain en publicitaire* (Rennes: Presses Universitaires de Rennes, 2018)

Bourdieu, Pierre. *La Distinction: critique sociale du jugement* (Paris: Éditions de Minuit, 1979)

Bourdieu, Pierre. *Les Règles de l'art: genèse et structure du champ littéraire* (Paris: Seuil, 1998) (Stanford: Stanford University Press, 1996)

Bourdieu, Pierre. *The Rules of Art: Genesis and Structure of the Literary Field*, trans. Susan Emanuel (Stanford: Stanford University Press, 1996)

Boyde, Melissa. 'The Modernist Roman à Clef and Cultural Secrets, or, I Know that You Know that I Know that You Know', *Australian Literary Studies* 24, nos. 3–4 (2009): pp. 155–66, doi: 10.20314/als.dfae519805

Boyde, Melissa. '"You for Whom I Wrote": Renée Vivien, H. D. and the Roman à Clef'. In *The Unsociable Sociability of Women's Lifewriting*, edited by Anne Collett and Louise D'Arcens (New York: Palgrave Macmillan, 2010), pp. 148–67

Bringer, Rodolphe. *Trente ans d'humour* (Paris: France-Édition, 1924)

Burin, Alexandre. 'The Harlequin Poetics: Fragmentation, Performance, and Scandal in Jean Lorrain' (PhD dissertation, Durham University, 2020)

Burin, Alexandre. '« Monsieur, JE JOUE MON PERSONNAGE » Jean Lorrain, construire sa propre légende', *Savoirs en prisme* 12 (Sept. 2020): pp. 235–52, doi:10.34929/sep.vi12.115

Carroy, Jacqueline, and Marc Renneville. *Mourir d'amour. Autopsie d'un imaginaire criminel* (Paris: Éditions La Découverte, 2022)

Chambers, Ross. 'Irony and Misogyny: Authority and the Homosocial in Baudelaire and Flaubert', *Australian Journal of French Studies* 26, no. 3 (1989): pp. 272–88

Chauvin, Agnès. 'Auguste Claverie, le parcours remarquable du propriétaire du château des Milandes en 1900', *Bulletin de la Société Historique et Archéologique du Périgord* 140, no. 3 (2013): pp. 357–62

Cook, Hera. *The Long Sexual Revolution: English Women, Sex, and Contraception 1800–1975* (Oxford: Oxford University Press, 2004)

Corbin, Alain. *L'Harmonie des plaisirs: les manières de jouir du siècle des Lumières à l'avènement de la sexologie* (Paris: Perrin, 2008)

Couégnas, Daniel. *Introduction à la paralittérature* (Paris: Seuil, 1993)

Counter, Andrew J. 'The Legacy of the Beast: Patrilinearity and Rupture in Zola's *La Bête humaine* and Freud's *Totem and Taboo*', *French Studies* 62, no. 1 (2008): pp. 26–38, doi:10.1093/fs/knm237

Counter, Andrew J. 'One of Them: Homosexuality and Anarchism in Wilde and Zola', *Comparative Literature* 63, no. 4 (2011): pp. 345–65, doi: 10.1215/00104124-1444419

Counter, Andrew J. 'Tough Love, Hard Bargains: Rape and Coercion in Balzac', *Nineteenth-Century French Studies* 36, nos. 1–2 (Fall–Winter 2007–2008): pp. 61–71, https://www.jstor.org/stable/23538479

Counter, Andrew J. 'Zola's *fin-de-siècle* Reproductive Politics', *French Studies* 68, no. 2 (2014): pp. 193–208, doi:10.1093/fs/knt302

Counter, Andrew J. 'Zola's Repetitions: On Repetition in Zola', *The Modern Language Review* 116, no. 1 (2021): pp. 42–64, doi:10.1353/mlr.2021.0073

Cragin, Thomas. *Murder in Parisian Streets: Manufacturing Crime and Justice in the Popular Press, 1830–1900* (Lewisburg: Bucknell University Press, 2006)

Culler, Jonathan. *Structuralist Poetics: Structuralism, Linguistics and the Study of Literature* (London: Routledge & Kegan Paul, 1975)

Diaz, Brigitte, ed. *L'Auteur et ses stratégies publicitaires au XIXe siecle* (Caen: Presses universitaires de Caen, 2019)

Didier, Bénédicte. *Petites revues et esprit bohème à la fin du XIXe siècle (1878–1889)* (Paris: L'Harmattan, 2009)

Dijkstra, Bram. *Idols of Perversity: Fantasies of Feminine Evil in Fin-de-Siècle Culture* (Oxford: Oxford University Press, 1986)

Dousteyssier-Khoze, Catherine. 'Rodolphe Salis et Émile Zola: rencontres chatnoiresques'. In *Le Rire moderne*, edited by Alain Vaillant and Roselyne de Villeneuve (Nanterre: Presses Universitaires de Paris Ouest, 2013), pp. 217–31

Downing, Lisa. 'The Birth of the Beast: Death-Driven Masculinity in Monneret, Zola and Freud', *Dix-Neuf* 5, no. 1 (2013): pp. 28–46, doi:10.1179/147873105790723321

Downing, Lisa. *The Subject of Murder: Gender, Exceptionality, and the Modern Killer* (Chicago: The University of Chicago Press, 2013)

Eger, Elizabeth. *Bluestockings: Women of Reason from Enlightenment to Romanticism* (Basingstoke: Palgrave Macmillan, 2010)

Feuillerat, Albert. *Paul Bourget: histoire d'un esprit sous la troisième république* (Paris: Plon, 1937)

Finn, Michael R. *Hysteria, Hypnotism, the Spirits, and Pornography: Fin-de-Siècle Cultural Discourses in the Decadent Rachilde* (Newark: University of Delaware Press, 2009)

Finn, Michael R. 'Imagining Rachilde: Decadence and the *roman à clefs*', *French Forum* 30, no. 1 (2005): pp. 81–96, https://www.jstor.org/stable/40552371

Fish, Stanley. 'Interpreting the *Variorum*', *Critical Inquiry* 2, no. 3 (1976): pp. 465–85, doi:10.1086/447852

Flint, Kate. *The Woman Reader, 1837–1914* (Oxford: Clarendon Press, 1993)

Forestier, Albane. 'La figure du petit-maître est-elle subversive?', *Apparence(s)* 12 (2022), doi:10.4000/apparences.4225

Forrest, Jennifer. *Decadent Aesthetics and the Acrobat in Fin-de-siècle France* (New York: Routledge, 2020)

Foucault, Michel. *Dits et écrits*, ed. Daniel Defert and others, 4 vols (Paris: Gallimard, 1994), I

Foucault, Michel. *Histoire de la sexualité I: la volonté de savoir* (Paris: Gallimard, 1976)
Frydman, Hannah, and Claire-Lise Gaillard. '"Les dessous des petites annonces": quand les intimités se marchandent à la quatrième page des journaux (IIIe République)'. In *Les Petites annonces personnelles dans la presse française (XVIIIe–XXe siècles)*, edited by Hannah Frydman and Claire-Lise Gaillard (= *Histoire, économie et société* 39, no. 3, 2020): pp. 45–66, doi:10.3917/hes.203.0045
Frydman, Hannah. 'Freedom's Sex Problem: Classified Advertising, Law, and the Politics of Reading in Third Republic France', *French Historical Studies* 44, no. 4 (2021): pp. 675–709, doi:10.1215/00161071-9248720
Gaillard, Claire-Lise. *Pas sérieux s'abstenir. Histoire du marché de la rencontre. XIXe–XXe siècles* (Paris: CNRS Éditions, 2024)
Geherin, David. *Scene of the Crime: The Importance of Place in Crime and Mystery Fiction* (Jefferson: McFarland, 2008)
Glinoer, Anthony, and Vincent Laisney. *L'Âge des cénacles. Confraternités littéraires et artistiques au XIXe siècle* (Paris: Fayard, 2013)
Glinoer, Anthony, and Michel Lacroix, eds. *Romans à clés: Les ambivalences du réel* (Liège: Presses Universitaires de Liège, 2014)
Goulet, Andrea. *Legacies of the Rue Morgue: Science, Space, and Crime Fiction in France* (Philadelphia: University of Pennsylvania Press, 2015)
Gougelmann, Stéphane. '« En littérature, ils ont le sexe changeant. » Jean Lorrain et l'émancipation des catégories de genre', *Romantisme* 179, no. 1 (2018): pp. 70–84, doi:10.3917/rom.179.0070
Grenfell, Michael, ed. *Pierre Bourdieu: Key Concepts* (London: Routledge, 2014, 2nd ed.)
Grivel, Charles. *Production de l'intérêt romanesque. Un état du texte (1870–1880), un essai de constitution de sa théorie* (The Hague: Mouton, 1973)
Grojnowski, Daniel, and Mireille Dottin-Orsini. 'La prostitution dans la presse parisienne à la fin du xixe siècle', *Littératures* 69 (2013): pp. 187–211, doi:10.4000/litteratures.159
Gubelmann, Marielle. 'La Visite à l'écrivain (1870–1940). Variations autour de la figure d'auteur sous la Troisième République' (Master's dissertation, University of Lausanne, 2007)
Halperin, Juan Ungersma. *Félix Fénéon. Aesthete & Anarchist in Fin-de-Siècle Paris* (New Haven: Yale University Press, 1988)
Harrison, Nicholas. *Circles of Censorship: Censorship and its Metaphors in French History, Literature, and Theory* (Oxford: Clarendon Press, 1995)
Haslett, Moyra. 'Bluestocking Feminism Revisited: The Satirical Figure of the Bluestocking', *Women's Writing* 17, no. 3 (2010): pp. 432–45, doi:10.1080/09699082.2010.508927
Hawthorne, Melanie. *Rachilde and French Women's Authorship: from Decadence to Modernism* (Lincoln: University of Nebraska Press, 2001)
Holmes, Diana. *French Women's Writing, 1848–1994* (London: The Athlone Press, 1996)
Holmes, Diana. *Middlebrow Matters: Women's Reading and the Literary Canon in France Since the Belle Époque* (Liverpool: Liverpool University Press, 2018)
Holmes, Diana. *Rachilde: Decadence, Gender and the Woman Writer* (Oxford: Berg, 2001)
Holmes, Diana, and David Loosely, eds. *Imagining the Popular in Contemporary French Culture* (Manchester: Manchester University Press, 2013)
Holub, Robert C. *Reception Theory: A Critical Introduction*, new edition (London: Routledge, 2003)
Horsley, Adam. *Libertines and the Law: Subversive Authors and Criminal Justice in Early Seventeenth-Century France* (Oxford: Oxford University Press, 2021)
Humphreys, Karen L. '*Bas-bleus, filles publiques*, and the Literary Marketplace in the Work of Jules Barbey d'Aurevilly', *French Studies* 66, no. 1 (2012): pp. 26–40, doi: 10.1093/fs/knr204
Iser, Wolfgang. 'The Reality of Fiction: A Functionalist Approach to Literature', *New Literary History* 7, no. 1 (1975): pp. 7–38, https://www.jstor.org/stable/468276
Jauss, Hans Robert. 'Literary History as a Challenge to Literary Theory', trans. Elizabeth Benzinger, *New Literary History* 2, no. 1 (1970): pp. 7–37, https://www.jstor.org/stable/468585
Jullian, Philippe. *Jean Lorrain ou Le Satiricon 1900* (Paris: Fayard, 1974)

Kalifa, Dominique. *L'Encre et le sang. Récits de crimes et société à la Belle Époque* (Paris: Fayard, 1995)

Kalifa, Dominique. 'Enquête et « culture de l'enquête » au XIXe siècle', *Romantisme* 149, no. 3 (2010): pp. 3–23, doi:10.3917/rom.149.0003

Kalifa, Dominique. 'Les lieux du crime. Topographie criminelle et imaginaire social à Paris au XIXe siècle', *Sociétés & Représentations* 17, no. 1 (2004): pp. 131–50, doi:10.3917/sr.017.0131

Kalifa, Dominique. *Paris: Une histoire érotique d'Offenbach aux sixties* (Paris: Payot, 2018)

Kalifa, Dominique and others, eds. *La Civilisation du journal: histoire culturelle et littéraire de la presse française au XIXe siècle* (Paris: Nouveau Monde, 2011)

Kerley, Lela F. *Uncovering Paris: Scandals and Nude Spectacles in the Belle Époque* (Baton Rouge: Louisiana State University Press, 2017)

Kohnen, Myriam. *Figures d'un polygraphe français. Hector Malot (1855–1881)* (Paris: Honoré Champion, 2016)

Koos, Leonard R. 'Improper Names: Pseudonyms and Transvestites in Decadent Prose'. In *Perennial Decay: On the Aesthetics and Politics of Decadence*, edited by Liz Constable and others (Philadelphia: University of Pennsylvania Press, 1999), pp. 198–214

Kosofsky Sedgwick, Eve. *Between Men: English Literature and Male Homosocial Desire* (New York: Columbia University Press, 1992)

Krakovitch, Odile. 'Robert Macaire ou la grande peur des censeurs', *Europe: revue littéraire mensuelle* 703–4 (Nov.–Dec. 1987): pp. 49–60

Ladenson, Elisabeth. *Dirt for Art's Sake: Books on Trial from* Madame Bovary *to* Lolita (Ithaca: Cornell University Press, 2007)

Larson, Sharon. '"Elle n'est pas un 'bas-bleu', mais un écrivain": Georges de Peyrebrune's Woman Writer', *Nineteenth-Century Contexts* 40, no. 1 (2018): pp. 19–31, doi:10.1080/08905495.2018.1393734

Latham, Sean. *The Art of Scandal: Modernism, Libel law, and the Roman à Clef* (Oxford: Oxford University Press, 2009)

Laville, Béatrice. *Une poétique des fictions autoritaires. Les voies de Zola, Barrès, Bourget* (Pessac: Presses Universitaires de Bordeaux, 2020)

Leclerc, Yvan. *Crimes écrits: la littérature en procès au XIX$^e$ siècle* (Paris: Plon, 1991)

Lemaire, Marion. *Robert Macaire: la construction d'un mythe. Du personnage théâtral au type social, 1823–1848* (Paris: Honoré Champion, 2018)

Le Naour, Jean-Yves, and Catherine Valenti. *Histoire de l'avortement. XIXe–XXe siècle* (Paris: Éditions du Seuil, 2003)

Lerner, Bettina. *Inventing the Popular: Printing, Politics, and Poetics* (London: Routledge, 2018)

Lewis, Philippa. *Intimacy and Distance: Conflicting Cultures in Nineteenth-Century France* (Cambridge: Legenda, 2017)

Lucey, Michael. *Never Say I: Sexuality and the First Person in Colette, Gide, and Proust* (Durham: Duke University Press, 2006)

Lyons, Martyn. *Readers and Society in Nineteenth-Century France: Workers, Women, Peasants* (Basingstoke: Palgrave, 2001)

Maitron, Jean. *Le Mouvement anarchiste en France. 1. Des origines à 1914* (Paris: Maspero, 1975)

Malavié, Jean. 'Présence du directeur de conscience dans les couples de La Comédie humaine', *Les Lettres Romanes* 56, nos. 3–4 (2002): pp. 223–33, doi:10.1484/J.LLR.3.53

Marcus, Sharon. *Between Women: Friendship, Desire, and Marriage in Victorian England* (Princeton: Princeton Unviersity Press, 2009)

Martin, Marc. *Trois siècles de publicité en France* (Paris: Éditions Odilie Jacob, 1992)

McCabe, Alexander. 'Dostoevsky's French reception: from Vogüé, Gide, Shestov and Berdyaev to Marcel, Camus and Sartre (1880–1959)' (PhD dissertation, University of Glasgow, 2013)

McGuinness, Patrick. *Poetry and Radical Politics in Fin-de-Siècle France: From Anarchism to Action Française* (Oxford: Oxford University Press, 2015)

McLaren, Angus. *A History of Contraception: From Antiquity to the Present Day* (Oxford: Basil Blackwell, 1990)

McLaren, Angus. *Sexuality and Social Order: The Debate Over the Fertility of Women and Workers in France, 1770–1920* (New York: Holmes & Meier, 1983)

McNab, Christopher. 'Psychological Novel and Roman d'analyse'. In *Encyclopedia of the Novel*, edited by Paul Schellinger and others, 2 vols (London: Fitzroy Dearborn, 1998), II, pp. 1057–9

Meizoz, Jérôme. *Postures littéraires. Mises en scène modernes de l'auteur* (Geneva: Slaktine Érudition, 2007)

Mendes Gallinari, Melliandro. 'La "clause auteur": l'écrivain, l'*ethos* et le discours littéraire', *Argumentation et Analyse du Discours* 3 (2009), doi:10.4000/aad.663

Mesch, Rachel. *Before Trans: Three Gender Stories from Nineteenth-Century France* (Stanford: Stanford University Press, 2020)

Mesch, Rachel. *Having It All in the Belle Époque: How French Women's Magazines Invented the Modern Woman* (Stanford: Stanford University Press, 2013)

Mesch, Rachel. *The Hysteric's Revenge: French Women Writers at the Fin de Siècle* (Nashville: Vanderbilt University Press, 2006)

Mesch, Rachel. 'Trans Rachilde: A Roadmap for Recovering the Gender Creative Past and Rehumanizing the Nineteenth Century', *Dix-Neuf* 25, nos. 3–4 (2021): pp. 242–59, doi:10.1080/14787318.2021.2017562

Mitterand, Henri. 'The Genesis of Novelistic Space: Zola's *La Bête Humaine*', trans. Anne C. Murch. In *Naturalism in the European Novel: New Critical Perspectives*, edited by Brian Nelson (New York: Berg, 1992), pp. 66–79

Nelson, Brian. 'Blood on the Tracks: The Uses of Space in Zola's *La Bête humaine*' *Australian Journal of French Studies* 43, no. 1 (2006): pp. 13–18, doi:10.3828/AJFS.43.1.13

Nora, Olivier. 'La Visite au grand écrivain'. In *Lieux de mémoire*, edited by Pierre Nora, 3 vols (1984–92), II (1986), pp. 563–87

Nye, Robert. *Crime, Madness and Politics in Modern France: The Medical Concept of National Decline* (Princeton: Princeton University Press, 2014)

Oxford English Dictionary (Online)

Paré, Sébastien. 'Les avatars du Littéraire chez Jean Lorrain', *Loxias* 18 (2007), doi:10670/1.1hmvhm

Pernot, Denis. *Le Roman de socialisation, 1889–1914* (Paris: Presses Universitaires de France, 1998)

Pick, Daniel. *Faces of Degeneration: A European Disorder, c. 1848–c.1918* (Cambridge: Cambridge University Press, 1989)

Platten, David. *The Pleasures of Crime: Reading Modern French Crime Fiction* (Amsterdam: Rodopi, 2011)

Polette, René. 'Mélodrame et roman-feuilleton sous le second Empire', *Europe: revue littéraire mensuelle* 703–4 (Nov.–Dec. 1987): pp. 82–9

Ponton, Rémy. 'Naissance du roman psychologique: capital culturel, capital social et stratégie littéraire à la fin du 19e siècle', *Actes de la recherche en sciences sociales* 1, no. 4 (1975): pp. 66–81, doi:10.3406/arss.1975.3421

Proulx, François. *Victims of the Book: Reading and Masculinity in Fin-de-Siècle France* (Toronto: University of Toronto Press, 2019)

Queffélec-Dumasy, Lise. 'De quelques problèmes méthodologiques concernant l'étude du roman populaire'. In *Problèmes de l'écriture populaire au XIXe siècle*, edited by Roger Bellet and Philippe Régnier (Limoges: Presses universitaires de Limoges, 1997), pp. 229–66

Reverzy, Éléonore. *Portrait de l'artiste en fille de joie: la littérature publique* (Paris: CNRS Éditions, 2016)

Rexer, Raisa. '*L'Année pornographique*: The French Press and the Invention of Pornography', *Romanic Review* 111, no. 2 (2020): pp. 260–87, doi:10.1215/00358118-8503476

Rexer, Raisa. *The Fallen Veil: A Literary and Cultural History of the Photographic Nude in Nineteenth-Century France* (Philadelphia: Philadelphia University Press, 2021)

Rodemacq, Maxence. 'L'Industrie de l'obscénité à Paris', *Romantisme* 167, no. 1 (2015): pp. 13–20, doi:10.3917/rom.167.0013

Rodemacq, Maxence. 'L'Industrie de l'obscénité: commerce pornographique et culture de masse à Paris (1855–1930)' (Master's dissertation, Sorbonne University, 2010)

Rogers, Juliette. *Career Stories: Belle Époque Novels of Professional Development* (Pennsylvania: Penn State University Press, 2007)

Ronsin, Francis. *La Grève des ventres: propaganda néo-malthusienne et baisse de la natalité française (XIX– XXe siècles)* (Paris: Éditions Aubier Montaigne, 1980)

Rosario, Vernon A. *The Erotic Imagination: French Histories of Perversity* (Oxford: Oxford University Press, 1997)

Sachs, Leon. 'Literature of Ideas and Paul Bourget's Republican Pedagogy', *French Forum* 33, nos. 1–2 (Winter–Spring 2008): pp. 53–72, https://www.jstor.org/stable/40552494

Sadoun-Édouard, Clara. *Le Roman de* La Vie parisienne *(1863–1914): Presse, genre, littérature et mondanité* (Paris: Honoré Champion, 2018)

Sanchez, Jean-Lucien. 'Les Lois Bérenger (lois du 14 août 1885 et du 26 mars 1891)', *Criminocorpus*, Histoire de la criminologie. Autour des *Archives d'anthropologie criminelle* 1886–1914, 3. Criminologie et droit pénal (2005), doi: 10.4000/criminocorpus.132

Sapiro, Gisèle. *La Responsabilité de l'écrivain: littérature, droit et morale en France (XIXe–XXIe siècle)* (Paris: Éditions du Seuil, 2011)

Schellenberg, Betty A. 'Bluestocking Women and the Negotiation of Oral, Manuscript, and Print Cultures'. In *The History of British Women's Writing, 1750–1830*, edited by Jacqueline M. Labbe (Basingstoke: Palgrave Macmillan, 2010), pp. 63–83

Schellinger, Paul, and others, eds. *Encyclopedia of the Novel*, 2 vols (London: Fitzroy Dearborn, 1998)

Schmidt, Arnold Anthony. 'Review: Bluestockings, George Eliot, and Nineteenth-Century Sociability', *Nineteenth Century Studies* 25, no. 1 (2011): pp. 271–8, doi:10.5325/ninecentstud.25.2011.0271

Schuh, Julien. 'Les Dîners de la Plume', *Romantisme* 137, no. 3 (2007): pp. 79–101, doi:10.3917/rom.137.0079

Schwartz, Vanessa. *Spectacular Realities: Early Mass Culture in* Fin-de-Siècle *Paris* (Berkeley: University of California Press, 1998)

Scott, Maria. *Empathy and the Strangeness of Fiction: Readings in French Realism* (Edinburgh: Edinburgh University Press, 2020)

Seys, Pascale. 'Maître ou complice? La philosophie de Taine dans *Le Disciple* de Paul Bourget'. In *Le Chant de Minerve: Les écrivains et leurs lectures philosophiques*, edited by Bruno Curatolo (Paris: Éditions l'Harmattan, 1996), pp. 35–47

Shapiro, Ann-Louise. *Breaking the Codes: Female Criminality in Fin-de-Siècle Paris* (Stanford: Stanford University Press, 1996)

Silverman, Willa Z. *The New Bibliopolis: French Book Collectors and the Culture of Print, 1880–1914* (Toronto: University of Toronto Press, 2008)

Speller, John R. W. *Bourdieu and Literature* (Cambridge: Open Book Publishers, 2011)

Staples, Amy. 'Primal Scenes / Primal Screens: The Homosocial Economy of Dirty Jokes'. In *High Anxiety: Masculinity in Crisis in Early Modern France*, edited by Kathleen Perry Long (Pennsylvania: Penn State University Press, 2002), pp. 37–54

Starobinski, Jean. *Portrait de l'artiste en saltimbanque* (Geneva: Albert Skira, 1970)

Suleiman, Susan Rubin. *Authoritarian Fictions: The Ideological Novel as a Literary Genre.* (Princeton: Princeton University Press, 1993, 2nd ed.)

Tallent, Alistaire. 'Intimate Exchanges: The Courtesan Narrative and Male Homosocial Desire in *La Dame aux camélias*', *French Forum* 39, no. 1 (Winter 2014): pp. 19–31, doi:10.1353/frf.2014.0001

Thérenty, Marie-Ève. 'La Réclame de librairie dans le journal quotidien au XIXe siècle: autopsie d'un objet textuel non identifié', *Romantisme* 155, no. 1 (2012): pp. 91–103, doi:10.3917/rom.155.0091

Thérenty, Marie-Ève, and Adeline Wrona, eds. *L'Écrivain comme marque* (Paris: Sorbonne Université Presses, 2020)

Tinguely, Frédéric. *La Lecture complice: Culture libertine et geste critique* (Geneva: Droz, 2016)

*Trésor de la langue Française informatisé*, http://www.atilf.fr/tlfi, ATILF: CNRS and Université de Lorraine
Vaillant, Alain, and Yoan Vérilhac, eds. *Vie de bohème et petite presse du XIXe siècle. Sociabilité littéraire ou solidarité journalistique?* (Nanterre: Presses universitaires de Paris Nanterre, 2018)
Van Nuijis, Laurence. 'Postures journalistiques et littéraires', *Interférences littéraires* 6 (May 2011): pp. 7–17, http://www.interferenceslitteraires.be/index.php/illi/article/view/573/444
Varias, Alexander. *Paris and the Anarchists: Aesthetes and Subversives During the Fin de Siècle* (Basingstoke: Macmillian, 1997)
Verdelhan, Arielle. 'L'Animal et l'animalité dans *Nono* (1885), avatars de la vérité'. In *Rachilde ou les aléas de la postérité: de l'oubli au renouveau*, edited by Thierry Poyet, Minores XIX–XX, 5 (Paris: Lettres Modernes Minard, 2023), pp. 187–200
Vérilhac, Yoan. *La Jeune Critique des petites revues symbolistes* (Saint-Etienne: Publications de l'Université de Saint-Etienne, 2010)
Viala, Alain. *La France galante: Essai historique sur une catégorie culturelle, de ses origines jusqu'à la Révolution* (Paris: Presses Universitaires de France, 2008)
Voisin-Fougère, Marie-Ange. 'Émile Zola et Paul Bourget: Une amitié littéraire'. In *Champ littéraire autour de Zola*, edited by Béatrice Laville (Pessac: Presses Universitaires de Bordeaux, 2004), pp. 177–91
Walbecq, Éric. 'Le Procès de Jeanne Jacquemin contre Jean Lorrain en mai 1903'. In *Jean Lorrain, produit d'extrême civilisation*, edited by Éric Walbecq and others (Mont-Saint-Aignan: Publications des Universités de Rouen et du Havre, 2009), doi:10.4000/books.purh.1251
Watelet, Jean. *La Presse illustrée en France, 1814–1914*, 2 vols (Lille: Atelier national de reproduction de thèses, 1998)
Weisberg, Gabriel P. 'Louis Legrand's Battle over *Prostitution*: The Uneasy Censoring of *Le Courrier Français*', *Art Journal* 51, no. 1 (1992): pp. 45–50, doi:10.1080/00043249.1992.10791551
Whidden, Seth, ed., *Models of Collaboration in Nineteenth-Century French Literature: Several Authors, One Pen* (Farnham: Ashgate, 2009)
Ziegler, Robert. 'The Author of Public Opinion in Jean Lorrain's *Les Lépillier*', *Dalhousie French Studies* 26 (Spring 1994): pp. 39–47, https://www.jstor.org/stable/40799306

# Index

(Figures are indicated by an italic *f* following the page number.)

abortion, 188–192, 207. *See also* sexual politics
advertising
  columns in newspapers, 196–197, 199–200, 201*f*
  indirect or veiled. *See réclame*
  posters, 90–91
  small ads (*petites annonces*), 117, 200–205
agony aunt column, 184–189
anarchism
  legal suppression of, 33–34. *See also lois scélérates*; Trial of the Thirty
  violent forms of, 32–33. *See also* propaganda by the deed
aphrodisiacs, 205–208
art for art's sake, 3–4, 194
assassination of President Sadi Carnot, 32
author function, 8–9, 30
authorial responsibility, 21–22
avant-garde
  literary groups, 122–124. *See also cénacle*
  literature, definition of, 1–2 n.3
  periodicals, 4–5, 117–120

bad influence, model of literature, 15, 20–21, 38–40, 46–47, 76–77, 96
Balzac, Honoré de, 3–4, 49
Barrès, Maurice, 57–58, 164–165
*bas bleus. See* bluestockings
Beaubourg, Maurice
  *Contes pour les assassins*, 111–114
  'Littérature des assassins, La', article in *La Revue blanche*, 106–109
Bérenger, René, 194–195
birth control, 189–191, 197–198. *See also* sexual politics
bluestockings, 131–136, 138–140
Bonald, Louis de, 49
Bonbons Vert-Galant. *See* aphrodisiacs
Bonnet, Alfred Hippolyte, 192, 194–195
Bonnetain, Paul, 142–143
Bourdieu, Pierre, 9–12
Bourget, Paul, 15, 39

brows, cultural and literary
  crossing boundaries between, 17–18
Brunetière, Ferdinand, 76–77

canon, literary
  reassessment of, 7, 18. *See also* brows
Casario, Sante, 32
*cénacle*, 123–124
censorship, 33, 81–82, 180–181, 193–194. *See also lois scélérates*; Press Freedom Law of 1881
Chambige, Henri, 66–67
Champsaur, Félicien, 144–146
*Chat Noir, Le* (cabaret and periodical), 117–120
Christianity, 46, 51–52, 55, 65, 74–75
*Chronique de Sapho, La. See* agony aunt column
Claverie
  Charles Auguste, 196
  Maison A., 196–200, 197*f*
competitions, in newspapers, 176–179
*complaisance* (moral complacency), 57–66, 73. *See also directeur de conscience*
complicity
  collaboration, as a form of, 21–22, 34–36, 119–120
  *connivence*, compared with, 7–8. *See also* reader, targeted
  critics' complicity in what they critique, 10–11, 76–77, 210–211
  dictionary definitions of, 2
  incitement, as a form of, 19–21, 81–82, 91–92, 105–106, 119–120, 189
  legal definitions of, 19–22
  male homosocial forms of, 12–13, 63, 92–93. *See also* homosociality
  tool for literary study, 5–6
confession
  legal strategy, 99–100
  literary practice, 60–62, 70–72. *See also* oratory literature
  religious practice, 59, 70–71

source of complicity between characters, 95–98
*connivence*, 7–8
Coolus, Romain
'Théorie rationnelle de l'assassinat propre', article in *La Grande Revue*, 114–116
correctional courts, 24–25, 28, 33, 37, 192, 197–199
correspondence
reader-to-reader, 200–204. *See also* advertising, small ads
writer-to-writer, 163–166
Couturier, Édouard, 171–172, 184, 192
crime fiction
genre, 15–16, 79–80, 82–83
medium for crossing generic boundaries, 82–83
target of criticism and censorship, 81–82
crimes, press-related, 4–5, 19–20, 33–34. *See also lois scélérates*
criminal association, concept of, 34–35
criminality, theories of, 80–81, 102–104
Culler, Jonathan, 7–8. *See also* reader, competent

*Décadent, Le*, 162–163
Delaville, Camille, 131–132 n.47
*déshabillage*
autobiographical unveiling, 147–150, 161–165
erotic titillation, 148–149, 181–183, 185*f*, 187–188
dialogism, 172
*directeur de conscience* (spiritual director), 58–66, 72–74
*Don Juan* (periodical), 169–172

Emery, René, 26–31, 169–171
*enquêtes*. *See* questionnaires
Estoc, Gisèle d', 142–143
ethos. *See* self-image
eugenics, 190–191. *See also* neo-Malthusianism
experimental literature, 50–52. *See also* Zola, *Le Roman expérimental*

*Fin de siècle, Le*, 26–31, 169–171
Fish, Stanley, 7–8. *See also* reader, competent
frame texts, 48–52, 67–69, 109–111
France, Anatole, 76–77
free indirect discourse, 70, 89–93, 100–101, 157–158

Gautier, Théophile, 3–4
gender identity, 11–12, 138–139

gender norms
critique of, 93–95, 184–186
Gide, André, 1, 66
good influence, model of literature, 55
Gyp (Comtesse de Martel de Janville), 148

homosexuality, 139–140, 149–150, 152–154, 157–158
homosociality
female, 13–14, 183–184, 188
male, 12–13, 42–43, 141–142, 177–178, 181–184, 188

industrial literature, 3–4
Iser, Wolfgang, 6–7. *See also* reader, implied

Jauss, Hans Robert, 6–7. *See also* reader, implied; strategies, textual
*Journal des Assassins*, 116–120, 118*f*

literacy rates, 4–5
literary trends, 4–5, 39
*littérature des assassins, la*. *See* murderer literature
little magazines. *See petites revues*
*lois scélérates, les* (anti-Anarchist laws), 33–34. *See also* anarchism; Trial of the Thirty
Lorrain, Jean, 125–127
correspondence with Oscar Méténier, 163–164
*Dans l'oratoire*, 60–63, 65, 164–165
depictions of, 143–146, 151–152, 158–164. *See also* Méténier, 'Aventure de Marius Dauriat'
'Encore les réclamations', article in *Le Zig-Zag*, 144–146, 149–150
intertextual exchanges with Oscar Méténier, 159–162
intertextual exchanges with Rachilde, 164–166
*Modernités*, 139
'Troisième Sexe, Le', article in *Le Zig-Zag*, 135–136, 138–141, 147–148

Malot, Hector, 84–85 n.24
*Complices*, 84–85, 94–95, 99–100, 104–105
mass media
concerns over, 25–26
metaliterature, 105–106, 113–115, 117–120
Méténier, Oscar, 150–152
'Aventure de Marius Dauriat, L", in *La Chair* (1885), 151–160
correspondence with Jean Lorrain, 163–164
'Décadence', in *La Grâce* (1886), 151–152, 154–157

Méténier, Oscar (*Continued*)
  intertextual exchanges with Jean Lorrain, 159–162. *See also* strongman; *réclame*
  intertextual exchanges with Rachilde, 162–163
methodologies, for literary analysis, 5–6, 14
Michelet, Jules, 58–60
middlebrow, 17–18. *See also* brows
Mirbeau, Octave
  *Jardin des supplices, Le*, 109–110, 113
  newspaper articles about murder, 108–109
  newspaper articles about Paul Bourget, 57–58, 63–65
*mise en abyme*, 54–55, 108, 154–155, 184, 203–204
*mise en page*, 136–137, 205–208
*mise en scène*, 143–144
misogyny, 62–65, 92–93, 138–140. *See also* complicity, male homosocial forms of
monstrosity, 139–141
murder
  art form, 108–109, 113–114, 119–120. *See also* murderer literature
  depictions of, 85–91
  moral imperative, 110–113
  natural urge, 106–112
  profession, 114–121, 118f
murderer literature (*littérature des assassins*), 15–16, 106–109

Natalism, 190–191, 207. *See also* sexual politics; neo-Malthusianism
neo-Malthusianism, 189–192
networks
  erotic commercial networks, 26, 198–199
  literary groups as networks, 52–53, 123–124, 133
  periodical culture networks, 106–107 n.66, 194–195, 205–206
  sociological approaches to literature, 9–10, 210–211. *See also* Bourdieu
nudity. *See déshabillage*

obscenity
  definitions of, 23
  industry of, 26
oratory literature, 60–63, 65
Orfer, Léo d', 130–131
outraging public decency (*outrages aux bonnes mœurs*), 23–26
  law of 1882, 23–25
  law of 1898, *Contre la licence des rues*, 199–200
  legal definition of, 23
  trials of, 26–31, 169–171, 192–195, 197–199

*petites annonces*. *See* advertising, small ads
*petites revues*, 128–130
pimp journalism (*proxénétisme*), 17, 195–196, 200–204. *See also* prostitution
priests, depictions of, 58–66. *See also* complaisance; Michelet
popular literature
  definitions of, 79–80
  denigrated aesthetic form, 81–82, 90–91
posturing. *See* self-image
Press Freedom Law of 1881, 4–5, 19–22, 35–36
*procès des trente, le*. *See* Trial of the Thirty
propaganda by the deed, 32. *See also* anarchism; Ravachol
prostitution
  literature as, 195–196
psychological novel, 52–53
publicity. *See réclame*

questionnaires, in newspapers, 178–181

Rachilde (Marguerite Eymery), 125–127
  approach to gender identity, 134–135 n.63
  contribution to murderer literature, 106–108
  correspondence with René Emery, 169–171
  depictions of, 140–143, 151–152, 154–157
  'Guichet de réclamations', article in *Le Zig-Zag*, 136–137, 142–143
  intertextual exchanges with Jean Lorrain, 164–166
  intertextual exchanges with Oscar Méténier, 162–163
  *Nono*, 83–89, 97–102, 104–105
  *Sanglante Ironie, La*, 110–111
  'Une fois pour toutes!', article in *Le Zig-Zag*, 131–132, 134–135, 147
  'Zig-Zag Parade', article in *Le Zig-Zag*, 131–132, 143–144, 148–149
  'Zig-Zag Parade. Auteurs et décors', article in *Le Zig-Zag*, 145–146
Ravachol (François Claudius Koenigstein), 32. *See also* anarchism
Reader
  actual, 6–8
  competent, 7–8. *See also* Fish; Culler
  implied, 6–7, 92–93. *See also* Jauss; Iser
  potential criminal, 20–21
  targeted, 7–9, 172
  victim, 20–21, 24
reading
  education, 41–43
  erotic encounter, 41–43, 60–62, 68–69, 172–177, 200–204
  pact, 71–73, 75–76

seduction, 69–70, 172–176
source of moral contagion, 44–45, 47–48, 54–55, 68–70. *See also* bad influence
reception of authors by their peers
Bourget, 56–58, 60–66, 75–77
Rachilde, 88–89
Zola, 90–92, 96–97
reception, theories of, 6–9
recidivism, 28–30, 169–171
*réclamation* (complaint/protestation), 137–138, 144–146
*réclame*
self-promotion, 124–125, 137–138, 142–145, 161–167
veiled advertising, 124–125, 137–138, 168–169, 204–208
*revue légère* (saucy magazine), as a genre, 168–169
Robin, Paul, 189–191. *See also* neo-Malthusianism
*roman à clef* (biographically revealing fiction), 123–124, 127–128, 148, 158–159, 162–163
*roman feuilleton* (serial fiction), 90–91

saucy magazine. *See revue légère*
Secrétan, Charles, 55
seduction
fictional depictions of, 68–70, 88–89, 138–139
literary appeal, form of, 172–174
self-exposure. *See déshabillage*
self-image, 122–125, 159–160
self-promotion. *See réclame*, self-promotion
sexual desire
links with violence, 89–90, 95–97, 101–102
sexual politics, 188–192. *See also* abortion; birth control
sex toys, 196–199
slumming, 158

small ads. *See* advertising, small ads
social art, 3–4
strategies
authorial, 9–10, 22, 49–50, 122–125, 160–167, 209–210. *See also* Bourdieu
legal, 26–31, 38
textual, 6–7. *See also* Jauss
striptease. *See déshabillage*
strongman, 152–154, 159–161
structural parallelism, 89–90
*style indirect libre. See* free indirect discourse
surveys, in newspapers. *See* questionnaires, in newspapers

Taine, Hippolyte, 40–41, 45–46, 52–53
thesis novels, 51–52
Third Republic France, 4–5, 31–32, 39, 79–80
Trial of the Thirty, the, 34–38
Trials
fictional depictions of, 100–106
real-life, 26–31, 34–37, 66–67, 169–171, 192–195. *See also* obscenity; *Fin de siècle*; Trial of the Thirty

Vaillant, Auguste, 32
verisimilitude
lack of, 56, 88–91
vulnerability, in the construction of authorial identity, 126–127, 150–151, 158–167

women readers, 177–178, 199–200

*Zig-Zag, Le*, 130–132
Zola, Émile
*Bête humaine, La*, 84, 89–97, 100–103, 105–108
*Roman expérimental, Le*, 45–46, 50–52, 82. *See also* experimental literature